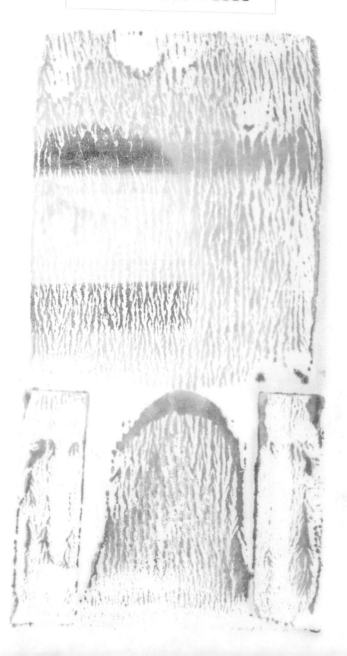

Reprinted from the edition of 1912, Philadelphia
First AMS EDITION published 1969
Manufactured in the United States of America

Library of Congress Catalog Card Number: 71-99249
SBN: 404-00608-6

AMS PRESS, INC.
New York, N.Y. 10003

THE RELATIONS OF PENN-SYLVANIA WITH THE BRITISH GOVERN-MENT, 1696-1765

BY

WINFRED TREXLER ROOT,

AMS PRESS
NEW YORK

CONTENTS

PREFACE

Until recent years,— the last two decades,— it was the fashion for historians of our colonial era to treat the English possessions in America in the domain of American history. This practice to a large degree ignored the fact that the colonies were parts of a great Empire.[1] A predominant interest in provincial development and a lack of the requisite material on this side of the water are the factors chiefly responsible for the neglect to study the old British colonial policy. A few writers have not failed to understand that the colonies were subject to an elaborate imperial system, neither have they been handicapped by the lack of the material necessary to study the imperial relation, but their work has been seriously marred by a show of the traditional American prejudice which views the British policy toward her first dependencies as something tyrannical and oppressive. Various forces have been at work, and are still active, tending to clear away the older parochial and democratic points of view. The advance of sound historical scholarship in America has substituted for narrowness of vision and false notions of patriotism, a catholic attitude, the spirit of the judge, and the desire of the investigator to leave nothing undone to elicit the truth in full. In the field of colonial history the advance has meant the substitution of the modern and normal imperial point of view for the old provincial attitude. In order to understand clearly and to pass judgment im-

[1] Andrews, *Some Neglected Aspects of Colonial Hist.*, (an address delivered before the N. J. Hist. Soc., May, 1900); Andrews, *American Colonial History*, (Amer. Hist. Asso., *Reports*, 1898); Osgood, *Study of American Colonial Hist.*, *ibid;* Conference on Research in American Colonial Hist., *ibid.*, 1908, I; Osgood, *American Colonies*, I, xxvi-xxvii.

partially on England's first colonial policy, American scholars are laboring patiently with material hitherto practically unexplored and neglected. The results have been embodied in histories and monographs clearing away erroneous notions and casting a flood of light on phases and periods of British American history once obscure and slighted.[2] Praiseworthy efforts have been made by English and American scholars to elaborate guides to the vast mass of material in English repositories, beckoning on the investigator to labor in new and interesting fields.[3] Much has been done to make this material accessible in America in the form of printed collections and transcriptions, but much remains to be done.[4] Great credit is due to Professor C. M. Andrews of Yale, Professor H. L. Osgood of Columbia, and Dr. Beer, the pioneers in this field, for their admirable work in calling attention to neglected points of view and unexplored material, and for interpreting the relation of the colonies to the Empire in a scholarly and scientific manner.

In the following work the province of Pennsylvania is singled out for particular investigation in order to elucidate the nature of British imperialism in its political and administrative features during the eighteenth century. It is the purpose to describe both the organization and activity

[2] Beer, *Origins of the British Colonial System, 1578-1660* (1908), and *British Colonial Policy, 1754-1765*, (1907); Andrews, *British Committees, Commissions, and Councils of Trade and Plantations*, (Johns Hopkins Studies, XXVI, 1908); Osgood, *American Colonies*, III, (1907), is a masterly treatment of the imperial system in the 17th. century, based chiefly upon printed material readily accessible. Professor Osgood is now engaged on a continuation of the work, based largely upon new material, viewing the subject from the standpoint of the colonies.

[3] Andrews and Davenport, *Guide to the Manuscript Materials for the History of the United States to 1783, in the British Museum, in Minor London Archives, and the Libraries of Oxford and Cambridge*. (Washington, 1908.)

[4] For a detailed list of the printed material and transcripts, see the bibliography appended.

of the central institutions of colonial control and the work of the royal officials in the colonial service administering imperial policies. Since the colony is considered from the point of view of the Empire, the study falls largely in the field of English history. Indirectly it is a part of American history, for a general knowledge of provincial development is essential to a proper appreciation of the continual action and interaction of imperial and local interests and ideals. The study will limit itself to that neglected middle period of colonial history extending roughly from the reorganization of the system of colonial administration in 1696 to a second reorganization at the close of the last French war. The material on which the work is based was drawn chiefly from the transcripts of the Board of Trade Papers and Journals in the library of the Historical Society of Pennsylvania and the originals in the Public Record Office, London. In addition, manuscript sources, such as the Penn Papers in the library of the above society, and published collections, such as the colonial records, parliamentary papers and journals, and the writings of English and American statesmen, have been fully searched.

This work is the result of investigations begun in a seminary course conducted by Professor Herman V. Ames, at the University of Pennsylvania. It was first accepted in partial fulfillment of the requirements for the degree of Doctor of Philosophy at this university, and has since been expanded in the light of more complete investigations.

I cannot close this preface without acknowledging the debt of gratitude I owe to Professor Andrews and to Professor Ames for their constant interest, encouragement, and counsel; their kindly criticisms and suggestions have saved me from many errors. My thanks are due also to the officials of the Historical Society of Pennsylvania for various courtesies; to the Publication Committee of the University of Pennsylvania for considerate attention; to Professor F. L. Paxson of the University of Wisconsin for reading my manuscript and suggesting alterations; and to my wife whose inspiration and encouragement have created the hope that this study will not be without value.

WINFRED T. ROOT.

Madison, Wis.,
    October, 1911.

CHAPTER ONE

INTRODUCTION

In undertaking to set forth the relations between the chartered colony of Pennsylvania and the central government, it is realized that the British system of colonial administration will not be as clearly revealed as in the case of the royal province. In the latter the powers of the home government were exercised immediately through the responsible agents of the crown; in the former they were exercised indirectly through the officials of proprietors and corporations. But the charter to William Penn contained provisions, peculiar to itself, which drew the province into intimate connection with the central government. Furthermore, the inception of a stricter control over the colonies in 1696 made this connection still stronger. A study of the charter and the system of administration established in 1696 will reveal the nature of these relations.

The charter to William Penn and his heirs of March, 1681, passed the seals at a time when English officials at home and in the colonies had learned by bitter experience the glaring deficiencies of the earlier charters viewed from the standpoint of imperial ideals. These defects arose from the difficult problem of enforcing imperial policies through officials not amenable to direct royal control. England's pioneer work in colonization had been accomplished chiefly by private enterprise and initiative, authorized by royal charter. The statesmen who drew these charters, unable to forecast the development of a well-defined imperial policy, bestowed upon the grantees large privileges and liberal powers of government and took no thought of making provision for a close supervision of colonial progress by the central government. The result was that the colonists, untrammeled by interference from home and exhibiting all the characteristics of a true pioneer and frontier people, fashioned their institutions as they saw fit and ordered their affairs according to their own conceptions, all of which was done with little regard for the interests of the Empire. But as the economic theories of the earlier part of the seventeenth century with regard to colonization found formal and definite expression in law by the passage of the acts of trade and navigation of the Restoration period, then English statesmen came to a thorough realization of the defects of the early charters. It became obvious that the development of the colonies toward self-control must be checked.[1] Their separatist and independent tendencies came clearly to light in the case of the New England colonies, especially Massachusetts.[2] They were charged with passing laws contrary to the statutes of Parliament, with transgressions of the laws of trade, with denying appeals to England, and with a general tendency toward independence. In the very year that Penn received his charter, that of Massachusetts was threatened with judicial proceedings grounded on such irregularities. With these facts fresh in mind, it is not hard to understand the reasons which led to the insertion of provisions in Penn's charter looking to an intimate supervision of colonial concerns by the central government.

First,[3] provision was made for a strict observance of the acts of trade by the requirement that the proprietor should appoint an agent to reside in London ready to answer before the English courts for any violations or will-

[1] Osgood, *Amer. Cols. in 17th. Cent.*, III, 22-24, 515-521.

[2] *Ibid.*, 228-240, 309-335, 395-399; Andrews, *Colonial Self-Government*, 256-268.

[3] Thorpe, *Amer. Charters, Constitutions, etc.*, V, 3035-3044; Poore, *Charters and Constitutions*, II, (2d. ed.) 1509-1515; *Pa. Col. Recs.*, I, 17-26.

ful neglects permitted by Penn or his heirs against the laws. This agent was required to pay within a year any damages awarded by the courts, and if for the space of a year Penn neglected to provide an agent or if he failed to make payment, the government of the province might be resumed to the crown until the obligations were fulfilled. Second, provision was made for the exercise of the royal veto on colonial legislation by the requirement that all laws should be submitted to the Privy Council within five years after enactment, such laws to remain in full force if not acted upon under the privy seal within six months after delivery. Third, the right of the colonists to appeal from the decisions of the colonial courts to the king was expressly guaranteed. Fourth, the right of the imperial Parliament to exercise concurrent jurisdiction with the colonial assembly in the matter of levying taxes in the colony was maintained by the clause that no taxes or impositions could be levied '' unless the same be with the consent of the pprietary, or chiefe Governour and assembly, or by Act of Parliament in England.'' No provision was made for colonial representation in the English Parliament. Fifth, the right of the bishop of London to appoint ministers for the colony, upon application to him by the inhabitants thereof to the number of twenty, was clearly stated, and that these appointees should be allowed to reside in the colony, '' without any deniall or molestation whatsoever.'' This was an express guarantee of the bishop's jurisdiction in a dissenting colony. This group of provisions put Pennsylvania in close touch with the home government and placed the colony on a footing unlike that upon which stood the other charter colonies as far as English control was concerned. Through the royal veto and appeals pressure could be brought to bear to make colonial development conform to English ideals, the supremacy of Parliament in matter of taxation was clearly affirmed, a due observance of the acts of trade was provided for, and finally, the interests of the Anglican Church were carefully guarded.

In other respects the Quaker colony was made a fief or proprietorship on much the same lines as those created in Maryland or Carolina. On the territorial side Penn and his heirs were constituted " true and absolute Propriataries " within the area set by the charter, which was erected into the " Province and Seigniore " of Pennsylvania, to be held of the crown by free and common socage at a nominal yearly rent. Penn was at liberty to grant or lease the lands to settlers in fee simple or fee tail, and under such services and rents as seemed best to him. All lands were to be held of the proprietor and not of the crown. To Penn was given power to erect manors, towns, and counties, to incorporate cities and boroughs, and to constitute all ports. An equal share of governmental powers was bestowed upon him. Penn and his heirs, or their deputies, were granted authority to make laws for the province with the advice and consent of the freemen or their deputies. Thus a modicum of participation in government was given to the freemen of the colony, but under serious limitations. The qualifications of freemen, the nature of the assembly as well as the time and place of meeting, were questions not provided for by the charter and therefore were left to the determination of the proprietor or to the force of circumstances. Moreover, the proprietor was given the power, modeled upon that possessed by the royal prerogative, to issue ordinances without the consent of the freemen, in times of emergency or when it was not deemed expedient to call together the people. Ordinances were required to be agreeable to English statutes, and could not deprive the inhabitants of life and property. This power gave the proprietor or his governor a way to legislate without popular consent, and in fact, there were times when the governor availed himself of this authority to offset a refractory legislature.

The proprietor was authorized to appoint all officials necessary for the due execution of the laws and to constitute all courts without limitation as to kind for the administration of justice. Finally, Penn, though as a Quaker he preached the iniquity of all war, was created a captain-general with all the powers pertaining to that office and was empowered to levy, muster, and train the inhabitants for military service and employ them in defensive war for the security of the province. Such, in a general way, was the system of government devised by the charter for the colony,— a system thoroughly undemocratic in character. The people were subject to prerogative power exercised either directly by the crown or placed in the hands of private individuals. The proprietor was both the absolute lord of the soil and the source of all political power, and the crown by reason of the veto power and appellate jurisdiction formed part of the legislative and judicial machinery of the province. This subjection to royal control will appear still more clearly in the light of the system of colonial administration devised by the English statute of 1696.

The tightening of the machinery of administration originated chiefly in a realization of the futility of depending upon officials outside the sphere of royal control to enforce the imperial laws.[4] The home government at first seemed content to rely upon the machinery of government devised under the royal charters, thus placing the execution of the laws in the hands of officials over whom the crown enjoyed slight control. Upon the governors devolved the duty of caring for the registry of ships, of granting bonds, of inspecting certificates and invoices, and, in general, of enforcing obedience to the laws of trade. Upon the judiciary of the colonies fell the office of punishing transgressors of the laws. This decentralized system threw the burden of executing imperial

[4] Osgood, *Amer. Cols.*, III, 210 ff.; Andrews, *Col. Self-Gov't.*, 31-40.

policies upon officials who, under the conditions, could refuse to enforce them or only imperfectly comply. Few
royal customs officers had been present in the colonies till
the passage of the act of 1672 which levied a duty upon
the exportation of enumerated commodities to other colonies. Thereafter, as occasion demanded, royal customs
officials were appointed for the colonies.[5] These officials
forced to rely upon the local government for assistance
encountered insurmountable difficulties in the path of their
duties. The evidence of such royal agents as Randolph,
surveyor-general of the customs, Nicholson, a royal governor, and others is of one piece on this point. The local
courts, both judges and jurors, believed to be prejudiced
in favor of illegal trade, consistently refused to condemn
breaches of the law.[6] The governors of the chartered colonies were found to be men of inferior ability who countenanced illegal trade and piracy.[7] In fine, the experience
of the royal agents is replete with instances where the
colonies by their laws and actions effectually and indirectly counteracted the laws of trade. At the same time
it was found that the customs service itself called loudly
for a thorough reorganization. Many of these officials
were of an indifferent sort, and the performance of the
duties of their office was fearfully lax. Randolph became
painfully aware of this deplorable condition on his survey
through the southern colonies in 1692.[8] Moreover, it may
be said that the prevalence of illegal trade is good and
sufficient evidence of the inadequacy of the existing system
to enforce the laws of trade. One cannot read the records
of the time without being impressed with the large amount

[5] Andrews, *Col. Self-Gov't.*, 32-34.

[6] Osgood, *op. cit.*, III, 230-234; *Cal. State Paps. Col.*, *1689-1692*,
524; 1693-1696, 509, 511, 520, 654; 1696-1697; 58, 74; *B. T. Paps.*, *Pl.
Gen.*, IV, pt. I, A 7-12.

[7] *Cal. State Paps., Col.*, 1696-1697, 72-74; *B. T. Paps.*, *Pl. Gen.*,
IV, pt. 1, A 11.

[8] *Cal. State Paps., Col.*, 1689-1692, 656-660; 1693-1696, 511, 654;
1696-1697, 71-72.

of illegal trade.[9] That between Scotland and the colonies in contravention of the laws of trade was especially large.[10] It was under such circumstances that English imperialists realized that it was necessary to institute reforms in the system of administration and to restrict the powers of government in the chartered colonies in the interest of home control.[11] Such was the purpose of the act of 1696.[12] It was of capital necessity in order to secure a maximum of efficiency in colonial administration.

In the main the act of 7 and 8 William III, chapter 22, was an administrative measure intended to correct the evils laid bare in the colonial system. It required that all governors of chartered colonies should receive royal approbation and take the oaths enjoined by the acts of trade before entering upon the duties of office. Neglect to take the oath or neglect of the duties imposed upon the governors by the laws carried a penalty of dismissal from office and a fine of £1000. The naval officer, the governor's agent in matters of trade, was obliged within two months after his entrance upon office, to give security to and be approved by the Customs Board in England. Until these obligations were absolved the governor was held liable for the neglects of his agent. To the Lords of the Treasury or its subordinate board, the Commissioners of the Customs, was given power to constitute such ports

[9] *Cal. State Paps., Col.*, 1689-1692, 153, 1693-1696, 511, 520; Mass. Hist. Soc., *Proceedings*, XII, 113-117.

[10] Keith, *Economic Causes for the Scottish Union* (English Hist. Rev., Jan., 1909); also *Scottish Trade with the Plantations* (Scottish Hist. Rev., Oct., 1908); *House of Lords Mss.*, n. s., II, 441-442, 462-463, 465-466; *Cal. State Paps., Col.*, 1685-1688, 353-354; 1693-1696, 323, 510, 519; 1689-1692, 657-660.

[11] *Jour. of House of Commons*, XI, 188, 195; *Jour. of House of Lords*, XV, 611; *Cal. State Paps., Col.*, 1693-1696, 279-280, 308, 321, 399; *B. T. Paps., Pl. Gen.*, IV, pt. 1, A 16.

[12] For the details in regard to the passage of the act of 1696, see *Jour. of Commons*, XI, 409, 440, 501, 505, 523; *Jour. of Lords*, XV, 712, 714, 720, 732; *House of Lords Mss.* n. s. II, 233-234; *Cal. State Paps., Col.*, 1693-1696, 639-640.

and customs officials in any places in the colonies as seemed
needful to them. The customs establishment in America
was put upon the same footing as that in England by
clothing the officers with the same power and authority
and placing them under the same penalties for maladministration. Provision was made for the trial of breaches
of the acts of trade in vice-admiralty courts to be established in the colonies. Finally, the supremacy of Parliament was maintained by the clause which declared null
and void all colonial laws and customs contrary to English laws, passed or to be passed, in which the colonies were
mentioned. It was also during this movement for reform
that the English merchants expressed dissatisfaction with
the management of colonial affairs in England. The colonial business was in the hands of a committee of the Privy
Council, known as the Lords of Trade. This resulted in
the creation of the Board of Trade and Plantations by
royal commission of May, 1696, whose members should be
experts in matters of colonial business.

Legislation looking to reform was now secured and that
prompt execution of the law should follow was a matter
of pressing necessity. The Customs Board, the newly created Board of Trade, Randolph, surveyor-general for the
colonies, and Parliament itself, acted vigorously to this
end. A system of vice-admiralty courts with royal officials was settled in the colonies; the customs service was
increased and put upon an orderly footing; governors
were obliged not only to be approved by the crown and
to take the oath to obey the acts of trade, but were also
required to give security for the due performance of their
duties as agents of the crown in matters of trade; naval
officers were required to give security; new and detailed
instructions with regard to the acts of trade were issued
to the governors and royal officials. Such was the system
inaugurated for centralizing and making more efficient and
complete colonial administration. It meant an abridgment

of the powers of the charters in several points. The full power to appoint or elect their governors, to establish ports, and to constitute all manner of courts was now curtailed by the force of the act of Parliament.

When we consider therefore the peculiar provisions of Penn's charter together with the provisions of the act of 1696 we are able to see clearly the intimate relation between the colony and the central government. In the light of these facts it may not be deemed unprofitable to study the working out of these relations, notwithstanding the fact that Pennsylvania was governed under a charter and not directly by the crown. Before 1696 the provisions of the charter were apparently not enforced, but the inception of the new system and the infusion of new vigor into colonial control witnessed an effort to require obedience to the requirements of the charter. Moreover, these relations between colony and mother country take on an added significance when viewed in several other respects. The long series of wars between England and France for colonial and commercial supremacy in North America involved the colony as part of the Empire in the important question of imperial defense. The development of the Anglican Church in the colony in the eighteenth century brought on a bitter conflict between the Quakers and Churchmen over matters of religion, which took on the nature of a struggle between a dissenting colony and the state-church system in England. Moreover, we note the increased activity of Parliament in colonial matters after the Revolution of 1689, legislating for the colonies in a number of ways. In fine, in matters of trade, war, religion, finance, justice, legislation, both local and imperial, the will of the home government was felt in the colony.

From the standpoint of the colonists all this meant a greater subjection to a system not of their own choice and a decrease in local self-control; a subserviency of distinctly local interests and desires to the interests and needs of the Empire. Furthermore, it is essential to bear in mind that the government provided for the colony by the charter was monarchical in character. Hence, if the proprietary system had adhered closely to the lines laid down in the charter and had the imperial system been enforced to the full, the province would never have become democratic. But the social and economic conditions precedent for the effectual establishment of a monarchical and imperial system were not present.[13] Soon after the founding of the province, the living forces of democracy, favored by the benevolent attitude of the first proprietor toward popular rights, finding themselves out of sympathy with proprietary and imperial interests and hampered in their growth toward self-control by outside authorities, at once took up the task of transforming the government in the direction of greater autonomy.[14] The relations of proprietors to the people as lords of the soil and the source of political power brought on bitter and prolonged struggles over questions of popular rights and proprietary interests and power, which form much of the staple of colonial history.[15] But in this larger struggle the fact must not be forgotten that there was also an opposition to royal control and imperial interests as well. The people were working in the direction of independence from any outside power whatsoever. This study is an attempt to make clear the interaction and opposition of conflicting interests and ideals. As a result of this conflict of opposing forces emerges the American Revolution and the disruption of the Empire.

[13] Osgood, *Amer. Cols. in 17th. Cent.*, II, 13-15.

[14] *Ibid.*, II, 252-276.

[15] Wrote Franklin in 1764, " Pennsylvania had scarce been settled Twenty Years, when these Disputes began between the first Proprietor and the Original Settlers; they continued, with some Intermissions, during his whole Life; his Widow took them up, and continued them after his Death. Her Sons resum'd them very early, and they still subsist." *Works*, (Smyth ed.) IV, 227-228.

CHAPTER TWO

CENTRAL INSTITUTIONS OF COLONIAL CONTROL

It is obvious that a knowledge of the central institutions of government as organized to deal with colonial affairs is requisite to a proper conception of the colonial system of administration. Some idea of the nature and functions of the organs of imperial control will not only help to an understanding of the manner in which colonial business was transacted at home, but also to some appreciation of the legal and political relations which existed between the mother country and the colonies. This subject for the sake of convenience of treatment readily divides itself into two parts, executive and legislative control.

The crown was the chief branch of the English government concerned with the colonies. The organs through which executive control over the colonies was exercised were the king, the Privy Council, the Secretaries of State, the Lords of the Treasury, and the Lords of the Admiralty. Besides these departments of state, the royal power was exercised through subordinate boards, such as the Board of Trade and the Commissioners of the Customs. Chief among the executive boards was the Privy Council, which included the great ministers of state and some not otherwise holding office. Although many of the powers of the prerogative over the colonies were placed in the hands of the high officers of state, yet the Privy Council never parted with two important functions. One the legislative function of expressing approval or disapproval of colonial enactments, the other the judicial function of hearing and determining appeals from the colonial courts, powers which the council enjoys to this day.[1] The council performed its work chiefly through committees, such as the Committee for Hearing Appeals, and the Committee for Plantation Affairs.[2] Professor Andrews points out that these were not standing or separate committees, "but the same committee, that is, the whole Council sitting under different titles."[3] In fact, for the two decades prior to 1696 the management of colonial business was placed in the hands of a committee of the whole council, known as the Lords of Trade.[4]

The usual form in which the Privy Council expressed its will was the "order in council." Osgood says, "Within the sphere of the executive they hold a position of importance corresponding to that of the statute within the province of the legislature." Such orders were issued concerning a variety of matters which came properly within the competence of the council, whether it was a minor matter of referring business to another office or the important function of appointing a royal governor or expressing a decision on a colonial law or appeal.

Besides the Privy Council, much of colonial management was vested in the offices of the Secretary of State, the First Lord of the Treasury, and the First Lord of the Admiralty. They were great ministers of state, sworn of the Privy Council, and members of the Cabinet, the inner circle of the council. These offices, like the council itself, existed for the realm as well as the dominions and were the representatives of royal authority within their respective departments, acting in the name and on behalf of the crown. In the sphere of war and foreign relations

[1] *Acts of Privy Council, Col.*, II, vi-vii, 826-853; III, 840-853.
[2] *Ibid.*, II, vi-vii.
[3] Andrews, in *Amer. Hist. Rev.*, XVI, 120-121; *Acts of Privy Council, Col.*, III, viii-ix.
[4] Andrews, *British Committees, Commissions, etc.*, Johns Hopkins Studies, XXVI, 111-113; *Acts of Privy Council, Col.*, I, II; *Journals of Lords of Trade*, 8 vols., Feb., 1675 to April, 1696.

the colonies fell chiefly under the administration of the secretary of state for the southern department and the secretary at war.[5] This control was considerable when it is remembered that during the period of 1689 to 1763, England was involved in a long series of wars and diplomatic negotiations with France. On these matters the civil and military officials in the colonies corresponded chiefly with the secretary of state, and from him they received orders to proclaim war or peace, to raise troops and military supplies, and on allied matters.[6] In the field of colonial patronage the secretary of state also enjoyed considerable power. Even in times of peace a general oversight of colonial administration came within the purview of this office. The royal governors corresponded with him on almost all matters of ordinary concern,[7] and to the secretary were referred many petitions and memorials from the colonies. From 1696 to 1724 this post was held by no less than thirteen successive incumbents with an average tenure of a little over two years each. Under conditions which made the secretaryship subject to the vicissitudes of party politics and rapidly changing ministries, continuity of administration was possible only because of the permanency of the under-secretaries. From 1724 to 1748 the office was held continuously by the Duke of Newcastle. Horace Walpole in his memoirs has accused Newcastle of an extreme negligence of colonial business and of an ignorance of colonial affairs, but it may be said that a closer inquiry into this matter will probably show that his attention to colonial management was greater than is

5 Todd, *Parliamentary Gov't. in England*, (2d. ed.), II, 606-612 · Anson, *Law and Custom of the Const.*, (2d. ed.), II, 152-160.

6 Kimball, *Corres. of Wm. Pitt with Col. Govs.*, etc., 2 vols.

7 See the correspondence of Governors Morris of N. J. (N. J. Hist. Soc., *Coll.*, IV); Dinwiddie of Va. (Va. Hist. Soc., *Coll.*, III, IV); and Belcher of Mass. (Mass. Hist. Soc., *Coll.*, sixth ser., VI). They corresponded with the secretary on almost all questions of colonial concern.

commonly supposed.[8] From 1748 to 1768 there were no less than nine successive secretaries. For five of these twenty years the office was ably administered by William Pitt, and during the Seven Years' War English arms, under his guidance, won renown in every quarter of the globe. Outside of Pitt's tenure, the office was the sport of politics, handed about frequently to men of decidedly mediocre ability in order to meet the plans of the various combinations of the Grenville, Rockingham, and Bedford factions of the Whig party.

As already stated part of colonial administration fell within the competence of the treasury and admiralty departments, both of which were composed of boards of ministerial rank, presided over by a First Lord of the Treasury and a First Lord of the Admiralty. The treasury board and its subordinate board, the Commissioners of the Customs, had charge of the execution of the acts of trade, and under their control came the customs officials in the colonies, such as the surveyors-general, collectors, naval officers, and the governors in matters of trade and revenue.[9] The admiralty board exercised control over the navy in American waters, and vice-admiralty officials were commissioned by the judge of the High Court of Admiralty on warrants issued by the admiralty board.[10] The chief board of non-ministerial rank concerned with the colonies was the Board of Trade. Of this office, its personnel, functions, and relations to the other departments of government we shall now treat.

Prior to 1696 colonial management was vested in the Lords of Trade, a committee of the whole Privy Council.

[8] Walpole *Memoirs*, I, 396-397. For a defense of Newcastle see Channing, *Hist. of U. S.*, II, 238, 433; Temperly, *The Age of Walpole*, Cambridge Modern Hist., VII, 54.

[9] *Customs Books* (Public Record Office); *Cal. Treas. Paps.*, 1557-1696, xiv-xvi; *ibid.*, 1702-1707, vii; *ibid.*, 1708-1714, vii; Todd, *op.. cit.*, II, 523; Anson, *op. cit.*, II, 164.

[10] *Admiralty Books* (Public Record Office); Todd, II, 762; Anson, II, 176.

The initial impulse toward the creation of a subordinate board, separate and distinct from the council, came from the merchant classes.[11]   In 1694 they began to complain loudly of the prevalence of illegal trade in the colonies. Parliament, acting under their influence, sought to establish a colonial office under its own control.   The London merchants resented the fact that colonial affairs were entrusted to " courtiers without experience."   In the next session of the legislature, the merchants renewed their attempt.   Under pressure of this movement the king decided to create a separate board by royal commission.   But it seems that after the laborers were chosen and the patent was ready, he refused to affix his signature.[12]   Again Parliament took up the matter and on December 14, 1695, ordered a bill to be introduced providing for a legislative council of trade.[13]   The Bristol merchants employed agents to lobby for the bill and the commercial towns sought to gain representation on the new board.[14]   The measure was stoutly resisted by William III who was very zealous of the royal powers.   He saw in this effort of Parliament a serious encroachment on the appointive power of the crown and the setting of a very dangerous precedent.[15] The agitation, however, had a salutary effect, for on May 15, 1696, was issued a royal commission creating the Board of Trade and Plantations under the control of the crown.[16] This bureau had an existence of varied fortune which came to an end with the disruption of England's first Empire in the West.

The work of the board, as outlined in the commission,[17]

11 Andrews, *British Commissions*, etc., Johns Hopkins Studies, XXVI, 113.   12 Fox-Bourne, *Life of John Locke*, II, 348.

13 Cobbett, *Parl. Hist.*, V, 977.

14 Andrews, *British Commissions*, etc., 113.

15 Cobbett, *Parl. Hist.*, V, 978.

16 *Cal. State Paps., Col.*, 1693-1696, 632; *Acts of Privy Council, Col.*, II, 299.

17 For a copy of the commission see, *B. T. Jour.*, IX; *House of Lords Mss.*, n. s., II, 416; *N. Y. Col. Docs.*, IV, 145-148.

was two-fold; the supervision of trade and the supervision of colonial administration. In the province of administration, in which we are chiefly interested, it was the duty of the board to examine the instructions issued to the governors in order to make them full and complete; to require an annual statement from the governors as to their administrations and to report the essential matters to the Privy Council; to consider of the qualifications of persons proposed for colonial offices, such as governors, deputy-governors, councilors, secretaries, and attorneys-general, and to present their names to the council; to weigh and examine colonial laws and to represent the " Usefulness or Mischief thereof to our Crown "; to hear complaints from the colonies and to advise the council of the proper action to be taken thereon, and other matters. All opinions and findings of the board were required to be drawn up in writing over the hands of five members and presented to the Privy Council. It is obvious at a glance that the board was invested with no power of execution or final action, but stood merely as a bureau of reference and examination, entirely subordinate to the Privy Council and the secretary of state. Herein, as we shall see, lay one of the essential imperfections in the organization of this office.

The board was composed of two classes of members, eight *ex-officio* members who were high officers of state, such as the principal Secretaries of State, the Lord High Admiral, and the Lord High Treasurer; and eight active members of non-ministerial rank. The first class were not required to be in attendance unless their presence was requisite or the public business permitted. The active membership, upon which the burden of the work fell, was to be composed of " knowing and fitt persons," according to the words of the commission. The constant laborers received a yearly compensation of £1000 each.[18] The

18 It is evident that Lord Monson, 1737-1748, and the Earl of

staff of the bureau consisted of secretary, deputy-secretary, seven clerks, and was completed by a force of two messengers, a porter and a janitress.[19] The entire establishment cost the government in salaries about £12,000 a year.[20] Prior to 1718, the crown lawyers acted in the capacity of legal advisers to the board, but the expanding business of the colonial office required the appointment of a special counsel.[21] The board still continued to consult the attorney-general and solicitor-general on questions of particular import. One of the most important officials of the board was the secretary. This post was held continuously by a member of the Popple family, father, son, and grandson, from 1696 to 1737.[22] The permanency in tenure of the board's staff, such as the secretaries, counsel, and clerks, afforded that unbroken continuity in administration in the midst of frequent changes in the personnel of the board itself and of the vicissitudes of ministries.[23]

For the first decade after the founding of the board, the intention to appoint to that office men of knowledge and ability in all matters pertaining to trade and colonial administration was fairly well realized. The Earl of Bridgewater, Lords Stamford and Dartmouth, who together held the presidency for fifteen years, had been active members of the former colonial office and had gained

Halifax, 1748-1761, each received an additional compensation of £500 a year as president of the board. *Bedford Corres.*, I, 505-506.

[19] *B. T. Jour.*, IX, 8, 11; XIV, 194; XXXIV, 115, 190; XL, 204; LXXII, 348.

[20] *Ibid.*, XX, 23; *Cal. Treas. Paps.*, 1729-1730, 540, 558, 595, 596; 1731-1734, 152, 155, 164, 176, 180; 1735-1738, 572, 587, 604, 611, 615; 1742-1745, 802, 815.

[21] *B. T. Jour.*, XXVII, 133, 203. This post was held by Richard West, 1718; Francis Fane, 1725; Matthew Lamb, 1745; and Richard Jackson, 1770-1782. Chalmers, *Opinions of Eminent Lawyers* (ed. 1858), 9-11.

[22] *B. T. Jour.*, IX, 7; XIX, 165; XXXII, 100.

[23] In the period from 1696 to 1714 there were no less than thirty different incumbents; and in the period 1715-1760, about fifty. For a convenient list of members see *N. Y. Col. Docs.*, III, xv-xvii.

a knowledge of colonial affairs.[24]   In fact, the first board was a capable and experienced body of men. Blathwayt [25] and Locke,[26] as secretaries of former colonial boards, and by their keen interest in colonization, were well fitted for their tasks. Stepney, a diplomat, Meadows and Pollexfen, economists of note and public servants of a high type, Hill, a man of science,— all thoroughly interested in trade and colonies,— formed a strong and efficient colonial bureau.[27] But by 1707 these first incumbents had given place to others of less ability and experience with the consequent result of a dwindling of force and activity in the powers of the board.[28] In general, down to the accession of the House of Hanover, the board exhibited a vigor and an interest in its work which cannot be said of the office in the days prior to the presidency of the efficient Halifax, 1748-1761. Frequent meetings were held,[29] colonial laws were thoroughly examined and many were disallowed, the act of 1696 was carried into execution, great care was shown in the drafting of the governors' instructions, the qualifications of persons for colonial office were carefully examined, and a well-defined policy of vacating the colonial charters in the interest of efficient administration was formulated and vigorously pursued. In many other ways the effectiveness of its work was felt both at home and abroad. But the period after 1714 tells a different story. With the accession of George I and the rise to power of the Whig mercantile interests under the leadership of Walpole, there came a change in the personnel and con-

24 *Jour. of Lords of Trade*, I-VIII, *passim.*

25 Channing, *History of United States*, II, 218-219.

26 Fox-Bourne, *Life of John Locke.*

27 *Dict. of Nat. Biog.*, XXVI, 389; XXXVII, 192; XLVI, 62.

28 In 1707, on the accession of the Tory party to power, the personnel of the board underwent an entire change.

29 In the first ten years the board met on an average about fifteen times a month, but after 1708 there seems to have been difficulty at times in securing a quorum of members. *B. T. Jour.*, XX, 35; XXI, 225, 234.

sequent activity of the board.[30] It was a change for the worse viewed from the standpoint of effective administration. In 1714 a keen critic of the board wrote that many were appointed to that office " for reasons different than their ability." [31] Later Horace Walpole wrote that during the premiership of his father the board " had very faultily been suffered to lapse almost into a sinecure." [32] Burke characterized the period as one of " salutary neglect." There is little reason to doubt that in that age of low political morality, when the spoils of office were used to support the existing administration, the Board of Trade, like other offices, offered convenient places to settle and reward faithful politicians and henchmen.[33] The consequence is clear to be seen. In comparison with the board of the earlier period, meetings were held less frequently,[34] fewer attended, the transaction of business was slower, legislation was less carefully scrutinized, in some cases correspondence between the board and colonial governors was lax,[35] and the policy of vacating the colonial charters was less persistently urged. With these facts in mind one is able to appreciate Burke's criticism that the lack of effective administration from home suffered " a generous nature to take its own way to perfection." In the first period the colonies were on the defensive, for they felt the aggressive powers of the board, but during the second period, untrammeled by interference from home,

[30] Chalmers, *Introd. to Revolt of Cols.*, II, 4.

[31] *B. T. Paps., Pl. Gen.*, IX, K 39; *No. Car. Col. Recs.*, II, 154-166.

[32] Walpole, *Memoirs*, (2d. ed.) I, 396-397.

[33] Said Burke in 1780 of the Board of Trade, " This board is a sort of temperate bed of influence; a sort of gently ripening hot-house, where eight members of parliament receive salaries of a thousand a year, for a certain given time, in order to mature, at a proper season, a claim to two thousand, granted for doing less, and on the credit of having toiled so long in that inferior, laborious department." *Works*, (Bohn Lib.), II, 109.

[34] They averaged about ten a month.

[35] *N. Y. Col. Docs.*, VI, 270-271; *No. Car. Col. Recs.*, IV, 173, 756, 797, 870.

they made rapid strides in curtailing the power of the imperial government and in fashioning their institutions as they saw fit without much regard for the interests of the Empire. The Walpolian era was one of commercial dominance and if the colonies were liberally and laxly administered in the province of politics, a greater effort was made to develop commerce and trade. The reports of the board to the king and Parliament on colonial manufactures, currency, trade, and similar subjects show a deep insight into the economic features of colonization.[36] Walpole fell from power in 1742 and Newcastle relinquished the post of secretary in 1748, and after this one becomes aware of a decided increase of interest in colonial politics. From 1748 to 1761 the board under the presidency of the able and energetic Halifax exhibited a renewed interest in its work.

From a theoretical standpoint the plan of the colonial office was fairly well conceived. A bureau composed in one part of active laborers possessing ability and experience in colonial matters, acting in close coöperation with *ex-officio* members, who represented royal authority in the colonies and who were included in the ministry, was well-designed to secure unity of purpose, consistency of action, and dispatch of business. Ideally considered the arrangement was calculated to bring together heretofore disunited departments of government, to obviate inter-departmental frictions, and to secure centralization of authority. In actual practice the original plan was in no ways approximated. In view of the remoteness of the colonies from the metropolis and the tedious and slow means of communication in that age, harmony and dispatch in the working of the central machinery of government was eminently necessary. Only under such a system would the authority and power of the imperial gov-

---

[36] Andrews and Davenport, *Guide to the MSS. material in the British Archives*, 192 ff.

ernment be felt and heeded. The ideal was not realized till the very close of our period. Quite to the contrary the system in actual practice was cumbersome and complex. The ministers, in whose departments colonial business fell, seldom attended the board as *ex-officio* members.[37] Each department in general pursued its own way without much regard for the Board of Trade or other offices. The result was a weak system of divided responsibility, interdepartmental jealousy and friction, and no one office became a center for all colonial business. The naval officers and customs officials corresponded with the Customs Board, the admiralty officials with the admiralty board, the governors and military officials with the secretary of state on matters of foreign relations and war, and the civil officials with both the Board of Trade and the secretary of state on questions of general concern.[38] Under this system where coöperation was lacking and a general direction of affairs was not vested in one office, unity of action and harmony of administration were out of the question. Everybody's business was liable to be nobody's business, or if taken up by anyone it was liable to create jealousy in another. Evidence on this point is not lacking. In 1697 the Customs Board petulantly rejected a proposal of Robert Quary to fit out an armed cruiser to check illegal trade in Delaware Bay because he had slighted its authority by first applying to the Board of Trade.[39] This jealousy brought to naught a wise proposal and the colonial service suffered accordingly. In 1707 the Earl of Sutherland, secretary of state, called the board to account for reporting on a matter to the Privy Council before it had been brought to his attention and directed the offending

[37] On rare occasions they were called in. *B. T. Jour.*, X, 424; XXIV, 16. At times the board was called to attend the Privy Council. *Ibid.*, XIV, 446; XV, 104; XVII, 8; XXXIX, 263; XLI, 287; LIX, 74.
[38] Pownall, *Administration of Cols.*, (ed. 1768), 14.
[39] *B. T. Jour.*, X, 271-274, 346.

board to report on no matter relating to his department until he was first acquainted.[40] The situation was serious when the Earl of Shelburne, president of the board, could write in 1763 that " it frequently happened that contradictory orders were given by different officers on the same points, and more frequently in affairs of difficulty and delicacy no orders were given at all, the responsibility of both officers being set aside by each having it in his power to throw the blame on the other."[41] Shelburne resigned from the board because of friction between his office and that of the secretary of state. The failings of the whole system were thoroughly realized not only by various members of the board itself but by royal officials in the colonial service, and they continually agitated and worked for a system of centralized authority.

Moreover, the Board of Trade, designed as the chief office for colonial management, enjoyed no executive power whatever. It found itself in a position subordinate to the Privy Council and the secretary of state. Two evils resulted from this. Thomas Povey wrote of an earlier colonial board " that whatsoever Council is not enabled as well to execute as advise, must needs produce very imperfect and weak effects. It being, by its subordination and impotency obliged to have recourse to Superior Ministers, and Counsels filled with other business, wch ofttimes gives great and prejudicial delays and usually begets new and slower deliberations and results, than the matter in hand may stand in need of, by wch means the authority and virtue of this council became faint and ineffectual."[42] Burke said, "Seas roll and months pass between the order and the execution; and the want of speedy explanation of a single point is enough to defeat a whole system."[43]

[40] B. T. Paps., Pl. Gen., VIII, I, 24.

[41] Fitzmaurice, Life of Shelburne, I, 270.

[42] Andrews, British Commissions, etc., Johns Hopkins Stud., XXVI, 112.

[43] Burke, Works, (Bohn Lib.) I, 468.

Under the circumstances promptness was a most valuable asset, but under the system it was lightly regarded. The board did not have immediate access to the king, but received its orders in writing either from the Privy Council directly or through the secretary of state; it reported its opinions in a " representation," drawn up by the secretary of the board and signed by five members, either to the Privy Council directly or through the secretary of state. The arrangement was not conducive to promptness.[44] Moreover, a body which had not the power to appoint one of the lowest of officials, but only the power of recommendation, to consider colonial laws but no authority to disallow them; in short a bureau which had no plenary executive power whatever would scarce enjoy the respect of the colonial officials. Governor Pownall wrote, " even the meanest of its officers in the plantations looking up solely to the *giving power*, will scarce correspond with the *directing*; nay, may perhaps make court to the one by passing by the other."[45] Pownall probably knew from experience whereof he spoke. Royal officials such as Quary and Randolph wrote that the Quakers of Pennsylvania " cared naught for the lords of trade and looked elsewhere for the confirmation of their rights."[46] They counted on the influence of William Penn, and in fact he was able to secure

[44] In its report of 1721, the board summarized the situation, "The present method of dispatching business is lyable to much delay and confusion, there being no less than three different ways of proceeding therein; that is to say (1) by immediate application to Your Majesty by one of Your Secretaries of State (2) by Petition to Your Majesty in Council and (3) by Representation to Your Majesty from this Board: from whence it happens that no one Office is thor'ly informed of all matters relating to the Plantations, and sometimes Orders are obtained by surprize, disadvantageous to Your Majesty's service; whereas, if the Business of the Plantations were wholly confined to one Office, these inconveniences would be thereby avoided. *B. T. Paps., Pl. Gen., Entry E*, ff. 286 *et. seq.*, *N. Y. Col. Docs.*, V, 630.

[45] Pownall, *Adm. of Cols.*, (ed. 1768) 17-18.

[46] *B. T. Paps., Prop.*, II, B 34; *ibid., Pl. Gen.*, IV, pt. 2, C 18.

favorable action by appealing to superior ministers in the face of adverse reports by the Board of Trade. Governor Belcher of Massachusetts wrote that " The Lords of Trade are not very mighty lords; nor are they able to administer life or death." [47] The thousand leagues which separated the mother country from the colonies may account for many of the failures to execute imperial policies and is no doubt responsible for the development of mutual misunderstanding, but it is by no means sufficient to account for the imperfections and failings of the colonial organization at home.

One other point demands our attention here. The success with which colonial business was handled depended not only on a simple and harmonious machine and on the ability and integrity of the men appointed to manage colonial affairs, but even to a greater extent on the appointment to office of men who had a knowledge gained from actual experience in the colonies. It was of the greatest importance that the members of the board should have an intimate knowledge of the needs, the laws, the customs, and the temper of the colonists gained from intimate experience so that official action might be wisely adapted to the colonial situation. It is true that men like Blathwayt, Locke and Bladen had a good knowledge of colonial affairs, but it was not gained by service in the colonies. In fact, there never sat at the board as a member anyone with a first-hand knowledge of the colonies, and after the first decade even those who were appointed thereto were generally men of inferior ability. William Penn summed up the situation admirably when he wrote in 1701 that there was " so little of an American understanding among those whose business it is to superintend it. All places as well as

[47] Belcher, *Letters*, II, 240, (Mass. Hist. Soc., *Coll.*, 6th. ser.). Wrote Belcher in 1731, " the Lords of Trade have not been very friendly in these matters. . . . We must treat them with good manners, and if they be unreasonable we must endeavour to do our business with the King & his immediate ministers." *Ibid.*, I, 38-39.

people and languages have their peculiarities, and a just
consideration thereof contributes much to proper methods
for their respective benefit.'' He expressed the wish '' that
there were added to those ingenious persons that superintend the Colonies some of their former governors that
served well. For besides that they deserve notice, they
must needs supply the rest with that knowledge their experience has given them; that they who have never been
in those parts of the world, cannot, though otherwise ora-
cles, comparably understand.'' [48] In a similar vein wrote
a memorialist in 1714.[49] '' No part of the British dominions '' said he, '' has been hitherto so little understood and
so much neglected,'' and he held that it was impossible
for a board to form a proper judgment of colonial affairs
unless some of the members had a perfect and personal
knowledge of colonial life. Like Penn, he suggested the
employment at the board of former governors of good
service. It is true that the board always laid hold of
every opportunity to accumulate all the information possible before making its report on a colonial matter. One
of its chief sources of knowledge of colonial conditions was
the colonial agent.[50] Its dependence upon this source is
illustrated by a letter from the board to the governor of
New York in 1698 urging the appointment of a permanent
agent for the colony in London '' whom we may call upon
for further information as may be requisite upon occasion;
the want thereof has occasioned delays in public affairs.'' [51]
Most of the colonies employed such agents and they were
frequently called into consultation by the board. But
some of the agents were not colonists themselves and were
employed solely to protect the interests of the colony which

[48] *Duke of Portland, Mss.*, IV, 30, (Hist. Mss. Com., *Report* 15,
pt. 4).
[49] *B. T. Paps., Pl. Gen.*, IX, K 39; *No. Car. Col. Recs.*, II, 154-166.
[50] Tanner, *Colonial Agencies, (Political Science Quarterly*, XVI,
24-49).
[51] *N. Y. Col. Docs.*, IV, 297; V, 361, 473.

they represented.   They stood rather as advocates of colonial interests than as judges.   Official action was taken by those who looked upon the colonies solely from the English point of view and who knew not American conditions by actual contact.   The board also availed itself of the information offered by proprietors, ex-governors, and English merchants trading to the colonies.   To a very great extent the board relied upon the information gained from the correspondence of royal officials, such as governors, customs and admiralty officials.   There was grave danger in a dependence upon this sort of evidence.   Many of the royal appointees in the colonies were not colonists, but Englishmen, and in some cases of an inferior sort and of a narrow and partisan cast of mind, who spent a few short years in the service and went out, as Governor Morris, himself a colonist, wrote, " generally to repair a shattered fortune or acquire an estate." [52]   This information was very apt to be *ex-parte* in character, yet we find that the Board of Trade was content to accept it at full value.   The lack of expert knowledge of colonial affairs at home contributed in no small degree to the friction, estrangement, and misunderstanding which existed between the colonies and the mother country.   In several respects the Board of Trade challenges comparison of an unfavorable sort with the English East India Office [53] of to-day or the Spanish Council of the Indies of former days.[54]   The former is a ministerial office presided over by a secretary of state for India who is assisted by a council whose members hold office for ten years at least and are chosen from those who have resided in India not less than ten years.   In Spain, the old Council of the Indies was a great department of state, entrusted with the royal authority in all matters relating to

[52] *N. Y. Col. Docs.*, V, 887.   Cf. Franklin, *Works*, (Smyth ed.), V, 83; *No. Car. Col. Recs.*, II, 158; Greene, *Prov. Gov.*, 47-48.

[53] Reinsch, *Colonial Government*, 292.

[54] Roscher, *Spanish Col. System*, (Bourne tr.), 25-26; Bourne, *Spain in America*, 222-227.

the colonies and whose members were chosen preferably from those who had held high office in New Spain with distinction. In England of the eighteenth century, authority was divided, the Board of Trade had no executive powers and was not composed of those trained by long experience in the field. It is fair to say that had the Board of Trade approximated either of the other organizations, colonial administration would have been more efficient and there would have existed more of an *entente cordiale* between the two parts of the Empire.

Still another criticism demands our attention here, and that is the ill-effects of the fee system on administration. Of the iniquities of the fee system in the colonies we shall deal in later pages. But it is a sad commentary on English colonial administration when the Board of Trade could write to a royal governor in 1716 that the laws of the colony could not be considered and reported on till an agent was appointed to pay the fees and " it is the same case with respect to Councillors; For if the Board had reported . . . that the persons you had recommended should be appointed Councillors by his Majesty, nothing would have been done therein, for want of a person to pay the fees in the Council and Secretaries Office." [55]   Governor Belcher of New Jersey was unable to secure his instructions till he disbursed £200 in fees and " this unexpected Supply set the Wheels into Motion." [56]   This statement is characteristic of the evidence on this point, but it is sufficient to illustrate to what an extent the political morality of the age cast its harmful influence on prompt and efficient administration.[57]

[55] *N. Y. Col. Docs.*, V, 361, 473. For the fees paid by the agents of Conn. at the various offices in England on the Intestacy Law and Mohegan case, consult the *Talcott Papers*, I, 244-245, (Conn. Hist. Soc., *Collections*).

[56] Greene, ·*Provincial Governor*, 47 and note.

[57] In 1731 the Privy Council adopted a table of fees which was posted in the office of the Board of Trade. *B. T. Jour.*, XLI, 230; *Acts of Privy Council, Col.*, III, 319-320.

The imperfections of the whole system were thoroughly realized by royal officials on both sides of the Atlantic. The board itself,[58] such efficient members of the board as Martin Bladen,[59] and such of its presidents, as Halifax, Shelburne,[60] Hillsborough,[61] and Dartmouth,[62] were alive to the faults of the system and its impotency. Economists, such as D'Avenant,[63] or such colonial officials as Thomas Pownall[64] and Sir William Keith,[65] were fully aware of its failings. These imperialists through reports and memorials laid bare the whole system and suggested remedies. Through personal influence they sought to bring about a reform. In order to centralize authority two remedial measures were repeatedly urged. As far as the colonies were concerned, they urged that royal government should be substituted for chartered control in order to bring all colonial administration under the immediate direction of the crown. This phase of the subject we leave for subsequent treatment. As far as England was concerned they proposed the substitution of centralized for divided responsibility by centering all colonial management in the office of the Board of Trade and by erecting that office into a department of state, whose president should be admitted into the ministry on the same footing as the other great ministers of state. Efficient control demanded one undivided department which should enjoy not only executive powers but should be the center for the transaction of all colonial business. This could be ac-

58 Report of the board of 1721, *B. T. Paps., Pl. Gen., Entry Bk. E*, 286 ff., *N. Y. Col. Docs.*, V, 629-630.

59 *No. Car. Col. Recs.*, II, 634-635.

60 Fitzmaurice, *Life of Shelburne*, I, 269-275.

61 *Grenville Corres.*, III, 294-296; *Dartmouth Mss.*, III, 179, (Hist. Mss. Com., *Report* 15, pt. 1).

62 *Dartmouth Mss.*, III, 182.

63 D'Avenant, *Works*, (Whitworth ed.), II, 29-30.

64 Pownall, *Administration of the Cols.*, (ed. 1768), 11-27.

65 Keith, *Short Discourse on Plantations*, (ed. 1740), 182-184; *B. T. Paps. Pl. Gen.*, X, L 105.

complished either by carrying out the remedy proposed above or else by giving all control over into the hands of the secretary of state and placing the board in a position of entire subordination to that office. The importance of American affairs certainly demanded the creation of a separate department of state. But in this respect the best interests of the Empire remained neglected and nothing was done to reform the system till the colonies had so far advanced to a position of political independence that adequate reforms in the direction of centralized authority would have little or no effect in restraining them.

Under the presidency of the Earl of Halifax, (1748-1761), new vigor was infused into the Board of Trade through the force of his personality and ability. Halifax took steps to put his office on a basis of efficiency and dignity such as the importance of American affairs demanded. In 1751 he urged that the board should be raised to the rank of a department of state whose president should be created secretary of state for America.[66] His suggestion was not acted upon at the time, but his persistency was productive of one step in the right direction. In March, 1752, an order in council was issued vesting the patronage of all colonial offices, except those under the direction of the Customs Board or Admiralty Board, solely in the hands of the Board of Trade. For the sake of " greater regularity and dispatch of business " the colonial governors were required to correspond exclusively with the board, except in cases of importance and of such a nature as to require the immediate attention of the secretary of state or in cases where the governors received the orders of the secretary, in which instances the correspondence was to be directed solely to the latter.[67] These exceptions referred to questions of war and diplomacy which fell properly within

[66] Walpole, *Letters*, (Cunningham ed.), II, 252, 258; Walpole, *Memoirs*, I, 199, 220.

[67] *B. T. Paps., Pl. Gen.*, XV, O 105, 107; *N. Y. Col. Docs.*, VI, 756-759; *R. I. Col. Recs.*, V, 350-354.

the secretary's office. On the formation of the Pitt ministry in 1756, Halifax again urged that he should be invested with the office and powers of a secretary of state for America. Pitt refused to consent to this division of his office and Halifax resigned.[68] The refusal to take this step at that time was no doubt wise. England was then engaged in the world-wide struggle with France for colonial and commercial supremacy and the militancy of the times demanded the entire concentration of affairs in the hands of the great secretary, William Pitt. Although Halifax was again not successful in his efforts, yet the matter was compromised and as president of the board he was admitted to a seat in the Pitt-Newcastle ministry of 1757. Horace Walpole may accuse Halifax of an overweening ambition, but the fact remains that the failings of the colonial organization at home and the critical position of American affairs is sufficient justification for an ambition so wisely directed. In 1761, with the fall of Canada, a backward step was taken. The Earl of Bute, the personal friend of the new king, George III, was admitted to the cabinet, and to appease Pitt, who was not consulted in the matter, American affairs were partly restored to his department.[69] An order in council of 1761 revoked the order of 1752 except in that part which related to the subject of correspondence.[70] But a turn in the wheel of politics was to bring a better order of affairs. In March, 1763, the Earl of Shelburne entered the Grenville ministry as president of the Board of Trade and the order of 1752 was restored.[71] But his tenure was of short duration. In September he resigned because of a lack of sympathy with Grenville's plans for America and because of friction with the Earl of Egremont, secretary of state, over questions of

[68] Walpole, *Letters*, III, 21, 84, 87; Walpole, *Memoirs*, III, 34; *Bedford Corres.*, II, 249-250.
[69] Walpole, *Letters*, III, 380, 383, 386.
[70] *N. Y. Col. Docs.*, VII, 459.
[71] *B. T. Jour.*, LXXI, 116.

their respective powers in colonial management.[72] The office with its old insignificance was bestowed upon the Earl of Hillsborough.[73] In 1765, upon the formation of the Rockingham ministry, Lord Dartmouth was made president of the board. Hillsborough, fully aware by actual experience of the evils of divided responsibility, warned his successor " that it is absolutely necessary that the same powers in every respect with regard to Trade and the Colonies should be delegated to Lord Dartmouth, as are vested in the First Lords of the Treasury and Admiralty with regard to their respective departments. Without this Lord Dartmouth will suffer continual disappointments and too probably undergo undeserved disgrace." [74] Dartmouth strongly urged what Halifax had attempted before, but to no avail and he resigned.[75] In 1766, the Earl of Shelburne entered the Grafton-Pitt ministry as secretary for the Southern department and Hillsborough was restored to the presidency of the board. An agreement was reached between the two, at Hillsborough's suggestion, whereby all colonial business was to center in the secretary's office, the board acting solely as a bureau of reference on all matters referred to it for consideration.[76] The order of 1752 was rescinded in full and the governors were directed to

[72] Fitzmaurice, *Life of Shelburne*, I, 268-278; Walpole, *Letters*, IV, 113.

[73] *B. T. Jour.*, LXXI, 211.

[74] *Dartmouth Mss.*, III, 179, (Hist. Mss. Com., *Report* 15, pt. 1).

[75] Earl of Chesterfield wrote Dartmouth, " You must be Secretary of State in all the forms and privileges of that office. . . . If we have no Secretary of State with full and undisputed powers for America, in a few years we may as well have no America." Dartmouth replied that he would not concur in any plan " that is not calculated to give dignity and credit, as well as effectual authority to the person who may undertake to preside over that Department." *Dartmouth Mss.*, III, 182, (Hist. Mss. Com., *Report* 15, pt. 1). *Narrative of Changes in the Ministry, 1765-1769, told by the Duke of Newcastle*, 96-97, (Camden Soc., *Publications*, 1898).

[76] *Cal. State Paps., Home Office*, 1766-1769, no. 256; Fitzmaurice, *Life of Shelburne*, II, 2-3: *Grenville Corres.*, III, 294-296.

correspond with the secretary, sending only " duplicates " to the board, except in cases of war and diplomacy.[77]   This plan was well-conceived and was without doubt calculated to give colonial concerns the undivided attention they deserved.   But the reform did not go far enough.   The critical posture of American affairs which followed in the wake of the Stamp Act demanded not only wise statesmanship but the creation of a separate and distinct department of ministerial standing for the control of the colonies.   Steps leading to a realization of this object were taken in 1767. Such was the design of Pitt in 1766,[78] but his illness rendered him incapable of business and forced him into retirement which left the ministry in the hands of the Grafton wing of the Whig party.   Grafton anxious to detach the Bedford faction from opposition, sought to make way for the inclusion of some of Bedford's followers in the ministry.   With this object in view Shelburne was approached on the question of separating American affairs from his office.[79]   Unable to secure the advice of Chatham in his retirement, Shelburne acquiesced.   The plan was consummated in January, 1768, and the Earl of Hillsborough became the first secretary of state for America.[80]

The reform came too late.   The efforts to strengthen the system of colonial administration which followed the close of the French and Indian war and the elevation of American affairs to the dignity of a department of state came at a time when the colonies had practically attained

[77] *N. Y. Col. Docs.*, VII, 848.

[78] *Grenville Corres.*, III, 235.

[79] Fitzmaurice, *Life of Shelburne*, II, 67-77; Walpole, *Letters*, V, 75, 77; *N. Y. Col. Docs.*, VIII, 7.

[80] Said Burke in 1780, " the history of this office is too recent to suffer us to forget, that it was made for the mere convenience of the arrangements of political intrigue, and not for the service of the state; that it was made, in order to give a colour to an exorbitant increase of the civil list; and in the same act to bring a new accession to the loaded compost heap of corrupt influence." *Works*, (Bohn Lib.) II, 109.

the position of political independence and were too far
beyond the point where they could be controlled by any
sort of a system except their own. From the point of
view of the colonists the lack of system was of great advantage to them. It left them free to develop their institutions in a normal and natural way, unhampered by
vigorous English control and interference. The inherent
difficulties of the geographical situation, which placed the
center of government so far away from the colonies, indeed accounts much for the failure to carry into effectual
execution imperial control and paved the way for final
separation. But it may be said that the lack of vigor at
home due to the complexity of machinery of administration,
the inferior character of the officials and their lack of an
intimate knowledge of colonial conditions, the vicissitudes
of party politics and factional struggles at home, all combined to prevent a real and effective control of the colonies by the imperial government.

Prior to the outbreak of the Civil War in England in
1641, the crown was the only organ of government concerned with the colonies; Parliament had not yet come to
exercise a power to legislate for them. This exclusive
connection between crown and colonies was a result of
the fact that at that time the crown stood as the embodiment of sovereignty in the English state.[81] Land in
America was seized in the name of the king, all charters
to commercial and colonizing companies were issued under
his name and seal, the powers and privileges bestowed
upon the patentees were granted away in accordance with
his will, and control over the colonies was exercised solely
by the king. But the tie which bound together the colonies and England was in no sense of a purely personal nature, such as the personal union between England and
Scotland before 1707, or between England and Hanover
after 1714, simply held together loosely by reason of al-

[81] Beer, *Origins of British Col. System, 1578-1660*, 300-303.

legiance to the same prince. The relations were far more
intimate.[82] The colonies were dominions or territories,
not incorporated into the realm of England as was Wales
by the Act of Union, but in the status of dependent communities, subordinate to the sovereignty of England and
subject to the absolute power of the central government
to determine their political and governmental rights.
With the founding of permanent colonies Parliament denied the crown's claim to exclusive jurisdiction over the
colonies, holding that it had a right to legislate for them.
But during the early part of the seventeenth century
Parliament had not yet determined the extent of its power
over England. Colonial control formed simply one of
the fundamental questions at issue in the struggle between
the crown and Parliament over their respective fields of
government. Until the Civil War the crown was able to
uphold its high monarchical pretensions, but during that
war and the Cromwellian era Parliament established its
right to deal with the colonies, and in fact emphatically asserted this claim in the words of the act of 1650.[83] It reads,
" Whereas the islands and other places in America, where
any English are planted, are and ought to be subject to
and dependent upon England and both ever since the
planting thereof, have been and ought to be subject to the
laws, orders, and regulations as are and shall be made by
the parliament." This is precisely the view of the supremacy of Parliament and the subordination of the colonies stated over a century later in the words of the De-
claratory Act.

After the Restoration the right of Parliament to
legislate for the colonies was not disputed in England
and during the period of the later Stuarts this power was
exercised directly by the passage of the famous acts of

[82] Osgood, *American Cols. in 17th. Cent.*, III, 6-12.
[83] Beer., *op. cit.*, ch. xii; Osgood, *op. cit.*, III, 115-118.

trade and navigation which laid down the principles along which the colonies were to be administered. The status of the colonies and the power of Parliament over them were well defined by the court of common pleas in the time of Charles II. Sir John Vaughan, chief justice, said in the case of *Craw vs. Ramsay,* that "Ireland is a dominion belonging to the Crown of England, and follows that it cannot separate from it, but by Act of Parliament, no more than Wales, Gernsey, Jersey, Berwick, the English Plantations, all which are belonging to the Realm of England, though not within the Territorial dominion or Realm of England, but follow it, and are a part of its Royalty." [84] In another case the same justice declared that Ireland, the Channel Islands, and the colonies over-sea "are of the dominions of England . . . all of which may be bound by Laws, made respectively for them by an English Parliament." [85] These clear cut expressions of opinion are comparable with the words of the act of 1650. They show in clearest terms that the union between the colonies and England was in no sense personal, but that the colonies were territories, outside the realm and subject to the sovereign power in the English state. Furthermore, these statements emphasize the right of Parliament to legislate for the colonies. But the question of the legal sovereignty in the English state was by no means established till the eighteenth century. The revolution of 1689 which saw the culmination of the long and bitter struggle between the crown and Parliament over questions of government was followed by the passage of the great remedial statutes, such as the Bill of Rights and the Act of Settlement, which guaranteed the liberties of the subjects against the arbitrary exercise of the royal prerogative, and hedged about with serious limitations the ancient powers of the crown.

[84] *Reports and Arguments of Sir John Vaughan,* (1720), 300.
[85] *Ibid.,* 400-401.

With the gradual transfer of power from the crown to Parliament in the direction of parliamentary supremacy [86] there never arose any question at home of the right and power of the imperial legislature to deal with the colonies. Therefore, until Parliament exercised the right to incorporate the colonies into the realm or to provide a government for them, they remained either under the direct control of the crown or were governed under the royal charters subject to the controlling power of the crown as provided by the royal grants.

After 1689 Parliament came more and more to exercise its power over the colonies. This interest in colonization is largely accounted for by the increasing influence of the mercantile classes and a consequent growing attachment to the principles of the laws of trade. It was the influence of the merchants acting through Parliament which secured the passage of the act of 1696 and which sought to obtain control of colonial management by the creation of a Parliamentary council of trade. In an administrative way Parliament exercised some control over the colonies. It repeatedly called upon the Board of Trade to submit reports on the questions of colonial administration, finance, trade, defense, manufactures and other interests.[87] Parliament appointed committees from its own members to investigate colonial conditions. In a positive way its administrative power is exemplified in addresses to the crown directing the execution of certain orders. By such means two laws of South Carolina were vetoed, the governors of the charter colonies were required to give bond for the proper performance of their duties in execution of the acts of trade, and governors were directed not to as-

[86] McIlwain, *The High Court of Parliament and its Supremacy*, chap. v, gives an admirable and clear account of the political history of parliamentary supremacy.

[87] For a list of the reports to Parliament, consult Andrews and Davenport, *Guide to the Mss. Materials for Hist. of U. S. in English Archives*, 192 ff. See the reports of 1702 and 1703 in the Bulletins of the N. Y. Public Lib., X, no. 5; XI, no. 10.

sent to laws creating a paper currency without the suspending clause.   In the sphere of actual legislation Parliament passed about sixty acts directly affecting the colonies in the period 1689 to 1765.   At least two-thirds of this
number related chiefly to an extension of the principles of
the acts of trade and navigation.   A few concerned more
intimately internal affairs, such as the post-office laws, the
acts concerning specie and paper currency, and the acts
restricting colonial manufactures.   On the whole Parliament confined itself mainly to the regulation of external
trade and matters which concerned the interests of the Empire at large, and left direct taxation and distinctly internal affairs to be regulated by the colonial governments.
But this legislation stands as positive evidence of the
right of the imperial legislature to make laws for the
colonies in every way whatever.   Moreover, that it was
within the competence of Parliament to alter or abolish
the colonial charters is evidenced by the act of 1696, was
shown conclusively by the several bills intended either to
vacate or modify them, and was repeatedly stated in the
opinions of the crown lawyers.   In the minds of Englishmen at home there was no doubt of the legal supremacy
of Parliament over the colonies.   In point of law and precedent this view was absolutely unassailable.[88]

The supremacy of Parliament meant the subordination
of the colonial governments.   In law the colonial corporations and the provinces were on the same plane respectively
as corporate municipalities and provinces in England.
This was the view commonly accepted by English statesmen.   As Burke said, '' at the first designation of the assemblies, they were not intended as anything more,

[88] Burke wrote, " When I first came into a public trust, I found
your parliament in possession of an unlimited legislative power
over the colonies.   I could not open the statute book without seeing
the actual exercise of it, more or less, in all cases whatsoever.
This possession passed with me for a title." *Letter to the Sheriffs
of Bristol, Works,* (Bohn Lib.) II, 26.

. . . than the municipal corporations within this Island, to which some at present love to compare them.'' [89] A clause of the act of 1696 expressly stated the doctrine of the supremacy of Parliament and the subordination of the colonial assemblies by declaring null and void any '' Lawes, By Laws, Usages and Customes '' which are repugnant to any statute made or to be made '' in this Kingdome soe far as such Law relate to and mention the said Plantations.'' [90] Considering the respective positions in law of Parliament and the colonial assemblies, what then was the ground upon which the colonists at a later period so stoutly resisted the right of Parliament to legislate for them on all questions? What was the basis of the colonial claims to legislative independence? Had the colonies been incorporated into the realm and had the crown and Parliament dealt with the colonies as directly and intensively as they did for the provinces at home, these questions would not have arisen at a later time to vex and disrupt the Empire. But such was not the case. Parliament never saw fit to define beyond the shadow of a doubt the status of the colonies in the imperial system. That it was within its power to do so is without doubt, but that it neglected definitely to ascertain the nature of the constitution of the Empire is equally true. This constitution was left to develop along normal lines and according to a natural growth. The colonists were left to fashion their own institutions and governments free from parliamentary interference and vigorous control of the crown due to the cumbersome and weak administrative system.

[89] Bladen, a member of the Board of Trade, wrote, "we are to consider them as so many Corporations at a distance, invested with an ability to make temporary By Laws for themselves agreeable to their respective Scituations and Climates, but no ways interfering with the legal Prerogative of the Crown, or the true Legislative Power of the Mother State." *No. Car. Col. Recs.*, II, 629-630. Cf. Burke, *Works*, II, 33; Andrews, *The Connecticut Intestacy Law,* *(Yale Review,* Nov., 1894, 281-287).

[90] 7 and 8 Wm. III, c. 22, sec. 8.

From the fact that the colonies were never made a part
of the realm there developed a distinction between the dominions and realm. This principle is best stated in the
words of Attorney-General Yorke in 1729 that statutes
of Parliament passed since the settlement of a colony " and
are not, by express words, located to the Plantations in
general, or to the Province in particular, are not in force
there, unless they have been introduced and declared to
be laws, by some acts of the Assembly of the Province."[91] This principle was supported by actual practice and commonly accepted in the colonies.[92] The fact
that Parliament passed very few acts which expressly mentioned the colonies and did not interfere with the internal
polity of the colonies to any great extent, left the bulk of
legislation to the colonial assemblies. In Rhode Island
and Connecticut the government under the royal charters
was democratically organized and these two corporate colonies possessed all the organs of representative government
necessary to independent political existence. In the provinces, both royal and proprietary, the source of political
power was not in the people; the political and governmental privileges shared by them depended to a large extent upon the will of the crown or proprietor. In the
royal province, the predominant type of colony in the
eighteenth century, the old prerogatives of the crown found
expression in the commissions to the royal governors.[93]
Since Parliament devised no government for them they remained subject to the controlling power of the crown.
The royal power in this respect was in no way limited by
the Revolution of 1689. The fundamental statutes which
limited the royal prerogative and gave greater emphasis

[91] Chalmers, *Opinions of Eminent Lawyers,* (ed. 1858), 208, also
209-232.

[92] Osgood, *American Cols. in 17th. Cent.,* III, 8-9. See the pre-
amble to the Pennsylvania law of 1718, *Pa. Statutes at Large,*
III, 199.

[93] Greene, *Provincial Governor,* 93-95.

to the rights of Englishmen at home, made no mention of the colonies and consequently were of no force there. But the crown had already recognized the triumph of the representative principle in government and granted the colonists the right to elect deputies to make laws for the colony in conjunction with the royal governor and council. In Pennsylvania, the people from the very first were granted large powers of self-government. William Penn was a fond believer in popular government. After two decades of constitution making, there was evolved the Charter of Privileges of 1701 which stood as the embodiment of the organic law of the province till 1776. This written constitution granted the people a representative assembly with power to choose its own speaker and officers, to judge of the qualifications of its own members, prepare bills to be passed into laws, redress grievances and to " have all the Powers and Privileges of an Assemby, according to the Rights of the Free-born Subjects of England." [94] In 1706 these powers were formally enacted into law which was passed upon by the crown and confirmed.[95] Thus the incipient parliament of the province received the legal sanction of the home government. Still the provincial assembly was not the dominant factor in politics. The extent of its power and its position in government was still to be determined. The relation of the representative bodies in the provinces to the crown or proprietor was in many ways analogous to that of Parliament to the crown prior to 1688. In the eighteenth century not only did Parliament become the sovereign power in the English state, but the House of Commons arrogated to itself more and more the political supremacy in government at the expense both of the Lords and crown. There was a steady advance toward the modern system of

[94] For Charter of Privileges, see *Pa. Col. Recs.*, II, 56-60; Poore, *Charters and Constitutions*, II; Thorpe, *Amer. Charters, Consts., etc.*, V, 3076-3081.

[95] *Pa. Statutes at Large*, II, 218.

responsible government by which the crown acts only on the advice of ministers chosen from the ruling party in the Commons. The means by which this was effected was the control of the purse strings by the Commons. By a course of development remarkably like that in England, the colonial assemblies became the dominant organs in provincial politics. To obtain this position, the representative branch of the assembly, like the Commons in England, used the effective whip of the money power. The position which the assembly of Pennsylvania sought to attain was that of the assemblies in the corporate colonies of New England or that of the House of Commons in England. In 1707 Robert Quary wrote to the Board of Trade of the bitter struggle in Pennsylvania between the governor and assembly in which the latter " resolved to have all the Government and powers into their own hands, they insist to have the sole regulation of all Courts, and the nomination of all officers, to sett when and as often and as long as they please on their own adjournments, they have filled a volume with Votes and Privileges so that they have banished all Prerogative & Government but what is lodged in the Assembly." [96] In 1741 Governor Thomas wrote that the assembly was " vested with Powers of Government so ample as to render the Governor a Cypher or no more than nominal." [97] What is said here of the assembly of Pennsylvania is equally true of all the provinces, and shows unmistakably that the constitutional development of the colonies was in the direction of responsible government. The lower house in the provinces, like the Commons in England, eventually became the controlling factor in the colonial governments.

[96] *N. Y. Col. Docs.*, IV, 1051. Wrote Logan to Penn, " Ours here (i. e. the assembly) contend for the whole power and leave the Governour only a name; and they aver 'tis their right from thy first charter granted them in England, which is obligatory upon them." *Penn-Logan Corres.*, II, 182.

[97] Governor Thomas to John Penn, May 14, 1741, *Penn. Mss., Official Corres.*, III.

Owing to the fact that Parliament confined itself chiefly to the regulation of external affairs and left to the colonial assemblies the greater part of legislation and regulation of internal affairs, it is not to be wondered that the people looked upon their assemblies as having the same powers and authority as the English Parliament. In these legislatures the people were represented and through their delegates expressed their desires and sentiments. Naturally enough they became attached to their own representative bodies and deemed them more important than Parliament in which they were only virtually represented. It was from such a course of development that was evolved the theory of "actual representation." Since the colonists had no voice in the election of members to the English Parliament, they denied the right of that body to tax them or to regulate their internal affairs. In 1754 Franklin opposed a plan to raise a fund by act of Parliament to support the charges of defense in the colonies on the ground that the colonists were unrepresented in that body.[98] Of such evidence there is not a little,[99] but this view did not become wide-spread till after the passage of the Stamp Act.

This tendency toward political independence was thoroughly realized by royal and proprietary officials and they persistently urged the home government to take measures to check it. In 1703, Robert Quary wrote of Virginia, "The Assembly concludes it is entitled to all the rights and Privileges of an English Parliament; and search into the records of that house for precedents; These false and pernicious notions, if not timely prevented, will have a very ill consequence."[100] Or as Governor Hamilton of

---

[98] Franklin, *Works*, (Smyth ed.), III, 209, 231, 232-241.

[99] Chalmers, *Intro. to Revolt of Cols.*, I, 284, 285; *N. Y. Col. Docs.*, IV, 71; Beer, *British Col. Pol., 1754-1765*, 41; Greene, *Prov. Amer.*, 186.

[100] *N. Y. Col. Docs.*, IV, 1051. Belcher, governor of Mass., wrote, "our Assemblies are sometimes made to think by their leaders that they are as big as the Parliament of Great Britain, but surely

Pennsylvania wrote, in 1761, that the assembly claimed
" to be entitled to all the priveledges of a House of
Comons, (tho' I am expressly advised to the Contrary by
his Majesty's Attorney-General of England)."[101] Time
and time again the assembly of Pennsylvania based its
claim to powers and privileges upon parliamentary precedents which is good evidence that it looked upon itself
as clothed with the same authority as the Parliament at
home.[102] Prior to 1765 there was apparently no friction
between the colonial assemblies and Parliament, although
they exercised the same functions. That they did not
clash was due to the fact that they confined themselves
to different spheres of activity; the one mainly to the
general interests of the Empire, and the other to internal
affairs.[103]

From these facts we are able to point out the nature
of the imperial constitution as it stood in 1765. The colonies had advanced from the legal position of provinces
with power to make by-laws to the actual position of autonomous governments with parliaments of their own co-
ordinate with the English Parliament. Great Britain, as
far as the colonies were concerned, was moving in the direction not of a consolidated and centralized empire, but
of a federal empire. It was composed of a number of in-

as occasions require, I can't help thinking we shall always to our
loss & cost find otherwise." *Letters*, II, 388, (Mass. Hist. Soc.,
Coll., sixth ser.). For like opinions see, *N. Y. Col. Docs.*, IV, 1059,
1121; V, 255-256.

[101] Kimball, *Corres. of Pitt with Col. Govs.*, II, 433.

[102] *Pa. Col. Recs.*, VI, 581, 708, 717; VII, 752; VIII, 74, 106.

[103] Burke wrote, " . . . neither part felt any inconvenience from
this double legislature, to which they had been formed by imper-
ceptible habits, and old custom, the great support of all the governments in the world. Though these legislatures were sometimes
found perhaps performing the very same functions, they did not
very grossly or systematically clash. In all likelihood this arose
from mere neglect; possibly from the natural operation of things,
which, left to themselves, generally fall into their proper order."
Works, (Bohn Lib.), II, 33.

dependent political units bound together into a loose confederation, owing allegiance to the same king, and controlled as to their external affairs by the imperial legislature. The permanence of the Empire depended upon a recognition of this historic growth.

CHAPTER THREE

ADMINISTRATION OF THE ACTS OF TRADE

In treating of the administrative relations between the colonies and England it is essential to bear in mind that the basis of the English colonial system was economic rather than political. The creation of a commercial rather than a political empire was the chief consideration. Colonization was looked upon as a means of lessening the economic dependence of the metropolis upon foreign countries and of developing national power and prestige.[1] This policy took definite shape with the passage of the acts of trade and navigation in the Restoration period, whereby the economic life of the colonies was regulated and controlled in the interest of a self-sufficient commercial empire.[2] Two principles lay at the basis of this system; that of confining all colonial shipping to national bottoms, and that of restricting colonial export and import trade to England as the staple. The laws provided that all ships trading to or from the colonies should be owned and built in England or the colonies, and that the master and three-fourths of the crew should be English or colonial born. As to the staple it was stipulated that colonial importations from Europe should first be landed in England before shipment to America, and that the exportation of certain colonial products, specified by law, should be shipped in the first instance to England. The carrying into effect of these laws called for an adminis-

[1] Callender, *Selections from Economic Hist. of U. S.*, 85-120; Beer, *British Col. Policy, 1754-1765*, 193-205, 209-210; Andrews, *Colonial Self-Gov't.*, 3-21; Osgood, *Amer. Cols.*, III, 193-239.

[2] 12 Chas. II., c. 18; 14 Chas. II., c. 11; 15 Chas. II., c. 7; 25 Chas. II., c. 7; 7 and 8 Wm. III., c. 22.

trative machinery of some sort. In this chapter it is the purpose to deal with the customs service, and in the next with the vice-admiralty courts established in the colonies under the act of 1696.

At the head of the customs service was the Lords of the Treasury and its subordinate board, the Commissioners of the Customs. By the act of 1696 they were authorized to designate all ports in the colonies and to appoint all needful officials thereto.[3] The Customs Board exercised a general superintendence over the customs officials both in the colonies and in England. This board commissioned officers on warrant from the Lords of the Treasury, issued instructions to the customs officials, and carried on a correspondence with them relative to the execution of the acts of trade.[4] There was also an auditor-general òf the colonial revenues, whose duty it was to audit and inspect all accounts of rents, revenues, and duties payable to the royal exchequer. He was empowered to appoint deputies for the colonies and to make proposals to the treasury board concerning the better management of the revenues. The office carried with it a yearly compensation of £500, payable out of the revenues arising in several of the colonies. This office was created in 1680 with William Blathwayt as the first incumbent, succeeded in 1718 by Horatio Walpole.[5] At the head of the American service was a surveyor-general, an office first established in 1683. Of the work of the first incumbents, William Dyer and Patrick Mein, there is little knowledge at hand.[6] But with the appointment of Edward Randolph to that post in 1691, the office stands out in clear relief.[7] The surveyor-general

---

[3] 7 and 8 Wm. III., c. 22, sec. 10.

[4] *Customs Books*, Public Record Office, London, contain the entries of commissions issued, warrants for salaries, etc.

[5] Commission to Blathwayt, *B. T. Paps., Pl. Gen.*, VIII, I 55; to Walpole, *ibid.*, IX, K 108.

[6] Osgood, *Amer. Cols.*, III, 236; Andrews, *Col. Self-Gov't.*, 34.

[7] *Customs Books*, XI, 353.

was empowered to inspect and control the management
of all inferior customs officers in the colonies, to suspend
from office for good cause, to appoint to vacancies, but
in either case to report the matter at once to the Customs
Board. A yearly salary of £365 attached to the office,
together with £50 a year for a clerk and £80 for the hire
of a boat and boatmen.[8] For twenty-five years the duties
of the office extended over all the continental colonies and
the Bermuda Islands. In 1709 the Customs Board reported to the Lords of the Treasury that recent information had brought to light gross frauds in the service, due
to the fact that it was practically impossible for one man
to control and inspect the offices and keep them to a proper
performance of their duties over such a wide-extended
territory.[9] As a result of this report the office was divided
in 1709 and two surveys created; one embracing the colonies of Newfoundland, New England, New York and
New Jersey; the other included Pennsylvania, the mainland
colonies south, Jamaica and the Bermudas, each under a
surveyor-general receiving the same salary and allowances
as allowed the former surveyor.[10] Of these officials none was
more active and zealous in the discharge of his duties than
Edward Randolph. At first he was surveyor for New England where he was unweary in his efforts to enforce the
laws of trade.[11] When his powers were given a wider scope
in 1691, the colonies to the south felt the rigors of his tire-
less efforts to bring offenders to justice. In his surveys of
1691-1695, he placed forfeited bonds in suit, brought action
against illegal traders, dismissed delinquent and corrupt
customs officials, and infused new vigor into the service.[12]

---

[8] *Customs Bks.*, XII, 268, 371. At first Randolph received only £200
a year, but in 1696 he petitioned for and was granted the salary
of £365, which had been allowed his predecessors. *Ibid.*, 268.

[9] *Ibid.*, XIV, 179.

[10] *Ibid.*, XIV, 181.

[11] Osgood, *Amer. Cols.*, III, 228-235.

[12] *Cal. State Paps., Col., 1689-1692*, 656-660.

In 1695 he was in England bending his energy to secure the passage of the act of 1696. In 1698 he was again in the colonies and during his surveys of the next two years he installed the new customs officials, visited all the colonies once, and in some cases twice, from New Hampshire to the Bermudas.[13] In the latter part of 1700 he was again in England actively engaged in support of the bill in Parliament to vacate the colonial charters in the interest of more efficient colonial administration. His correspondence with the Customs Board and the Board of Trade was frequent and voluminous, and it was accepted at home with implicit faith.[14] On his death in 1703, he was succeeded by Robert Quary who stood high in the estimation of the boards of trade and customs.[15] At the time of his appointment he was judge of the vice-admiralty court and surveyor of the customs for Pennsylvania and New Jersey. Quary was continued surveyor-general for the southern district when the office was divided in 1709. He was an official of much the same type as Randolph, although he lacked his predecessor's ability. Quary was succeeded by Sir William Keith, afterwards governor of Pennsylvania.[16] Keith served for the short space of a year and a half, but he has left a record of his work which throws some light on the administration of his office.[17] He left England in June, 1714, and landed in Virginia, where he visited and inspected all the customs offices; in January, 1715, he sailed for Jamaica where he recovered £8000 in revenue due the crown for nine years and in grave danger of being lost; thence he sailed in June to South Carolina, where he put the customs offices on a good footing. Keith's

13 *B. T. Paps., Pl. Gen.*, V, pt. 2, D 49.

14 For the letters and papers of Randolph see the 7 vols. in the publications of the Prince Society.

15 *Customs Books*, XIII, 296; Toppan, *Edward Randolph*, V, 291, 292-293. Quary's commission is printed in the Mass. Hist. Soc., *Proceedings*, 2d. ser., IV, 148.

16 *Customs Books*, XV, 58, 81.

17 *B. T. Paps., Props.*, X, pt. 1, Q 87.

report not only reveals the character of the work performed by the surveyor-general, but illustrates the looseness which characterized much of the customs service.

Before taking up the work of the officials directly under the control of the Customs Board and surveyor-general, it will be well to describe the duties of the governor and the naval officer as administrators of the laws of trade. As we have already pointed out, the act of 1696 contained provisions intended to draw the governor and naval officers in the chartered colonies more directly under royal influence.[18] The governor was required to give bond and take the oath binding him to a faithful performance of his duties with regard to the trade laws; failure to do either was made punishable by removal from office and a fine of £1000. The naval officer, appointed by the governor, was also required to give bond to the Customs Board, and until this obligation was absolved, the governor was held liable for the neglects of his appointee. By far the most effective hold on the governor possessed by the crown was contained in the clause, that "All governors nominated by proprietors entitled to make such nominations should be approved by his majesty." Randolph busied himself at once in efforts to see the provisions carried into effect. A draft of a commission to administer the oath was drawn up by the attorney-general at Randolph's request.[19] The Board of Trade advised the Privy Council of the necessity of issuing these commissions.[20] This report was approved by the council in August, 1696, commissions were drawn up and placed in the hands of Randolph, soon to depart for the colonies, to see that they were put into force.[21] The com-

[18] See page 7.
[19] B. T. Jour., IX, 28-29; B. T. Paps., Pl. Gen., Entry Bk. A, 25-26.
[20] B. T. Jour., IX, 23, 43, 45; B. T. Paps., Pl. Gen., IV, pt. 1, A 4; Entry Bk. A, 19.
[21] B. T. Paps., Pl. Gen., IV, pt. 1, A 63; C 41; Entry Bk. A, 27; House of Lords Mss., n.s., II, 426.

mission for Pennsylvania empowered three of the provincial council together with the collector at Philadelphia, or three of the persons named therein to administer the oath to the governor.[22] The matter of the royal approbation of the governors was not pressed at the time, but meanwhile steps were taken to bind the proprietors and governors by restrictions which formed no part of the act of 1696.

In February, 1697, a committee of the House of Lords intimated to William Penn that in view of the gross irregularities committed in the chartered colonies it may be found necessary to place such colonies under direct royal control.[23] To meet this threat Penn suggested that his governor should give security for good behavior.[24] In consequence the Lords addressed the crown directing that the proprietors should give bond in England obliging their governors to " observe and obey all Instructions that shall be sent to them from Your Majesty, or any acting under Your Authority, pursuant to the several Acts of Trade relating to the Plantations."[25] This measure went further than Penn contemplated, for he only proposed that the governors appointed by the proprietors, and not the proprietors themselves, should enter into security. The Board of Trade acted promptly on the address. The attorney-general was called upon to draw up a suitable bond and the Customs Board was asked to fix the sum.[26] Early in May, 1697, the proprietors and colonial agents were directed to appear before the board and fulfill the obligation.[27] At

[22] B. T. Paps., Props., IV, D 31; Pl. Gen., IV, pt. 2, B 42.

[23] House of Lords Jour., XVI, 94; House of Lords Mss., n.s., II, 410.

[24] House of Lords Mss., n.s., II, 413, 414.

[25] House of Lords Jour., XVI, 125-126, 127-128, 131.

[26] B. T. Paps., Props., Entry Bk. A, 62, 64, 68, 79; B. T. Jour., X, 64-65, 66, 69, 94. For draft of bond see Props., Entry Bk. D, 165. The Customs Board reported that the amount of the bond should be from £2000 to £5000, according to the importance of the trade of the colony.

[27] B. T. Paps., Props., Entry Bk. A, 74-75. Earl of Bellomont,

once they protested. Thornburgh, agent for the Carolina proprietors, answered that the patentees could not be expected to give security for persons approved by the crown, neither was there any law which required it.[28] Penn took the same stand. He thought " it hard that the Proprietarys should give security for the Deputys of the King's approbation; Since it is the same thing for therefore we should be excused because the King approves or disapproves our Nomination." [29] He held that if the appointment was entirely in the hands of the proprietor there was reasonable grounds for requiring him to give security for his governor. The matter was not pressed again till 1700 in connection with the appointment of a governor for the Bahamas. At this time the Board of Trade took further ground, insisting that both the proprietor and his governor should enter into a bond.[30] The legality of the question was referred to the attorney-general who held that there was no law which required the proprietors to enter into such obligation.[31] With this the effort to include the proprietors was dropped, but deputy-governors upon confirmation by the crown were required to give security.

Considerable difficulty was experienced by the Board of Trade in enforcing the provisions requiring the royal confirmation of the governor of chartered colonies. There were two serious defects in the act of 1696 in this respect, pointed out by Randolph.[32] No penalty was provided for patentees who refused or neglected to present their nominees for royal approval, and, after the royal will had once been expressed, the crown had no power to remove a gov-

governor of N. Y., was instructed to execute bonds for the governors of Rhode Island and Connecticut. *Ibid.*, 108, 112.

[28] *B. T. Paps., Props.*, Entry Bk. A., 80; *B. T. Jour.*, X, 103-104.

[29] *B. T. Paps., Props.*, II, B 8; Entry Bk. A, 189, 194; *B. T. Jour.*, X, 117, 119, 385.

[30] *B. T. Paps., Props.*, Entry Bk. B, 213, 214. 216.

[31] *Ibid.*, 243.

[32] *House of Lords Mss.*, n.s., II, 488-490.

ernor and insist upon the nomination of another. On the other hand the crown lawyers on several occasions gave the opinion that the crown had a right to appoint a royal governor in a chartered colony, a right which was exercised several times.[33] In February, 1698, the Board of Trade reported to the Privy Council that because of the irregularities committed in the chartered colonies and because the proprietors had not presented their governors for royal approbation nor given security, the charters should be vacated by legislative action.[34] Meanwhile Randolph complained that none of the governors had secured the royal sanction.[35] In October, 1699, the board wrote to the proprietors asking what steps they had taken to absolve the obligation.[36] The Privy Council directed the attorney-general to report on a measure to enforce this obligation on the proprietors.[37] It was proposed to remedy the matter by a clause in the piracy act of 1700, but it was omitted. In January, 1701, the attorney-general advised the passage of a special act,[38] but again no such law found its way to the statute books. The only solution of the problem was the vacation of the charters and the establishment of direct control by the crown. A bill to this effect was introduced into the House of Lords in March, 1701, but it never passed beyond the second reading.[39]

Even before this the crown assumed a power to remove a governor by requiring Penn in 1699 to dismiss Governor Markham and nominate another in his stead. Markham was charged with countenancing piracy and smuggling, with opposition to the admiralty court, and with not having the royal confirmation. Penn went to the province and took

[33] See pages 338, 339.
[34] *B. T. Jour.*, X, 444.
[35] *Ibid.*, XII, 98; *B. T. Paps., Pl. Gen.*, IV, pt. 2, B 40.
[36] *B. T. Jour.*, XII, 221, 240-241.
[37] *B. T. Paps., Props.*, IV, D 18; *Pl. Gen.*, IV, pt. 1, D 3.
[38] *B. T. Jour.*, XIII, 293, 315; *B. T. Paps., Props.*, V, F 56.
[39] See page 344.

upon himself the duties of governor. In 1701 he returned hastily to England to defend his charter against parliamentary attacks, and appointed Andrew Hamilton governor. Robert Quary, then in England, charged that Hamilton was unqualified to act, not having the royal approval nor given security.[40] In answer Penn said that he had directed his son in England to secure a royal order confirming Hamilton, but it was not done because of the doubtful issue of the bill against the charters.[41] In justification of Hamilton's appointment Penn held that it was necessary to leave someone to care for the interests of the crown and proprietor until royal sanction could be secured, and in support of this contention he produced the opinion of Chief Justice Atwood of New York that the appointment was good until the royal will was expressed. Penn then petitioned the crown to approve Hamilton.[42] His name was also under consideration as governor of the new royal province of New Jersey. Quary and Randolph both opposed the nomination on the ground that Hamilton had connived at violations of the acts of trade opposed the admiralty court, and had shown great favoritism to the Quakers.[43] On this evidence the Board of Trade reported against Hamilton and in July, 1702, the Privy Council sustained the report.[44] Penn appealed to members of the ministry asking that Hamilton be confirmed for one year as necessary to the security of English and colonial interests.[45] The crown was disposed to grant the request, and the board seized the occasion to fasten upon Penn two conditions; that his governor should provide security in the sum of £2000, and that the royal confirmation should in no way

40 B. T. Paps., Props., VI, pt. 2, I 28; VII, M 21.
41 Ibid., VI, pt. 2, I 19, K 8.
42 Ibid., VI, pt. 2, K 13; B. T. Jour., XV, 111.
43 B. T. Paps., Props., VI, pt. 2, K 6, 7; N. J. Archives, II, 479, 481.
44 B. T. Paps., Props., VI, pt. 2, K 49; Entry Bk. D, 102, 220.
45 B. T. Paps., Props., VI, pt. 2, K 51; Entry Bk. D, 233; Penn-Logan Corres., I, 136.

prejudice the right and title of the crown to the soil and government of Delaware.[46]   Penn fulfilled the conditions. He signed a statement with regard to Delaware according to the wishes of the board and left with the Lords of the Treasury the names of Hamilton's bondsmen.   In January, 1703, a certificate was issued from the office of the Remembrancer of the Exchequer showing that the bond had been executed.[47]   Thereupon Hamilton was approved by order in council as governor of Delaware at the pleasure of the crown and of Pennsylvania for one year.[48]   This in general was the procedure which obtained in the case of all governors nominated by Penn or his heirs for their dominions. The attempts to enforce the obligations of the bond and royal confirmation upon the governors of the corporate colonies of Rhode Island and Connecticut illustrate the imperfections of the law in 1696.   In these colonies the charters called for yearly elections of the governors and the short tenure and great distance from England practically nullified any attempts to enforce the provisions.   This fact was repeatedly urged in support of the policy to vacate the charters.[49]   The whole situation revealed the serious difficulties in the way of administering colonies governed under charters in the interests of the Empire.

At first the Board of Trade inquired very carefully into

[46] *B. T. Jour.*, XV, 259; *B. T. Paps., Props.*, Entry Bk. D, 237, 239-240.

[47] *B. T. Jour.*, XV, 296, 297, 310, 315, 316; *B. T. Paps., Props.*, Entry Bk. D, 262, 267, 277, 278; *Props.*, VII, L 6, 10-12, 17.

[48] *B. T. Paps., Props.*, VI, pt. 2, K 53; *B. T. Jour.*, XV, 279.

[49] *N. Y. Col. Docs.*, V, 599-600.   In 1723, the agent for Rhode Island objected to the royal order sent to the governor of Massachusetts to demand a bond and to require an oath of the governor of the colony on the ground that they were "inconsistent with the Priviledges granted them in their Charter" and "would be attended with very Great Inconveniences." *Acts of Privy Council, Col.*, III, 45.   In 1730 and 1734, the Board of Trade complained that the corporate colonies had not obeyed these requirements and recommended action against the charters.   Andrews, *Conn. Intestacy Law, Yale Review*, Nov., 1894, 291; *Talcott Papers.* II, 446, in Conn. Hist. Soc., *Collections.*

the qualifications of Penn's nominees. We have already noticed the case of Hamilton. In 1703, when the name of John Evans was presented for confirmation, the board asked Penn to give some account of a person wholly unknown to its members. Not until Penn and his agent, Lawton, had testified to the good character of Evans was his name proposed to the crown for approval.[50] In the case of Charles Gookin nominated in 1708, Penn and General Erle, in whose regiment Gookin had served, wrote in words of commendation of the nominee.[51] Keith, who was proposed in 1716, found it necessary to justify his dismissal from the surveyor-generalship by giving an account of the zeal he displayed in that office.[52] But after this the records show that the board apparently made no effort to inquire into the merits of the persons proposed by the sons of William Penn. By the time of George I this bureau had entered upon a period of decline and consequently decidedly less interest was shown in colonial administration.

The duties of the governor as administrator of the acts of trade were set forth in a list of instructions issued to him at the time of his confirmation.[53] It was simply a collection and exposition of the duties which devolved upon him by the acts of trade. The bond stipulated that if he refused to obey all instructions issued by the crown or its agents pursuant to the laws, the security was to be forfeited.[54] One article of the instructions required the governor to enter into a bond of £500 forbidding him during his administration to act as a merchant or factor in any

50 *B. T. Paps., Props.*, VII, L 39-44; Entry Bk. D, 345, 350; *B. T. Jour.*, XVI, 177.

51 *B. T. Paps., Props.*, IX, P 32-34, 39, 44-46; Entry Bk., F, 44, 45, 46; *B. T. Jour.*, XX, 164.

52 *B. T. Paps., Props.*, X, pt. 1, Q 87.

53 For the instructions to Gookin, 1709, see *B. T. Paps., Props.*, Entry Bk. F, 100-127; to Gordon, 1726, *ibid.*, Entry Bk. G, 363-395; to Hamilton, 1748, *ibid.*, Entry Bk. H, 285-350.

54 For the bond given by Governor Hamilton, see *B. T. Paps., Props.*, Entry Bk. H, 267-281.

mercantile pursuit or as owner of any trading vessel. This precaution was taken to place him above the temptations of using his office for personal advantage. This obligation was apparently not fulfilled for many years. In 1726 the Board of Trade complained that the governors had paid no attention to it, and for the future it was inserted as part of the larger bond given by the governors.[55] The principal duties of the governor were three. He was to see that all vessels trading to or from the colonies were English or colonial built and owned, whereof the master and three-fourths of the crew were English or colonial born, and that no ship shall be deemed qualified to trade unless the persons claiming property in the same had duly registered the vessel. As to the colonial export trade the governor was not to permit a vessel to lade the enumerated articles unless the master had given bond to discharge his cargo in the realm. In case of vessels coming from the realm a certificate showing that a bond had been given to the chief officer of the port whence the vessel sailed was sufficient, but if from any other port the governor was to demand a bond and was required to return a list of them semi-annually to the Customs Board. To provide against false or suspicious papers, the governor was directed to examine with great care all certificates of discharge and of security given in England, and in case he felt doubtful as to their validity, he was to demand a new bond in the former case and not to cancel the bond in the latter case until he had notified the Customs Board and received directions. If a certificate of discharge of cargo in the realm was not produced within eighteen months from date of bond, the governor was to sue for the security. He was to take care that all bondsmen were persons of residence and of property sufficient to meet the obligations of the bond. As to the colonial import trade, no vessel was allowed to discharge her cargo until the master had notified

55 *B. T. Paps., Props.*, Entry Bk. G, 352-353.

the governor or the naval officer of the arrival of the ship, her name and his own, and had produced a true invoice of the goods, where laden, and proof that the ship was legally qualified. Furthermore, the governor was to see that before discharge of cargo the master had first produced to the collector of the customs a certificate under the seal of the customs house where the goods were reshipped, and that no goods should be unladed except by permit of the collector and in the presence of an officer by him appointed. In addition the instructions included a long list of statutes which imposed various duties upon the governor. He was instructed to aid the customs officials in the discharge of their duties, to correspond with the Customs Board, advising it of mismanagement in the service or giving information of value. He was empowered to fill vacancies in the custom house in the province pending action by the surveyor-general or the Customs Board. He was to exempt all customs officials from jury or militia duty, except in extreme cases, or from service in any provincial office likely to hinder them in a discharge of their duties. As compensation the governor was allowed by law one-third of all fines and forfeitures arising from violations of the acts of trade, which was augmented by certain fees fixed by colonial law for the registry of vessels, inspecting invoices, granting clearance papers, and taking bonds.[56] Governor Evans, (1703-1709), estimated that his income amounted yearly to £250 from fines and forfeitures, and £50 from fees.[57]

The governor's agent was the naval officer. It is evident that the obligation of giving bond to the Customs Board, imposed on the governor's appointee by the statute of 1696, was not highly regarded. In 1725 the Customs Board informed Governor Gordon that several naval officers, appointed by him, had not given bond, and he was

[56] *Pa. Statutes at Large*, II, 347; III, 110.
[57] *B. T. Paps., Props.*, X, pt. 1, Q 53.

instructed to execute the bonds and submit a list of the officers to the surveyor-general to be sent to England for approval.[58] This order was not obeyed, for in 1733 Gordon was again directed to send home the names and qualifications of the naval officers, and to require the latter to name bondsmen in England to give security for them.[59] Whether this order was obeyed is a matter of conjecture, but these instances illustrate the laxity of management in the customs service prior to 1763. The duty of the naval officer was to make an entry and keep an account of all exports and imports, of all vessels with tonnage and guns, whence they came, whither bound, and to submit his accounts quarterly to the Customs Board.[60] As compensation he was allowed certain fees by colonial law.

In 1696 the Customs Board urged upon the Privy Council and the Lords of the Treasury the necessity of appointing many new customs officers for the colonies and of granting them fit compensation in order to obviate the temptation to connive at illegal trade.[61] On November 20, 1696, the Lords of the Treasury approved the list of nominees and salaries, submitted to it by the Customs Board, and ordered the persons named to be commissioned.[62] This act marked the beginning of an orderly customs service for the colonies. Nearly thirty officials, including a surveyor-general, local surveyors, collectors, and comptrollers, were appointed at a yearly outlay of £1605. By 1724 the staff had increased to forty and the charges to £3540, and in 1760 the establishment cost £4000.[63] Three col-

58 *Pa. Archives*, I, 1st ser., 185-186.

59 *Ibid.*, 395.

60 *Cal. State Paps., Col.*, 1677-1680, 1590; *British Museum Additional Mss.*, 22617, ff. 143-144, (Lib. of Cong. Transcripts). For an account of the duties of this office, see *Talcott Papers*, I, 229-330, in Conn. Hist. Soc., *Collections*.

61 *B. T. Paps., Pl. Gen.*, IV, pt. 1, A 9, 10; *House of Lords Mss.*, n.s., II, 451-454; *Cal. State Paps., Col.*, 1693-1696, 640.

62 *Customs Books*, XII, 301-302.

63 *Ibid.*, XVII, 488-490; XVIII, 49.

lectors were appointed for Penn's territories: one each for
the ports of Philadelphia, Newcastle, and Lewes.[64] As the
power to establish ports was vested by the act of 1696 in
the Customs Board, these places became the official ports
for the entrance and clearance of all ships. There was
also a local surveyor. In 1698 Randolph appointed John
Jewell to be surveyor and searcher of the customs for
Pennsylvania and Delaware.[65] In 1701 Robert Quary was
commissioned by the Customs Board as surveyor-general
for Pennsylvania and New Jersey at a yearly salary of
£200.[66] This office was discontinued in 1703 when Quary
became surveyor-general for all the colonies. In 1703
Quary appointed a " riding surveyor " for Delaware Bay,
and three years later the office was placed upon the permanent establishment at a salary of £50 a year.[67] In 1721
the Customs Board commissioned a comptroller of the customs with headquarters at Philadelphia at a yearly salary
of £40. His duty was to " keep the journal, & assist the
Coll[rs] sign the Acco[ts] & dispatches with him & goe quarterly to Newcastle and Lewis & examine & sign those Coll[rs]
Acco[ts]."[68] At the time of appointment the collector was
given a commission and a set of instructions, the former
delegating to him power and authority in general terms,
the latter setting forth in great detail the duties of his
office.[69] The navigation act of 1696 extended to the col-

[64] List of collectors at Philadelphia: John Bewley, 1696; John
Moore, 1704; W. E. Fox, 1728; Grosvenor Bedford, 1732. At New-
castle: Matthew Birch, 1696; Francis Birchfield, 1701; Samuel
Lowman; Daniel Moore, 1726; Alexander Keith, 1729; Thomas
Graeme; William Till, 1748. At Lewes: William Massey, 1696;
Samuel Lowman, 1698; Henry Brooke, 1700; Thomas Forbes, 1737;
Richard Metcalfe, 1738.

[65] *Pa. Col. Recs.*, I, 538.

[66] *Customs Books*, XIII, 126.

[67] *Ibid.*, 432.

[68] *Ibid.*, XVI, 429-430. This office was held by William Alexander,
1721; William Bully, 1727; Alexander Barclay, 1749.

[69] Commission to Matthew Birch, collector at Newcastle, *Pa. Col.
Recs.*, I, 534. Copy of instructions in *House of Lords Mss.*, n.s.,

onies the force of the act of 14 Chas.II.,c.21, whereby the
customs officials were given the same powers and placed
under the same penalties for maladministration provided
for the customs officers in England. By this act and his
commission the collector was authorized to visit and search
all vessels, take their entries, seize and bring ashore all
uncustomed goods, or to search any house, store or other
place for contraband goods. To bind him to a faithful
discharge of his office the collector was obliged to take an
oath before the governor of the colony and to give bond
to him in the king's name in the sum of £500. The collector was empowered to appoint deputies for such places as
he deemed necessary and to send home promptly a list of
places and officers appointed. The deputies were required to
take the oath before the governor, but the collector was held
answerable for the neglect of his agents. The collector was
instructed to keep an exact account of all duties collected,
specifying the name of ship and master, contents of cargo,
and whither bound. At the end of every twelve months he
was to send to the Customs Board a general account of the
management of his office and the revenues collected, attested
by the comptroller or surveyor. As far as possible all
duties were to be collected in specie and not in kind.
Duties paid in specie or bills of exchange were to be remitted to the receiver-general of customs at London, and
all goods accepted in lieu of money, if not sold to advantage in the colony, were to be forwarded to the ware-
house keeper at London. It is evident that the collector
acted as a check upon the governor and naval officer. His
instructions directed him to see that these officers enforced
the provisions of the laws with regard to the qualifications
of vessels, the taking of bonds, the inspection of bonds,
ship registries, certificates of discharge and security, invoices, and other papers. The collector was directed to make

II, 472-481; *British Museum Additional Mss.*, 28089, ff. 71-79,
(Lib. of Cong. Transcripts).

a duplicate of all bonds taken by the governor and send them to the Customs Board by separate passage. The local surveyor was empowered to act as a check upon the collector and his deputies.[70] He was authorized to inspect the entries of all collectors and deputies within his survey, examine and sign the collectors' accounts before they were transmitted to the Customs Board, to make a duplicate of all entries, to see that no vessel laded a greater quantity of goods than the collector's permit warranted, to compare the ship's cargo with the collector's entry, to visit frequently all ships in order to prevent and discover illegal trading. William Penn wrote of the system, that where the "King has approved of a Deputy Governor no more than if he named him, especially if he is obliged to give security for the faithful discharge of his duties to the laws of trade, . . . besides the King has already his Vice-Admirals, Judges of the Admiralty, Advocates, Collectors, Surveyors, and Auditors in each proprietary government . . . I must think so many spies cannot be but a security."[71]

In any attempt to pass in review the actual enforcement of the acts of trade it is essential to bear in mind that the English commercial system was based on abstract and general principles. The whole system was framed to meet the economic needs of the mother country; it was not a system of the colonists' own choosing nor the outgrowth of their own economic needs. Hence in the execution of laws which regulated the trade of the colonies in artificial channels, it was possible that the customs officials would come into conflict with the colonists who sought to evade laws which ran counter to their economic welfare. This is evidenced by the illegal trade which thrived between Penn's colonies and Scotland on the one side, and the Dutch West Indian pos-

[70] Instructions to a local surveyor, *British Museum Add. Mss.*, 28089, ff. 83-85, (Lib. of Cong. Transcripts).
[71] *Duke of Portland Mss.*, IV, 19, Hist. Mss Com., *Report*, 15, pt. 4.

sessions of Surinam and Curaçoa on the other.[72] There is little doubt that the restrictive character of the mercantile system was responsible for these evasions. It is a matter of extreme difficulty to estimate the amount of this unlawful commerce, but one cannot read the records of the period following the Revolution of 1688 without being forcibly impressed with the extent of the illegal traffic directly with Scotland.[73] The reasons for this are clear. The restrictions of the English laws and the liberal concessions granted to Scotch industry enabled the Scotch merchant to undersell the fair English or colonial trader. On the other hand the colonists found a more profitable market for their tobacco in Scotland.[74] This trade was also furthered by a goodly number of Scotch merchants and factors resident in Pennsylvania, Delaware, Maryland, New Jersey, and Carolina.[75] The Scots were excluded from colonial trade by the requirement that the owners, master, and three-fourths of the crew must be English or colonial born. But from the letters of Quary, Randolph, and other customs officials, the Scotch and Dutch trade persisted in spite of the reorganized customs service.[76] On the other hand the right of the Scots to participate in the colonial trade was sanctioned by opinions of the crown lawyers. On several occasions they held that in law Scotsmen were natural-born subjects of England.[77] These opinions opened the colonial trade to the Scots and tended to nullify the provisions designed to exclude them. As a result, wrote Quary in Au-

---

72 *Cal. State Paps., Col.*, 1693-1696, 511, 520.

73 *House of Lords Mss.*, n.s., II, 462-466.

74 Keith, *Economic Causes for the Scottish Union, English Hist. Rev.*, XXIV, Jan., 1909, 44-60; also *Scottish Trade with the Plantations, Scottish Hist. Rev.*, Oct., 1908, 32-48.

75 *Cal. State Paps., Col.*, 1685-1688, 353-354; 1689-1692, 656-660; *N. Y. Col. Docs.*, IV, 1055; *N. J. Archives*, II, 288.

76 *B. T. Paps., Props.*, III, C 26, no. 2.

77 *Cal. State Paps., Col.*, 1697-1698, 293-294, 516; *N. J. Archives*, II, 251.

gust, 1698, the Scots grow more numerous than ever.[78] He also instanced another difficulty in the enforcement of the law. This arose from the practice of the governors granting letters of denization to foreigners. Quary expressed the fear that by the ease with which Scotch, Dutch, and French were able to secure such qualifications it would soon be impossible to man colonial shipping with properly qualified mariners. In one case the admiralty court rejected a letter of denization and decreed the ship forfeited according to law.[79] Quary also cited two cases of illegal trade between Pennsylvania and Curaçoa. The statements of Randolph and Quary must be taken at a discount because of their enmity to the colonial charters, but on the other hand it is true that the failure of the English government to deal successfully with the Scotch trade was a prominent factor in promoting the union of England and Scotland in 1707.[80] With this the question of illegal trade with Scotland came to an end.

There was also an illegal trade of a more lawless and defiant sort. The records of the period of King William's War likewise impress one with the prevalence of piracy.[81] It was a temporary phenomenon, the outcome of a condition of war. Piracy was closely connected with privateering. Ships were equipped and manned in colonial ports and cleared away under privateering commissions granted by the governors authorizing them to prey upon the commerce of the enemy. A number of such vessels sailed away, not bent upon legitimate prize, but to prey upon the commerce of any nation irrespective of flag. The granting of commissions for corrupt purposes implied collusion on the part of colonial governors. Especially singled out for this offense were Fletcher of New York and Trott of the Baha-

[78] B. T. Paps., Props., II, B 29, 30.

[79] See page 101.

[80] Keith, Economic Causes of the Scottish Union, as cited.

[81] Cal. State Paps., Col., vols. for 1693-1698, see the prefaces and the indexes at Piracy.

mas.[82] It was not the restrictive character of the trade
laws which led to piracy under color of law, but purely
greed and corruption.   It was charged that the governors
of the chartered colonies connived at piracy, allowed ships
for this purpose to be fitted out in their ports, and permitted the freebooters to return to the colonies to enjoy
their ill-gotten gains in peace.[83] These privateersmen
turned pirates were known as Red Seamen or Madagascar
pirates, because the scene of their operations lay in the eastern waters where the rich commerce of the orient offered
the most attractive prize.[84]   In 1698 Parliament passed
an act against piracy and an English squadron, on complaint of the East India Company, was dispatched to the
east to check the nefarious trade.[85]   Governor Markham
and the officials of Pennsylvania were accused of ignoring
the royal proclamation to apprehend the pirates then living
in security in the province and Delaware.   Such was the
charge of Robert Snead, a local justice, in a letter submitted to the Board of Trade in 1698.[86] He said that
Markham's daughter had married James Brown, a member
of the notorious pirate crew of Every, and that when several old-time pirates were seized, justices Shippen and Morris released them on bail, allowing one pirate to give security for another.   Thomas Robinson charged the governor
and magistrates with undue leniency to these old offenders.[87]   Randolph and Quary substantiated the charge, the
former accused Markham of taking protection money from
one Miller, a quondam pirate, the other claimed that the
governor kept in his possession the goods of a pirate allowed to escape.[88]   In 1699 Quary wrote home that resi-

[82] *Cal. St. Paps., Col.*, 1696-1697, 259-264; 1697-1698, 108, 224-229,
279-288, 506.

[83] *Ibid.*, 1693-1696, 519; 1696-1697, 20, 44, 379, 557.

[84] *Ibid.*, 1697-1698, 97, 106-108, 112-113.

[85] *Ibid.*, 1697-1698, 126, 139, 407, 410, 418, etc.

[86] *B. T. Paps., Props.*, II, B 14; *Pl. Gen.*, IV, pt. 2, 114; *B. T.
Jour.*, X, 268.

[87] *B. T. Paps., Props.*, II, B 35.

[88] *Ibid., Pl. Gen.*, IV, pt. 2, B 40, 42.

dents of Delaware had given assistance to a pirate crew under the famous Captain Kidd and had resisted the efforts of the customs officials to apprehend the pirates and their booty.[89] On the other hand, Markham and the members of the provincial council and assembly in 1698 united in an address to the crown in vindication of the government against the accusations '' our enemies have maliciously charged against us.''[90] An absolute disclaimer was made that they countenanced illegal trade with the Scotch and Dutch, or that they ever sheltered any pirates except those allowed to settle there under Fletcher when the province was under royal administration, who were seized and confined to jail as soon as the royal proclamation was made public. In conclusion serious charges were brought against Randolph. He was accused of accepting money from the pirates by holding out offers of pardon, and of acting in a most abusive manner to the governor and magistrates. In submitting this memorial, Penn also denied the charges of illegal trade and piracy made against his colony, and characterized Randolph's insinuations as malicious.[91]

Aroused by these complaints royal orders were issued to the colonial governors in 1699 directing them to send to England for trial all pirates, their effects, and the evidence against them, also to see that the laws of trade were properly executed and that the customs and admiralty officials were supported in the discharge of their func-

---

[89] *B. T. Paps., Props.*, III, C 30, 31; *B. T. Jour.*, XII, 138; *House of Lords Mss.*, n.s., IV, 342-345.

[90] *Pa. Votes of Assembly*, I, 107; *B. T. Paps., Props.*, II, B 18. For Markham's letters of vindication, *B. T. Paps., Props.*, II, B 3, nos. 11, 12; V, F 40. Francis Jones of the province, in a letter to Penn characterized Snead as a person of " hot temper, unworthy of your notice, being of little or no reputation, . . . a fellow that has little or no credit given to his words." Penn wrote of Snead, that he "ran away in my debt, and I suppose in other people's." *Penn-Logan Corres.*, I, 12.

[91] *B. T. Paps., Props.*, II, B 38.

tions.[92]   As we have seen summary action was taken against
Markham.   The Privy Council approved the report of the
Board of Trade which recommended the dismissal of the
governor and two other officials accused of opposition to
the admiralty court.[93]   Penn fully aware of the hostility
of the home government to the charters, hastened to his
province, took upon himself the office of governor, dismissed Morris and Lloyd, the offenders against the admiralty court, and turned out of office a sheriff who allowed
a pirate to escape.   Penn impressed his provincial council
with the necessity of calling a special session of the assembly to enact measures against illegal trade and piracy.[94]
In January, 1700, Penn met the assembly, submitted the
royal orders, and fully related '' the Odium cast upon the
Government in that Case; also how earnestly these Things
were urged by our Superiours at home.'' [95]   In response the
assembly expressed an abhorrence of piracy and a willingness to proceed against it and illegal trade.   Two laws
were passed, the one to suppress piracy and the other to
prevent unlawful commerce.[96]   The house also expelled
James Brown, returned from Kent county, because charged
with piracy.[97]   Those who aided Captain Kidd's crew in
1699 were apprehended and forced to give bond awaiting
instructions from England as to their disposal.[98]   In the
spring of 1700 Quary wrote home in warm praise of the
proprietor's zeal for the royal interests.[99]

Quary's praise soon turned to words of condemnation.
In November, 1700, he informed the home government that
Penn had invaded the proper jurisdiction of the admiralty
court and that the government continued to countenance

[92] B. T. Paps., Props., IV, D 4; Entry Bk. A, 471; Pl. Gen., V, pt.
1, C 45, 46, 52.
[93] Ibid., Props., Entry Bk. B, 20-32, 98-102, 102-104.
[94] Pa. Col. Recs., I, 572, 573-574, 591.
[95] Pa. Votes of Assembly, I, 112-117.
[96] B. T. Paps., Props., III, F 25; Pa. Col. Recs., I, 594.
[97] Pa. Votes of Assembly, I, 114-115.
[98] B. T. Paps., Props., V, F 23-27.
[99] Ibid., V, F 5, 34; House of Lords Mss., n.s., IV, 345-346.

piracy and illegal trade.[100] Randolph alleged that an illicit trade overland from one colony to another caused great loss to the royal revenue.[101] He estimated that 370 hogshead of tobacco were carried illegally from Pennsylvania to other colonies and that the greater part of Delaware's crop was sent directly to Scotland. On the basis of these complaints a bill was introduced into the House of Lords in 1701 to vacate the charters.[102] Penn in August, 1701, from his colony, wrote in refutation of the unjust charges made against his province.[103] He said that doubtless there were faults committed in an infant colony, but held that for the most part the colonists and the government could not be held responsible for them. He said that he had brought to justice the pirates allowed to settle in the province in Fletcher's time and denied that any illegal trade was carried on during his presence there except two small vessels from Curaçoa, which were seized and duly condemned. Penn felt very bitter, and justly so, against those officials who were '' unnecessarily busy for the King, taking his name in vain to serve every turn of advantage or revenge . . . that by overacting their parts, unreasonably and unjustly, they may recommend their zeal as meritorious to the Commissioners of the Customs, or the Lords of Trade.''[104] It seems that every chance irregularity, every ignorance of the law's exactness, was seized upon and dressed up to represent the prevalence of illegal trade. The purpose was to secure the overthrow of the charter and the establishment of royal government. Again in 1702, Quary in person before the Board of Trade made serious charges against Pennsylvania.[105] He claimed

100 B. T. Paps., Props., V, F 57, 64 no. 10; House of Lords Mss., n.s., IV, 341-342.

101 B. T. Paps., Pl. Gen., V, pt. 2, D 48; Toppan, Randolph, V, 230.

102 See page 344.

103 B. T. Paps., Props., VI, pt. 1, G 39.

104 Duke of Portland Mss., IV, 30, Hist. Mss. Com., Report 15, pt. 4.

105 B. T. Paps., Props., VI, pt. 2, I 10.

that an illegal trade flourished worse than ever and that no care was taken to execute either the laws of Parliament or the colony against it. He charged that sloops were employed purposely to meet incoming vessels outside the capes and to land their cargoes secretly. In proof of this he cited several vessels which carried on a direct trade with Curaçoa. Before the board Penn admitted the charge but held that it was impossible to check this trade because of the convenience of the coast line and refuted the charge that the government of the province was privy to these violations.[106] Likewise the council of the colony replied to Quary's charges which were believed to be leveled solely against the Quaker government.[107] Quary was charged to give one instance of illegal trade since 1699, except the two small vessels from Curaçoa, or one instance where the provincial officials did not readily lend assistance to the royal agents. For the sake of vindicating the magistrates and merchants of the province, both Penn and the council asked for a full investigation of the charges on the ground. In conclusion, the council said that it was hard that those who had borne no share in settling a colony so prosperous and so profitable to the mother country, should, instead of acting in a just manner, shamefully slander and misrepresent it to the crown.

The fact is that neither the local or royal officials were to blame for the ease with which illegal trade was carried on. A glance at a map showing the character of the colonial coast line will reveal the difficulties inherent in the situation. The long tide-water area, the numerous arms of the sea, broad harbors and navigable rivers, and the relative situation of the colonies all conspired to facilitate frequent evasions of the law. It was little trouble for a vessel to drop anchor in Delaware Bay out of reach of the customs officers, discharge a cargo of uncustomed goods

---

106 *B. T. Paps., Props.,* VI, pt. 2, I 19; *B. T. Jour.,* XV, 29-35.
107 *B. T. Paps., Props.,* VII, M 21.

or lade a cargo of prohibited goods with the aid of small craft, and then sail away unmolested.[108]   A few revenue cutters judiciously stationed would have been far more serviceable as sentinels of the law than a host of customs officials on land.   Cruisers were stationed in Delaware and Chesapeake Bays for a short time in 1695, and again in 1697 the admiralty ordered the frigate *Swift* to duty on the coast.[109]   The next year this vessel was lost off North Carolina and again the home government was implored to provide a revenue cutter.[110]   When Quary in 1700 complained of the prevalence of illegal trade he said that he did not make any charge against the provincial government or the royal agents, for no matter how diligent the officers or stringent the laws, it could not be checked without the aid of armed vessels.   Finally, Quary said he would say nothing more since the admiralty paid no attention to his entreaties.

One of the most radical defects in the customs service, as in the whole English administrative system in America, was the method by which royal officials were compensated. In order to render English agents independent of colonial

108 Randolph wrote in 1692, " every vessel runs into a different bay, so that it is endless work for a diligent officer to keep an eye on them (i.e. illegal traders), and he has nothing to satisfy him that the master had been trading legally, but his oath." *Cal. State Paps., Col.,* 1689-1692, 660.

109 *Cal. State Paps., Col.,* 1693-1696, 308, 321, 399, 496, 497, 499, 509-510; *Cal. Treas. Paps.,* 1697-1702, 301; *N. Y. Col. Docs.,* IV, 300-302; *B. T. Jour.,* X, 198, 199, 203, 248.

110 *B. T. Paps., Props.,* III, C 26 no. 1; V, F 34; *Pl. Gen.,* V, pt. 1, D 41; *House of Lords Mss.,* n. s., IV, 326-328, 345-346.   In 1700, Penn informed the Customs Board that the trade in provisions from Pennsylvania to Curaçoa offered a great temptation to bring back Holland goods, but that there was no way to check it on account of the length of the bay; he asked advice. *Pa. Archives,* 1st. ser., I, 139.   Spotswood of Va., in reply to the complaints of the illegal trade to Curaçoa, said that " the want of Guard ships so frequently has given encouragement to the carrying on this Trade, . . . in my Opinion nothing can more effectually break that trade than haveing Guard ships constantly attending here."   Spotswood, *Letters,* I, 15, 29.

influence and to place them above temptation, they should have been rewarded with adequate salaries. This very desirable position was never realized.. The customs officers received compensation from three sources, salaries allowed by the home government, certain fees provided by colonial acts, and one-third of fines and forfeitures granted to informers by the acts of trade. The collector at Philadelphia received a salary of £160 a year, and the collectors at Newcastle each received £90.[111] Out of this they were required to keep a boat and boatmen and to maintain their offices. The colonial laws of 1711 and 1715 allowed certain fees for granting permits to lade or unlade, certificates of discharge, entrance and clearance papers.[112] Preferential treatment was accorded vessels owned in the colony, in which cases the fee abated one-fourth. The law required that the table of fees should be publicly posted and provided penalties for those demanding a fee greater than fixed by law. The government found it necessary to take this precaution to prevent the extortion of exorbitant fees. The low amount of the fees and the meager salary left little over for compensation when the expenses of office had been deducted. Under such circumstances it was possible that customs officials would resort either to the exaction of unwarranted fees, to collusion with illegal traders, or else to unjust and rigorous action against fair traders in order to supply the lack of a proper reward or to satisfy unscrupulous greed. In 1701 Penn voiced the evils of this system when he wrote that "It were to be wished . . . that both governors and inferior officers were men of good estates, good morals, and character at home, or they are a punishment in lieu of a benefit, and to encourage them to go so far, let them have double pay, and

[111] At first the collector at Philadelphia received £200 a year, and the collectors at Newcastle and Lewes each £80, but in 1700 the salaries were fixed at the figures named in the text. *Customs Books*, XII, 301-302; XIII, 89.

[112] *Pa. Statutes at Large*, II, 346; III, 109-110; V, 174.

make all gratuities and perquisites punishable.''[113]   In fact Penn held that '' the notion men had at an office or two is in disfavor of proprietary governments,'' thereby implying that the motive which impelled Quary and others to attack the charters was the desire for more lucrative offices under royal control.[114]   In August, 1701, Penn wrote to the Board of Trade in complaint of those who '' thinking themselves Secure under the awful Language of Serving the King's Interest have stopt at no piece of Rigour, that would turn a penny their own way, of which Instances may be given that would be tolerated I must believe by no King's Govern[r] in America.''[115]   In 1702 he laid before the Privy Council charges of bribery, corruption, and rigorous conduct against the admiralty and customs officials in Pennsylvania.   This matter will be treated at length in the following chapter,[116] but suffice it to say here the whole situation illustrated well the evils of the fee system.   Much complaint was made against John Moore, royal customs collector at Philadelphia for twenty-four years.[117]   In 1705 the merchants complained to the Board of Trade and Customs Board of the unjust conduct of Moore and other collectors.[118]   On several occasions masters of vessels appealed to the provincial council or

[113] *Duke of Portland Mss.*, IV, 30; Hist. Mss. Com., *Report* 15 pt. 4.

[114] Penn wrote, "I think the commission of the Customs is not changed upon every trick a merchant plays in trade." *Ibid.*, 19. Jeremiah Dummer wrote, "If it were true that some persons did now and then concern themselves in an illegal trade, can it be thought just or reasonable that the whole community should suffer for their private fault? Nobody will say that the acts of trade are perfectly observed in the provinces immediately under the Crown, or in Great Britain itself." *Almon Tracts*, I, 56.

[115] *B. T. Paps., Props.*, VI, pt. 1, G 39.

[116] See page 112.

[117] *Customs Books*, XIII, 331; XVIII, 264. Moore secured the collectorship through the influence of the bishop of London. *B. T. Paps., Props.*, VII, M 46; *B. T. Jour.*, XVII, 164.

[118] *Penn-Logan Corres.*, I, 322, 360, 371; II, 90, 314.

assembly for relief from the arbitrary conduct of Moore and Quary.[119] Moore's rigorous conduct is seen especially in the case of the *Richard and William*, bound from Portsmouth, England, with freight for Philadelphia.[120] The master, ignorant of the American trade and not informed by the collector of the port of sailing, failed to take out a ship's registry, and consequently his ship was promptly seized by Moore. Although the master and consignees offered ample security to produce a registry within eighteen months, Moore would not allow the ship to proceed on her voyage, but detained her and instituted condemnation proceedings. The case was appealed to the Board of Trade and Customs Board and Moore's action was not sustained.[121] Whether his conduct was due to a high regard for the letter of the law or to a desire to enhance his income by an unjust vexation of a fair trader is hard to say. But it is evident that he had no regard for the equity of the case. We know also that Governor Keith in 1724 wrote to the Board of Trade and the Duke of Newcastle saying that Moore had shown himself to be a " negligent, collusive and insufficient officer " who should be dismissed from office.[122]

Another factor which conduced to inefficiency and corruption in the customs service was the practice of making the principal collectorships sinecures. In 1728 Moore was superseded by W. E. Fox, and in the next year Fox was granted the place by royal patent.[123] In 1732 Grosvenor Bedford was appointed to the post by royal patent.[124] Bedford was secretary to Horace Walpole, son of the great

[119] *Pa. Col. Recs.*, II, 240; III, 240; *Pa. Votes of Assembly*, II, 110.

[120] *B. T. Paps., Props.*, XII, R 93.

[121] *Ibid.*, Entry Bk. H, 2.

[122] *Ibid., Paps.*, XI, R 52; Pa. Bundle, *Am. and W. I.* 28, XXIV, 9, (Public Record Office).

[123] *Customs Books*, XVIII, 264, 373.

[124] *Ibid.*, XIX, 310; Walpole, *Letters*, (Cunningham ed.), IV, 113.

premier, and it was doubtless through these connections that he secured the collectorship. The actual appointees remained in England and farmed the office out for what it would bear. Bedford let the office to a deputy for £130 a year, thus receiving not only a salary of £160 but the rental in addition for performing no services.[125] Such a system simply placed a premium on vexatious dealings with fair traders and collusion with illegal traders. This is evidenced by the petition of the merchants of Philadelphia to the assembly in 1736 setting forth that several vessels had left the port for other colonies rather than suffer the annoyances put upon them by the deputy-collector.[126] This vexation, said the petitioners, was due to the fact that the chief collector resided in England and farmed his office to a deputy for a greater sum than the place would bear. Peter Razer, surveyor and searcher for Delaware Bay, has left us a good description of the lax manner in which the office at Philadelphia was administered.[127] In October, 1755, he wrote, " illicit trade is much encreased and carried on in a most barefaced and Shamefull manner." He said that although the collector was required to maintain a boat and boatmen, yet this had not been done since the year 1741. He asked, " what can a Collector and Comptroller do or know in so large a trading City as this whose business is at home in their proper offices without an Assistant at the water side to see what Ships arrive and examine their Cargo, which they might compare with the Master's report and see if they agree; for want of such an officer Ships have unloaded here before they have entered at the Custom house." The laxity of management is also evidenced by the letter of Peter Randolph, surveyor-general for the southern district, to the

125 *British Museum Add. Mss.*, 34728, f. 36, (Lib. of Cong. Transcripts).

126 *Pa. Votes of Assembly*, III, 287.

127 *British Museum Add. Mss.*, 34728, ff. 21, 36, 52, 54, (Lib. of Cong. Transcripts).

deputy collector at Philadelphia stating that the Customs Board has made complaint that no accounts had been received from that port for 1739-1750, except for several quarters.[128] Randolph was ordered to instruct the officials that unless the accounts were submitted regularly in the future the salaries would be withheld. Thus it is evident to what an extent the corrupt patronage system in England of this period cast its baneful influence upon efficient colonial administration.

The lack of evidence makes it hard to come to any conclusion as to what extent the colonists evaded that part of the system which confined their export and import trade to the mother country. It may be fair to conclude from the yearly increase in the purchase of English manufactures that the colonists found their best market at home and had no reason to violate the law forbidding direct trade in European commodities.[129] As the northern colonies produced practically none of the enumerated articles for exportation the opportunity for illegal trade in this respect was slight. It is fair to assume that had the colonists found these measures contrary to their economic welfare they would have evaded them as they did the Molasses Act of 1733. There seems to be little doubt that this law was responsible for much illegal trade.

By reason of similarity of climate and soil the mother country and the northern colonies produced like commodities. Under these conditions the northern colonies became competitors of the mother country instead of supplement-

---

[128] *Customs House Paps.*, I, (Mss. in Lib. of Hist. Soc. of Pa.).

[129] Value of exports from England to Pennsylvania.

1698-1704	£ 57,573	
1723	15,992	
1730	48,592	*B. T. Paps., Props.*, VIII, pt.
1737	56,690	2, O 99, 100.
1742	75,295	Franklin, *Works*, (Smyth
1747	82,404	ed.), IV, 68. Cf. Dickin-
1752	201,666	son, *Writings*, I, 218.
1757	268,426	

ing her economic needs. Hence the colonists were compelled to find other markets where in turn they would be able to exchange their products for other commodities and a cash balance to carry to England in a second exchange for manufactured goods. This market was found in the West Indies and to a less extent in Southern Europe and the islands of the Atlantic.[130] A considerable trade was built up between the northern colonies and the foreign West Indies. The rapid growth of population and expansion of settlement in the northern colonies created a surplus of products which more than supplied the need of the British sugar islands. The slow growth of the latter resulted in a failure to meet the demands of the northern colonies for rum, sugar, and molasses. The inability of the British sugar planters to compete successfully with their foreign rivals in the West Indies led to complaints which were satisfied by the passage of the Molasses Act of 1733.[131] This statute laid a prohibitive duty on the importation of foreign rum, sugar, and molasses into the colonies. A rigid enforcement of this law would practically have deprived the colonies of a market sufficient to their needs. It would have worked injury to British industry and commerce by closing the channels through which the colonists were enabled to take off British manufactures. Hence the colonists would be forced either to manufacture for themselves, unprofitable in new communities and contrary to the mercantile system, or else to evade the law. The latter method was utilized and the Molasses Act remained a dead letter. Of course it is well-nigh impossible to find tangible evidence of a trade which was purposely and successfully concealed, but it is generally recognized that this statute was treated with scant cour-

[130] Callender, *Selections from Econ. Hist. of U. S.*, 51-56; *B. T. Paps., Props.*, XI, R 7, 42, 47, 78; XIII, S 34.

[131] Beer, *British Col. Pol., 1754-1765*, 33-34, 292-293; Beer, *Commercial Policy of England toward the Cols.*, 107-122, (Columbia College Studies, III).

tesy.[132] Moreover, the lack of adequate salaries, the vicious fee system, the sinecures, the want of revenue cutters, and the convenience of the coast line all lent themselves readily to evasions of the law.[133] The very fact that the law was not enforced implies great laxity in the customs service. Even if an official was faithful, his efforts could not overcome the difficulties of enforcing a law so contrary to colonial interest. In many cases the royal officials found it far more profitable, and indeed at times more conducive to personal safety, to connive at the trade than to insist upon a due obedience to the law. The thriving of this trade during the last French war brought very clearly to light the disregard for the law and the venality of the customs officials.

As a result of a condition of war all commercial relations with the enemy should have ceased. But in spite of this the evidence shows that the colonists, especially in the north, carried on a reprehensible trade with the French. Such a trade flourished to a remarkable degree in the final struggle between England and France for supremacy in America. In 1755 Governor Dinwiddie wrote that the French were able to carry on their invasion of the Ohio Valley by means of provisions supplied from

132 Mr. Beer shows that the revenue collected under the Molasses Act during the twenty-two years from 1734 to 1755 averaged only £259 a year, but when especial efforts were made to stop the illegal trade in 1760 and 1761, the receipts arose to £1170 and £1189 respectively. Beer, *British Col. Pol.*, *1754-1765*, 115-116.

133 Hutchinson of Mass. wrote in 1763, "The real cause of the illicit trade in this province has been the indulgence of the officers of the customs, and we are told that the cause of their indulgence has been that they are quartered upon for more than their legal fees, and that without bribery and corruption they must starve." Quincy, *Mass. Reports*, 430. James Otis said, "it has been observed, that a very small office in the customs in America has raised a man a fortune sooner than a Government. The truth is, the acts of trade have been too often evaded; but by whom? Not by the American merchants in general, but by some former custom-house officers, their friends and partisans." *The Rights of the British Cols. Asserted, Almon Tracts*, I.

Philadelphia and New York.[134] In the same year Commodore Keppel informed Governor Morris of Pennsylvania that "From the Accounts that I have received I find the carrying Stores and Provisions to the French constantly practised by the Gentlemen of the Colony in your Government."[135] It was realized by imperial officials that to a great extent the success of the French in the final struggle depended upon their ability to secure food supplies from the English colonies.[136] The superiority of the British sea power checked the dispatch of provisions and stores of war from France to her troops and fleet in America; and the failure of the French colonies to produce food-stuffs made the enemy dependent upon the English colonies. Formal war against France was not declared till May, 1756, and during the two years previous, although the two nations were at sword's points in America, trade with the enemy was not illegal, but reprehensible and unpatriotic. In order to check the trade in this time of nominal peace it was necessary for the colonial or English governments to declare it prohibited.

Commodore Keppel, acting under royal orders, directed his captains to seize vessels bound for French ports.[137]

[134] *Dinwiddie Papers*, I, 473, 476.

[135] *Pa. Col. Recs.*, VI, 323. In March, 1755, Gov. Morris of Pa. wrote to DeLancey of N. Y., "I am told there were, last summer, no less than forty English vessels at one time in the harbour of Louisburg, that had carry'd Provisions there. The great supply, I am afraid, will last them all the next summer, and enable them to maintain an Army on the back of us, which they could not otherwise have done." *Pa. Archives*, 1st. ser., II, 261-262.

[136] Dinwiddie wrote, "This is a very pernicious Trade, as they c'd not conduct their unjust Invas's on His M'y's Lands with't this Supply." *Dinwiddie Papers*, I, 473. Shirley said, "nothing we can do seems likely to tend more, by the blessing of God, to defeat the schemes of the French to swallow up all his Majesty's Dominions on the continent of America than that all governments should agree in the most effectual means for stopping all supplies of provisions and warlike stores being sent out of any of these colonies" to the enemy. *Pa. Col. Recs.*, VI, 309.

[137] *Pa. Col. Recs.*, VI, 323.

General Braddock was instructed to take measures to prevent "the continuance of all such dangerous Practices."[138] Governor Dinwiddie by executive action laid an embargo on the exportation of provisions to the French as a precedent for other colonies.[139]   Shirley of Massachusetts secured the passage of an act of three months' duration requiring masters to give bond to carry provisions to British ports only.[140]   The efficacy of such measures depended on a general concurrence by all the colonies. Shirley wrote to the other governors soliciting the passage of a similar law.   In March, 1755, the governor of Pennsylvania, with the advice of his council, instructed the collectors and naval officers at Philadelphia, Newcastle, and Lewes to require masters of vessels laden with provisions to give bond obliging them to discharge their cargoes in British ports or in countries in amity with England.[141] In April, the assembly sanctioned the executive action by a law to continue for three months, and on expiration it was continued for a year.[142]   In June, 1755, Shirley notified the governors that his assembly had laid a general embargo for three months provided the other colonies passed similar measures.[143]   The purpose of a general embargo was to distress the French fleet at Louisburg, "for there is great reason to think," wrote Shirley, "that the French there as well as at Canada are but scantily supplied with provisions."   The assembly of Pennsylvania claimed that the law just passed was sufficient, and since this prohibition was only partial, the governor instructed the collectors and naval officers to enforce a general embargo until further notified.[144]

---

138 *Pa. Archives*, 1st. ser., II, 206.
139 *Dinwiddie Papers*, I, 526-527.
140 *Pa. Col. Recs.*, VI, 309; *Sharpe Corres.*, I, 169.
141 *Pa. Col. Recs.*, VI, 319-320.
142 *Ibid.*, 321; *Pa. Statutes at Large*, V, 184, 188.
143 *Pa. Col. Recs.*, VI, 439.
144 *Ibid.*, 450-451, 453, 511, 555, 587, 601.

The prohibition upon the exportation to French ports only did not suffice. The enemy was able to secure provisions from the English colonies indirectly through the neutral ports in the Spanish and Dutch West Indies.[145] Governor Hardy of New York prevailed upon his assembly to pass a law to check this indirect trade, but with the proviso that it should not become operative until Pennsylvania and New Jersey enacted similar measures.[146] In May, 1756, the assembly of Pennsylvania passed a similar law, to be of force when New Jersey and Delaware enacted such measures.[147] New Jersey responded, Delaware passed an act to continue for one month only, thus invalidating the laws of the other colonies.[148] In May, 1756, formal war was declared against France whereby all commercial relations with the enemy became treasonable. In October, 1756, the Board of Trade instructed the colonial governors to lay an embargo on all vessels clearing out with supplies except those bound for some British port, in which case the master was to give bond to the collector at the port of sailing to discharge his cargo in a British port and to produce within twelve months of the date of bond a certificate of discharge.[149] Governor Denny of Pennsylvania promptly transmitted the order to the collectors within his jurisdiction and then called upon the assembly to enact the order into law.[150] In February, 1757, the assembly presented the governor with a bill which differed from the order. The order

---

145 *N. Y. Col. Docs.*, VII, 81-82, 117, 163-164, 225, 226, 272, 273.
146 *Ibid.*, 81-82, 117; *Pa. Col. Recs.*, VII, 122, 130.
147 *Pa. Col. Recs.*, VII, 125-126; 129.
148 *Ibid.*, 183, 197-198.
149 *Ibid.*, 386-387; *N. Y. Col. Docs.*, VII, 162; *Sharpe Corres.*,
I, 529-530. In March, 1756, Henry Fox, secretary of state, wrote the colonial governors that, " The King would have you recommend it in the Strongest manner to your Council and assembly to pass Effectual Laws for prohibiting all trade and Commerce with the French." *Pa. Col. Recs.*, VII, 179-180.
150 *Pa. Col. Recs.*, VII, 388.

restricted the exportation of provisions to British ports only, the bill left open the trade to neutral Europe. The assembly held that the purpose of the order was answered by preventing the French from securing supplies indirectly through neutral ports in America, and declared that it was unreasonable to check the trade of the province to neutral Europe and thereby ruin colonial commerce and lessen the financial resources in this time of crisis. The difference was not compromised and the law did not find its way to the statute book.[151]

What could not be done by concert of action among the disunited and jealous colonies was effected by an act of the imperial legislature. Early in 1757 Parliament passed a law to prohibit during war the exportation of provisions from the colonies " unless to Great Britain or Ireland or to some of the said Plantations and Colonies." [152] Also on several occasions the governors laid a general embargo for the purposes of securing transports and supplies for particular enterprises.[153] But the act of 1757, like the Molasses Act, ran counter to the economic interests of the colonies. The activity of the British fleet in American waters was sufficient to check a direct trade with the enemy, but the vigilance of the fleet was neutralized by the ingenuity of the colonists. Two methods were utilized to circumvent the act of 1757. Trade was carried on directly with the French under commissions known as " flags of truce." These were issued by the governors to masters of ships to effect an exchange of prisoners. These commissions, like the privateering commissions issued in King William's War, were turned to illegitimate uses. Instead of

---

[151] *Pa. Col. Recs.*, VII, 408, 409, 418-420, 444.

[152] 30 Geo. II., c. 9; *Pa. Archives*, 1st. ser., III, 97.

[153] In 1756-1757, Lord Loudoun ordered a temporary general embargo; in March, 1757, General Abercrombie, and in 1762, General Amherst issued similar orders. *Pa. Col. Recs.*, VII, 235, 270, 429-430, 606, 608; VIII, 38-39, 713-714; *Pa. Archives*, 1st. ser., III, 364; IV, 79.

carrying prisoners to the French islands, the masters carried provisions to the enemy. Such a use implied crass negligence or corruption on the part of the governors. Governors Wentworth of New Hampshire and Fauquier of Virginia disdained to accept large bribes for flags of truce to be used improperly, but Denny of Pennsylvania was not of such stuff of which honest men are made.[154] Of his venal conduct, Hamilton, his successor, has left a good account. In a letter to Pitt, November, 1760, he wrote that the practice began in 1759 when Denny sold flags of truce in small numbers under the pretense of exchanging French prisoners " of whom 'tis well known we have not had more during the whole War than might have been conveniently embarked in one, or at most, two small ships; yet M^r. Denny or his agents received for each flag so granted, a Sum not less than three to four hundred pistolen, and once having relished the sweets of this Traffick, he became more undisguised, and as it were open'd shop at lower prices to all Customers as well of our own as of the neighboring Provinces, to which they came and purchas'd freely: But toward the end of his administration, the matter was carried to such a pitch, that he scrupled not to set his name to & dispose of blank flags of Truce, at the low price of twenty pounds sterling or under; some of which were selling from hand to hand at advanced prices, several months after my arrival."[155]

By the second device, a master cleared his vessel laden with provisions by properly giving bond to carry the cargo to some British port, but when the high seas were reached

154 Fauquier said that he refused to grant flags of truce for fraudulent purposes, although "I was given to understand I might have 400 Guineas if I would license a Flag of Truce." Wentworth wrote that he was offered "Considerable Sums of Money, yet I ever treated the Applications with the greatest Contempt and disdain." Kimball, *Pitt Corres.*, II, 349-351, 362-363.

155 *Ibid.*, II, 351-352. Gov. Hopkins of R. I. granted about thirty flags of truce, and confessed that some of the masters used these commissions for illegitimate purposes. *Ibid.*, II, 375.

the course of the ship was altered toward a neutral port
in the West Indies, such as Monte Christi in Spanish
Santo Domingo, or to the Dutch possessions of Curaçoa,
St. Thomas, and Eustatia. These vessels brought a return cargo of foreign rum, sugar, and molasses. By this
course of commerce the enemy was supplied with provisions and found a market for their products. This trade
was carried on under color of law. Masters were able to
produce not only proper certificates of discharge, but also
certificates of lading and clearance papers from some British port, although there was every indication that the vessel had not touched at the designated ports. Hamilton
of Pennsylvania said with regard to entries inward that
masters brought " certificates and Clearances from some
other English Port, such as Jamaica, Providence, New
York, Port of Newcastle or Lewes." [156]   Such was also the
evidence of Governor Colden of New York.[157]   Hamilton
said that " it is next to impossible that the Clearances &
Certificates above-mentioned could have been obtained but
by the most shocking Perjury and Corruption." [158]   It
is clear evidence of the prevalence of gross corruption and
rottenness in the customs service. This treasonable trade
was confined chiefly to the northern colonies, especially
Rhode Island, New York, and Pennsylvania. Hamilton
said that he found a " very great part of the principal merchants of the city (Philadelphia) engaged in a trade with
the French Islands in the West Indies." [159]   Colden wrote
that he was persuaded that the " New York Merchants
have been too generally concerned in this illegal trade, and

[156] Kimball, *Pitt Corres.*, II, 354.

[157] *Ibid.*, II, 348-349, 358-359.

[158] *Ibid.*, II, 354.

[159] *Ibid.*, II, 352. In 1759, Thos. Penn informed Pitt, that the
Delaware River at Phila. swarmed "with shallops unloading illegal
cargoes, brought at their return, and cheating the King of his
dutys, besides carrying provisions and ready money to the Enemy."
Quoted in Beer, *British Col. Pol., 1754-1765*, 91.

the Philadelphia Merchants more so.'' [160]   The fact is that the corrupt customs service, for which the home government was wholly responsible, facilitated the continuance of this most reprehensible traffic.

This trade worked injury to English arms. In August, 1760, Pitt wrote to the governors sharply rebuking the colonists for carrying on '' an Illegal and most pernicious Trade '' whereby the French were supplied with provisions which enabled them '' principally, if not alone, . . . to sustain this long and expensive War.'' [161]   While the trade succored the enemy and protracted the war on one side, it hurt the English cause by enhancing the price and creating a scarcity of provisions for the English forces.[162] Furthermore, the need of using British cruisers to break up the trade tended to weaken the naval power in America.[163]   If loyalty implies the element of sacrifice, then it may be said that there existed little sentiment of loyalty to the Empire among a considerable number of colonial merchants and traders.[164]

In order to check the trade Pitt ordered the governors to detect the guilty parties and bring them to justice. The navy was instrumental in breaking up the illegal intercourse.[165]   But under the conditions by which the trade

---

[160] Kimball, *Pitt Corres.*, II, 348.

[161] *Ibid.*, II, 320-321; *Pa. Archives*, 1st. ser., III, 753. In Dec., 1759, General Crump wrote from the West Indies to Pitt, "it is very certain that the French Islands have entirely subsisted" by the treasonable trade carried on from the English islands. *Kimball, Pitt Corres.*, II, 228-229. Cf. the evidence of Commodore Moore, *ibid.*, 207-208.

[162] Beer, *British Col. Pol.*, *1754-1765*, 112-113.

[163] Kimball, *Pitt Corres.*, II, 55. In 1758 the armed sloop, *Charming Polly*, was stationed in Delaware River to enforce the embargo. *Pa. Col. Recs.*, VIII, 58.

[164] Colden of N. Y. said that the merchants engaged in this illegal trade "consider nothing but their private profit"; and Gov. Bull of S. C. wrote that the trade was "so lucrative as to attempt many to engage in it." Kimball, *Pitt Corres.*, II, 395; *N. Y. Col. Docs.*, VII, 499.

[165] For the activity of British cruisers and privateers in breaking

was carried on it was hard to suppress it. It was difficult to secure convictions because the trade was effected under such plausible pretenses of law. If a master was able to secure proper papers in every case, whether on exportation or importation, he was practically beyond the reach of the courts. For this reason, wrote the governor of South Carolina, the admiralty court has dismissed vessels coming from Spanish ports with French products.[166] In Pennsylvania the court dismissed two such cases, and the captors, ready with other vessels suspected of illegal trade, grew discouraged and released them.[167] From the letters of General Amherst in 1762 it appears that the trade had not been checked in the chartered colonies of Rhode Island and Pennsylvania.[168] In the royal provinces of Massachusetts and New York the activity of the royal officials was sufficient to stop the trade. The Boston merchants laid plans to annihilate the powers of the customs and admiralty officials, and the New York merchants complained bitterly that the same care was not shown in Delaware Bay with the result that the Philadelphia merchants were able to undersell them.[169]

The return to a condition of peace in 1763 saw the revival of an imperial sentiment in England, not unlike that which followed the Revolution of 1688. In both cases the events of the war made clear the looseness which characterized the colonial administrative system. Questions of trade, defense, and administration became of prime importance. The close of King William's War witnessed the reorganization of the colonial system by the act of 1696, and the termination of the last French war was to see a

up the trade, consult Kimball, *Pitt Corres.*, II, 344, 353, 349, 584-585; *N. Y. Col. Docs.*, VII, 273.

166 Kimball, *Pitt Corres.*, II, 394-395.

167 *Ibid.*, II, 352.

168 *Pa. Col. Recs.*, VIII, 713, 714; *Pa. Archives*, 1st. ser., IV, 79; *R. I. Col. Recs.*, VI, 311-312.

169 Beer, *British Col. Pol.*, *1754-1765*, 116-125; Kimball, *Pitt Corres.*, II, 584-585.

further strengthening of the administrative system. The acquisition of new dominions to the Empire required a modification of the laws of trade, the prevalence of illegal trade and the defects in the customs service and vice-admiralty courts demanded a reformation of the administrative system, and the failure of the requisition system called for a standing army in the colonies supported in part by a colonial revenue. The whole fabric of the colonial system needed reënforcement; efficiency demanded imperial cohesion and centralization.

The colonial system was reconstructed on both the administrative and economic sides. In 1763 Parliament authorized the use of the navy in American waters to enforce the laws of trade.[170] The good service rendered by the naval commanders in breaking up illegal trade during the war no doubt formed the basis of this law. In July, 1763, the Earl of Egremont, secretary of state, directed the governors to coöperate with the naval commanders, at the same time forwarding a list of ships stationed on the American coast with commissions from the Customs Board and instructions from the Lords of the Admiralty.[171] Thus at last the English government was forced to adopt a measure which had been urged long before by royal agents in the colonies. In the same year the vicious practice of absenteeism in the customs service was terminated. The statesman responsible for this reform as well as others was George Grenville, Prime Minister and First Lord of the Treasury. Parliament had made heavy complaints that the cost of maintaining the customs establishment in America was four times greater than the receipt of revenues. "This, it was urged, arose from the practice of making all these offices sinecures in England." The Customs Board made the same charge and Grenville at once ordered all officials to their posts and directed the Cus-

170 3 Geo. III., c. 22.
171 Sharpe Corres., III, 102-103; R. I. Col. Recs., VI, 376.

toms Board to appoint others in place of those who refused to comply.[172]   Horace Walpole interceded for Grosvenor Bedford, who held the collectorship at Philadelphia since 1732, but Grenville saw no reason to waive the order in this case.[173]   In October, 1763, the Board of Trade instructed the governors " in the strictest manner " to suppress illegal trade, to lend all possible assistance to the customs officials, and finally to report on the state of trade and the conduct of persons empowered to execute the laws so that abuses might be corrected and delinquent officials punished.[174]   This order was the outcome of a report of the Lords of the Treasury to the crown declaring that the revenues collected in the colonies was not sufficient " to defray a fourth part of the expense necessary for collecting it; and that through neglect, connivance and fraud, not only the revenue is impaired, but the commerce of the colonies is directed from its natural course, and the salutary provisions of many wise laws are in great measure defeated." Furthermore, the officials of the customs service and admiralty courts were strengthened in position and power.   By act of Parliament the colonies were forbidden to lower the fees of customs officials and provision was made against subjecting them to damage suits in cases where the court saw fit to release a vessel seized for illegal trading.[175]

The extension of colonial territory as a result of conquest made necessary some changes in the laws of trade in order to bring the new dominions within the scope of the mercantile system.   The statute which embodied the principal economic reform was the Sugar Act of 1764.   Its purpose was two-fold; the creation of a colonial revenue

[172] *Grenville Corres.*, II, 113-114; Kimball, *Corres. of Govs. of R. I.*, II, 355.

[173] *Grenville Corres.*, II, 113; *Walpole Letters*, (Cunningham ed.), IV, 113.

[174] *R. I. Col. Recs.*, VI, 375.

[175] 4 Geo. III, c. 15; 5 Geo. III., c. 45.

to support an army in America, and a reform in the administrative and economic features of the colonial system. Certain products peculiar to the conquered area were added to the enumerated list.[176] But that part of the law which concerned the northern colonies most vitally was the extension of the principles of the Molasses Act. The importation of foreign rum was now prohibited, the duty on sugar was increased, the impost on molasses was lowered from six to three pence per gallon, and in addition colonial lumber and iron were placed on the enumerated list. The reorganized and strengthened customs service would no longer allow for evasions of the law as occurred in the case of the Molasses Act under the former ill-organized and venal customs establishment.

The reformations in the colonial system, which tended toward imperial centralization, at once came into collision with the trend of colonial life toward complete self-control. The immediate effect was to crystallize colonial discontent into unity of action. In May, 1764, on receipt of the news of the passage of the Sugar Act and the intention to levy a stamp tax on the colonists, the assembly of Massachusetts instructed its London agent to secure the repeal of the one and to remonstrate against the passage of the other, and appointed a committee of correspondence to solicit the coöperation of other colonies in the protest.[177] Rhode Island adopted a similar course.[178] The solicitations from these colonies spurred the assembly of Pennsylvania to action. Richard Jackson, the London agent, was ordered to unite with other colonial agents in opposing the measure.[179] Not only a majority of the colonial assemblies passed resolutions of protest, but memorials of public meetings and the pamphlets of colonial leaders, such as John Dickinson, Stephen Hopkins, and James Otis,

[176] Beer, *British Col. Pol., 1754-1765*, ch. x.
[177] Minot, *Hist. of Mass.*, II, 146-149.
[178] *R. I. Col. Recs.*, VI, 403, 414-416.
[179] *Pa. Votes of Assembly*, V. 355-356, 363-364, 376, 377-378.

joined in the common opposition.[180]   The basis of opposition was two-fold, constitutional and economic.   The avowed object of the Sugar Act and the proposed stamp tax was to create a colonial revenue to support in part an army to protect the new dominions.   Heretofore the colonies had enjoyed by long continued usage the power of self-taxation, hence the creation of a colonial revenue by act of Parliament struck a decidedly new note in the colonial policy.   The violation of a well established custom created great alarm in the colonies, for it threatened the very basis of colonial self-government.   It drew into discussion the very nature of the constitution of the Empire and led to the colonial theory of legislative independence in the matter of taxation.   The colonists also protested against the extension of the powers of the vice-admiralty courts which threatened to deprive them of the right to the benefits of the common law and jury trial, rights dear to the hearts of Englishmen.   But the main objection to the Sugar Act was economic.

The opposition to the Sugar Act came chiefly from the northern colonies and was similar in character to that made against the Molasses Act, upon which the new statute was based.   We have seen how necessary was the trade of the colonies to the foreign West Indies.   The very prosperity and wealth of the northern colonies depended upon the trade to foreign ports.   Although the duty on foreign molasses, the chief article demanded of the sugar islands, was lowered one-half, yet the colonists contended that it amounted to a prohibition.[181]   Furthermore lumber, a chief item in the West Indian trade, was now restricted to the English market.   The colonial remonstrances placed em-

---

[180] John Dickinson, *The Late Regulations, Writings*, I, 209-245; Stephen Hopkins, *The Rights of the Cols. Exam., R. I. Col. Recs.*, VI, 416-427; Jas. Otis, *The Rights of the British Cols. Asserted, Almon Tracts*, I,

[181] *R. I. Col. Recs.*, VI, 415, 421; Callender, *Econ. Hist. of U. S.*, 135.

phasis on two points. They declared that closing the channels of trade to the foreign markets not only undermined
the prosperity of the northern colonies but also worked serious injury to the mother country herself. The economic interests of metropolis and dependencies were so intimately
associated in the development of a commercial Empire that
to contract the trade of the colonies was to prejudice English industrial and mercantile interests.[182] For example,
the assembly of Pennsylvania declared that the consumption of British manufactures in the province exceeded the
exportation of colonial products to England by £400,000 a
year, which balance against the colony was liquidated only
by means of the foreign trade.[183] Therefore, contended
the colonists, any legislation which restricted this trade deprived them of the means to pay the debts then due at
home and to continue the consumption of British wares.
This appeal to the industrial interests of the mother country had its effect at a later time. The Sugar Act was
simply a piece of class legislation in favor of the British
sugar islands. As Dickinson said, " The statutes made
to restrain the trade of this continent in favour of the
islands, seemed to tend toward promoting *partial* rather
than *general* interests." The fact that the interests of a
group of West Indian planters was allowed to outweigh
those of the mainland colonies created an intense feeling
of dissatisfaction with the English system of control. The
whole procedure clearly illustrates one of the most fundamental defects in the imperial system. Instead of inquir-
ing into the actual conditions of colonial economic life,
or of heeding the opinions of the colonists, English statesmen built up a system on artificial principles. The fact
that Parliament estimated so lightly colonial interests was

[182] Callender, *Econ. Hist.*, 133-137; *R. I. Col. Recs.*, VI, 415, 421;
N. Y. Col. Docs., VII, 612; *Conn. Col. Recs.*, XII, 651; *No. Car.
Col. Recs.*, VI, 1034, 1261; Kimball, *Pitt Corres.*, II, 376-381; Dickinson, *The Late Regulations, Writings*, I, 213-218.
[183] *Pa. Votes of Assembly*, V, 377-378.

without doubt one of the prominent factors in provoking opposition to its power.[184]   It was felt, and justly so, that Parliament by reason of a lack of an intimate knowledge of colonial life was not fitted to legislate for the colonies.

Discontent revealed itself not only in the constitutional method of petition for redress of grievances, but in acts of violence. Acts of Parliament could be resisted and nullified only by popular resistance. The economic distress caused by the late war,[185] the enforcement of restrictions upon their trade and industry by a reorganized customs service, and the dangers which threatened their rights as Englishmen provoked the colonists to acts of violence. In Rhode Island they attacked the British cruisers and the customs officers who dared to enforce the law, forcing the latter to flee to the decks of the former for protection.[186] In Massachusetts the customs officials were subject to similar treatment and in Maryland a collector was forced to go armed in fear of violence.[187]   John Dickinson wrote that the unwise measures of the mother country taught the colonies " to make a distinction between her interests and our own." The conflict between imperial and provincial economic and political interests revealed a defiant and united America.

[184] Hopkins of R. I. wrote, " The colonies are at so great a distance from England, that the members of Parliament can generally have but little knowledge of their business, connections and interest, but what is gained from people who have been there; the most of these have so slight a knowledge themselves, that the information they can give, is very little to be depended on, though they may pretend to determine with confidence, on matters far above their reach." *R. I. Col. Recs.*, VI, 420-421.

[185] Dickinson, *Late Regulations, Writings*, I, 227-228.

[186] *R. I. Col. Recs.*, VI, 427-430, 453-459.

[187] Beer, *British Col. Pol., 1754-1765*, 288-290, 301-302.

CHAPTER FOUR

THE COURT OF VICE-ADMIRALTY

Experience had proven beyond the shadow of doubt that little dependence could be placed upon the common law courts of the colonies to administer justice where the imperial laws were concerned. Randolph wrote in 1695 " that the illegal trade of the plantations was supported and encouraged by the Generall partiality of Courts and Jurys (byassed by private Interest) in causes relating to the Crown." [1] This condition of affairs called for a system of maritime courts under the direct control of the crown. With this purpose in view a clause was inserted in the act of 1696 providing that certain forfeitures and penalties under the acts of trade should " bee recovered in any of His Majesties Courts at Westminster, or in the Kingdom of Ireland, or in the Court of Admiralty held in His Majesties plantations." [2] The words employed here seem to indicate that admiralty courts were already in operation in the colonies contrary to fact. Randolph at once coöperated with the Board of Trade and Customs Commissioners to secure the institution of such tribunals. [3] In July, 1696, the Customs Board recommended to the Lords of the Treasury the advisability of erecting such courts for the good of the plantation trade. [4] This report reached the Privy Council which in turn referred it to the

---

[1] *B. T. Paps., Pl. Gen.*, IV, pt. 1, A 7, 10, 12; *Cal. State Paps., Col.*, 1693-1696, 509-510, 511, 654; *Osgood*, III, 230-234.

[2] 7 and 8 Wm. III, c. 22, sec. 6.

[3] *B. T. Paps., Pl. Gen.*, IV, pt. 1, A 7, 9; *B. T. Jour.*, IX, 269.

[4] *Cal. State Paps., Col*, 1693-1696, 639-640; *B. T. Paps., Pl. Gen.*, IV, pt. 1, A 5.

Board of Trade.[5] The board consulted Randolph in the matter.[6] He gave it as his opinion, based upon personal experience, that where the laws of trade were concerned the colonial courts denied justice. The judges and jurors were implicated in illegal trade and that he had been unable to carry a conviction in a single case. Randolph insisted that the only remedy was the establishment of admiralty courts, each with a full complement of officers commissioned from England.[7] Convinced of the needs of this measure, the Board of Trade in its report to the Privy Council expressed full concurrence in the recommendations of the Customs Board.[8]

On November 19, the Lords of the Admiralty made a report to the Privy Council in the matter. This body seemed to look unfavorably upon the establishment of special courts by the home government. They held that the governor's commission as vice-admiral was sufficient.[9] A vice-admiralty commission empowered the governor to punish all offenders against the maritime laws and for that purpose to maintain admiralty courts and to appoint the requisite officials.[10] It was found that no such commissions had been granted to the governors of chartered colonies. The Board of Trade was then directed to consider to what other colonies such commissions should be issued for the better execution of the acts of trade.[11] The board evidently did not consider a vice-admiralty commission in these jurisdictions as an adequate remedy and asked the attorney-general to examine the charters

5 *B. T. Jour.*, IX, 24.

6 *Ibid.*, 25.

7 *Ibid.*, 25, 26, 28; *Paps., Pl. Gen.*, IV, pt. 1, A 7, 9.

8 *B. T. Jour.*, IX, 49, 50; *Paps., Pl. Gen.*, Entry Bk. A, ff. 27-28; *House of Lords Mss.*, n.s., II, 427.

9 *B. T. Paps., Pl. Gen.*, IV, pt. 1, A 25.

10 For a copy of a vice-admiralty commission, see Benedict, *American Admiralty*, ch. 9, (3d. ed.) ; *N. J. Archives*, IX, 195. Cf. Greene, *Provincial Governor*, 105-106.

11 *B. T. Paps., Pl. Gen.*, IV, pt. 1, A 25.

and give an opinion whether the crown had the right to constitute admiralty courts in the chartered colonies.[12] On December 4, Attorney-General Trevor replied that upon an examination of the charters he found nothing therein, Massachusetts excepted, that debarred the crown from this right.[13] The authority to establish courts and to appoint all judicial officers delegated by the charters carried with it no limitation in either respect and in this light it is hard to understand upon what ground the crown lawyer based his opinion. The act of 1696 no doubt gave the crown this right, but to say that the charters did not restrain the crown is an assumption rather unwarranted. William Penn, Fitz-John Winthrop, and other representatives of colonial charters appeared before the Board of Trade and during several hearings insisted that to establish admiralty courts by royal prerogative was to infringe the patents by which the crown had invested the grantees with power both " by land and by sea." They held that this covered maritime jurisdiction. In order to protect their powers they offered to establish admiralty courts by their authority, if such tribunals were deemed necessary.[14] In a formal paper embodying these statements, they further declared that since the laws of trade provided for the trial of breaches of the law in the common law courts, maritime courts had not been thought necessary, except for the trial of prize cases, of which there were few or none, or else to occasion additional heavy expenses. Again they expressed themselves willing to erect these courts, to appoint efficient officers, and zealously endeavor to force an obedience to the acts of trade.[15] This defense left the Board of Trade doubtful as to the extent of the admiralty jurisdiction of

12 *B. T. Jour.*, IX, 241.
13 *Ibid.*, 263; *Props.*, Entry Bk. A, ff. 13, 14; *House of Lords Mss.* n. s., II, 428.
14 *B. T. Jour.*, IX, 269, 271, 275, 279-280.
15 *B. T. Paps.*, *Props.*, Entry Bk. A, f. 15, *House of Lords Mss.*, n. s., II, 428-429.

England, and unwilling to make a decision in the matter, submitted the question to the determination of the Privy Council.[16] The proprietors and agents of the chartered colonies then petitioned the king to grant their governors vice-admiralty commissions.[17] Such a procedure was hardly calculated to meet the needs of the situation. To leave the organization of these courts to the colonial authorities by virtue of the charters or to their governors by virtue of vice-admiralty commissions was not an adequate remedy. The chief difficulty lay in the fact that the chartered governments were not sufficiently subject to the will of the crown. A due administration of the law required special courts and officers immediately under the royal will. It seems likely that this was the view of the Privy Council for on February 24, 1697, it directed the Board of Trade and the Customs Commissioners to prepare a list of persons properly qualified for employment in the vice-admiralty courts.[18] Randolph was at once consulted and it was his list of nominees which was accepted.[19] On April 27, the Lords of the Admiralty issued warrants to Sir Charles Hedges, judge of the High Court of Admiralty, to grant letters patent under the seal of his court to the list of persons proposed.[20] Seven vice-admiralty jurisdictions were created for the mainland colonies. Pennsylvania, Delaware and West Jersey formed one district.[21] For this area the following officers were commissioned,

[16] *B. T. Paps., Props.*, Entry Bk. A, ff. 16, 17; *Jour.*, IX, 285; *House of Lords Mss.*, n. s., II, 427-428.

[17] *B. T. Paps., Props.*, Entry Bk. A, f. 31.

[18] *B. T. Jour.*, X, 6.

[19] *Ibid.*, X, 9, 11, 14; *Paps., Pl. Gen.*, IV, pt. 1, A 46, 49; *Props.*, Entry Bk. A, ff. 109, 111-116.

[20] *Admiralty Books* (Public Record Office), III, 101; *Pa. Col. Recs.*, I, 353.

[21] Pa. and West Jersey were made one district, and Del. was made part of the Maryland district. Penn opposed this division of his dominion and his request that Del. be included in the former district was granted. *B. T. Jour.*, X, 38, 44; *Paps., Pl. Gen.*, IV, pt. 1, A 54.

Robery Quary, judge; Edward Chilton, advocate; William Rodney, register; and Robert Webb, marshal.

In the resolution of the home government to secure obedience to the laws of trade the opposition of those who stood for chartered rights was overborne, the charters were abridged and the colonists were to become acquainted for the first time with courts not of their own making officered by persons not of their own selection. From the standpoint of imperial interests such courts were a capital necessity. A review of the power and jurisdiction vested in these courts is necessary to an understanding of their subsequent history.

The terms of the commission [22] to the judge invested the court with a jurisdiction as wide and with powers as liberal as ever claimed by the admiralty in England in the heighth of its vigor. Territorially considered it was very broad, drawing within its competence all causes or offenses committed upon or by the high seas, arms of the sea, navigable rivers and all ports, harbors and creeks within the ebbing and flowing of the tide below the first bridges. Its jurisdiction embraced all causes, civil or maritime, such as charter parties, bills of lading, policies of assurance, debts, exchanges, complaints, all matters relating in any way to freight, transport money, maritime loans, and bottomry. In fine, it was comprehensive enough to include all classes of persons in any way connected with maritime transactions. The act of 1606 provided no definition of the limits of these courts either in point of territory or jurisdiction, but simply gave them competence over certain violations of the laws of trade. In the absence of statutory definition of limits, the judges' commissions contained the source, extent, and definition of vice-admiralty jurisdiction in America. Moreover, it is essential to bear in mind that

[22] Benedict, *American Admiralty*, ch. 9 (3d. ed.), contains a translation of the commissions to the judges of the district of New York, Conn., and East Jersey.

the admiralty court was a prerogative court which employed the civil law, a code of foreign origin.[23]

The business of the admiralty court at home was limited. It consisted chiefly of piracy, salvage, collision, wages and bottomry under certain limitations.[24] This is in striking contrast with the powers and jurisdiction of the similiar courts in America by statute and commission. Furthermore, in England causes growing out of the revenue or customs came before the Court of Exchequer which practised the common law and employed juries. In the colonies similiar cases could be tried in the civil courts. The decline of the admiralty at home was due to the powerful attacks upon it as well as other courts of special jurisdiction employing foreign codes of law by the common law courts.[25] The judges of the latter court considered themselves the proper guardians of the lives, liberty, and property of Englishmen. On the other hand the people demanded the right to be tried by the common law of the country and before juries,— rights dear to the hearts of Englishmen. When the expansion of the jurisdiction of the civil courts threatened to curtail the powers of the common law courts, the antagonism of the latter was thoroughly aroused. The peculiar instrument by which the admiralty court was attacked was the " prerogative writ " of prohibition issuing out of the superior Court of King's Bench.[26] This writ was designed to correct the improper assumption of jurisdiction by inferior courts. The contest between the opposing courts went on with varying success till the time of the Restoration when the admiralty yielded in an unequal struggle and its business

[23] Holdsworth, *History of English Law*, I, 313-332.
[24] *Ibid.*, 325-326; Marsden, *Select Pleas in the Court of Admiralty*, I, lxxix in Selden Society, *Publications;* Benedict, *American Admiralty*, (3d. ed.) ch. 7, secs. 111-113.
[25] Holdsworth, *op. cit.*, I, 321-325.
[26] *Ibid.*, 92-93.

rapidly declined.[27] In America a similiar contest was waged. The basis of colonial opposition was well stated by Penn in 1701. '' Our settlements are upon the freshes of navigable rivers and creeks, where the river may be from two to three miles over, to a stone's cast over, and 100 miles from the ocean, and the Court of Admiralty by virtue of the seventh and eighth of the king, pretends not only to try cases that relate to the King's revenue as to unlawful trade or piracy, but whatever is done in the rivers or creeks other ways, as debts for victuals, beer, sails or anything relating to the building of small craft; so that they have swallowed up a great part of the Government here, because our commerce, by reason of the nature of our settlements, is so much upon the river and small creeks of it; and determining these causes without a jury, gives our people the greatest discontent, looking upon themselves as less free here than at home, instead of greater privileges, which were promised.'' [28]

From the outset the admiralty courts met with the sturdiest sort of opposition in the chartered colonies. In Rhode Island, the governor rendered the commission of the new judge ineffectual by refusing to administer to him the oath of office.[29] The governor of Connecticut refused to recognize the commission, holding it to be an infringement of the charter.[30] The judge in South Carolina complained of great discouragement offered him by the government.[31] The governor and council in the Bahamas openly denounced the commission, and the judge in fear of his life was forced to flee.[32] In no colony was the opposition more general or persistent than in Pennsylvania. No sooner had

[27] Holdsworth, *op. cit.*, 321-325; Marsden, *Select Pleas*, II, xli-lvii, lxxix; Benedict, *op. cit.*, 3-4.

[28] *Duke of Portland Mss.*, IV, 31, Hist. Mss. Com., *Report 15*, pt. 4.

[29] *B. T. Jour.*, XI, 256-257.

[30] *B. T. Paps.*, *Props.*, Entry Bk. A, ff. 201, 203.

[31] *Ibid.*, Entry Bk. C, f. 335; *Props.*, IV, pt. 1, H 5, 6, 7.

[32] *Ibid.*, Entry Bk. C, f. 292; *Props.*, IV, pt. 1, G 42.

Quary arrived with his commission than there developed a bitter hostility to his power. In 1698 the assembly enacted a law providing that all actions involving breaches of the trade laws should be judged according to the common law and before juries returned from the district where the offense was committed.[33]   Such a measure of course nullified Quary's commission. But there was some justification for it. Section ten of the statute of 1696 states that upon all suits where the acts of trade were concerned '' there shall not bee any jury but of such only as are Natives of England, or Ireland or are borne in His Majesties said Plantations.''   The object of this clause was to exclude the Scots in the colonies from jury duty. But the words justify the contention of the colonists that the admiralty courts were to employ the common law and juries. In August, 1699, Penn secured the opinion of Roger Mompesson, an English lawyer, that this clause meant that the admiralty courts were to employ juries.[34] It is probably nearer the truth, as Sir John Cook, advocate-general, pointed out in 1702 that the clause meant that where an action was brought before a common law court the jurors must be so qualified and not that the civil court should try by jury.[35]   This was undoubtedly the intention of the framers, but the act was carelessly drawn. According to Penn it could not be otherwise when only '' Com. Chaddock and Ed. Randol were the framers of it.''[36]   In fact the very reason for the creation of admiralty courts in the colonies was to do away with the prejudices of juries. Randolph sent home the colonial law of 1698 saying '' that it damns the Admiralty,'' and Quary asked for directions how to proceed in the face of it.[37] The law was vetoed

[33] B. T. Paps., Props., III, C. 26, no. 8; Charter and Laws of Pa., 268-274.

[34] B. T. Paps., Props., VII, M 15.

[35] Ibid., VI, pt. 2, K 32.

[36] Duke of Portland Mss., IV, 31; Hist. Mss. Com., Report 15, pt. 4.

[37] B. T. Paps., Pl. Gen., IV, pt. 2, C 18; ibid., Props., II, B 22; Jour., XI, 259.

in August, 1699.[38] But the veto availed little where the interests of the colonists were concerned. The law of 1700 provided that no freemen should be tried or condemned in any case whatever but by the "lawful judgment of his equals or by the laws of the province." This too was disallowed as contrary to the statute of 1696.[39]

Quary was unable on his arrival to put his commission into practice. This was due to the absence of the advocate, Edward Chilton, in England.[40] Meanwhile, in June, 1698, Matthew Birch, collector of the customs at Newcastle, seized some European goods on board the sloop *Jacob*, alleging the lack of certificate of reshipment in England. The goods were turned over to the custody of Robert Webb, marshal of the court. John Adams, claimant, secured the promise of the collector to recover his goods on appraisement until the court met. Shortly after this Adams received from New York the lacking certificate, but Quary refused to recognize it, saying that a thousand certificates would avail nothing and that the goods could only be recovered by suit. Adams offered to give security to the amount of appraisement set by Quary to make answer at court, but this the judge also arbitrarily refused. The claimant then appealed to Governor Markham for redress, but the latter wisely refused to meddle in the concerns of the new court.[41] Taking advantage of Quary's absence, Adams applied to the county court of Philadelphia for a writ of replevin to recover the goods out of the hands of the marshal. The marshal was haled before the court and ordered to show on what authority he held the goods. He replied by producing his com-

---

[38] *B. T. Jour.*, XII, 156-157; *Props.*, Entry Bk. B, f. 82.
[39] *Penn'a. Statutes at Large*, II, 18, 451. Laws of New York and Mass. were vetoed for similar reasons. *Cal. State Paps., Col.*, 1699, 38; *Acts and Resolves of Mass. Bay*, I, 287, 307.
[40] *B. T. Paps., Props.*, II, B 22.
[41] *Pa. Col. Recs.*, I, 541 *et seq.*

mission.[42]   David Lloyd, leader of the democracy in the
province, took the document, held it aloft, and pointing
to the king's picture on it, exclaimed scornfully '' here is
a fine baby, a pretty baby, but we are not to be frightened
with babies.''[43]   These words afford a good illustration of
the scant respect shown by the colonists for the royal authority.   Anthony Morris, one of the justices of the court,
at Lloyd's instigation issued a writ of replevin and the
sheriff by virtue thereof seized the goods out of the marshal's custody.[44]   According to Quary, the court was
pleased with Lloyd's sarcasm.   He was also charged with
saying that all who gave countenance to this court '' were
greater enemies to the Liberties & properties of the people
than those that sett up Shipp Money in King Charles the
firsts time . . .''   Governor Markham was charged
with refusing to restore the goods when an appeal was
made to him.   In fact, said Quary, the entire government
was privy to the whole affair.   '' Their dependance ''
wrote he, '' is so great on Mr. Penn's Interest at Courte
that they conclude that they may do anything.''   He characterized the Quakers as a '' perverse, obstinate and turbulent People '' who will submit to no laws but of their own
making nor acknowledge any of England but such as particularly mention the province.[45]   There is no doubt that
Quary's statements were colored by a feeling of intense resentment, yet they may be taken as a good indication of
the colonial sentiment toward the new court.   The charge
that the whole government connived at the opposition is
manifestly unfair.   The governor not only refused to restore the goods to Adams, but the governor and council,
on Quary's complaint, held that the procedure of Morris
was not an act of the government and censured the court

[42] *B. T. Paps., Props.*, II, B 34.
[43] *Ibid.*, B 40; III, C 17, no. 1.
[44] *House of Lords Mss.*, n. s., IV, 318-319.
[45] *B. T. Paps., Props.*, II, B 30, 34.

for allowing Lloyd's words to pass without reprimand.[46]
It was rather the expression of resentment felt by the common law courts against a new and extensive jurisdiction
which threatened the very jurisdiction of the former.
The first session of the court was held at Newcastle, November 10-12, 1699.[47] The sloop *Jacob* was libeled by
collector Birch for importing uncustomed goods. The case
was continued by the court on the plea of David Lloyd,
counsel for the claimant, that his client was absent. But
the matter was reached another way. John Bewley, collector at Philadelphia, exhibited information against Jacob
Basset, master of the said sloop, alleging that he as a
Frenchman was not qualified to navigate the ship according
to the laws of trade. The law required that the master and
three-fourths of the crew must be English or colonial born.
Moorehead, owner of the vessel, tried to block the proceedings by insisting upon a jury trial as provided by the act
of 1696 and the law of the colony. The court properly
rejected this claim. He then presented a certificate of
Basset's denization, but this too the court refused as contrary to law. The court decreed the ship and cargo condemned. Moorehead moved for an appeal to the High
Court of Admiralty, but refusing to give security, the court
ordered the decree to be executed. At the same session
the prize case, the *St. Louis*, came up for adjudication.[48]
David Lloyd, by order of the governor, claimed that the
vessel was a castaway and therefore by charter became forfeited to the proprietor. The claim was overruled, the
ship was judged lawful prize and ordered delivered into
the hands of John Moore, deputy prize-agent. Quary
charged that the sheriff of Newcastle, acting under the
governor's orders, refused to deliver up the ship. Such
were the devices of the local authorities to thwart and nullify the powers of the admiralty court. After making

[46] *Pa. Col. Recs.*, I, 544, 545-546; *B. T. Paps., Props.*, V, F 40.
[47] *B. T. Paps., Props.*, III, C 17, no. 4.
[48] *Ibid.*

due allowance for the *ex parte* character of Quary's charges, it seems clear from a general survey of the evidence in this and other colonies that the colonial governments were bitterly opposed to the exercise of admiralty jurisdiction and used every means to reduce it to a cipher. Quary wrote home that attempts were made to persuade the grand jury to represent the admiralty officers as enemies to the government and that he was afraid of taking fees for fear of imprisonment.[49]

In May, 1699, Quary held another session of the court.[50] When Morris was ordered to restore the goods seized out of the hands of the marshal, it is alleged that he replied that the court of common pleas had custody of the goods and that no action would be taken until directions were received from England. When the marshal, on the order of Quary, requested the governor to deliver the prize *St. Louis,* Markham is charged with the reply that " when he sees any power to call him to account he will give answer to it." · At this sitting was tried the case of the ship *Providence,* libeled by John Moore, advocate of the admiralty court, as not duly registered according to law.[51] It appears that the crew, bound from England to Maryland, was forced by stress of weather to put in at the nearest haven, Newcastle on the Delaware. The king's collector demanded sight of the certificate of the ship's registry. Unfortunately the paper was either mislaid or lost and the vessel was seized. Shortly after this, Lumby the master, secured from the governor of Maryland a list of vessels duly registered, which included the *Providence.* The collector accepted this evidence and released the ship. Not so Quary, who ordered the vessel seized and libeled in his court as unregistered. The evidence in the

---

49 *B. T. Paps., Props.,* III, C 16, 28.

50 *Ibid.,* C 28.

51 *House of Lords Mss.,* n. s., IV, 338-340; *B. T. Paps., Props.,* III, C 28, no. 2; VI, pt. 1, H 15.

case is conflicting and hardly allows of impartial judgment. The master and several of the crew testified that the ship was properly registered in England and produced the Maryland list in evidence. On the other hand several of the crew testified that they knew nothing of the ship's registry. Quary held the Maryland list irrelevant and ordered the ship and cargo condemned according to law.[52] Quary charged that the Quaker magistrates supported Lumby in this case " not out of kindness to the man or his cause, but prejudice to the jurisdiction of the admiralty."[53] The decree was strictly according to law, but out of regard for the equity in the case Quary left the ship to the master's care and ordered the cargo into the king's store in order to allow the master and owners to secure redress in England. When it became evident that there was no hope of recovery at home, Quary ordered the cargo sold, but at the solicitation of the master, the sale of the vessel was deferred until word could be received from the owners. Later, at the master's request, Quary proceeded to the sale of the ship and tried to effect a plan by which the former could buy up the vessel on easy terms.[54] Quary accused the Quakers of persuading the master not to agree to this plan on the promise to get the ship for him without cost.

The frequent complaints from Quary convinced the Board of Trade that stern measures were necessary. In August, 1699, the board advised the Privy Council to order that Governor Markham be dismissed from office for lack of royal confirmation and opposition to the admiralty

---

[52] Thomas Smith, supercargo, made affidavit that the ship did not break bulk, but only put into Newcastle by stress of weather; on the other hand, Jeremiah Basse, royal agent in West Jersey, made affidavit that the vessel did break bulk. *B. T. Paps., Props.,* VI, pt. 1, H 15; *Jour.* XIV, 337, 341, 351.

[53] *House of Lords Mss.,* n. s., IV, 332.

[54] *Ibid.,* 333, *B. T. Paps., Props.,* V, F 58; VI, pt. 1, G 4, H 15; *Pa. Archives,* 1st. ser., I, 136.

court; that David Lloyd, for ridiculing the king's commission, should not be allowed to continue in any office
whatever; and that Anthony Morris, the justice, who of-
fended by issuing the writ of replevin, should be expelled from his office. As Penn was about to repair to
the province he should be directed to obey the instructions, redress the wrongs suffered by the admiralty court,
and see to it that the admiralty and customs officials were
supported in their duties.[55] The council approved the
recommendations and on September 12 Penn received instructions.[56] The execution of these orders depended
solely upon the determination of the proprietor. By the
royal charter he enjoyed the power to nominate all officers
within his province. But the ceaseless hostility of the
home government to colonial charters was a cogent reason
why Penn should obey. Then again Penn probably appreciated the justification for the measures. Penn set
foot in his colony late in 1699 and promptly fulfilled the
instructions. Before the provincial council Morris surrendered his commission as magistrate and his action was
rebuked by Penn as " rash and unwarrantable " and beyond justification. Morris acknowledged his error, Penn
promised to restore the appraised value of the goods, and
Quary seemed satisfied.[57] Lloyd was suspended as coun-
cilor until he cleared himself of the charges made against
him.[58] Penn showed a willingness to uphold the new
court and to protect imperial interests in other respects.
In March, 1700, Quary wrote home approvingly of Penn's
zeal.[59] But it proved to be only a truce. In November,
Quary wrote both to the Board of Trade and the Lords of

[55] B. T. Jour., XII, 137; Paps., Props., II, B 20; Entry Bk. B,
ff. 20-32.

[56] Ibid., Props., IV, D 3; Entry Bk. B, ff. 84, 98-102; Jour., XII,
156-157.

[57] Pa. Col. Recs., I, 565-566, 576.

[58] Ibid., 602; B. T. Paps., Props., V, F 23, 26.

[59] B. T. Paps., Props., V, F 5; House of Lords Mss., n. s.; IV, 323-
326.

the Admiralty that the court never labored under worse difficulties and that Penn's sincerity had proven a delusion.[60] The basis of the complaint was that the proprietor had granted commissions to the high-sheriffs investing them with the powers of " water-bailiffs " whereby the proper jurisdiction of the admiralty was invaded. At the same time there arrived in the province two writs from the High Court of Admiralty inhibiting the execution of Quary's decrees in the cases of the *Jacob* and *Providence*. Quary claimed that these orders were secured through the efforts of Penn and the Quakers in order to thwart the detested court. The granting of the water-bailiff commissions and the issuing of the inhibitions raises two questions; the respective limits of the common and civil law jurisdiction in the colony, and the relations between the admiralty court in the colony and the High Court of Admiralty at home.

It appears that the owners of the *Jacob* and the *Providence* carried their causes on appeal to the High Court of Admiralty. The owners in the first case were able to secure an order forbidding Quary from executing the decree of condemnation and a commission empowering the appellants themselves to carry it out. In the second case the decree of the court was ordered suspended till the matter could be heard and determined by the admiralty at home.[61] The question arises, did the High Court of Admiralty possess an appellate jurisdiction where the acts of trade were concerned? The commission to the colonial admiralty judge makes reservation for appeals home but that instrument does not cover the acts of trade in express terms. Furthermore, since the act of 1696 gives the admiralty at home no original jurisdiction over breaches

[60] *B. T. Paps., Props.*, V, F 57, 58, 64, no. 10; *House of Lords Mss.*, n. s., IV, 331-336.

[61] *House of Lords Mss.*, n. s., IV, 334-346; *B. T. Paps., Props.*, V, F 58.

of the law, could it claim a right to entertain cases on appeal? In fact, the act of 1696 was very carelessly drawn in several particulars. Was it that the maritime court in the colonies should employ juries? Was it the purpose that these courts should have jurisdiction solely over breaches of the laws of trade or to the fullest extent of the commission? Was the High Court of Admiralty to enjoy appellate jurisdiction over the laws of trade? Of the question of juries we have already treated. Quary, in his perplexity, sought from English counsel an interpretation of the law of 1696 with regard to juries and appeals.[62] They gave the opinion that according to the law juries were to be employed in the colonial admiralty courts, and since the admiralty in England was given no original jurisdiction over the acts of trade it possessed no jurisdiction on appeal. This opinion was justified by a strict interpretation of the law of 1696 and in the light of these facts the procedure of the court at home in the cases of the *Jacob* and *Providence* may be considered illegal. Sir Charles Hedges, judge of the High Court of Admiralty, gave Quary the opposite opinion as to appeals.[63] Quary wrote to the Lords of the Admiralty expressing the hope that Parliament would '' explain that dark, contradictory act, not only in that particular, but in several other points, and that the authority of the Admiralty will be asserted beyond all objections and contradictions.''[64] The admiralty in England asserted the right to hear cases on appeal for in October, 1701, it affirmed Quary's decree *in re Providence* and the owners were cast for costs.[65] In 1715 Advocate-General Lloyd gave the opinion that in common maritime cases appeals from the colonial admiralty courts lay in the High Court of

[62] *House of Lords Mss.*, n. s., IV, 332.
[63] *Ibid.*, 332.
[64] *Ibid.*, 326.
[65] *B. T. Paps., Props.*, V, F 26.

Admiralty.[66] But the practice was not uniform, for we note that the Privy Council heard and determined cases on appeal from the courts of admiralty in the colonies.[67] These inhibitions no doubt caused great joy to the enemies of the admiralty court. Quary claimed that they were secured by Penn and the Quakers for the sole purpose of working injury to the court. He said, " All this clamor and intrigue is carried on in masquerade by the inveterate enemies of the Admiralty Jurisdiction " and " they have already raised all the reflections and affronts on the King's advocate and myself, giving out that we are sent for to England and there to be found to our ruin and that whatever we have or shall do will be made void at home." [68] On the other hand Penn declared that because the colonists saw fit to protect the owners of the *Providence* from the rigorous decree of the court it is imputed to them as opposition.[69] There is little reason to doubt that the granting of these inhibitions had the effect of lessening the influence of the court.

With regard to the water-bailiffs' commissions it appears that Quary was absent from the province for five months by reason of illness and private business and that during this time some offenses were committed on the river at Philadelphia.[70] According to his commission the admiralty judge had jurisdiction here. But in order to preserve peace the high-sheriff of Philadelphia county was commissioned water-bailiff, which empowered him to execute all processes on the waters of the county. On his re-

---

[66] Chalmers, *Opinions of Eminent Lawyers* (ed. 1858), 531, 532.
[67] *Acts of the Privy Council, Col.*, II, 356, 378; III, 84, 87, 127, 252, 270, 459, 485.
[68] *House of Lords Mss.*, n. s., IV, 333-335; *B. T. Paps., Props.*, V, F 58, 64, no. 10.
[69] *House of Lords Mss.*, n. s., IV, 348; *B. T. Paps., Props.*, VI, pt. 1, G 4.
[70] *House of Lords Mss.*, n. s., IV, 349, 337-338; *B. T. Paps., Props.*, V, F 58, 57, 60, 64, no. 10; V, pt. 2, I 19; *Jour.*, XV, 54-56.

turn Quary at once complained that the commission was a serious infringement of the jurisdiction of the admiralty court. He declared that the effect of this commission was to restrict the jurisdiction of his court to the high seas beyond the capes of the Delaware, thereby nullifying the power of the court. Penn issued the commission, claimed Quary, in violation of his promise not to invade the rights of the admiralty court until the respective limits of the common and civil law jurisdictions were determined at home, but was forced to break his pledge by a Quaker assembly which threatened to withhold all supplies till the obnoxious court was banished from the province. To satisfy Quary, Penn revoked the offending commission although scarcely four warrants had been issued. Penn justified his granting of it on the ground that if Quary had been home or deputed one to serve in his stead it never would have been issued. Indeed Penn's action appears in a most defensible light. If writs issuing out of the common law courts could not be executed on the Delaware, criminals or debtors fleeing before the law would be able to bid defiance to the civil powers merely by stepping off a wharf on board a vessel. This would be extremely serious if the admiralty judge was absent and left none to exercise the powers of the court. Penn expressed bitter feelings toward a court which claimed a jurisdiction so wide as to threaten the very existence of the common law courts and which deprived his people of the benefits of the ancient common law and jury trial. He wrote to the Admiralty Board in 1700 saying that he did not conceive that the civil courts set up in the colonies for the trial of breaches of the acts of trade " were ever designed to extend so far that nothing should be done a foot off shore in any creek or river but by its power," and asked that " the just boundaries of the civil and maritime powers, where they border upon one another " should be determined.[71] To his agent Law-

---

[71] *House of Lords Mss.*, n. s., IV, 349-350.

ton, Penn wrote expressing the hope that he would live to see these men who cast away other men's estates without a jury punished " though not so rigorously as Empson and Dudley." [72] It was the old conflict over again in the new world,— a conflict between a court exercising the common law so dear to the hearts of Englishmen and a court bitterly hated because it employed a foreign code and denied jury trial. The dispute was now carried to England.

In 1702 both Penn and Quary were in England. In April of this year Quary submitted to the Board of Trade a bill of charges against the province.[73] This list included the complaint that the admiralty jurisdiction had been invaded by the common law courts, which assumed the right to try breaches of the trade laws, and by the issuance of the water-bailiff's commission. Penn answered the charges in writing [74] and both sides were given a hearing before the board.[75] Edward Randolph and Jeremiah Basse, both royal agents, appeared to substantiate Quary's statements. The dispute was referred to the crown lawyers who were asked to submit an opinion on the following queries.[76] Do the common law courts enjoy concurrent jurisdiction with the civil courts over the acts of trade? May any other court judge a case after the admiralty has once taken cognizance of it? Does a water-bailiff's commission infringe the admiralty jurisdiction? The joint opinion of Sir John Cook, advocate-general, and Sir Edward Northey, attorney-general, was favorable to Penn's contentions.[77] It held that the indefinite wording of the act of 1696

---

[72] *Pa. Archives*, 1st. ser., I, 139-141; *B. T. Paps., Props.,* V, F 26.

[73] *B. T. Paps., Props.,* VI, pt. 2, I 17, 28; VII, M 21.

[74] *Ibid.,* VI, pt. 2, I 20.

[75] *B. T. Jour.,* XV, 54-56, 75-76.

[76] *Ibid.,* XV, 82, 87; *Props.,* VI, pt. 2, K 4.

[77] *B. T. Paps., Props.,* VI, pt. 2, K 24 gives both queries and answers. Sir John Cook was also called into consultation by the board. *Jour.,* X, 128, 131.

seemed to give both the common and civil law courts jurisdiction over forfeitures under that statute and that the informer was not restricted to the admiralty court. But when once the latter court had taken cognizance of a case, pending action, no other court might interfere. A water-bailiff's commission did not infringe the admiralty jurisdiction since such officers were simply sheriffs whom Penn had the right by charter to appoint. In conclusion, they held that although Penn had no right to erect an admiralty court, he had the right to constitute judges to try causes arising within the body of the province but not on the high seas. If the latter held good then the territorial limit of the admiralty court was restricted to the high seas beyond the Delaware Capes. This practically meant that ships seized within the Delaware bay and river for violating the laws of trade could be tried solely in the common law courts. This fact drew from the board further pertinent questions. Do the colonial admiralty courts enjoy greater powers than the High Court of Admiralty? In a case of a violation of the laws of trade may the admiralty take cognizance of it? In case a ship sails up the river with uncustomed goods consigned to the colony, or· in case of illegal exportation of goods from the colony, does the action lie in the civil or in the common law courts, or may the informer choose his court? The opinions of Cook and Northey were delivered separately; [78] the former showing himself to be a true exponent of the civil law and the latter a zealous advocate of the common law. Northey held that none of the acts of trade prior to 1696 gave the admiralty courts in the colonies any power over those laws for the terms used therein applied solely to " courts of record " which excluded the admiralty. As to the High Court of Admiralty, the navigation act of 1660

[78] B. T. Paps., Props., VI, pt. 2, K 32 for queries and answer of Cook; K 48 for answer of Northey. See also Chalmers, Opinions, (ed. 1858), 499-502, 504-507.

gave it competence over a vessel seized on the high seas, the act of 1663 gave it no jurisdiction whatever, and the act of 1670 power only over offenses against that particular law. On the other hand Cook held that " courts of record " included the civil courts and that therefore by the laws of trade both the admiralty at home and in the dominions enjoyed competence over all of the acts of trade. As to the act of 1696 it was the opinion of Northey that offenses against this law were triable only in the common law courts in England, but in the colonies the jurisdiction was divided. The admiralty court had sole jurisdiction over all offenses except in cases of ships not legally owned, built, manned and commanded, in which cases the common and civil law courts possessed concurrent jurisdiction. Cook upheld the right of the admiralty at home and in the colonies to hear and determine cases of illegal exportation or importation as established by the laws of 1670 and 1696, but seemed inclined to the opinion that the common law courts shared concurrent jurisdiction in such cases. These opinions are diametrically opposed to each other. When crown lawyers disagreed over the interpretation of the acts of trade so loosely worded and were unable to meet on common ground as to the respective limits of the opposing courts, it may be appreciated what an ill-effect this would have upon the standing of the admiralty courts in the colonies. What directions were given as a result of these opinions the records do not lay bare. Evidence shows that the common law courts in Pennsylvania assumed the right to hear and determine not only causes involving violations of the navigation law proper but also breaches of the acts of trade in other respects.[79]

As a result of the dispute Penn was able to secure Quary's dismissal from the post of admiralty judge by exhibiting charges of a most serious character against him.

[79] *B. T. Paps., Props.*, XI, R 52; XII, R 19 no. 8; R 93; VI, pt. 2, I 20.

These accusations disclose the loose lines along which England administered her colonies. To put the admiralty court upon a footing of independence and efficiency called for several requisites of high necessity. The administration of justice ever demands men of the highest integrity, of knowledge and experience in the law, and free from those private interests which are liable to sway their opinions as judges. In the case of an admiralty judge these qualifications were especially to be desired. It was a grave and serious matter to put the property of a litigant at the mercy of a single judge who, according to the civil law, decided both the law and the facts in the case, unrestrained by the rules of the common law and juries. Under this system a court composed of inferior officials might use its power for personal and mercenary ends. Then again the admiralty officers should have been rewarded by salaries paid from the English exchequer equal to the dignity of the post in order to free them from temptation and dependence upon the colonial governments. Lastly, the limits and powers of the civil courts should have been fixed with certainty by act of Parliament in order to prevent a recurrence of the conflict between the common and civil law courts. These ideals were in no ways approximated and a review of the charges against Quary reveal these facts. In June, 1702, Penn presented to the Privy Council a series of charges against Quary.[80] He alleged that Quary's ignorance of the civil law and his lack of education rendered him unfit for a trust wherein the property of the people was so deeply concerned. He charged him with stretching the powers of his court to include causes properly cognizable at common law; with being the greatest merchant and factor in the colony although holding the offices of admiralty judge and surveyor of the customs; and finally, with using his power for mercenary ends. In

[80] *B. T. Paps., Props.*, VI, pt. 2, K 9; VI, pt. 1, G 4; *House of Lords Mss.*, n. s., IV, 348-349.

support of the last charge Penn instanced several cases in which he held Quary guilty of corrupt practices. Quary entered a flat denial of corruption and brought counter-charges of a similiar character against Penn.[81] Both statements were undoubtedly colored by a feeling of resentment, and in the absence of other evidence nothing can be proved one way or another. But the fact remains that no definite salaries were allowed the admiralty officers by the English government. They were made dependent for compensation upon a percentage of the proceeds of vessels and cargos condemned and sold. Men of little honor and dependent upon the pickings of office for support would not be loath to promote litigation and pronounce unjust decrees for lucre's sake. As Burke said of this system many years later, " a court partaking of its own condemnation is a robber." But Quary himself made several confessions of a damaging character. He acknowledged his ignorance of the civil law and did not deny that he acted as a merchant and factor in the colony; and he declared that he would have continued as such had he not been discouraged by " an infamous illegal trade." [82] There is a strange incongruity in permitting a judge of the admiralty court to serve also as a customs official, as in Quary's case, for it allowed him to sit in judgment on his own seizures. Neither was it proper that a judge should pursue the calling of a trader, for the charge that the colonial judges were partial because implicated in illegal trade is of equal force in Quary's case. John Moore, the advocate, likewise confessed to an ignorance of the civil law and was equally guilty of being both an officer of the court and customs collector for Philadelphia.[83] Quary wrote to the Lords of the Admiralty in 1700 to request that some person be

81 *B. T. Paps., Props.*, VI, pt. 2, K 10.
82 *Pa. Col. Recs.*, I, 562; *Cal. Treas. Paps.*, 1697-1702, 91.
83 *House of Lords Mss.*, n. s., IV, 337; *B. T. Paps., Props.*, V, F 61.

sent from England " that is well read in the law and in all respects duly qualified for the discharge of this difficult place." [84]   Of the marshal and register, Quary wrote in condemning terms. " One lives more than a 100 miles from this place, and the other is a perfect sot. I am forced in some cases to be Marshal and Register, else all things must be in confusion." [85]   These men were the nominees of Randolph, and apparently no effort was made to inquire into their qualifications.[86]   It may hardly be said that such officials were of the proper sort to be entrusted with administering the imperial system or to win the allegiance of the colonists to a system imposed from without.

Penn succeeded in having Quary deposed from the office of judge and secured the appointment of Roger Mompesson in March, 1703.[87]   Quary wrote to the Board of Trade that he was glad to be relieved, yet he thought it very strange that one should be preferred who gave an opinion unfavorable to the admiralty court.[88]   Perhaps with a view to inciting the board to anger, Quary wrote that the Quakers declared Penn would be able to carry his designs in spite of the board's hostility to him because of his greater influence at court. At once the board wrote to the secretary of state and the Lords of the Admiralty in Quary's favor, and at the same time submitted the offending opinion of Mompesson.[89]   The outcome of the whole

[84] *House of Lords Mss.*, IV, 335.

[85] *Ibid.*, 326; *B. T. Paps., Props.*, II, B 22.

[86] Wrote Penn, " So miserable are the Queen's poor Industrious Subjects in Pennsilvania under such Officers; And for that Reason, They and I beg to be delivered from 'em; unless a Colony, and they that made it, are of less Importance to the Crown, than an Insolent & Vexatious, as well as Uncapable Officer." *B. T. Paps., Props.*, VI, pt. 2, K 34.

[87] *Admiralty Book*, V, 141; *Penn-Logan Corres.*, I, 163.

[88] *B. T. Paps., Props.*, VII, L 51.

[89] *Ibid., Props.*, Entry Bk. D, ff. 384-386; *Penn-Logan Corres.*, I, 376.

affair was that Quary was restored as judge in November, 1703.[90] Indeed, further favors were heaped upon him by his appointment in the same month to succeed Randolph as surveyor-general of the customs.[91] Quary continued to cause uneasiness in the colony. In May, 1704, Penn appeared before the board to request that Quary should be directed to live peaceably with the colonial authorities and not cause unnecessary trouble.[92] The board granted the request and wrote the meddlesome official to this end.[93] Again in 1709, Penn received a letter from Logan, his secretary in the province, asking that Quary and the other royal officials be requested to cease their annoyance.[94] In 1713 Quary died and for some years all went smoothly as far as the court was concerned. This is perhaps accounted for by the fact that there was no judge till 1718. In that year William Asheton was appointed, to be succeeded by Josiah Rolfe in 1724.[95] As both of these men were colonists of high character and members of the provincial council, little friction was likely to ensue. On the death of Rolfe in 1724, one Joseph Browne, an outsider, was appointed and again there was trouble. This friction is not only a further illustration of the iniquitous fee system but also clearly exhibits the means by which the colonial courts were able to attack the admiralty and subject it to humiliating correction.

In 1717-8 John Menzies, judge, and James Smith, advocate, of the admiralty court in New England, made complaint to the home authorities that the provincial judges encroached on the powers of the admiralty court by releasing prisoners committed to jail by the latter court and by setting aside appeals to the High Court of Ad-

90 *Admiralty Books*, V, 189, 193.
91 *Customs Books*, XIII, 296.
92 *B. T. Jour.*, XVII, 34.
93 *Ibid.*, 36; *Props.*, Entry Bk. D, f. 31.
94 *Penn-Logan Corres.*, II, 309.
95 *Admiralty Books*, VIII, 82, 371.

miralty.[96] For example; two men, committed to jail by
the admiralty for insulting the court by public placard,
were released by writ of prohibition, and the proceedings
against a ship libeled in the admiralty for illegal exportation of wool were stopped by a similiar writ. As already stated this was the familiar weapon which the Court
of King's Bench in England used with such telling effect
against the admiralty at home. By a similiar process the
colonists attacked the admiralty in America. Indeed the
granting of writs of prohibition was not at all confined
to chartered colonies. In the royal provinces they were
issued as well, which is good proof that royal control was
not a panacea for the ills of chartered jurisdictions. Fundamentally it was a struggle of the forces of democracy
against centralization and imperialism. The Lords of the
Admiralty complained of these encroachments to the Privy
Council, saying that there was " little or no regard had
to the authority and jurisdiction of the admiralty abroad,"
and praying that the colonial governors should be directed
to restrain the provincial judges. The report was referred
to the Board of Trade which in turn passed it on to Richard West, counsel to the board, for his opinion.[97] West
shared all the prejudices of the adherents of the common
law and his opinion is especial hostile to the admiralty
courts. In his report of 1720 [98] West declared that a consideration of the complaints of Menzies and Smith plainly
show that the basis of the dispute is nothing but the desire
of the civil court to extend its jurisdiction by denying the
right of the provincial courts to issue writs of prohibition
and in holding that the only redress against a decree of
the admiralty court was by appeal to the High Court of
Admiralty. Said West, this position is untenable, for the
right of the courts of the colonies to issue writs of

[96] B. T. Paps., Pl. Gen., IX, K 146; X, L 29.
[97] Acts of Privy Council, Col., III, 38, 57.
[98] B. T. Paps., Pl. Gen., X, L 10; Chalmers, Opinions, (ed. 1858),
510-521.

prohibition was founded on the common law, which is the heritage of Englishmen wherever they go. Furthermore, continued West, the admiralty courts in America enjoy not a whit more power than the admiralty in England, for the statutes of Parliament which affirm the common law and restrict the admiralty courts in England, passed prior to the settlement of a colony, extend thither unless there exists a colonial law to the contrary. Therefore, the laws of 13 and 15 Richard II restricting the admiralty solely to the high seas and other acts defining the limits of the civil and common law West declared to be in force in the colonies.[99] And the fact of the matter is that the colonial courts did not hesitate to avail themselves of the force of these statutes.[100] The right of the superior courts of common law to issue writs of prohibition was further guaranteed by colonial statutes confirmed by the crown. Moreover, as West pointed out, should the admiralty in the colonies assume to itself the power to decide cases cognizable only at common law, what remedy had the colonist to vindicate his right to the common law if writs of prohibition were not allowed? Therefore, said West, to direct the governors to restrain the judges from issuing these writs was improper. But if it should be found, as was probably the case, that the colonists have used this power improperly to banish the admiralty from the colony then the remedy to apply is an act of Parliament reducing the admiralty jurisdiction to a certainty. The remedy proposed was never applied and the admiralty court was

[99] Holdsworth. Hist. of English Law, I, 317.

[100] In 1739 the supreme court of New York issued a writ of prohibition restraining the admiralty court in the case of the ship Margaret and Mary, seized for illegal importation of goods. The writ was based on the statutes of 13 and 15 Richard II, which limited the admiralty jurisdiction to the high seas. Such action practically nullified the competence of the maritime courts over breaches of the acts of trade, since all seizures were made " infra corpus comitatus." N. Y. Col. Docs., VI, 154-155. Cf. No. Car. Col. Recs., III, 224; Acts of Privy Council, Col., III, 703, 704, 720.

left to work out its own salvation in the face of a keen opposition. The colonists felt bitterly toward a court which deprived them of the common law and jury trial and which tended to draw unto itself causes which arose within the body of the country.[101] The danger was still greater, as Jeremiah Dummer pointed out in 1721, " where neither the Judge nor any of the Inferior officers of the Admiralty have Salaries, or perhaps other Dependance than upon what they get by their Fees, and therefore must be strongly tempted to receive all Business that comes before them, however improper for their Cognizance." [102]

John Moore, collector at Philadelphia, seized some uncustomed goods which were libeled in the admiralty court in the session of February, 1726.[103] When no claimant appeared, Judge Browne decreed the goods to be sold and the proceeds distributed, one-third each to the informer, governor, and king, according to law. Governor Gordon and Moore, the informer, objected to this method of distributing the proceeds and insisted on having their share in kind. The court overruled the objection and ordered the decree executed. Gordon thereupon, on the advice of

[101] Jeremiah Dummer wrote, in his *Defense of the New England Charters*, (London, 1721), "It had bin ever boasted as the peculiar Privelege of an Englishman, & the grand Security of his Property to be try'd by his County and the Laws of the Land; whereas this Admiralty Method of Tryal deprives him of both, as it puts his Estate in the Disposal of a single Person, and makes the Civil Law the Rule of Judgment; which though it may not perhaps be call'd Foreign, being the Law of Nature, yet 'tis what he has not consented to himself, or his Representative for him. A Jurisdiction therefore so founded ought not to extend beyond what Necessity requires, that is, to nothing but what is really transacted on the High Seas, which not being *infra Corpus Comitatus*, is not triable at Common Law. If some Bounds are not set to this Jurisdiction of the Admiralty, beyond which it shall not pass, it may in Time, like the Element to which it ought to be confin'd, grow outrageous & overflow the Banks of all the other Courts of Justice." 30-31. *Cf. No. Car. Col. Recs.*, III, 224-225.

[102] Dummer, *op. cit.*, 31.

[103] *B. T. Paps., Props.*, XII, R 112.

Moore, appointed a commission to distribute the goods according to their desires.[104] Likewise, Gordon, as chancellor, issued out of the court of chancery, a writ of injunction restraining the admiralty officers from executing the decree of that court under penalty of £2000 fine.[105] Gordon defended his action on the ground that he knew of no law which forced him to take his share in money if he wished it in kind. Furthermore, Browne was accused of exacting extortionate fees.[106] He claimed as a fee five per cent. on the sale and seven and one-half per cent. on condemnation, which on an appraisement of £591 on the goods would net him about £74. Browne was also charged with delaying proceedings in his court without pretense, with vexatious procedure, and with being obliged to quit the providence on suspicion of debt. Gordon's commission proceeded to carry out the decree and Browne was allowed only a three and one half per cent. fee. There is little doubt but that Gordon assumed unwarranted powers. He did not question the jurisdiction of the court or the legality of the decree of condemnation and it is hard to see upon what ground he could base his authority to carry out the decree in his own fashion or to regulate the fees. On the other hand, a twelve and one half per cent. fee on condemnation and sale was extortion. Browne produced evidence to show that in the neighboring colonies a seven and one half per cent. was allowed on condemnation, but to exact a further fee of five per cent. on sale was unreasonable. It is a clear illustration of the evils likely to be attendant where the officers of the court were dependent upon fees for support and where such fees were regulated by custom and not by authority of the home government.

In 1727, Gordon again exercised his powers as chancellor to obstruct the admiralty court. In July, Daniel Moore,

104 *B. T. Paps., Props.*, XII, R 115.
105 *Ibid.*, R 113.
106 *Ibid.*, R 116, 117, 118.

collector at Newcastle, seized the *Sarah* for irregular trad-ing.[107] The ship was first libeled before Isaac Miranda, acting as judge under deputation from Browne. The lat-ter found it necessary to revoke his commission to Miranda on a charge of gross proceedings. Peter Baynton, claim-ant, requested Browne to proceed in the case. Moore then appealed to Governor Gordon to issue a writ to stay the proceedings of that court. Gordon acquiesced and issued the desired injunction to restrain the admiralty court under penalty of £500 until the case was fully heard in the chancery court.[108] This action was based on Moore's com-plaint that Browne had shown favoritism to the claimant, and had put the informer to needless charges in prose-cuting the case, whereby the judge was rendered unfit to try the cause.[109] Later Gordon dissolved the injunction and requested Browne to proceed, but he refused. The case was then heard in the court of common pleas and the ship was acquitted.[110] Again in September, 1727, David Lloyd, chief justice of the supreme court, issued a writ of prohibition to restrain the admiralty from hearing a case of seamen's wages on the ground that the contract was made on shore and therefore cognizable only at common law.[111] This was in accordance with English practice in similiar cases.[112] This Lloyd, wrote Browne, is the same one who created opposition to the court in 1699.[113] In 1727 both Browne and Gordon sent home their respective versions of the whole dispute. Later Browne went to

[107] *B. T. Paps., Props.*, XII, R 119.

[108] *Ibid.*, R 120, 121, 122; XIII, S 27, 28.

[109] Gordon also brought civil action against Browne for slander and the latter was held on bail to the exorbitant sum of £2000, but the case never materialized. *Ibid.*, XII, R 111.

[110] *Ibid.*, R 122.

[111] *Ibid.*, R 126.

[112] Salkeld, *Reports of Cases adjudged in the Court of King's Bench . . . from 1 William and Mary to 10 Queene Anne*, I, 32, 33, III, 24.

[113] *B. T. Paps., Props.*, XII, R 126.

England, armed with affidavits, to urge his complaints in person.[114] In June, 1730, Sir Henry Penrice, judge of the High Court of Admiralty, made a long report in the matter. He characterized Gordon's conduct as high-handed and complained that the colonial courts by various methods infringed the admiralty jurisdiction as often as they pleased. He advised that the offending persons should be removed from office and that the " Penn family " should be instructed to see that the admiralty court was protected against attacks by the common law courts.[115] The report was referred to the Board of Trade. Browne submitted his case in writing to this bureau and was also granted a hearing.[116] The board reported to the Privy Council that as the evidence before it was *ex parte* in character, Gordon should be directed to submit his statements of the matter supported by proofs and affidavits and meanwhile should not interfere with the admiralty court.[117] The report was approved. Browne returned to the province and both sides prepared statements in defense of their actions.[118] In May and June, 1732, these papers were considered by the Privy Council and further than this there is no evidence that positive action was taken.[119] No colonial officials were removed, the admiralty court was given no support from home, all of which is in striking contrast with the vigorous measures taken in 1699.

This whole situation makes still clearer, what the events of Quary's incumbency have already shown, the serious defects in the organization of the system of admiralty courts. Of the merits of the controversy between Browne

[114] *Admiralty Books*, IX, 7.
[115] *B. T. Paps., Props.*, XII, R 111; *Acts of Privy Council, Col.*, III, 251, 272.
[116] *B. T. Jour.*, XL, 193, 209-210; *Props.*, XII, R 131; *Pl. Gen.*, XI, M 12.
[117] *Ibid., Props.*, Entry Bk. H, ff. 12-15; *Acts of Privy Council, Col.*, III, 287.
[118] *B. T. Paps., Props.*, Entry Bk. H, ff. 15-18; *Props.*, XIII, S 2.
[119] *Ibid.*, Entry Bk. H, ff. 48-53, 55-56.

and Gordon it is hard to pass judgment. Browne was charged with showing favoritism to a litigant, with creating needless delay in the trial of causes, with vexatious proceedings, and with claiming extortionate fees. If such charges were well founded they illustrate both the poor character of appointments to the colonial service and the evils of the fee system. On the other hand Browne submitted to the home authorities a certificate of good behavior signed by seventy-five men of prominence in the colony declaring that he was a man of integrity and free from private interest in the execution of his office, and that his conduct was commensurate with the duties of a judge.[120] Whatever may be the merits of the controversy, the whole situation laid bare two great defects in the system of imperial courts; the evils of the fee system, and the failure to define with certainty the jurisdiction of the admiralty courts by act of Parliament. The former subjected the officials to unscrupulous methods, the latter made it possible for the colonial courts to nullify the powers of the hated civil courts.

From 1728, when Browne left for England, down to the time of the last French war, no further trouble over the admiralty court was experienced. The reasons for this are simple. From 1728 to 1734 no admiralty court existed in the province.[121] After 1734 the admiralty posts were filled by colonists of ability and eminence. It became the custom for the Lords of the Admiralty, when vacancies in the court occurred, to consult the proprietors or governor and appoint their nominees [122] To the judgeship were appointed such men as Charles Reade, 1734;

[120] *B. T. Paps., Props.,* XII, R 124.

[121] Gordon refused to recognize Browne's commission as judge when the latter returned to the province. *B. T. Paps., Props.,* XIII, S 24.

[122] *Penn Mss., Official Corres.,* III, Wm. Allen to John Penn, March 26, 1737; *ibid.,* V, Thos. Penn to Gov. Hamilton, March 9, 1752.

Andrew Hamilton, 1737; Thomas Hopkinson, 1743; and Edward Shippen, 1752.[123] All of them were men of wide interests, of great experience in the law, and of prominence in the councils of the provincial government. Likewise the inferior posts were filled with colonists of ability and worth. The choice of such men, colonists themselves and therefore in hearty sympathy with colonial aspirations, precluded the probability of a clash between the admiralty and common law courts. Their predilections would lead them to adapt official action to the needs and desires of the colonists.

During the French and Indian war the latent hostility of the colonists toward the court as well as the defects in the court itself came clearly to light again.[124] In former pages we have seen by what means the colonists carried on an illegal and treasonable trade with the French West Indies. It was charged that the admiralty courts of South Carolina, New York, the Bahamas and Pennsylvania were prejudiced in favor of this trade.[125] On November 1, 1760, Governor Hamilton of the latter province wrote to Pitt[126] that he found the most eminent lawyers of Philadelphia " retained in favor of this Trade,'' and that on technical grounds " the Judge of the Court of Vice Admiralty had also decreed in its favor, in the only two instances that have been brought before him '' and had cast the costs of the suit on the captors. As a result, wrote Hamilton, several ships carrying flags of truce and laden with French provisions were seized by English cruisers and brought to the port of Philadelphia for condemnation, but were released without prosecution because of the attitude of the court and the lack of good lawyers to engage in the prosecution. Similar complaints came from

123 *Admiralty Books*, IX, 254, 347; X, 160.
124 Beer, *British Col. Policy, 1754-1765*, 117-123.
125 *Ibid.*, 126-127.
126 Kimball, *Corres. of Wm. Pitt with Col. Govs., etc.*, II, 352-353.

other colonies. In fact, the judge of the admiralty court in the Bahamas was under a retainer from the Philadelphia merchants to release any vessels of the colony brought there for condemnation.[127] The efforts of Pitt to check the trade aroused the merchants of Massachusetts and Rhode Island to a bitter hatred of the customs officials and admiralty courts. They therefore concerted measures calculated to nullify and destroy the powers of these royal agents. To accomplish this design they relied on the common law courts and the prejudice of colonial juries. In Rhode Island the execution of a decree of the admiralty was stopped by a writ of prohibition issuing out of the superior court of the colony and suit was instituted in the inferior court to recover money awarded by a decree of the admiralty. Judge Andrews wrote that " all proceedings of said vice-admiralty court, not only in this but in all other causes, have been stopped; although there are now causes of great consequence pending before the said vice-admiralty court, unfinished." [128] In Massachusetts at least five actions were instituted in the admiralty court designed to cripple the customs and admiralty officials in the performance of their duties. The latter cases, however, were finally settled in a fashion tending to uphold the court and customs officials.[129] The basis of this opposition may be gleaned from a letter of Governor Bernard. He wrote that this conduct was a part of a preconceived plan of the Boston merchants " to destroy the Court of Admiralty and with it the Custom House which cannot subsist without that Court," and that it was the avowed intention to discourage " a Court immediately subject to the King, and independent of the Province and which determined property without a jury." [130]

On the return of peace the whole administrative system

127 Beer, *op. cit.*, 127.
128 *R. I. Col. Recs.*, VI, 371-372.
129 Quincy, *Massachusetts Reports*, 541-547, 557.
130 *Ibid.*, 555.

was strengthened. October 4, 1763, the Lords of the Treasury reported to the Privy Council that it was highly necessary to establish by law a better method for the condemnation of seizures in the colonies. As the acts of trade varied so much as to the mode and place of trial, the prosecutor or informer was at times in great doubt as to the method of procedure, it was advised that a uniform system for the trials of breaches of the law should be established.[131] Accordingly the act of 1764 provided that all violations of the laws of trade may be tried in any common law or admiralty court in the colonies, or in any court of admiralty which may be established with jurisdiction over all America, at the option of the informer.[132] Pursuant to this act the Lords of the Admiralty ordered the appointment of a vice-admiral for America and of a judge of a general vice-admiralty court with jurisdiction over all the colonies.

The extension of admiralty jurisdiction and powers as well as the intention of the English government to tax the colonies directly created widespread alarm and aroused profound discontent in the colonies. The pamphlet literature, resolves, and petitions of the numerous colonial assemblies were of one accord in protesting against measures which were designed to deprive Englishmen in America of the two most precious rights of all Englishmen; the right to grant money by their own consent and the right to the benefits of the common law and jury trial.[133] The petition of Rhode Island to the king in 1764 well sums up the colonial contention.[134] '' The extensive powers given . . . to the courts of admiralty in America have a tendency in a great measure, to deprive the col-

131 B. T. Paps., Pl. Gen., XVIII, Q 74.

132 4 George III, c. 15, sec. xli.

133 Hopkins, Rights of the Cols. Examined. in R. I. Col. Recs., VI, 422; John Dickinson, Writings, I, 175, 195. Cf. Beer, British Col. Policy, 1754-1765, 289-290.

134 R. I. Col. Recs., VI, 415.

onists of that darling privilege, trial by juries, the inalienable right of every Englishman; and subjects the inhabitants to other great hardships and intolerable expenses; as the seizor may take the goods of any person, though ever so legally exported and carry the trial to a distant province." These protests also voiced the evils of the fee system.[135] There was in fact much justification for the opposition on this ground. As Edmund Burke put it "courts incommodiously situated, in effect, deny justice; and a court partaking in the fruits of its own condemnation is a robber. The Congress complain, and complain justly of this grievance." On the other hand, it is evident in the light of past events that the English government was forced to widen the powers and strengthen the position of the admiralty courts for the security of the acts of trade. These courts were a necessity because of the intense prejudice of colonial common law courts and juries.[136] The continual opposition of the colonists to these courts, like the struggle of the colonial assemblies against the powers of the royal and proprietary governors,

[135] Gov. Bernard of Mass. wrote in 1764, " . . . the objection to the Judge of the Admiralty being paid by the poundage of condemnation is very forcible; for thereby it is his interest to condemn, rather than to acquit. The present Judge of this Province is, I Believe, as uncorrupt as any one the King has; but he has frequently complained to me of his office being supported by such means" Bernard, *Select Letters on Trade, etc.*, (London, 1774), 16-17. Wm. Allen wrote to John Penn, that an honest admiralty judge cannot make £5 a year out of the office, but one of a different turn will hold court every day and annoy the masters of vessels in every petty dispute with the sailors. *Penn Mss., Official Corres.*, III, March 26, 1737. Cf. John Adams, *Works*, III, 466; James Otis, *Rights of the British Cols.*, (Boston, 1764) 53.

[136] Gov. Bernard wrote in 1764, "the reason for putting these causes into a course of trial without jury, undoubtedly arose from an apprehension that the juries in these causes were not to be trusted. The force of this reason may have abated, but I cannot think that it is wholly destroyed: no candid man, I believe, will take upon him to declare, that an American jury is impartial and indifferent enough, to determine equally upon frauds of trade." *Select Letters*, 16. *Cf. N. Y. Col. Docs.*, VI, 155.

simply illustrates the determination of the colonists not to submit to any outside jurisdiction whatever. Their hearts were embittered against courts not of their own making, to officials not of their own choice, and to a code of law which put their property at the hazard of a single judge and deprived them of a trial at common law. The opposition to the admiralty courts was simply one manifestation of the general movement toward home rule and independence.

CHAPTER FIVE

THE ROYAL DISALLOWANCE

In taking up the subject of the royal disallowance, I propose to describe the attitude of the central government toward the colonial laws submitted to it for examination; to consider the number of laws disallowed and the reasons for this action; and to come to some conclusion as to the effectiveness of the crown's check on colonial legislation. Subsequent chapters will take up the attitude of the province toward the royal disallowance and instructions in regard to laws which affected particular interests of the colony; such as the judicial system, the questions of coinage and currency, and the tender subject of the Quaker religious principles.

First a few words as to the extent and nature of the power over legislation possessed by the province and crown. By the charter the proprietor and the freemen of the province were empowered to make laws '' for the raising of money for the publick use of the said province, or for any other End apperteyning unto the publick state, peace or safety of the said Countrey, or unto the private utility of perticular persons.'' It was stipulated that these laws should be consonant to reason, and not contrary, but as near as may be agreeable, to the statutes and rights of the realm. All laws were to go into operation when published under the seal of the proprietor. On the other hand, the crown's check on these laws was provided for by the clause which made it incumbent upon the proprietor and his heirs to send all acts to the Privy Council within five years after passage, and if the said laws were not disallowed under the privy seal within six months after delivery to the council they were to stand in full force.[1] It is obvious that this power was not a veto in the sense that all laws required the royal sanction before becoming operative, neither was it a repeal because the laws were not regularly annulled by the legislature. The king and council sat rather as a supreme court with power to judge and interpret the colonial enactments, and in this capacity disallowed or annulled laws contrary to English statutes or imperial interests.

A review of the process through which the laws passed in England will throw some light on the methods of colonial administration. Prior to 1696 little effort was made to enforce obedience to the obligation to send the laws to the council. In that year new vigor was infused into colonial management by the creation of the Board of Trade. One of its specified duties was to "examin into, and weigh such Acts of the Assemblies of the Plantations respectively as shall from time to time be sent over or transmitted for Our Approbation." The king in council reserved to itself the power of final action, and to the board was delegated power only to examine the laws and make report.[2] The consideration of colonial laws constituted a large part of the board's work as evidenced by the journals and the great collection of laws stowed away in the Public Record Office.[3] The new board acted promptly in the days of its youth. In December, 1696, Penn was called to attend the board and directed to submit the laws of his province as soon as possible.[4] A year later, when no laws were forthcoming, Penn, as well as the agents of the Jerseys and Carolinas, were directed by letter to lay before the board

[1] Poore, *Charters and Consts.*, II, 1512; Thorpe, *Amer. Charters Consts., etc.*, V., 3039.

[2] *Acts of Privy Council, Col.*, II, III, Appendix.

[3] For a list of journals and acts of the thirteen original colonies, preserved in the Public Record Office, London, edited by C. M. Andrews, see Amer. His. Asso., *Report*, 1908, I, 399-509.

[4] *B. T. Jour.*, IX, 275.

at once a collection of the laws of their respective colonies.[5] In the same month Penn responded by delivering a full collection of the laws.[6] It does not appear that any positive action was taken at the time on this body of laws. Two years later, December, 1702, Penn again laid before the board a body of one hundred and five laws passed in the latter part of the year 1700.[7] Final action on them was not taken till February, 1706, after a lapse of a little over three years after delivery and five years and two months after enactment.[8] This long delay was no doubt occasioned by the pending negotiations between Penn and the crown looking to a surrender of his powers of government. But with this exception the board acted with a fair measure of promptness on the laws which came before it. For example, fifty laws submitted in April, 1709, had received final action in October of the same year, and twenty-nine laid before the board in July, 1713, had been either confirmed or disallowed by the order in council of February, 1714; and in fact, rarely more than seven months on an average intervened from the time of submission to the time of final action.[9]

The board did not presume to pass upon the laws in point of legal accuracy and expediency, but passed them on to the crown lawyers, and after 1718, to the standing counsel to the board. The opinions of the counsel show much care and thought in their consideration of the laws and it was usually upon the basis of their opinions that the board framed its report to the Privy Council.[10] Thus it may be said that the fate of colonial laws rested really

5 *B. T. Jour.*, X, 373, 377.

6 *Ibid.*, 386; XI, 438; XII, 78, 115; *B. T. Paps., Props.*, II, B 6, 7.

7 *B. T. Jour.*, XIV, 289; XV, 327.

8 *Pa. Statutes at Large*, II, 449.

9 *Ibid.*, II, 524-534; 541-556; II—V, Appendices, *passim.*

10 For the reports of the crown lawyers and counsel to the board on the laws of Pa. see the *Pa. Statutes at Large*, II—V, appendices; also Chalmers, *Opinions of Eminent Lawyers*, (ed. 1858).

in the hands of the counsel. Not all the laws were sent to
the counsel, as for example, twenty out of over a hundred
considered 1705 were reported for disallowance on the
sole examination of the board; [11] and in 1709 only five
out of fifty were referred to the attorney-general.[12] These
were the exceptions rather than the rule. After the report of the counsel was at hand, the board took up the
laws for consideration in point of practical expediency.
Were they prejudicial to the mercantile system, were they
contrary to English statute, or did they infringe upon the
power of the crown over the colonies. The board treated
the laws with a fair degree of attention, took them up at
various sittings for examination, and laid hold of every
available opportunity to secure the information requisite
to rational action.[13] The board showed a desire to consider the interests of all concerned in the laws. To secure information the colonial agents and proprietors were
frequently called to attend the board.[14] In fact, the work
of supporting the laws formed the chief burden of the ac-
tivities of the colonial agents. William Penn during his
active life frequently appeared before the board in support of the laws of his province,[15] and after his incapaci-
tation in 1712, two of the mortgagees of the province,
Joshua Gee and Simon Clement, performed this duty.[16]
Not till 1731 did the colony appoint a permanent agent
to reside in London to look after its interests.[17] Prior
to this special agents were employed as occasion demanded

[11] *Pa. Statutes at Large,* II, 464-467.
[12] *Ibid.,* 527-528.
[13] In 1717, in order to facilitate the dispatch of business, the
board fixed upon the following routine: Mondays for reading letters and papers from the colonies; Tues. and Weds. for plantation business; Thurs. for trade; and Fridays for colonial legislation. *B. T. Jour.,* XXVI, 438.
[14] *Pa. Statutes at Large,* II—V, appendices; *B. T. Jours, passim.*
[15] *Pa. Statutes at Large,* II, appendix, *passim.*
[16] *Ibid.,* III, appendix, *passim.*
[17] *Pa. Votes of Assembly,* III, 150, 151.

to secure the royal sanction of favorite laws.[18]   The board consulted other interests as well.   Merchants, trading to the colonies were consulted on laws likely to effect their interests; [19] the bishop of London was called upon for advice on laws which touched Anglican interests in America; [20] laws which concerned the colonial post-office, the vice-admiralty courts and the customs service were sent respectively to the Postmaster-general, the Lords of the Admiralty and the Customs Board for examination.[21]   At times it was necessary for the colonial agents or proprietors to employ counsel to support particular laws attacked by special interest.   In 1731 the Penns engaged special counsel to defend a law to establish the colonial judiciary which had been attacked by the customs officials in the colony,[22] and in 1760 both the proprietors and assembly employed eminent counsel to argue before the board on several laws which concerned conflicting interests in the province.[23] On the whole the board did not act in a summary or arbitrary manner, but showed a desire to deal fairly and to secure all needful information before acting, and usually gave the colonial agent or the proprietors fair opportunity to answer objections and to clear away misconceptions.

When the board's examination had reached an end, the result was embodied in a report, drawn up by the secretary and signed by the members, to be submitted to the Privy Council.   It was customary for the council to accept fully the board's report.   In two cases the colonial agent appealed from the report of the board to the Privy Council,

18 See pages 193, 194, 252.
19 Pa. Statutes at Large, IV, 481; B. T. Jour., XLIX, 26, 30.
20 B. T. Jour., XV, 17, 71; XI, 48, 57; XXXXIV, 243; Pa. Statutes at Large, II, 458, 461, 512.
21 Pa. Stat. at Large, II, 475-476, V, 508-509; Acts and Resolves of Mass., I, 364; II, 67-68.
22 Pa. Statutes at Large, IV, 448.
23 Ibid., V, 691-692.

which granted a hearing to both sides concerned.[24] In one case the report of the board was upheld and in the other a compromise was reached. Final action was taken by means of " orders in council "; the usual method of expressing the royal will, confirming some and annulling others. The charter does not specify that laws should be confirmed by positive action, but that all laws not vetoed within six months after their delivery to the Privy Council should stand in full force. In some cases laws reported favorably were confirmed by order in council, and in others no action was taken and they stood confirmed by lapse of the six months.

It appears that there was considerable expense connected with the negotiation of colonial affairs at home. We have already stated that English subordinate officials received meager salaries and their chief dependence for support was upon fees. It seemed well-nigh impossible to secure the passage of reports and other papers through the colonial office without a large outlay of fees. In 1732, the agent of Rhode Island advised the colony to oppose a bill in Parliament to oblige the colony to send home the laws on the ground that it would entail a great expenditure of money yearly " at the Council office and the Board of Trade to get Acts through here, in fees for Petitions, Reports, References and Royal Orders, besides the tedious delays that may happen." [25] Indeed, the board informed the governor of New Jersey that several laws " will lye forever in their hands for want of an agent to pay their fees." [26] Penn wrote to the colony in 1704 for " 50 guineas, if not 100, to get a favorable report on the laws "; and later wrote that the report of the attorney-general was held up for want of a large fee to him.[27] It was by

24 *Pa. Stat. at Large*, V, 654; *Penn Mss., Letter Bk.*, I, 82, Thos. Penn to Gov. Gordon, July 23, 1731.
25 Kimball, *Corres. of Govs. of R. I.*, 55-56.
26 *N. Y. Col. Docs.* V, 361, 473.
27 *Penn-Logan Corres.*, I, 297, 342; *Pa. Col. Recs.*, II, 193.

such a low order of affairs at home that colonial concerns, which called for prompt attention by reason of the great distance of the colonies from the center of government, were delayed. It illustrates to what an extent efficient control was affected by the arbitrary and cumbersome system of administration at home. The organization of government in England was ill-adapted to the ordering of a great empire.

In several respects this procedure on the laws of Pennsylvania was not strictly according to the charter. The disallowance by means of the order in council was irregular as the charter required that it should be done under the privy seal. This fact came to light in 1733 in the case of *Hamilton vs. Richardson,* argued before the English court of chancery, where the plaintiff held that none of the laws had been legally vetoed. The court did not decide the question.[28] The error had crept in through careless copying of the original charter. The charter called for annulment under the privy seal, the transcripts by order in council. The consequence was that there were many laws, once disallowed, likely to be in force because of this error to the possible creation of much confusion and litigation. Lord Wilmington, president of the council, suggested to the Penns that the matter be remedied by an act of Parliament. To such a measure the proprietors promptly dissented. They said, "we Cannot tell but they [Parliament] may think Severall other clauses want Explanation, when once they have gott it into the house; and it is also a very Ill Precident for any matter relating to the Plantations to be considered by Parliament."[29] Fully aware of the hostility expressed in Parliament to the colonial charters, the Penns had no wish to jeopardize their interests by such a false move. The discrepancy was

---

[28] *Penn Mss., Letter Bk.,* I, 90-91, John Penn to Thos. Penn, August 3, 1733.
[29] *Ibid.*

remedied by act of the provincial assembly which confirmed the disallowance of all laws by order in council.[30] But in spite of this irregularity, the order in council continued to be the method of expressing the veto.[31] This error brought to light another. It became the custom to lay the laws in the first instance before the Board of Trade, although the charter specifies that they should first be delivered to the Privy Council. Hence the laws did not come to the notice of the council until it received them together with the board's report thereon. After 1735 we note that the laws were regularly laid before the Privy Council and then referred by it to the Board of Trade.[32] In fact, the board sought to take advantage of the irregularity in order to secure the disallowance of several laws of long standing. In 1746 several laws dating back to 1722 and 1729, which were considered prejudicial to the act of Parliament permitting the transportation of convicts to the colonies, were reported for disallowance on the ground that they had been delivered originally to the board and not to the council. The proprietors, aware of the dangerous consequences of establishing such a precedent, petitioned against such action. Upon their promise to see that the assembly passed a new law clear of the objections and repealed the old ones, the matter was allowed to drop.[33]

The six months clause was a serious limitation upon the effectiveness of the veto power. In the first place, this narrow period hardly offered sufficient time for a careful scrutiny and a proper judgment of a large collection of laws. The situation is well stated by the board in its re-

[30] Pa. Stat. at Large, IV, 257-260, 452, 453; Votes of Assembly, III, 205-206; B. T. Jour., XLV, 20; Props., XIII, S 46.

[31] In 1735, West gave the opinion that no veto was valid, according to the charter, except under the privy seal. B. T. Paps., Props., XIII, S 59.

[32] Pa. Statutes at Large, IV, V, Appendices, passim.

[33] Pa. Archives, 1st. ser., I, 716-723; Pa. Col. Recs., V, 499-501; Pa. Statutes at Large, III, 505-513; Penn Mss., Letter Bk., II, 179, Thos. Penn to Gov. Gordon, March 5, 1747.

port of 1714, that " it may so happen as in the collection
of laws passed in Pennsylvania in 1705, that so great a
number of laws may at one time be transmitted that it
will be difficult if not impossible considering the other
business that may intervene to examine the same as they
ought to be.'' [34] During the period when the laws were
first submitted to the Board of Trade, the legal adviser
held that the time during which the laws were in that office
formed no part of the six months, which only began when
they were sent with the report of the Privy Council.[35]
Under such circumstances a longer period was allowed
for examination.   After 1735 the laws were regularly submitted to the council in the first instance, hence the time
allowed the Board of Trade for examination of the acts
counted as part of the six months so that prompt action
was necessary to prevent the confirmation of objectionable
laws by lapse of time.   By 1735 the Plantation Committee
of the Council became active in colonial affairs.   The council first referred the laws to the committee, which in turn
by '' order of reference '' submitted them to the board
for consideration and report.   The committee received the
board's report, considered it with care, and at times consulted the crown lawyers, and finally the report reached
the council.   This additional check was probably demanded
by the necessity of obtaining an adequate examination of
the laws within the unreasonably short time allowed.   In
the second place, the charter allowed the crown no opportunity to veto laws which at a later time might prove to
be harmful to British interests.   If no action was taken
within the six months the laws stood confirmed and laws
which later might prove objectionable could not be repealed or altered except by action of Parliament or the
provincial assembly.   In either case redress was likely to

---

[34] *Pa. Statutes at Large*, II, 555; *B. T. Paps., Props.*, IX, 35.

[35] Chalmers, *Opinions*, 336-337; *B. T. Paps., Props.*, X, pt. 2, Q
171; *Pa. Statute at Large*, II, 473-474.

be secured only with considerable difficulty. In the royal province this condition did not obtain, for after a law was once examined by the board and its counsel, no further action was taken if not found immediately objectionable or unless disallowance or confirmation was necessary. The general method was to order the laws " to lye by probationary " which gave the crown an opportunity to use the veto power at any future time on laws which had been found harmful in their operations.[36] In fact, it was not uncommon for the crown to veto laws dating back over a considerable period.[37] The charter of Pennsylvania precluded the crown from any such hold on the laws of this province.

Having pictured the method of procedure, our attention will be directed to the inquiry of how far the charter gave the home government the desired effectual check on colonial legislation. This question involves the attitude of the colonists toward the veto and the measure of obedience paid by the proprietor or colonists to the obligation to send home their laws within five years after enactment. In the first few years after its organization, the board required of Penn prompt compliance in the submission of the laws, but after this it was not quite so insistent and the laws were not transmitted so promptly. Still the laws were delivered within the five-year limit, for example, fifty laws passed in 1705 came to the board in 1709, and twenty-nine enacted in 1708-1712 were submitted in 1713.[38] During Penn's activity he acted as agent for the province and saw to it that the laws were duly laid before the board. But in 1712 Penn was rendered incapable of further business by reason of a paralytic stroke and the year of his misfortune coincides roughly with a decadence in the powers of the Board of Trade. In 1716 Governor Keith sent

[36] For example, see *B. T. Jour.*, XXXIX, 255, XXXVII, 6.
[37] *Ibid.*, LXII, 141, 253, XLIII, 262; *No. Car. Col. Recs.*, V, vi, vii, 155, 166.
[38] *Pa. Statutes at Large*, II, 525-526, 544-545.

to England a body of laws passed in 1713-1715 which did
not reach the board till 1718.[39] In fact, the neglect to
submit the laws would doubtless have been passed un-
noticed had not the attention of the languishing board
been directed to it by an anonymous letter of April, 1718,
charging the colonial authorities with improper motives
in withholding the laws.[40] Joshua Gee was called upon
for an explanation. He replied with a disavowal of any
such motives as imputed, and excused the tardiness on the
ground of Penn's illness and the mortgagee's unacquaint-
ance with the colonial business.[41] Three of the belated
collection had by this time passed beyond the five years
and were presumably in full force in spite of any action
of the crown to the contrary.[42] In general, it may be said
that all the laws of the period of 1696 to 1715 were regularly sent home and received careful attention.

The two decades from 1715 to 1735 tell quite a different
story. Of the one hundred and fifteen laws enacted during this period but fourteen were properly considered
by the home government. Here is evidence both of colonial
disregard for the obligation of the charter and of gross laxity in colonial administration at home. Conformity to the
requirement depended upon the disposition of the colonists
or the proprietor on one hand, and upon the vigor of the
home government on the other. The colonists, separatistic
in their tendencies, were little disposed to allow their laws
to come before the Board of Trade or Privy Council for
examination. English control was disliked for several reasons. The cost involved in the payment of fees, the labor,
the ignorance of colonial conditions at home, the long-

---

[39] Pa. Votes of Assembly, III, 189, 190.

[40] B. T. Paps., Props., X, pt. 2, Q 150; Pa. Statutes at Large, III,
441-442.

[41] B. T. Paps., Props., X, pt. 2, Q 155; Pa. Statutes at Large, III,
443-445.

[42] B. T. Paps., Props., X, pt. 2, Q 160, 161; Pa. Statutes at Large,
III, 445-454.

drawn out delay in acting upon the laws which left the colonies in a state of uncertainty, all contributed to make the colonists reluctant to submit their laws to the will of the crown. The assembly, moreover, felt that the obligation to transmit the laws rested upon the proprietor and not itself. This was the reply made in 1726 when Governor Gordon asked the house to appoint an agent to look after the laws.[43] This view of the matter was in accordance with the provision of the charter, but the sons of William Penn, unlike their father, were unwilling to bear the expense and seemed to be interested in the affairs of the province only so far as their interests as lords of the soil were involved. Furthermore, the laxity and inertia which characterized the work of the Board of Trade during the era of Walpole and Newcastle stands out in striking contrast with the vigor displayed in the earlier period. Hence, shielded by the charter, and favored by the neglect shown by the proprietors and the Board of Trade, the assembly ran its own course unchecked by the exercise of the crown's power of disallowance. In 1730 the board took notice that only a few laws of the province came before it and brought the neglect to the attention of the proprietors.[44] Thereupon John Penn instructed Governor Gordon to transmit promptly to England a collection of the laws passed during his administration, and for the future to send over two copies of the enactments of each assembly, one for the Board of Trade and the other for the proprietors.[45] In response the assembly appointed F. J. Paris London agent for the colony and dispatched a number of laws.[46] The decadence of the board is well illustrated by the treatment accorded this collection. Twenty-six laws passed during the years 1729-

---

[43] Pa. Votes of Assembly, II, 486, 488.

[44] Penn Mss., Letter Bk., I, 8, John Penn to Gov. Gordon, May 3, 1730.

[45] Ibid.

[46] Pa. Votes of Assembly, III, 150, 151.

1733 were found in 1739 after a tedious search by the colonial agent "laid up in a by-corner of the Board of Trade and covered very thick with dust."[47] Under such a régime the veto was of no effect whatever. The province was left to pursue its own course and consult its own desires, unhampered by restraint from England. The whole situation is a good illustration of the difficult problem of administering colonies governed under charters. The royal governors were instructed to transmit the laws of the respective provinces within three months after enactment and the journals of the board show that the laws were sent home in most cases with a fair degree of promptness, were examined by the board and its counsel, and objectionable acts were disallowed.[48] Over the officials of the chartered colonies the crown enjoyed no such control and the royal disallowance proved of force only when the administration at home acted with vigor. In 1739 a long list of acts dating back to 1717, except such as had been repealed by the assembly or temporary acts which had expired by limitation of time, were sent to Francis Fane, the board's counsel, for examination. In November, 1740, Fane submitted his report, but beyond this no action was taken.[49] In fact, no further action was possible. The charter is silent on the point whether those acts which have not been submitted within the five-year period should be on that account null and void, and it seems safe to assume that all laws once having passed this allotted time must be regarded as confirmed in spite of the irregularity. The charter lacked completeness in this as well as in other respects. A proper enforcement of the requirement to transmit the laws called for a provision in the charter making void all laws not promptly sent home or else laying a heavy penalty for disobedience.

[47] Pa. Statutes at Large, III, 493.
[48] For chances instances see B. T. Jour., XXXII, 156, XXXIII, 142, 150; XXXIV, 283; XXXVI, 210, 251, 252.
[49] Pa. Statutes at Large, III, 488-493, 495-505.

Increased administrative efficiency demanded the vacation of the colonial charters.

After 1740 the Board of Trade as well as the colonial authorities showed a greater interest in the obligation to send home the laws. From this date down to the close of our period all the laws, with very few exceptions, were regularly laid before the Privy Council. Rarely more than three years elapsed from the time of enactment till delivery to the council was made,[50] and especially after 1748, when the board was under the efficient presidency of the Earl of Halifax, seldom more than a year intervened. In 1758, and again in 1766, the board complained that certain laws had not been presented till three years after their passage, which shows that a watchful eye was kept on colonial legislation.[51] But the charter afforded other loop-holes for an evasion of the veto.

It is hard to see where the provisions of the charter gave the crown an adequate control over law-making in the colony. It lacked those elements of completeness and positiveness requisite for an effectual control. This is true as we have seen in the case of the transmission of the laws and with regard to the six months clause. It is also true in two other respects. The long five-year limit allowed for transmission afforded the assembly a good occasion to enact temporary measures within the period and by a process of reënactment keep within the letter of the law and ward off the veto. Then again, even though a law should be vetoed at home, there was nothing in the charter which forbade the reënactment of the very same offending law. The case was different in the royal province. Here the governor was bound by royal instructions not to assent to certain laws of an objectionable character, or to confirm temporary measures save in times of necessity, or to give his assent to laws of an extraor-

50 Pa. Statutes at Large, IV, V, Appendices, passim.
51 Ibid., V, 592, VI, 608; B. T. Jour., LXXIV, 178.

dinary nature without the insertion therein of a clause suspending the operation of the law till the royal pleasure was signified. In fact, the royal instructions were very detailed and explicit and by the crown's hold on the governor obedience to the royal orders could be exacted.[52] Thus the crown enjoyed in such colonies what may be called the anticipatory veto. Moreover, the interests of the Empire were further safe-guarded by the royal coun- cil which formed the upper house of the legislature.[53] In the chartered colony royal instructions requiring the suspending clause or forbidding the governor to assent to certain laws were always resisted by the assembly as con- trary to the charter which was interpreted as giving the freemen full legislative independence. The assembly showed no hesitation in taking advantage of the protection afforded by the charter to elude the veto power. No com- plaint was made of such evasions till 1714. Twenty-nine laws enacted 1709-1712 reached the board in July, 1713. Among them were discovered several temporary measures near expiration and several reënactments of laws once dis- allowed. The Board of Trade in its report to the council complained of these facts and cited a law which placed a heavy tonnage duty on all ships trading to the colony, except those owned or built in Pennsylvania, Delaware or West Jersey. This law, said the board, was objectionable as placing a burden on English shipping, and since it was near expiration it might be reënacted before the colony received notice of the veto.[54] The report was considered by a committee of the whole council which advised that the agreement pending between Penn and the crown for the purchase of the powers of government granted away by the charter should be perfected by act of Parliament

[52] Greene, *Provincial Governor*, 162-165, Appendix A gives in full the royal instructions to Governor Bernard of N. J., 1758.

[53] *Ibid.*, 72-90.

[54] *Pa. Statutes at Large*, II, 554-555; *B. T. Paps., Pl. Gen.*, IX, K 35.

and that provision should be made "for inconveniences complained of in passing and transmitting the laws by present tenor." The report was approved by order in council and the Lord Treasurer was directed to perfect the agreement to be laid before Parliament.[55] The Board of Trade was also instructed to report on the best ways and means to check similar practices in other colonies. The attorney-general was consulted and he replied that it could be prevented in the royal colonies by insisting on the governor's obedience to his instructions but in the charter colonies only by act of Parliament. He held that the latter colonies by their charters had a right to make their own laws which could not be put under any restraint other than the charter specified, except by action of the imperial legislature.[56] The board advised the Privy Council to secure the passage of an act of Parliament obliging those colonies not required by charter to submit their laws to do so hereafter.[57] The agreement between Penn and the crown never found its way into law because of the unsettled differences between the Penn family and the mortgagees of the province. Neither was a bill introduced to force all colonies under charters to send home their laws, probably due to the reorganization of government consequent upon the death of Queen Anne in 1714.

Other irregularities came to light a few years later. Twenty-four laws passed 1713-1715 were not delivered to the board till 1718 when it was found that three were temporary measures, several were reënactments of laws once vetoed, and several had passed beyond the five-year period.[58] Aroused by the violations of the spirit of the charter, if not the letter, the board, in March, 1719, sent the charter to Richard West, its counsel, with the request

[55] *B. T. Paps., Pl. Gen.,* IX, K 30; *Props.,* IX, Q 43.

[56] *Ibid., Pl. Gen.,* IX, K 35; *Jour.,* XXIV, 228, 270, 308.

[57] *Ibid., Pl. Gen.,* Entry Bk. F, ff. 418-421; *Jour.,* XXIV, 309, 314.

[58] *Ibid., Props.,* X, pt. 2, Q 160; *Pa. Statutes at Large,* III, 445-455.

for an opinion on the question whether the assembly could by charter reënact laws which the crown had once disallowed.[59] West answered a week later that the charter contained no provision which barred the assembly from reënacting the substance of any laws disallowed by the king. This dictum at once completely nullified the force of the veto power.[60] The only remedy, and one which the interests of the Empire demanded, was the vacation of the colonial charters and the substitution of royal government. This conclusion had been reached many times before by imperial administrators but it was not put into practice. In July, 1719, the board in its report to the council pictured the ill-effects of temporary laws and re-enactments "which is a practice they are guilty of in the very worst degree," and offered the opinion that the "plantations will never be upon a right footing till the dominions of proprietary colonies shall be resumed to the Crown." [61]

It was thoroughly recognized by the board itself and royal officials closely connected with colonial affairs that the charter colony was an anomaly in the imperial system. Again in 1721 the board called attention to the loose provisions of the Pennsylvania charter in regard to the laws and urged that the agreement for the purchase of Penn's powers of government be consummated.[62] Time and time again Parliament and the ministry were called upon to vacate the charters or curtail their powers of government for the sake of stricter royal control, but just as often

<hr/>

59 *B. T. Paps., Props.,* Entry Bk. G, f. 164; *Jour.,* XXVIII, 167.
60 *Ibid.,* Entry Bk. G, f. 165; X, pt. 2, Q 171; *Jour.,* XXVIII, 181.
61 *Ibid.,* Entry Bk. G, ff. 214-216; *Statutes at Large,* III, 467. In 1722 Gov. Keith, in a message to the assembly, expressed the hope that the house would no longer offend the crown by passing laws once vetoed, "a Practice too much in use in this Province heretofore, tho' never attempted in my Time and I hope never will be hereafter." *Pa. Votes of Assembly,* II, 300. *Cf. Acts and Resolves of Mass.,* I, 308.
62 *N. Y. Col. Docs.,* V, 603-604.

these appeals remained unanswered. For some years no further complaint was made. It was the period in which the board had fallen into a state of inertia and few laws of the colony reached England. But early in 1732 the board laid before the House of Commons a statement of colonial affairs, which pointed out the defects of the charters with respect to royal supervision of colonial legislation. " Connecticut, Rhode Island, and Maryland, being under no obligation to transmit their laws . . . it is not surprising that governments like these should be guilty of many irregularities. Pennsylvania has evaded her charter, having transmitted since the year 1715, no acts for the royal supervision, except occasionally an act or two " and that even royal governors neglected to transmit laws passed contrary to their instructions.[63] In April, 1734, the following resolutions were offered in the House of Lords designed to correct these evils. The laws of all colonies, both royal and chartered, should be sent home within a year after passage, that no law should be in force till approved by the crown, except such as were demanded by the exigencies of war, and that the crown should be empowered to veto any former laws, if found detrimental to imperial interests, except such as were already confirmed. Such a measure was a capital necessity for the security of the ideals of the Empire.[64] The resolutions were adopted and ordered to be framed into a bill to be considered at the next session of Parliament. When this news reached the ears of the colonists through the ever watchful colonial agents, there was great alarm. The passage of this bill meant a serious limitation upon their freedom of action enjoyed under the charters and a greater subjection to a foreign control. The agents of Rhode Island and Connecticut were instructed to spare no pains or costs to oppose this measure which endangered

63 Chalmers, *Introd. to Revolt of Cols.*, II, 118-119.
64 *Journals of House of Lords*, XXIV, 411.

colonial charters and privileges.[65] In Pennsylvania a committee of the assembly was appointed to represent to Parliament and the king "in the most lively Terms" the hardships the bill would place upon the colony and that it would be a violation of the royal charter. The addresses were drawn up and sent to Paris, the colonial agent, together with instructions to oppose the bill vigorously.[66] Lewis Morris, late chief-justice of New York, then on his way to England, was solicited by the assembly to join with Paris in opposing the bill.[67] The measure never found its way into law and it is fair to assume that the efforts and influence of the colonial agents was at least partly responsible for its failure.

The evasion of the veto by reënactment will be brought out more clearly in subsequent pages. Suffice it to say here that in the case of their religious beliefs the Quakers remained true to conscience and reënacted oft vetoed laws. Determined to fashion their judicial system as they saw fit the royal veto had no power which the assembly felt bound to respect. In the matter of regulating coin current in the colony the assembly did not scruple to set at variance the rate fixed by royal proclamation or act of Parliament in spite of the veto. Yet in many of these cases the constant exercise of the veto had its effect, for the assembly finally either partly acquiesced or else failed to reënact the objectionable laws. The same is true in other cases. The law of 1700 granted the freemen of the colony the benefit of the common law and jury trial in all cases whatsoever, and nowhere were the privileges and liberties of Englishmen more dearly cherished than in the Quaker province. The law was vetoed as interfering with the vice-admiralty court which employed the

---

[65] Kimball, *Corres. of Govs. of R. I.*, I, 63; *Talcott Papers*, Conn. Hist. Soc., *Coll.*, IV, 296-298.

[66] *Pa. Votes of Assembly*, III, 214, 215, 217.

[67] *Ibid.*, 227.

civil law and denied juries.[68] The law was reënacted with a proviso that nothing contained therein should act as a bar to the trial of causes properly cognizable by the admiralty court. Still the crown vetoed this law as liable to interfere with the maritime court.[69] The assembly reenacted the very same law only to have it disallowed again and this time the royal will was effective.[70] A law of 1700 gave preference to colonial creditors over others but was disallowed as unjust to the people of England.[71] The law was repassed in 1711, modified to some extent but yet to the same general purpose, but was again disallowed on the same grounds.[72] In this case the veto was at last effective for the law was not put upon the statute book again. These cases might be multiplied, but these few instances suffice to show that the power of the English government, like that of the potter, was limited by the sort of material it had to deal with. When bent on subserving their own interests, the colonists showed no hesitation in disobeying the will of a far distant authority and were abetted in this conduct by the loose and incomplete provisions of the charter. But in the long run it is true that the veto did have the effect of checking legislation undesirable from the point of view of English interests.

As to temporary laws many such were passed which concerned chiefly matters of internal economy and polity and which in no ways interfered with English interests. Of such laws no complaint was made. They had to do with the regulation of Indian affairs, or internal taxation for the sake of defraying the charges of government,[73] and in the last French war many laws of a military character demanded by the exigencies of the occasion were passed

---

[68] *Pa. Statutes at Large*, II, 18, 451, 467.
[69] *Ibid.*, II, 359, 543, 550.
[70] *Ibid.*, III, 31, 439, 463.
[71] *Ibid.*, II, 63, 494.
[72] *Ibid.*, II, 364, 550.
[73] *Ibid.*, II-V, *passim*.

for a year or for a shorter period.[74] But on the other hand various short-time laws were passed which were considered at home detrimental to English commercial interests and these called forth much complaint. This is illustrated in the case of the law of 1711, designed to run for three years, imposing a duty on the importation of wine, rum, and other spirits, except when imported by vessels owned or built in Pennsylvania, Delaware, and West Jersey; a tonnage duty on all vessels with similar exceptions; and a duty on the importation of negroes.[75] The law was vetoed in 1714 as burdensome to English trade and as unjust in its discrimination.[76] The veto was of no avail since the act was near expiration and before notice of the disallowance could be received in the colony, the law was revived for another three years with the exception of the tonnage duty.[77] It was again vetoed but only after the act had run its course.[78] In fact similar measures were passed subsequently, but apparently they were never submitted to the consideration of the crown.[79] The merchants began to complain of the discriminations and burdens placed on trade. In 1731 and 1732 the crown instructed the governor not to assent, under any pretense whatever, to laws putting the inhabitants of the colony upon a more advantageous footing than those of England, or which imposed a duty on the importation or exportation of negroes, or in any case where the trade and navigation of the kingdom might be affected.[80] After this no laws of this objectionable character appear.

What proportion of the laws were vetoed and what were

[74] *Pa. Statutes at Large*, V, *passim*.
[75] *Ibid.*, II, 382.
[76] *Ibid.*, II, 555.
[77] *Ibid.*, III, 112, 117.
[78] *Ibid.*, II, 459, 465.
[79] *Ibid.*, III, 150, 159, 165, 238, 268, 275.
[80] *Pa. Archives*, 1st ser., I, 306, 325; *B. T. Paps., Pl. Gen.*, X, L 45, 53.

the reasons for so doing? The years 1700-1765 may be
divided for this purpose into three periods, corresponding
roughly to the measure of vigor shown by the Board of
Trade. From 1700 to 1715, a period which coincides with
the youthful vigor of the board, eighty-nine, out of two
hundred and twenty laws passed, were vetoed; approximately forty per cent. From 1715 to 1735, during which
time the board had grown lax and careless in administration, only three out of one hundred and fifteen were vetoed.
From 1735 to 1765, a period of marked activity in colonial
administration, eleven out of about two hundred laws were
disallowed. Of the large number vetoed in the first period
fully one-half were disallowed, not on the ground that
they were essentially bad in principle, but because the
phraseology was loose and defective, or else the penalties
imposed were considered too heavy, or the common law
was not properly observed. The colonists lacked training
in the nicer points of law-making and the keen eye of a
skilled lawyer was needed to detect the loose wording and
defective drafting of colonial bills. The law officers of
the crown and the counsel to the Board of Trade pointed
out the confusion and litigation likely to follow from the
uncertain wording and lack of completeness in the laws
relating to the recording of deeds, descent of property,
wills, and other statutes affecting property interests.[81]
Some of the criminal laws were so defectively drawn as to
allow the court too broad a latitude for interpretation,
as for example, in the act against assault and battery the
words ''menace, write or speak slightingly, or carry themselves abusively '' were considered '' too general and uncertain and liable to be construed according to the humor
of the courts.'' [82] It was also held unreasonable to sell
a man into servitude if unable to pay a four-fold satisfac-

[81] *Pa. Statutes at Large*, II, 489-497. For a criticism of the
Conn. laws by Francis Fane, see Andrews, *Conn. Intestacy Law*,
Yale Review, Nov., 1894, 286-287.
[82] *Pa. Statutes at Large*, II, 464, 479-481.

tion for house-breaking or incendiarism, and besides "selling a man is a punishment not allowed by the law of
England."[83] Laws of this class were altered by the assembly to obviate the objections and were subsequently
confirmed at home.[84] To the exercise of the veto in this
way the colonists had no objections. It is obvious that
in these cases the veto power had the effect of clearing
away errors and defects in colonial laws and of making
them more conformable to English common law. To the
large bulk of laws which strictly concerned internal affairs
the home government made no objections. But when the
assembly passed laws which were contrary to the commercial policy of the Empire or to statutes in regulation
thereof; or were prejudicial to the interests of English
merchants, or curtailed royal control in matters of finance,
trade, war, and justice; or were detrimental to the welfare
of the Churchmen in the colony, then the royal veto was
exercised to uphold imperial as well as special interests.
Acts imposing a duty on the importation of convicts,
negroes, European goods, or a tonnage duty on vessels
trading to the colony, were vetoed as burdensome to the
shipping and navigation of the kingdom.[85] Several laws
of the earlier period regulating the rate of coin current
in the province were disallowed as contrary to the rate
fixed by royal proclamation or act of Parliament.[86] An
act of 1700 to prevent the sale of ill-tanned leather and
working it into foot-gear was disallowed "for it cannot
be expected that encouragement should be given to the
making any manufactures in the plantations, it being
against the advantage of England."[87] The royal check

[83] *Pa. Statutes at Large*, II, 491.

[84] In 1709 Penn was informed that various acts had been disallowed because of objectionable clauses while the acts themselves
were good and profitable. *B. T. Paps., Props.*, IX, P 80.

[85] See page 142.

[86] *Pa. Statutes at Large*, II, 445-446, 525, 530, 548.

[87] *Ibid.*, II, 481.

was exercised to safe-guard the interests of Englishmen
at home. The attachment law which condemned the goods
and lands only of non-residents was considered unjust to
owners of land and traders living in England; [88] the law
which gave preference to creditors of the colony before
all others was unfair to English merchants; [89] the law
which subjected a man to servitude for debt, where there
was no visible estate, was likely to work hardship to masters of vessels and others trading to the colony; [90] the
law which required masters of vessels to give bond not
to carry out of the province any person without a pass-
port was held to abridge the right of the people of England
to trade to the colony freely. [91] The prerogatives of the
crown were upheld by annulling several acts granting freemen the right of jury trial because the authority of the
admiralty court was thereby infringed; [92] a law making
Newcastle a port of entry because it abridged the right of
the Customs Board to establish all ports; [93] and a law
giving executive powers to the council upon the death or
resignation of the governor because it made possible an
evasion of the crown's right to confirm the nomination
of a governor. [94] During the French and Indian war two
acts which hampered the military service were vetoed: one
which extended to the colony a statute of Parliament
regulating the quartering of soldiers in time of peace and
not of war, the other because it did not require compulsory
enlistment and placed restrictions on the employment of
the troops. [95]

The proprietors also resorted to an appeal to the crown's
power of final assent or dissent to uphold their rights as

[88] *Pa. Statutes at Large*, II, 492.
[89] *Ibid.*, II, 494, 550.
[90] *Ibid.*, II, 496.
[91] *Ibid.*, II, 495.
[92] *Ibid.*, II, 479, 550.
[93] *Ibid.*, II, 480-481.
[94] *Ibid.*, II, 529.
[95] *Ibid.*, V, 532, 536, 537.

lords of the soil and governors of the province bestowed upon them by royal charter. They enjoyed no actual veto on colonial legislation. Up to 1704 Penn reserved to himself, according to his commissions to Governors Hamilton and Evans, " Our final Assent to all Such Bills as thou shalt pass into Law in the said Government." [96] There was thus the possibility of a triple veto; by governor, proprietor, and crown.[97] In this year the council and assembly protested against the proprietor's claim to a negative power. They came to the resolution that the above clause in the governor's commission was void and that all bills which the governor saw fit to pass into law under the great seal of the proprietor could not be annulled by the latter without the consent of the assembly.[98] In 1705 the Board of Trade sought from the attorney-general an opinion on the same point. He replied that all acts passed by the legislature and governor were absolute in law till vetoed by the crown and that the reservation of a veto power to the proprietor was contrary to the charter. It was held that under this instrument the power of law making must be exercised by the proprietor himself or by his deputy.[99] Although deprived of this essential power the same end was reached in an indirect way. The proprietors enjoyed what may be called an anticipatory veto. The governor was placed under a bond to obey all instructions from the proprietors.[100] By such means they were able to forbid the governor to assent to laws which in any way encroached upon their powers of government or prejudiced their landed interests. By force of instructions and by appeal to the royal veto, the Penns were in possession of two methods of controlling legislation. They lacked a third effective check which the crown possessed

[96] B. T. Paps., Props., VIII, pt. 1, N 45.
[97] Penn-Logan Corres., I, 268.
[98] Pa. Col. Recs., II, 146
[99] Pa. Statutes at Large, II, 373-374.
[100] Shepherd, Proprietary Gov't. in Pa., 474-475.

in the royal provinces. In Pennsylvania the provincial council, appointed by the proprietors, enjoyed no legislative powers, as did the royal council in the crown colonies. The Charter of Privileges of 1701, granted by Penn as the fundamental law of the province, made no provision for a bicameral legislature. All law making powers were vested in the representative assembly and the governor.[101] The only hold the council had on legislation was by way of influence on the governor and assembly. Then again, proprietary instructions did not afford an effective check for the simple reason that the assembly was in possession of the power over the purse. The charges of government and the support of the governor were thrown upon the people. The money power was an effective whip in the hands of the assembly and that body showed no hesitation in applying it with severity in order to force the governor to acquiesce in the wishes of the peoples' representatives. Governor Thomas well stated the situation when he wrote " as the governor of this province is and always had been dependent upon the assembly for a support every six months, he is not at liberty to exercise his own judgment upon any bills the assembly shall think fit to present to him, or even to assert His Majesty's just prerogative in any case whatsoever. Starve him into compliance or into silence is the common language both of the assembly and the people here when the governor refuses his assent to a bill or presses what they dislike, let the honor of His Majesty or the security of his dominions be ever so much concerned." [102] Thomas knew whereof he spoke for his salary was then badly in arrears because of a quarrel with the Quaker assembly over royal orders. Such was the means by which the governors were forced to acquiesce in laws contrary to royal or proprietary orders. Such was

[101] Shepherd, op. cit., 292-293; Osgood, Amer. Cols. in 17th. Cent., II, 275-276.

[102] Pa. Statutes at Large, IV, 475; Greene, Provincial Governor, ch. 9, especially p. 174.

the means by which the assembly was able to make itself the dominant and controlling power in the provincial government. This course of development was facilitated by a lack of interest in colonial administration both on the part of the sons of William Penn and the Board of Trade. Penn's incapacity from business from 1712 to his death in 1718 by reason of a serious illness, the minority of his heirs and their subsequent inattention to colonial affairs as long as their landed interests were not attacked, together with the inefficiency of the Board of Trade after 1714 were the factors which suffered the assembly to absorb most of the powers of government. To a less extent the same is true of the royal provinces.[103]   Said the Board of Trade with regard to Massachusetts in 1757, " Almost every act of executive and legislative power, whether it be political, judicial or military, is ordered and directed by Votes and Resolves of the General Court, in most cases originating in the House of Representatives." [104]   This statement is applicable to all the colonies. It is unmistakable evidence of the strong tendencies toward home rule and responsible government.

Under such conditions royal and proprietary instructions availed little. The proprietors enjoyed but one check upon colonial legislation, an appeal to the crown's power of veto. During the French and Indian war the assembly took advantage of the demand for large supplies to carry on military operations to secure the assent of Governor Denny to a number of laws contrary to the instructions of the Penns. Even the proprietors' hold on the governor was rendered nugatory. When Denny informed the house of his bond to the proprietors, it resolved to indemnify him in case the proprietors brought suit to recover the security.[105]   The Penns were now thoroughly aroused to ac-

103 Greene, *op. cit.*, chs. 9, 10.
104 *Ibid.*, 187, 193-194.
105 *Pa. Votes of Assembly*, V, 68.

tion because their landed interests were endangered. In March, 1760, they laid before the king a memorial protesting against the confirmation of eleven laws which "greatly affect your Majesty's prerogative, the powers and privileges vested in your petitioners by virtue of the royal charter and the properties of your petitioners in the said province."[106] Five concerned their interests as land-lords and six were considered serious encroachments upon their governmental powers. Several which had to do with the taxation of the proprietary estates and one which concerned the tenure of office of the provincial judges will be treated subsequently. Against three laws the Penns offered no objections in point of utility and expediency but opposed them solely on the ground that the assembly by naming therein the officers to carry the acts into execution had encroached upon the power of appointment vested in the proprietors by charter. Up to this time the proprietors had made no objection to this unwarranted assumption of power by the legislature, but it was thought "that now when the assembly are grasping at all power, it behooves the proprietors to be more watchful of every encroachment."[107] On June 24 the board sent its report on the laws to the Privy Council.[108] It is a long and able document, probably the work of Halifax, the efficient president of the board. It is eminently favorable to the contentions of the proprietors. The objections to seven of the laws were sustained and they were reported for disallowance. The board said that not a single law had been offered to the crown for disapproval, nor even one for confirmation, which did not encroach in some way either on the territorial or governmental rights of the Penns.[109] The board lamented the fact that the proprietors "instead of supporting the constitution of the colony and their own dignity as

[106] *Pa. Statutes at Large*, V. 661-663.
[107] *Ibid.*, 665, 729.
[108] *Ibid.*, V, 697-734; *Pa. Col. Recs.*, VIII, 524-552.
[109] *Pa. Statutes at Large*, V, 731; *Pa. Col. Recs.*, VIII, 549-550.

a very material part of the legislature, they seem to have considered themselves only in the narrow and contracted view of landholders in the province and to have been regardless of their prerogatives as long as their property remained secure and never to have felt for their privileges as proprietaries till by a diminution of those privileges their interests were affected as individuals.'' [110]   There is little doubt as to the justice of this censure, but may it not be said that it is equally applicable to the English government itself. The repeated warnings of officials of the colonial tendencies toward political independence fell upon deaf ears at home. The repeated measures urged by the Board of Trade designed to check these tendencies and to strengthen royal authority in the colonies proved of no avail. In conclusion, the board reported that it was necessary for the crown to interpose to restrain the assembly '' from becoming exorbitant beyond measure by its encroachments '' and to protect the royal prerogative '' which must always be invaded while the prerogatives of royalty are placed in the feeble hands of individuals.'' [111]   But here again may it not be said that the assemblies of the royal provinces had absorbed the powers of the crown placed in the hands of the governors to almost the same extent as was true of Pennsylvania? As a result of this report six laws were disallowed by order in council of September, 1760. [112]   On the seventh reported for disallowance, a compromise was reached between the agents of the assembly and the Privy Council. It is clear that the only check the proprietors possessed over legislation was by appeal to the crown.

In conclusion of the whole matter of the veto, it may be asked how far this power in the hands of the crown was effective. In the long run the crown was able to accom-

[110] Pa. Statutes at Large, V, 732; Pa. Col. Recs., VIII, 550.
[111] Pa. Statutes at Large, V, 734; Pa. Col. Recs., VIII, 552.
[112] Pa. Statutes at Large, V, 653-659; Pa. Col. Recs., VIII, 552-554.

plish what it desired. The chief difficulty lay in the fact
that it lacked immediate effectiveness. It was only after
repeated applications of the veto that the assembly acquiesced. This was due in great part to the incomplete
provisions of the charter. The crown enjoyed no authority to instruct the governor with regard to legislation.
Short-time laws and reënactments of laws once vetoed were
made possible under the loose requirements of the charter.
The inefficient administration of the Board of Trade after
1714 was another factor favorable to the freedom of the assembly in legislation. The whole situation reveals the extent to which the colonies disregarded the authority of the
crown. Little respect was shown for the veto when the
representative body was bent on carrying out its own programme. The jealousy of all outside interference led the
assembly to judge of the propriety of all laws regardless
of the interests of the proprietor or Empire and in spite of
the royal veto. These facts stand out more clearly in the
relations between the crown and assembly over questions of
religion, finance, and the provincial judiciary.

CHAPTER SIX

THE JUDICIAL SYSTEM AND THE ROYAL DISALLOWANCE

During the first century of colonization the settlers were to a large extent allowed to fashion their own institutions without pressure from the central government. The royal disallowance was not exercised and a system of appeals to the Privy Council was not definitely fixed till the latter part of the seventeenth century.[1] But with the establishment of a more definite control over the colonies in the years following the Revolution of 1689, and the evincing of a greater interest in colonial administration at home, the legislative and judicial powers of the king and council came to be exercised. Through the operation of these powers and the instructions to the governors of the royal provinces, the central government was able to mould and develop colonial institutions. Pennsylvania was not a royal province, but the express reservation of the veto power and appellate jurisdiction by charter to the Privy Council afforded the home government a good opportunity to check any radical departures of the colonists from English institutions. It was principally through the exercise of the crown's power of disallowance that it was able to control the judicial establishment of the province.

The charter bestowed on the proprietor or his deputy full power and authority to appoint all judicial officers and " to do all and everything and things, which unto the compleate establishment of Justice, unto Courts and Tribunalls, formes of Judicature, and manner of Proceedings doe belong." The power to create courts, define their jurisdictions, and to fix their forms and procedure was delegated

[1] Osgood, *Amer. Cols.*, II, 277-308.

to the patentees without any limitations whatsoever.[2] Whatever privileges, therefore, the assembly enjoyed with respect to the regulation of courts depended entirely upon the determination of the proprietor. But William Penn, in accordance with his liberal attitude toward popular liberties, early granted the freemen a large share in the regulation of the judiciary. Penn declared that one of the three fundamental rights of Englishmen was " An influence upon, and a real share in, the judicatory, in the execution and application thereof."[3] At an early date the assembly began to establish the courts by law, while the appointment of judicial officers, properly an executive function, was retained in the hands of the proprietor. For two decades after the founding of the colony the crown did not interfere in the regulation of the courts. But this desirable condition came to an end with the establishment of the Board of Trade in 1696, which insisted upon obedience to the requirements to send home the laws and for three decades thereafter the colony knew no peace by reason of the constant exercise of the veto on their laws to establish and regulate their courts.

It was not till the passage of the law of 1701 that the colonial judiciary received a definite form.[4] By this law there was created for each county a court of quarter sessions with justices appointed and commissioned by the governor. These were the courts of all work for the colony by virtue of their wide jurisdiction. Within the competence of these courts was brought all criminal causes, except the graver crimes, all civil suits, equity proceedings, orphan's court business, and all suits between merchants and seamen which according to the laws and usages of England were not properly cognizable by the admiralty court. There was also established a central or supreme

[2] Poore, *Charters and Consts.*, (2d ed.) II, 1511; Thorpe, *Amer. Charters, Consts., etc.*, V, 3038.

[3] Penn, *Works*, III, 218.

[4] *Pa. Statutes at Large*, II, 148.

court, composed of five judges commissioned by the governor, of which three were empowered to hold court twice a year at Philadelphia. It was also required that twice a year two of the judges should go on circuit into each county, according to the well known practice in England. By such means the administration of justice was facilitated and the complaints of the people of the expense, delay and inconvenience entailed by the journey up to the capital to transact judicial business were eliminated. It is interesting to note the position occupied by the provincial court. It enjoyed no original jurisdiction whatever, except the exclusive power over capital offenses; its chief function was to sit as a court to hear and determine causes brought before it from the county courts by appeal or writ of error. The governor and council were given no judicial powers except the authority to issue writs of error and other remedial writs. Thus very early in this province judicial functions became differentiated from the executive and were placed in the keeping of a separate and distinct court. The people were little disposed to leave any judicial powers in the hands of the proprietary agents over whom they exercised slight control.[5] In this respect Pennsylvania differs from the royal province where the governor and council enjoyed appellate jurisdiction in all civil suits involving more than a certain sum. The whole system was capped by the allowance of appeals to the Privy Council from the decisions of the supreme court as provided by charter. The law prescribed no limitation as to the amount involved to be appealed, but required that the appellant should give bond in double sum adjudged to be recovered against him to prosecute his cause with effect in England within twelve months. Such was the judicial system instituted by the colonists to meet their own ideas and the conditions of life in a newly settled community. Naturally they had recourse to the institutions under which

5 *Pa. Col. Recs.*, II, 38.

they lived in England, they did not break entirely with the past, but in many essentials they did depart widely from the judicial system of the mother country and the royal provinces. In the latter it was usual to invest the supreme court with all the powers and jurisdiction of the courts of King's Bench, Common Pleas, and Exchequer at Westminster, thereby giving them both original and appellate jurisdiction. In Pennsylvania the county courts and not the provincial court had the powers of the central tribunal in other colonies. The supreme court was simply empowered to rectify proceedings of the lower courts by appeal or writ of error. This fact is undoubtedly due to the desires of the people of the colony to have justice administered in the first instance by the county courts and under local justices who were thought to be best fitted to judge of the actions. Moreover, competent county courts of first instance would obviate the expense and delay created in carrying judicial business to a central court sitting so far away. Then again, since the assembly was averse to investing the governor and council with appellate jurisdiction, a litigant had no recourse for redress except to the Privy Council if the supreme court was given original jurisdiction. It was considered a hardship to force an aggrieved person to incur the heavy expense of an appeal to England because he could not appeal to a higher court in the province. These attempts to modify the English system in order to meet their own conditions received a decided check by the controlling power of the veto.

In his report of 1705 on a collection of provincial laws, the attorney-general made no observations on the judiciary act. Not so the Board of Trade. In its report to the Privy Council the opinion was offered that "This act [is] so far from expediting the determination of laws suits that we conceive it will impede the same."[6] It was no doubt felt that the supreme court was not of sufficient utility.

[6] *Statutes at Large*, II, 482-483.

To give it only jurisdiction in error and appeal without any limitation as to the amount involved simply paved the way for the multiplication of law suits and the creation of delay and expense in judicial business. Had the county courts been granted authority to hear and end all ordinary suits without appeal, the objection of the board would probably have been met. Thus for the first time the crown interfered in the regulation of the judicial institutions and inaugurated thereby a period of bitter dispute and great annoyance.[7]

The problem of establishing courts which now confronted the governor and assembly led to a violent controversy. The dispute engendered a bitter factional strife between the proprietary and anti-proprietary parties and occasioned a deadlock for six months to the detriment of a proper administration of justice. It was the desire of the governor and council to make the supreme court more useful by widening its jurisdiction and giving it greater power. With this purpose in view several bills were presented to the assembly.[8] In general the system devised was as follows: a system of county courts in which all causes, civil and criminal, should be tried, except graver crimes which should be heard and determined by special courts of oyer and terminer; a provincial court, which should go on circuit twice a year into the several counties and exercise a concurrent jurisdiction with the county courts in all civil suits involving over ten pounds; the removal of civil causes involving over this amount to the supreme court by writ of *habeas corpus* or *certiorari* before trial and by writ of error after trial in the lower courts; and conferring upon the governor and council a complete equity jurisdiction. This scheme in no ways conformed to the ideals of the assembly. Their standard was the system devised by the law which the crown had vetoed making the county courts

---

[7] *Pa. Statutes at Large*, II, 452.
[8] *Pa. Col. Recs.*, II, 254-255, 259, 262-266.

the chief tribunals.[9] The representatives were not inclined to give the supreme court any power further than
to sit on causes which had first been heard in the county
courts. The people wished justice administered in the
first instance by local courts and judges.[10] Should the
provincial court be invested with original jurisdiction
it would necessitate the transaction of some judicial business in Philadelphia, would involve expense, delays and
annoyance, and would deny redress on appeal except to the
Privy Council. The assembly would not listen to any plan
whereby the supreme court should be empowered to hear
a cause before trial in the lower courts or to remove a cause
to any other jurisdiction. Neither would it hearken to any
scheme to vest complete equity jurisdiction in the governor
and council, because it feared that this would afford that
body an opportunity to " Intermeddle in Civil Causes."
The governor thought it unreasonable and inconsistent that
the same judges should sit in law and in equity on the same
case.[11] After much bitter debate these differences in point
of jurisdiction were in a fair way to be compromised, but
on several other points the two sides remained obdurate.
The assembly sought to give the judges the power to grant
tavern licenses, to appropriate to the justices fines and
forfeitures, and to make the tenure of office of judges depend upon good behavior. To these proposals the governor turned a deaf ear, holding that assent to them would
be a serious infringement of the proprietary powers.[12]
For six months the two branches of government wrangled
on, often indulging in bitter recrimination and exhibiting

[9] *Pa. Col. Recs.*, II, 253-254.

[10] A member of the assembly from Phila. informed the governor
that "the chief difficulty among them was, that the members of the
other Counties could not be induced to agree that business should
be brought from these Counties and generally fixt in Philadelphia."
Ibid., II, 257.

[11] *Ibid.*, II, 266-276.

[12] *Ibid.*, 277-279, 282-283, 302-314, 328-335; *Penn-Logan Corres.*,
II, 180.

a spirit of malice. Robert Quary wrote to the Board of
Trade that "the war is hot . . . for here is the Assembly against Mr. Penn and his deputy, and they them,
the Deputy Governor has strangely incensed and disobliged
all sorts of people, on the other hand the assembly do carry
their resentment against him and the Proprietor to that
height, that they are resolved to have all the Government
into their own hands, they insist to have the sole regulation of all Courts, and the nomination of all officers,
. . . So that they have banished all Prerogative & Government but what is lodged in the Assembly."[13]   Governor Evans accused the house of a project to "take very
near the whole power, both in property and Govmt. out of
the hands of the Proprietr. and Govr. and lodge it in the
People."[14]   The ideal of the assembly in this as in many
other matters was the complete independence of the people's representatives at the expense of the powers of both
proprietors and crown.

The whole dispute was set at rest for a while by the
ordinance of February, 1707, issued by the governor, settling the judicial system.[15]   The assembly strongly protested against the exercise of this power, declaring that
under the charter the proprietor had power merely to appoint judges and outline the forms of the courts and left
the "jurisdictions and proceedings to be supported and
directed by law."[16]   But according to the charter, Governor Evans was clearly within his legal powers for the
proprietors were granted plenary powers in all matters
with respect to the constitution of courts. No compromise
seemed possible, though order demanded that the channels
of justice should be kept open and the governor under the
circumstances had acted with propriety. By this ordinance there was established a supreme court to be held in

[13] N. Y. Col. Docs., V. 17-18, 19-20.
[14] Pa. Col. Recs., II, 325.
[15] Pa. Statutes at Large, II, 500-506.
[16] Pa. Col. Recs., II, 272, 291, 296, 327, 336, 351.

each county twice a year having not only a jurisdiction
in error and appeal but in general authorized to administer justice in all cases as fully as the "justices of the
Court of Queen's Bench, common pleas and Exchequer, at
Westminster, may or can do." In each county there was
established a court of quarter sessions and common pleas
to adminster justice according to the course and procedure
of similiar courts in England. The same county justices
were to exercise an equity jurisdiction as near as possible
to the "practice and proceedings of the high court of
Chancery in England." For the trial of capital offenses
special courts of oyer and terminer and jail delivery were
to be commissioned. Thus it is clear that through the
exercise of the veto and ordinance power the tendencies
of the assembly to follow its own bent were given a decided
check. By this action the judiciary was made to conform
more closely to English forms of jurisdiction and procedure. The supreme court was made more useful by giving it an original as well as an appellate jurisdiction.

Governor Gookin proved a more pliable tool in the hands
of the assembly and the law of 1711, which again placed the
judiciary on a basis of law, was a decided victory for the
representatives.[17] In general the courts were organized
along much the same lines as had been laid down by the
law of 1701. The supreme court was authorized to issue
writs of error and all remedial writs, but was restrained
from issuing original writs or processes and from removing any indictment or presentment from the county courts
before trial there except under serious limitations. The
county courts of quarter sessions and common pleas were
given the same powers as these same courts enjoyed in
England but with due regard to the laws and constitution
of the province. The common pleas courts were also given
equity jurisdiction, "observing, as near as may be, the
rules and practice of the high court of chancery in Great

[17] *Pa. Statutes at Large*, II, 301

Britain.'' Appeals in equity cases involving over ten pounds lay to the supreme court, but it was not allowed to deal in equity business whenever remedy was possible in any other court. Moreover, if any cause in equity should come before the supreme court which was determinable at common law, the parties were to be referred to that law, or if matters of fact should arise the court was to send the case to trial in the county court where the facts occurred before proceeding to decree in equity. It is very evident that the assembly was able to carry out its programme in spite of the royal disallowance or the governor's ordinance power. This law was also vetoed by the crown. In 1713 Solicitor-General Raymond reported that he thought there were '' several things not proper to be established as law.'' [18] In the first place he objected to the law on the same ground the Board of Trade took in 1705, namely, that the supreme court's only business seemed to be to draw from the inferior courts by various writs what causes it thought proper. Raymond declared that since justice could be obtained in all particulars mentioned in the law in the county courts, the central court was designed only '' to multiply suits or make proceedings at law more dilatory and expensive.'' He also reported that the law was objectionable because it forbade the supreme court to decree anything in equity which could be determined at common law, and he further declared that the inability of the court to try any fact arising on hearing the case but to send it to an issue at law, would make '' proceedings in equity insufferably dilatory and multiply trials at law in the plain cases to no manner of purpose.'' Finally, he reported that the loose wording of certain clauses had a tendency to leave too much to the discretion of the judges, as for example, the extension to the colony of an English statute '' as far as circumstances will admit.'' The home government seemed unable to realize that what

18 *Pa. Statutes at Large*, II, 548-549.

the colonists wished was a supreme court with power simply to act in an appellate capacity, and to leave to the county courts original jurisdiction in all cases, except the graver crimes. By such an establishment the people would have the benefit of trial by local judges, obviate the expense and delay in carrying their business to Philadelphia, and secure a hearing on appeal in the colony before carrying a case to the Privy Council. The ignorance of colonial conditions at home made the people unwilling to submit their laws to the crown for review. On the basis of Raymond's report the law was vetoed by order in council of February, 1714.[19]

For the second time the course of justice was stopped by the exertion of the royal check. Again the governor resorted to the ordinance power to reëstablish the judicial system along the same lines as organized by the earlier ordinance.[20] But in 1715 the courts were again placed upon a statutory footing.[21] The various courts, their practice and proceedings, were now embodied in separate laws. The advantage of this method over the former plan of grouping all in one law, lay in the hope that if one or another escaped the royal disallowance, the others would remain in force and an entire cessation of justice would not ensue. But this hope was not realized. By the laws of 1715 the objection as to equity cases was now obviated. Equity jurisdiction was withdrawn from the county courts and vested in the supreme court. Furthermore, the veto and ordinance powers had further effect, for the supreme court was now given an original jurisdiction. In general, it was authorized to administer justice as fully as the common law courts at Westminster. Richard West, the board's counsel, offered no objection to the laws. But the board itself, after sitting four days in consideration of the

---

[19] *Pa. Statutes at Large*, II, 543.
[20] *Ibid.*, 556-561.
[21] *Ibid.*, III, 32, 33, 65, 69, 73.

laws, came to a different conclusion. In its report of July, 1719, to the Privy Council, it made the same objections as offered by Raymond against the former law.[22] The law to establish the supreme court was considered liable to the same defects. The same objection was made to the phrase '' as far as circumstances admit,'' because such wording '' may upon some occasions be made use of to serve an ill purpose.'' Six laws to regulate the judicial system were vetoed in July and August, 1719.[23] For the third time a cessation of justice resulted and again the executive power was used to keep the channels of justice open. Governor Keith had regard for the wishes of the assembly in not resorting to the ordinance power, but simply continued the work of the courts by issuing new commissions empowering the justices to hold court and determine pending actions on the days specified by the late laws.[24]

The act of May, 1722, revived the judicial system.[25] All loose wording such as the board objected to was now eliminated. In spite of the veto the jurisdiction of the supreme court was made the same as prescribed by the former act. The assembly was able to consummate its wishes despite the power of the crown. This law, liable to the same objections as the previous law in this respect, by good fortune escaped the veto, probably because it was one of the large body of laws which was not delivered to the board in its days of decadence and languor. But the worry and perplexity over the judiciary question was not yet ended. In the latter part of 1724 Governor Keith and John Moore, royal customs collector at Philadelphia, came to a dispute over the seizure and trial of the ship *Fame*. This vessel was seized by Moore for the illegal importation of European goods.[26] Under cover of night a band of armed men

22 *Pa. Statutes at Large*, III, 459, 461, 462, 463-468.
23 *Ibid.*, III, 439-440.
24 *Pa. Col. Recs.*, III, 90.
25 *Pa. Statutes at Large*, III, 298.
26 *B. T. Paps., Props.*, XI, R 53.

seized the ship out of the hands of the customs officers and anchored her down the river where the goods were secretly landed. The collector did not think it safe with the aid at hand to effect a reseizure but sent to New York for the help of an armed vessel. Keith took matters into his own hands, seized the ship and brought her back to port. After censuring Moore for a lack of courage, Keith ordered him to prosecute the ship before the court of common pleas in the absence of an admiralty court. Moore refused to do so on the ground that an inferior court was not a proper tribunal to hold pleas of the crown.[27] Keith thought differently and the ship was tried and condemned by special court of common pleas in November, 1724.[28] Moore carried the matter to the Privy Council which issued an order that he should be allowed to prosecute the seizure in the proper court. The collector consulted the crown lawyers who advised him that the supreme court of the province was the proper court for an action against both the ship and the offenders. Armed with this order and advice Moore proceeded against the vessel in the supreme court and condemnation was decreed in September, 1726.[29] Moore then instituted suit in the same court against Lawrence and others charged with running and concealing the goods. Thereupon the defendants petitioned the assembly asserting that the supreme court by law had no power to issue original processes. Moore presented a counter-petition justifying his proceedings in that court. After a careful consideration of the matter the house came to a unanimous resolution that the law of 1722 should be amended to deprive the supreme court of the power to issue original processes in civil causes.[30] Moore requested of the assembly that this court be given original jurisdiction in all pleas

27 *B. T. Paps., Props.*, XI, R 53.
28 *Ibid.*, XI, R 52.
29 *Pa. Statutes at Large*, IV, 429-431; *Acts of Privy Council, Col.*, III, 120-121.
30 *Pa. Votes of Assembly*, III, 8, 11.

of the crown. To this proposal the house would not listen. He then besought the governor not to assent to the act without the insertion of a suspending clause in order to allow the crown a chance to be heard before the law went into operation. Again the house refused to acquiesce.[31] In 1727 the law of 1722 was amended according to the resolution, but in order not to prejudice suits then pending in the supreme court the law was not made retroactive.[32] It is clear that the assembly had no mind to give the supreme court any original jurisdiction but was driven to it only by the constant application of the veto and ordinance power. Moreover, the amended law took from the supreme court all exchequer jurisdiction and vested it in the county courts so that all revenue cases were required to be brought in the inferior courts in the first instance. At once Richard Fitzwilliam, surveyor-general of the customs, wrote to the Board of Trade in strong protestation against the confirmation of the law.[33] He held that it was unreasonable to limit the customs officials to the inferior courts in cases which concerned the crown. These courts were not considered fit to hold pleas of the crown for the reason that the judges were men of inferior ability and small means and the jurors were inclined to favor transgressors of the acts of trade. On the other hand the supreme court justices were held to be men of ability and fortune and able to influence the juries against prejudiced verdicts. Fitzwilliam also asserted that the law was contrary to the act of 1696 which gave the informer the privilege of choosing the court of the colony in which to lay his action. Hence, if the assembly was allowed to legislate one court out of competence over the acts of trade the same means might be used to check all prosecutions of the crown and thereby render ineffectual English law. No action was taken at

31 *B. T. Paps., Props.,* XII, R 84, 87.
32 *Pa. Statutes at Large,* IV, 84.
33 *B. T. Paps., Props.,* XII, R 84; *Jour.,* XXXVIII, 135, 145; *Pa. Statutes at Large,* IV, 422-427, 428.

home till the law was presented to the board in the regular way in 1730. At once Moore laid before the Privy Council a petition reciting the history of the case and praying for the disapproval of the law.[34] The petition was referred to the Council Committee on Appeals before which the proprietors, in response to an order of that body, presented a counter-petition.[35] The respondents denied the charge that the law was passed by undue influence upon the governor and assembly in order to prejudice the action of Moore and pointed out that provision was made for pending cases. It was declared that the law was passed simply as a necessary and reasonable settlement of the several judicial jurisdictions in the province. The chief design was to divest the supreme court of an original jurisdiction since it was the intention that that court should sit simply to rectify the proceedings of inferior courts. The reasons given in support of this plan were the same as already alluded to. If an original jurisdiction was vested in the supreme court it would work to the prejudice of the people by forcing them to come a great distance to Philadelphia upon every action no matter how small. Then again, if a case was tried in the supreme court in the first instance, there was no appeal except to the Privy Council. This would not only cause great annoyance to the council since the law allowed an appeal in all cases, but would also work great injustice to a poor litigant since it would be in the power only of the wealthy to bear the expense of an appeal to England.

In May, 1730, the council committee considered both petitions but resolved not to make a final report until the Board of Trade had examined the matter.[36] The board sent the law to its counsel, Francis Fane, for examination.[37] Be-

---

[34] *Statutes at Large*, IV, 429-431; *B. T. Paps., Props.*, XII, R 110.

[35] *Pa. Statutes at Large*, IV, 431-440; *B. T. Paps., Props.*, XII, R 110; *Acts of Privy Council, Col.*, III, 257-258.

[36] *Pa. Statutes at Large*, IV, 441; *B. T. Paps., Props.*, XII, R 110.

[37] *B. T. Paps., Props.*, Entry Bk. H, ff. 8, 11; *Jour.*, XL, 89, 159.

fore him appeared Sharpe, solicitor for Moore, and Paris, the colonial agent.[38] At this hearing practically the same points were argued pro and con as already set forth in the petitions. Fane censured the assembly for rejecting the clause offered by Moore designed to give the supreme court an original jurisdiction in all pleas of the crown. He declared that this was a reasonable request because the judges of this court were men usually bred to the law and likely to be above the temptations that beset the judges of the lower courts, who were generally interested in mercantile pursuits and thus liable to be partial to the illegal trader. Moreover, he held it to be unreasonable to require an officer to lay his action in the county where the seizure was made and before a court whose jurisdiction was limited by the bounds of the county. In England an officer was at liberty to bring his action to Middlesex, though the seizure was made in another county. This liberty was found to be beneficial because of the partiality too often shown to transgressors in their own localities. This same inconvenience, declared Fane, was apt to arise in the colonies and it would have been prudent for the assembly to follow the English practice. To the argument that it was inconsistent to have the same judges sit as a court of first instance and a court of error, Fane replied that the law before them was open to that very objection and that it was an inconsistency never complained of in the court of King's Bench. Finally, Fane said that if the clause offered by Moore had been accepted he would have made no objections to the law, but under the conditions he reported it for disapproval. The matter was then argued before the Board of Trade but to no avail.[39] The board reported it for the veto as prejudicial to the customs service and as contrary to the act

[38] *B. T. Paps., Props.*, XIII, S 3; *Pa. Statutes at Large*, IV, 442-447.
[39] *B. T. Jour.*, XLI, 159, 164-165; *Pa. Statutes at Large*, IV, 448-449.

of 1696 which allowed the informer a choice of courts.[40] The Penns then appealed the case to the Privy Council and in spite of all the arguments made by Paris and two lawyers, the law was vetoed in August, 1731.[41] For the fourth time the veto checked the smooth course of justice in the province. When the governor notified the assembly of the veto, it drew up resolutions expressing regret that the Board of Trade had been so ill-informed as to the purpose of the act. It was resolved that the sole purpose was to give the supreme court only an appellate jurisdiction, for otherwise there would be no appeal possible except to England. It characterized the insinuation that the county courts were partial and that the law was passed by undue influence on the governor and assembly as " false and scandalous."[42] A law was passed to revive the law of 1722 which vested exchequer jurisdiction in the supreme court and the course of justice suffered no harm. This law was confirmed and at last the troubles over the judiciary question were at an end.[43] In several respects the disallowing power was effective. Under the repeated application of this power the supreme court was given a wider field of usefulness by investing it with original as well as appellate jurisdiction, but the chief contention of the Board of Trade and crown lawyers was not realized. Thrice the veto had been exercised because it was considered that the only business of the supreme court was to draw unto itself cases which could be finally decided in the county courts. But in spite of the veto the assembly succeeded in passing a law which allowed an appeal to

[40] *Pa. Statutes at Large*, IV, 449-450; *B. T. Paps., Props.*, Entry Bk. H. ff. 31, 32.
[41] *B. T. Paps., Props.*, XIII, S 7; *Pa. Statutes at Large*, IV, 421; *Penn Mss., Letter Book*, I, 32, Thos. Penn to Gov. Gordon, July 23, 1731.
[42] *Pa. Votes of Assembly*, III, 168.
[43] *Pa. Statutes at Large*, IV, 229.

the supreme court in all cases whatever no matter how small a sum was involved.

One other aspect of the judicial question deserves our attention. One of the most important changes which flowed from the constitutional struggle in England in the seventeenth century was the raising of the judiciary to a position of independence. The Act of Settlement made the tenure of office of the judges *quam diu se bene gesserint* and provided fixed and certain salaries. Such a change made for the purity of the bench, free from undue influence either on the part of the crown or Parliament. This was a course highly desirable in view of the arbitrary and corrupt means used by the Stuarts, especially James II, to make the judiciary entirely subservient to their wishes. The colonists reaped no benefit from the salutary operation of this act since it made no mention of the dominions. In the provinces the judges were usually commissioned by the governors to hold at the pleasure of the crown or proprietor while their salaries were granted for a short period by the assemblies. Such a course rendered the bench subject to the influence of both the governor and the assembly. Very early the colonists sought to give the courts the position of independence held by the English courts. Englishmen in America claimed the same rights and privileges as enjoyed by their brethren in England. In no province was this movement more strongly urged than in Pennsylvania. We have already stated that in 1706-1707 the tenure of the judges' office was one of the points involved in the conflict between Governor Evans and the assembly. The latter desired that judges should hold during good behavior and should be removed by the governor only on an address from the house. The assembly declared that such was the practice in England, and although the statute did not extend to the colonies, yet '' the People of this Province had a right to claim it.'' The assembly pointed to the arbitrary conduct of James II with regard to the courts which forced Parliament to put it out of the power of the crown to displace any judge except for official misbehavior. Such circumstances, argued the house, were likely to occur in this province, as for example in a dispute which involved the proprietor or governor, therefore, " it was fitt that Judges of the Difference should be under no awe or fear of loosing their places." [44] The governor firmly refused to yield to the wishes of the house, insisting that the conditions which gave rise to the practice at home did not hold in the colonies. He contended that since the assembly made no provisions for fixed and permanent salaries for the judges and vested in itself the power to remove them at pleasure, the judiciary was thereby rendered subservient to the legislature. Such a course, declared the governor, would allow a judge to proceed to the " greatest insolencys and plead Privileges or Law for it, and perhaps make a sufficient number of Representatives who may be acquainted with both, believe that he is really in the right, and then he stands secure." For two other reasons Evans refused his assent. In England there was a sufficient number of persons bred to the law from which to make a choice, but in the colony the lack of trained lawyers made it necessary that the removal of a judge should be as easy as possible in order to allow for the substitution of one better qualified when found. Then again, provincial judges by reason of the small salaries attached to the office, were dependent upon other pursuits for a livelihood, and an occasion might arise when a judge, because of outside business, would be unable to serve on a case, a full bench could not be secured, and a failure or delay of justice would follow. If, argued Evans, the judges could be removed only by judicial process it would be impossible for the governor to appoint others. For these reasons he refused his assent to

[44] *Pa. Col. Recs.*, II, 267, 277, 294, 310, 313.

any bill which provided a tenure of office other than at the pleasure of the governor or proprietor.[45]

But the movement did not abate with the failure of the assembly in this instance. In 1743 Thomas Penn wrote to the governor that it would be unwise " to make any statement in council concerning judges holding during good behaviour."[46] In 1751 the proprietors expressed a willingness to commission judges for good behavior provided the assembly granted them permanent salaries.[47] In this year the assembly of Jamaica enacted a law which provided a permanent tenure for judges. This law was disallowed by the crown on the opinion of the attorney-general that the change " effects the royal prerogative in point of great moment," and that the circumstances in the colony were not such as to make a permanent tenure for judges advisable either for the crown or colony.[48] Instructions were then issued to the royal governors directing that judges should be commissioned only to hold at the royal will and pleasure.[49] But the desire for an independent judiciary was wide-spread and the order was frequently violated. In New York an act to provide a permanent tenure was defeated only by the opposition of the governor. North Carolina succeeded in passing a similar law but it was disallowed by the crown.[50] In Pennsylvania through a judicious bribe, the assembly was able to secure the assent of Governor Denny to the law of 1759 making the tenure of office of the judges of the supreme and common pleas for good behavior and providing fixed salaries.[51] The proprietors at once petitioned the crown

[45] *Pa. Col. Recs.*, II, 264, 273, 288, 311, 313.
[46] *Penn Mss., Letter Bk.* II, Thos. Penn to Gov. Thomas, Aug. 21, 1743.
[47] *Ibid.*, III, Thos. Penn to Richard Peters, Feb. 24, 1751.
[48] Chalmers, *Opinions*, (ed. 1858), 433.
[49] Beer, *British Col. Pol., 1754-1765*, 189; Greene, *Prov. Gov.*, 135.
[50] Beer, 188-192; Greene, 134-136.
[51] *Pa. Statutes at Large*, V, 462.

against the confirmation of this law as a serious encroachment on their powers of government granted by the charter.[52] In its report the Board of Trade said that this subject was agitated " not only in the province of Pennsylvania but in every other colony of North America and the West Indies " and reminded the council of the decision taken on the Jamaica law.[53] On the supposition that the same opinion held good this law was offered for royal disallowance. In addition, this law was held to be an infringement of the proprietary powers, and it was not considered just to permit a law to be passed by the exercise of undue influence upon the governor and against the consent of the proprietors. In answer to the argument that the law was in conformity with English practice, the board replied that the cases of the colonies and England were not analogous. The board in support of this contention reverted to the same arguments as used by Governor Evans in 1707. In England the tenure of the judges was made permanent because of the arbitrary conduct of the crown toward the courts, but this condition was not likely to arise in the colonies. Upon what ground such an argument was based it is hard to see. The contention of the colonists that the " judges being subject to the influence and direction of the proprietaries and their governors, their favorites and creatures, the laws may not be duely administered and executed, but often wrested from their true sense, to serve particular purposes " was of the same validity in America as it was in England in the time of James II.[54] The board also employed the argument that the removal of a judge should be made as easy as possible in order to make way for the appointment of a man of greater ability when found. This principle held

---

[52] Pa. Statutes at Large, V, 661-663; B. T. Paps., Props., XX, W 40.

[53] N. Y. Col. Docs., IV, 474; Pa. Statutes at Large, V, 722-724; Pa. Col. Recs., VIII, 543.

[54] Franklin, Works, (Smyth ed.) III, 374-375.

good in the early days of the colonies when there was a dearth of men trained to the profession of the law but it was no longer true at a time when the colonies could boast of skilled lawyers, many of whom had been trained in the Inns of Court in England. The real purpose of the crown appears in the statement made by the Board of Trade in 1761 that the appointing of judges for good behavior was " subversive of the Interest of the Crown and People, and tending to lessen that just Dependance which the Colonies ought to have upon the Government of the Mother Country." [55] This is perhaps the view taken by the proprietors with regard to their powers. Finally, the board held that if the practice was allowed in Pennsylvania it would create jealousy in the other provinces where the principle was denied. The law was vetoed in September, 1760.[56]

After the passage of the law Governor Denny issued new patents, under the great seal of the province and in the name of the king, to five persons constituting them justices of the court of common pleas of the county of Philadelphia during good behavior.[57] When the governor was notified of the veto he held that it worked an annulment of the patents. He thereupon issued writs of *supersedeas* to vacate the patents issued under the law and granted commissions to five others to hold at the will and pleasure of the proprietors. The patent judges refused to recognize the writs on the ground that their patents were not based on the law just vetoed, but were good at common law and hence could not be vacated except for misbehavior in office. The governor held that they were based on the law of 1759 and its disallowance invalidated the patents. Furthermore, he was of the opinion that even though they were good at common law, all judicial

55 *B. T. Jour.*, LXIX, Nov. 5, 1761.
56 *Pa. Statutes at Large*, V, 655.
57 *Ibid.*, VI, 566-570.

offices terminated on the demise of the king. George II died in 1760 and since the patents were issued in his name, his death terminated the patents. Unable to carry his point in the colony, he laid the case before Attorney-General Pratt. The latter's opinion was asked on these points; were not the patents, issued after the passage of the law of 1759, vacated by its disallowance? was not the governor restrained from commissioning judges for good behavior as contrary to proprietary instructions? and were not the patents rendered void by the death of the king? In June, 1761, Pratt replied that the patents became void *ipso facto* on the veto of the act, but if granted before the law was passed they were good although passed contrary to the governor's instructions, and lastly he could not comprehend how these judges could be commissioned in the king's name since they were not king's judges and did not depend upon the king's life.[58] Through the exercise of the royal veto and the opinion of the crown lawyer the rights of the proprietor were upheld and the schemes of the assembly were checked. It was undoubtedly one of the factors which created great discontent, not only with the proprietary government, but also with the royal governments.[59] The same problem confronted the home government in the royal provinces, but there the colonists were forced to yield owing to the determined stand taken by the crown.[60] The ideal of the provincial assemblies was complete political independence.

[58] *Pa. Statutes at Large*, VI, 570-571.

[59] One clause of the Declaration of Independence runs: " He has made Judges dependent on his Will alone, for the tenure of their offices, and the amount and payment of their salaries."

[60] Greene, *Prov. Gov.*, 134-136; Beer, *British Col. Policy, 1754-1765*, 188-192.

CHAPTER SEVEN

Few questions stood out more conspicuously in the economic and political history of the Empire or have been more prolific of vexation and trouble than the financial relations between the colonies and the mother country. With the economic aspect of the monetary problem we are not primarily interested except as it throws light on the political relations. The two aspects of the situation are so closely interwoven that one cannot be properly understood without the other.

The lack of a sufficient supply of specie as a medium of exchange is a prominent characteristic of all newly settled areas. The abundance of land, the lack of capital, and the scarcity and scattered condition of labor renders manufacturing in such a community simply a make-shift. It is evident that under such conditions the settlers are forced to turn to the development of their natural resources and to the production of staple commodities in order to achieve wealth and prosperity. This in turn requires foreign markets where colonial products may be exchanged either for manufactured articles or for bullion with which to secure the needed finished products in other markets.[1] Not blessed with mines of precious metals, specie can only be secured by this round of exchange. But it must be borne in mind that the economic development of the colonies was not allowed to pursue its natural course; it was controlled by the principles of the English commercial laws in the interest of a self-sufficing commercial empire. England required that all commodities of the

[1] Callender, *Economic History of the United States*, 6-9.

production or growth of the colonies which supplemented the needs of the metropolis should be first brought to English ports. These became known as the "enumerated commodities." The colonies were obliged to laden and ship all European commodities in England. Thus England became the staple for colonial exports and imports. To safeguard the colonies as a market for home manufactures restrictions were placed on such industries in the colonies as in any way competed with those of England.[2] With this resumé of the mercantile system in mind one is able to understand its relation to the monetary problem.

Pennsylvania and the northern colonies had few of the enumerated articles to carry to England in exchange for manufactured products. Because of the similarity of climate and soil between England and the northern colonies the two sections produced like commodities. The result was that the northern colonies did not supplement the needs of the metropolis and were therefore forced by a tedious roundabout course of commerce to exchange their products in foreign markets and in other English colonies in order to secure the specie and cargo necessary to return to England in a second exchange for manufactured goods.[3] The bulk of the commerce of Pennsylvania as well as that of her northern neighbors found a vent in the British and foreign West Indies and to a less extent in southern Europe and the Madeiras.[4] Because of these indirect commercial relations the balance of trade was always against the colony. For the six years ending in 1704 Pennsylvania was indebted to English merchants in the sum of £34,350 and in 1765 this balance had reached the high figure of at least £300,000.[5] To secure a bal-

[2] Beer, *British Colonial Policy, 1754-1765*, 193-205, 209-210; Callender, *Economic Hist. of U. S.*, 85-121.

[3] *Callender, op. cit.*, 9-20, 51-63.

[4] *B. T. Paps., Props.*, XI, R 7, 42; XIII, S 34; Anderson, *Origin of Commerce*, III, 155, 171; *N. Y. Col. Docs.*, V, 616.

[5] *B. T. Paps., Props.*, VIII, pt. 1, N 51, 52, 53; pt. 2, O 100;

ance of trade in its favor was one of the vital principles of the English mercantile system. According to the theories of the English mercantilists and economists of that age a nation's wealth and power were measured in terms of gold and silver and hence every precaution was taken to secure a monopoly of them for the mother country and to guard the source of supply. England, not blessed with the rich mines in America which Spain possessed, found it necessary to effect this end by means of trade. Such was one of the cardinal objects of the acts of trade. But in this fact lay the root of much of the financial distress of the colonies. The prompt remittance to England of specie and bills of exchange acquired in the foreign markets to liquidate the balance against the colony caused a chronic lack of a sufficient currency of coin for domestic economy. The serious nature of the financial problem may be gathered from a letter of William Penn to the Board of Trade in 1701. " The whole continent labors under the want of money to circulate trade in the respective governments which has put Boston herself upon thinking of Tickets to supply the want of coin, and New York as well as this Province are following." [6]

The growing demands of a foreign market for colonial productions demanded a greater capital to aid in their development and exchange; a rapidly increasing population and the growing expenses of government requiring a circulating medium of some sort. Several courses were open to the colonists. To forbid the exportation of bullion secured in foreign markets and to employ it in domestic manufactures at once called forth the exercise of the royal

---

Franklin declared before the bar of the Commons in 1766 that the imports from Great Britain amounted to £500,000 a year while the exports from the colony in exchange for British goods did not exceed £40,000. These figures were without much question placed too high. *Works*, (Smyth ed.) IV, 416-417.

[6] *B. T. Paps., Props.*, VI, pt. 1, G 12.

veto as contrary to the mercantile system.[7] Another course was to supply the want of coin by currency in other forms, such as a system of barter or the use of paper money. Payment in kind was a device practiced by all the colonies in the earlier period. Massachusetts had her " country pay," Virginia and Maryland had their tobacco certificates, and Pennsylvania by the laws of 1683 and 1693 made hemp, flax, grain, pork, beef, and tobacco current pay in lieu of money.[8] Paper currency was an expedient resorted to by Pennsylvania long after the other colonies had been forced to it. But like her neighbors, Pennsylvania practiced another familiar expedient; that of inviting specie into the province by accepting it at a rate fixed by law higher than that set by other governments.

A law of 1683 provided that English money should pass current at an advance of twenty-five per cent., New England money at par and the Spanish piece of eight at six shillings.[9] The Spanish piece of eight, minted sparingly in the mother country but in great numbers in Mexico and Peru, was the coin of almost universal circulation in the colonies. In 1693 the rate of Spanish money was advanced and again still further in 1700 with the avowed object of " bringing in of money to promote trade and make payments more easy." [10] By the latter law a piece of eight of full weight was rated at seven shillings, ten pence, and punishment was provided for mutilation. The lack of a fixed and uniform standard for foreign money was highly prejudicial to intercolonial trade. In 1700 Penn met in conference with Governors Nicholson of Virginia and Bellomont of New York and it was agreed,

[7] Mass. in 1697 passed a law prohibiting the exportation of specie or bullion on the plea of scarcity of money and the heavy expenses of war. This was vetoed at home because of the lack of a clause permitting exportation to England. *Acts and Resolves of Mass.*, I, 306, 308.

[8] *Charter and Laws*, 162, 229.

[9] *Ibid.*, 145.

[10] *Ibid.*, 275; *Pa. Statutes at Large*, II, 87.

among other things, that measures should be secured to provide for a fixed and uniform standard.[11] It was a plan warranted by the situation but it required the force of an act of Parliament to secure its adoption. The end might have been attained in the royal provinces by means of the instructions from the crown to the governors, but over the chartered colonies the crown enjoyed no such control. Penn submitted the report of the conference to the Board of Trade but no immediate action was taken.[12] Again in 1703 Penn urged upon the board the necessity of taking action.[13] It was also urged in strong terms by Governor Cornbury and Robert Quary.[14] Quary asserted that the high rate of specie in Pennsylvania caused the people of neighboring colonies to migrate thither in hopes of greater wages. Cornbury complained of the injury to the trade of New York by the flow of coin into Pennsylvania. The board was now aroused to action and directed the attorney-general to give an opinion if the crown by force of its prerogative had power to settle the rate of coin for the colonies. In July, 1703, he replied in the affirmative, so far as the rate fixed did not infringe a colonial statute already confirmed.[15] The board then reported to the council the advisability of fixing the rate by proclamation and recommended that the Pennsylvania law of 1700 should be disallowed.[16] The report was acted upon and

[11] B. T. Paps., Props, VI, pt. 1, G 7, 8; N. Y. Col. Docs., IV, 757. This shows that a Spanish piece of eight was current in Boston at 6s., New York at 6s. 9d., Jersey and Pa., at 7s. 8d., Maryland at 4s. 6d., Va.. and Car. at 5s.

[12] B. T. Paps., Props., Entry Bk. C, ff. 40-42.

[13] Ibid., Props., VII, L 27.

[14] N. Y. Col. Docs., IV, 1047, 1059. Says a report from Virginia in 1697, "It will be well for a common standard of money to be established over all English colonies in America." Cal. State Paps., Col., 1696-1697, 645.

[15] Pa. Statutes at Large, II, 446-447; B. T. Jour., XVI, 143, 174.

[16] B. T. Paps., Props., Entry Bk. D, ff. 345, 361; Props., VII, L 46; Bulletin N. Y. Public Lib., Oct., 1907, 491-492; Pa. Statutes at Large, II, 445.

Isaac Newton, master of the mint, was directed to draw up a table fixing the rates of the various foreign coins current in the colonies. In July, 1704, this was proclaimed by the crown to be the standard.[17] The basis of the table was the Massachusetts law, already confirmed by the crown, which rated the piece of eight at six shillings. By the table, Mexico, Seville and Pillar pieces of eight of full weight (17½ pwt.), were to pass current at six shillings, Peru pieces of eight of full weight at five shillings, ten and one-half pence. Other coin of foreign origin, such as the Crusadoes of Portugal, the Rix dollars of the Empire and the Ducatoons of Flanders were also rated. The proclamation was very unskillfully adapted to actual conditions. No provision was made for contracts at old rates or for punishment of the mutilation of coin, so commonly practiced. Moreover, the table gave to coin an artificial value and arbitrary denomination not warranted by its commercial value as governed by the market price.[18] In the face of these facts there is little wonder that the proclamation was accorded scant respect. In October, 1704, James Logan wrote from the colony to Penn that the proclamation was at hand '' but will answer no one good end I know of, it is so very confused and perplexing,'' and in

---

[17] B. T. Paps., Pl. Gen., VII, G, 9, 10.

[18] Pownall, at one time gov. of Mass., wrote, '' . . . I could never comprehend to what general uses, or to what purposes of government, the proclamation which Queen Ann issued, . . . could be supposed to extend, while it endeavored to rate the foreign coins current in the Colonies by an artificial standard. It would seem just as wise, and answering to just as good purpose, if government should now issue a proclamation, directing, that for the future, all black horses in the Colonies should be called white, and all brindled cows red. The making even a law to alter the names of things, will never alter the nature of those things; and will never have any other effect, than that of introducing confusion, and of giving an opportunity to bad men of profiting by that confusion.'' Administration of Cols., (ed. 1768) 181. Cf. Sumner, Spanish Dollar and Colonial Shilling, in Amer. Hist. Rev., III, 607-619.

the next year he wrote that money passed at the old rate
and no one obeyed the royal proclamation.[19] In similiar
terms wrote Governor Evans, saying that the disobedience
was not due to any slackness in putting the proclamation
into force, but to the " liberty trading men will take in
their own bargains."[20] That it was not obeyed is evidenced by the fact that the merchants of New York complained to the home government of the injury to their
trade caused by the flow of specie to other colonies, especially to Pennsylvania, where it passed current at a
higher rate.[21] The royal orders of a distant government
availed little. In fact they were held in such slight es-
teem that the assembly of Pennsylvania had the temerity
to pass a law in 1706 providing for a uniform rate for the
province approximately one-third in advance of that set
by the Queen's table.[22] The excuse, as expressed in the
law, was that it was unjust for this colony to obey the royal
mandate when other colonies older in settlement and more
considerable in trade did not conform to it. On similiar
grounds Governor Evans justified his assent to the law.[23]
The prevalent disobedience to the proclamation now forced
the Board of Trade to further action. In June, 1706, the
attorney-general was asked for an opinion as to the best
method to be taken to exact obedience in the chartered
colonies.[24] He responded that the proclamation imposed
no legal obligations in private transactions, but that an act
of an assembly contrary to the royal order made the government guilty of high misdemeanor and the charter liable to forfeiture.[25] The remedy suggested was an act of
Parliament giving the proclamation the force of law as

[19] *Penn-Logan Corres.*, I, 325, II, 26.
[20] *B. T. Paps., Props.*, VIII, pt. 1, N 36.
[21] *N. Y. Col. Docs.*, IV, 1131-1135.
[22] *Pa. Statutes at Large*, II, 276.
[23] *Ibid.*, II, 510-511; *B. T. Paps., Props.*, VIII, pt. 2, O 66.
[24] *B. T. Paps., Pl. Gen.*, VII, H 20.
[25] *Ibid.*

was done in England under like conditions in 1694. No
action to this end was taken at the time because the board
was busy supporting the bill then in Parliament providing for the vacation of the charters. Upon the failure
of this bill the board took up the monetary question.
This action was occasioned by a complaint from Barbadoes
that the island colonies were drained of coin by those on
the mainland, especially the chartered colonies.[26] This
agitation resulted in the act of 1708 giving the proclamation the force of law and providing penalties for violations.[27] Acts of Parliament seemed to have no greater
fears for the colonies than royal commands. Not only
the chartered colony of Pennsylvania but the royal province of New York set at naught the law by rating money
contrary to it.[28] The law of Pennsylvania of 1706 rated
a piece of eight at eight shillings while the English statute
fixed it at six shillings. The theory of the assembly was
that the worth of specie depended upon its commercial
value and not upon any arbitrary denomination and that
a piece of eight called six shillings was of no less value
then one denominated eight and should purchase the same
amount of goods. On this principle the assembly did not
change the denomination of the coin but enacted in 1709
that since coin fell one-fourth in value by English law,
all prices, wages, and fees should abate in the same proportion.[29] This unique device to countervail the English
statute did not deceive the home authorities. The solicitor-general held that it rendered ineffectual the law of
Parliament '' because the lowering the price of goods in
consequence in respect to other colonies, the coin will be
raised to the old value.''[30] The act was vetoed by the

---

[26] B. T. Paps., Pl. Gen., Entry Bk. D, f, 143.
[27] Ibid., Pl. Gen., VIII, I 48, 50; 6 Anne, c. 30.
[28] N. Y. Col. Docs., V, 66, 67-68, 71.
[29] Pa. Statutes at Large, II, 294-297.
[30] Ibid., II, 547-548; Pa. Archives, 1st. ser., I, 156.

crown in 1714.[31]   Again in 1722 the assembly sent to the
governor a bill which provided a rating contrary to law
but he refused his assent.[32]   One is strikingly impressed
with the disregard shown by the colonists to royal orders
and acts of Parliament which ran counter to their economic
interests.   Like the evasion of the Molasses Act of 1733,
the coinage problem shows conclusively the utter futility
of trying to order the affairs of a community by artificial
measures which did not conform to the economic advantages of its members.   These methods also clearly exhibit
the means by which the colony of Pennsylvania nullified
the royal veto.   By a process of reënactment the colony
for a period of ten years was able to evade the will of the
English government.

To supply the lack of specie there seemed to be left but
one expedient,— paper currency.   From such a course the
colony had long held aloof.   Perhaps the loss caused by
the depreciation of notes in other colonies served to warn
this province against such ills.   It may be too that the
sound judgment of the Quaker business men prevented
any yielding to a cheap currency.   Then again Pennsylvania was not driven to it by the exigencies of war.   Her
happy situation geographically and her kindly policy toward the savages freed the province from the evils as well
as the expenses which followed in the wake of war.   The
border colonies on the north and south were forced to an
early issue of paper currency to erect forts, provide stores
of war, and equip troops to guard their dominions against
the French and Spanish and their savage allies.   But if
not forced to it by reason of war, the great increase in
population caused by the coming of the Scotch-Irish and
Germans in large numbers and a rapidly growing com-

---

[31] *Pa. Statutes at Large,* II, 543.

[32] In 1755 Gov. Morris declared that the act of parliament " was
shamefully slighted and disregarded in this Province," and that
for years a piece of eight passed current at 7s. 6d. while the English rated it at 6s. only. *Pa. Col. Recs.,* VI, 239.

merce demanded a circulating medium of some sort. By
1719 depression fell upon the province. To ease the situation the assembly proposed various remedies: to stay the
execution of debt, to prohibit the exportation of bullion,
to advance specie one-fourth contrary to law, to make produce a legal tender and to lower the rate of interest.[33]   In
1722 Governor Keith wrote to the Board of Trade picturing the economic distress, saying that the farmer brought
his produce to market but there was no money to give for
it, the export trade had decreased, ship-builders were idle,
law suits multiplied, and the jails crowded with debtors.[34]
As a result the question of a paper currency was agitated
in 1721, but as is usual the movement was resisted by the
more conservative classes.[35]   In 1723 the assembly yielded
to the petitions from the counties for paper currency and
passed a law to create £15,000 in bills of credit.[36]   These
bills were to be loaned out for eight years at five per cent.
interest and secured by mortgages on estates in fee simple,
lands, houses and ground rents at double or treble value.
Thus ample provision was made for funding and securing
the same.   Trade promptly revived and the results were
apparently so beneficial that an immediate demand came
for more of this balm of all economic ills.   In December
of the same year the assembly complied with a further issue
of £30,000 on the same terms and restrictions.[37]   It was
inevitable that the question of paper currency should find
its way into politics.

In 1722 Governor Keith wrote that the lawyers and a
few rich usurers were opposed to paper currency but that

[33] *Pa. Col. Recs.*, III, 173; *Pa. Votes of Assembly*, II, 313, 314,
335.   In 1723 two laws were passed to relieve the suffering; the
one to reduce the rate of interest from eight to six per cent., the
other to stay the execution of debts.   *Pa. Statutes at Large*, III,
338, 343.
[34] *B. T. Paps., Props*, XI, R 42.
[35] *Pa. Votes of Assembly*, II, 337; Proud, *Hist. of Pa.*, II, 150-172.
[36] *Pa. Statutes at Large*, III, 324.
[37] *Ibid.*, III, 389.

the farmers and merchants clamored for it.[38] Thus from the time when the colony launched out upon the sea of paper currency to the end of our period party lines were closely drawn on this issue. Around this question revolved much of the bitter struggle between the assembly and proprietors. It was also a matter which caused friction with the home government and created great opposition to royal authority. It created public disturbance, it bred factional strife, and brought forth prolonged deadlocks between the governors and assemblies in many of the colonies. The colonial party which was opposed to the unqualified issue of paper currency was composed of the proprietors, heirs to the wide dominions of Pennsylvania, other large property holders, and in general the wealthy and more conservative classes. This party was not opposed to a paper currency in general, and probably appreciated the need of a circulating medium, but it was stoutly opposed to all efforts to force a paper currency in payment of sterling obligations. The law required that the currency should be received in payment of all debts on the same basis as sterling money.[39] The currency had a strong tendency to depreciate in value and to give it a compulsory value in effect impaired the obligation of contracts. In 1723 this party petitioned the assembly, pointing out the rapid depreciation of such a currency in other colonies, and praying that provision be made to exempt all debts due the crown, to the English merchants, to the proprietors for rents and lands, and to guardians and trustees for orphans, widows and minors, and that such debts should be paid in sterling money or if in paper currency with the addition of so much exchange current at the time

---

[38] *B. T. Paps., Props.*, XI, R 42.

[39] Section eight of the act of 1723 stipulates that any one refusing to accept the bills of credit in discharge of debts, dues or demands, " according to their values and rates, . . . shall lose the said debt or debts, sum or sums of money so refused." *Pa. Statutes at Large*, III, 330.

between paper and sterling money.[40] But the petition was unanswered and the laws of 1723 made the bills of credit a legal tender in full payment of all debts and contracts calling for sterling money or Spanish coin. The paper money party was composed of the democratic classes, the farmers, the wage earners, and the debtor classes in general. It is a characteristic feature of colonial life that the tiller of the soil, the rent payer, and the wage-earner, destitute of specie and poor in this world's goods, usually stand for a cheap currency to supply the lack of specie. A cheap currency takes the place of stay and execution laws and affords the easiest method of alleviating economic distress. There was perhaps no intent to be fraudulent or dishonest, but the demand was simply a result of their economic situation. To them it seemed arbitrary and unjust to make a distinction between the debtor and creditor classes in money transactions. Moreover, to the paper currency party it appeared that to make any distinction in value between sterling money and bills of credit would at once have an ill-effect on the latter and conduce to depreciation. On these grounds any attempt to exempt sterling debts from payment in the legal tender paper currency was steadfastly resisted. On the other hand the proprietary party just as firmly refused to accept a depreciated currency in discharge of debts and rents due them unless some provision was made for the difference between currency and specie. The fiat money party had control of the assembly, the proprietary party of the governor and council. The governors were under instructions from the proprietors and were under bond to render obedience to them. Thus it was that the whole financial problem led to a bitter struggle between the people as represented in the assembly and the proprietors over questions of "Proprietary Interest and Power, and Popular

[40] B. T. Paps., Props., XI, R 67.

Liberty.''[41]   Still another element entered into this contention. The whole weight of the home government, acting under the influence of the English merchants, was thrown into the balance on the side of the proprietary party.

English merchants in general were hostile to colonial bills of credit on the same grounds as the proprietors. In 1720 the merchants trading to New York protested against a paper currency in that province as pernicious to the trade of England.[42]   They had no mind to receive an unsound money in payment of sterling debts contracted in England. As a result the crown instructed the royal governors not to assent to any further emissions of paper currency.[43]   In 1723 two laws of South Carolina and one of Barbadoes were vetoed by the crown on the protest of English merchants.[44]   Pennsylvania's obligation to send her laws home gave the crown an opportunity to check paper currency projects in this colony. Thus it may be seen that the question involved also the relations between the colony and home government. In May, 1725, the legal adviser to the board reported on the two currency laws of the province and recommended them for disapproval since the policy of the board was hostile to paper currency.[45]   The board consulted Joshua Gee, the eminent economist, who advised against the veto on the ground that the bills were already in circulation but that the governor should be directed to oppose further issues.[46]   The board wrote to Governor Gordon in 1726 pointing out the ill-effects of rapid depreciation in other colonies, especially the Carolinas, and warned him that any future laws from

[41] Franklin, *Works*, (Smyth ed.) IV, 227.

[42] *N. Y. Col. Docs.*, V, 539.

[43] *Ibid.*

[44] *B. T. Jour.*, XXXIV, 145, XXXIII, 96, 161, 245; Smith, *So. Car. as a Royal Prov.* 240; Chalmers, *Introd. to Revolt of Cols.*, II, 96-97; *Acts of Privy Council, Col.*, III, 55-56.

[45] *Pa. Statutes at Large*, II, 518.

[46] *B. T. Jour.*, XXXVI, 177-178.

his government would be vetoed.[47] Before the reception
of this letter the assembly had passed a law to reissue and
continue the sum created by the laws of 1723. This action contrary to the board's letter demanded some justification. A memorial was addressed to the board describ-
ing the good effects produced by the former issues, whereby
labor was again employed, commerce was revived and colonial purchases from England were increased and that the
colony was able to supply the mother country with greater
quantities of iron ore than was otherwise possible and
prayed that the law be confirmed.[48] Micajah Perry, a
merchant of London and a large trader to the colonies,
particularly Virginia, was employed to solicit the royal
confirmation.[49] In spite of the board's former declaration
the law was not vetoed.

Again in 1729 the currency problem created disturbance
in the province. The bills of credit had gradually been
withdrawn from circulation by the process of funding and
destroying, and economic depression fell upon the colony.
James Logan wrote that a greater cry for money was
scarcely ever heard.[50] In 1728 David Barclay wrote that
the people " seem to be mad " about paper money.[51] The
question precipitated a keen fight between the assembly
and governor, in which the latter was placed in an uncomfortable position. He was instructed by the proprietor
and bound by a bond to assent to no paper money bill unless due provision was made for exempting sterling debts,
and he was also bound by the board's letter of 1726. He
refused his assent at first to a new issue. The situation
was well described by James Logan, when he wrote that

[47] B. T. Paps., Props., Entry Bk. G, ff. 399-400; Pa. Statutes at
Large, III, 520-521.
[48] B. T. Paps., Props., XI, R 78.
[49] Pa. Votes of Assembly, III, 12.
[50] Penn Mss., Official Corres., II, James Logan to proprietors,
Apr. 30, 1729.
[51] Ibid., David Barclay to Thomas Penn, Oct. 27, 1728.

while the governor was "pinched on one hand by his Instructions, unsupportably clamour'd at on the other, and not one person will advise him agst. another emission, he has a very unpleasant time of it."[52] Gordon expressed a willingness to assent to an issue on two conditions, that provision should be made for sterling debts and proprietary quit-rents and that a clause be inserted in the law suspending its operation till the will of the king was known. The assembly would listen to no conditions or compromises and the governor was forced to yield.[53] The act together with an address to the king praying for royal confirmation was again forwarded to Micajah Perry and again no action was taken against the law.[54] In 1731 the assembly renewed the issue of £45,000 put in circulation in 1723.[55] Gordon again asked for the insertion of the suspending clause but to no avail and he yielded. This act was sent home but with many others passed in this period of the board's inertia was not considered and the colony profited thereby. If the central government took no action the proprietors did. In 1733 the governor was instructed not to assent to any future emissions of bills of credit without the suspending clause, giving as their reason the hostility of English merchants to this form of currency.[56] But that the Penns were more solicitous of their interests as lords of the soil than of the welfare of English merchants is evidenced by the fact that the instructions to Governor Thomas in 1739 said naught about the suspending clause but ordered him to assent to no bill unless provision was made for proprietary quit-rents according to the rate of exchange between London and Phila-

[52] *Penn Mss., Off. Corres.*, James Logan to proprietors, Apr. 30, 1729.

[53] *Ibid.*, II, Gov. Gordon to Penns, May 2, 16, 1729.

[54] *Pa. Statutes at Large*, IV, 98; *Votes of Assembly*, III, 88.

[55] *Pa. Statutes at Large*, IV, 197.

[56] *Penn Mss., Letter Bk.*, Instructions to Gov. Gordon, Jan. 28, 1733.

delphia.[57]   Therefore, when in 1739 a law was passed to
continue the outstanding notes and to create an additional
issue sufficient to bring the amount in circulation up to
£80,000, provision was made to compensate the proprietors for the loss resulting from the acceptance of their
rents in the paper currency.[58]   The Board of Trade consulted several merchants trading to the colony concerning
the new issue and "they rather thought them absolutely
necessary for the carrying on of commerce."[59]   The law
was accordingly confirmed.[60]

The full force of the enmity of the English merchants
was yet to be felt.[61]   In 1739 they began to agitate the
question in Parliament.   In March, the Board of Trade
submitted to the Commons, in response to an order of that
body, a statement of colonial currency.[62]   This report was
incomplete and the house directed the crown to submit
to it at the next session a full account of colonial currency
since 1700, its equivalent in sterling money and the process provided for funding it.   The board instructed the
governors to this effect[64] and in April, 1740, a full statement was laid before Parliament.[65]   It exhibited a wide
discrepancy between sterling money and fiat currency.
The ratio between a pound sterling and paper money was
one to fifty in North Carolina, one to five in New York,
Rhode Island and Connecticut, while in Pennsylvania it
stood in the very favorable proportion of about one to two.
In order to check depreciation the Commons directed the

[57] *Pa. Col. Recs.*, IV, 318.
[58] *Pa. Statutes at Large*, IV, 322, 344.
[59] *B. T. Jour.*, XLIX, 26, 30; *Pa. Statutes at Large*, IV, 481.
[60] *Pa. Statutes at Large*, IV, 479.
[61] See the complaint of 153 merchants of Liverpool, London and
Bristol in 1736. *B. T. Paps., Pl. Gen.*, XII, N 14.
[62] *Jour. House of Commons*, XXIII, 512, 517.
[64] *B. T. Paps., Pl. Gen.*, Entry Bk. G, ff. 255-256; *Pa. Col. Recs.*,
IV, 356, 359; *Pa. Votes of Assembly*, III, 355.
[65] *B. T. Paps., Pl. Gen.*, XII, N 40. Cf. Proud, *Hist. of Pa.*, II, 172.
For reports of Pa. currency see *Col. Recs.*, IV, 363-364; *Votes,,* III,
357-358; *B. T. Paps., Props.*, XIV, T 25; XV, T 47.

crown to instruct the governors not to assent to any further bills without the suspending clause.[66] This was accordingly done, but to little effect.[67] In the next year the board again reported to Parliament on the subject and suggested that the instructions to the royal governors should be repeated. Such orders will suffice in the royal provinces, said the board, but not in those colonies " who think themselves by their charters little dependent upon the crown and seldom pay obedience to royal orders."[68] The only action taken in that year was to place a quietus on the Massachusetts " land bank " which a recent investigator asserts was of greater influence in creating opposition to parliamentary power in that colony than the Stamp Act.[69] In 1744 the English merchants complained to the Commons that no obedience had been paid to the royal orders concerning paper currency.[70] The evidence on this point well warrants the complaint.[71] By the use of the money power the assemblies were able to starve the governors into compliance with the will of the people contrary to royal orders. To remedy the mischief a bill was brought into Parliament designed to prohibit the issue of bills of credit with the legal tender quality. But of far more serious portent was the insertion therein of a clause intended to give to royal instructions the force of law.[72] The passage of such a measure would in effect have empowered the crown to legislate for the colonies. This practically meant an annihilation of the legislative independence enjoyed by the colonial legislatures. It would

---

[66] *Jour. House of Commons*, XXIII, 518, 528.

[67] *B. T. Paps., Props.*, XV, T 34, 40, 48; *Pa. Col. Recs.*, IV, 471-472; *Votes*, III, 426.

[68] *B. T. Paps., Pl. Gen.*, Entry Bk. G, ff. 269-273.

[69] Davis, *Currency and Banking in Mass. Bay*, pt. 2, Pub. Amer. Econ. Asso., vol. II, 3d. ser., 256-261.

[70] *Jour. House of Commons*, XXIV, 658, 681; *Penn Mss., Letter Bk.*, II, 89, Thos. Penn to Gov. Thomas, May 5, 1744.

[71] Greene, *Provincial Governor*, 164-165.

[72] *Pa. Col. Recs.*, IV, 750.

have come into direct opposition to the strong movement of the colonies toward complete autonomy and produced disturbances not unlike those which followed in the wake of the Stamp Act. The colonies were quick to take alarm. The assembly of Pennsylvania resolved that the passage of this measure would be " destructive of all their Liberties, and likely to be attended with the most dangerous consequences to all the King's Subjects in America." [73] The colonial agent was ordered to oppose the bill with vigor and £100 was remitted to him for that service. Other chartered colonies took similiar action.[74] It was probably due to the activity of the colonial agents that the bill failed of passage.

This hostile attitude of the mother country nowise checked the demand for more paper currency in the province. In 1746 Governor Thomas gave his assent to two bills, the one to reissue the £80,000 put in circulation by law of 1739, and the other to create a further sum of £5000 to finance the raising of troops for the expedition against Canada. Neither contained the suspending clause although the governor urged it. The fact that Governor Thomas yielded in violation of the royal order created a precedent which the assembly used to advantage. Both laws were confirmed at home, the one because it did not augment the amount in circulation, the other because it was demanded by the stress of war and continued the bills only for five years.[75] In 1749 a bill similiar to that of 1744 was introduced into the Commons. Through the influence of Thomas Penn and Lord Baltimore the clause designed to give royal orders the force of law was eliminated.[76] Thomas Penn promised the Board of Trade and

[73] Pa. Votes of Assembly, IV, 3-4.
[74] Kimball, Corres. of Govs. of R. I., I, 255, 285-287, 311; R. I. Col. Recs., V, 97.
[75] Pa. Statutes at Large, IV, 469-470, 474-475.
[76] Penn Mss., Letter Bk., II, 268-270, Thos. Penn to Gov. Hamilton, June 6, 1749.

a few members of the Commons that no further issues of
paper money would be made in the province before the
whole question was considered at the next session of Parliament.[77]   This was the argument used by Governor Hamilton when the assembly presented to him a bill to create
a further issue.[78]   As a result of the agitation in England
the statute of 1751 forbade the New England colonies to
create bills of credit with a compulsory value, but allowed
them to issue treasury notes, redeemable in a short period
and without a forced circulation.[79]   Thomas Penn wrote
that Pennsylvania was not included in the law because of
the caution exercised in keeping within the bounds of moderation in amount and providing a firm foundation for
securing the currency.[80]   But the cry for more money increased.   During the war of the Austrian Succession the
trade to the West Indies declined, the markets in Europe
were closed to the merchants of the province, and depression fell upon the people.   In 1752 the assembly passed
a bill to reissue the £85,000 created by the laws of 1746
and to increase it by £40,000.   At first Governor Hamilton refused his assent on the ground that the province
had been left out of the statute of 1751 with difficulty and
the crown would certainly veto any further issues.[81]   When
the assembly persisted in its demands, he expressed his
willingness to assent to the bill provided the suspending
clause demanded by the royal order of 1740 was inserted
in the act.[82]   The assembly would not listen to this, the
governor refused to recede from his position and a bitter
debate ensued.

[77] *Penn Mss., Sup. Proceedings*, 35, Thos. Penn to Richard Peters,
August 2, 1749.
[78] *Pa. Votes of Assembly*, IV, 108, 116-117.
[79] 24 George II, c. 53.
[80] *Penn Mss., Sup. Proc.*, 85, Thos. Penn to Gov. Morris, May 10,
1755.
[81] *Pa. Votes of Assembly*, IV, 218, 240.
[82] *Ibid.*, 251, 252.

It has been shown that on the question of paper currency the interests of the proprietors and the English merchants were identical. This identity of interests afforded the Penns a splendid occasion to cloak their enmity to paper currency under cover of imperial interests and authority. By directing the governor to uphold the royal order the proprietors were able to protect their interests while at the same time make royal instructions the issue in controversy between the governor and assembly. The assembly without a dissenting voice resolved that the insertion of the suspending clause was " destructive of the Liberties granted to the People of the Province by the Royal and Provincial Charters, Injurious to the Rights of the Proprietaries," and without precedent in the law of the province.[83] The representatives claimed that the order of 1740 was simply a temporary expedient pending the action of Parliament which body, after a due consideration of the state of currency in the colony, did not include it in the act of 1751. All this was sufficient indication to the house that Parliament was satisfied with the currency of the colony, the instruction of 1740 had served its purpose, and the government was left in full possession of its power to issue bills of credit. The governor held that the order was not temporary but was still in force and insisted that he was guided by it.[84] The two branches of the government remained obdurate in their respective interpretations of the order of 1740 and no law to create paper currency was enacted.

In 1753 a new and vital element entered into the situation. It was the element of necessity attendant upon the outbreak of the French and Indian war. The province at last found itself heir to all the evils of foreign invasion and savage warfare which had befallen the border colonies to the north and south long since. The needs of defenses

[83] *Pa. Votes of Assembly*, IV, 254-256, 257-259, 262-264.
[84] *Ibid.*, 260-262, 284, 287-291.

entailed additional heavy expenses which could only be met by the creation of paper currency. The serious situation of affairs called for the sinking of all disputes and the uniting of all interests in order to protect the lives and homes of the people from the horrors of Indian warfare. But such was not to be the case. In February, 1754, the governor urged upon the house the necessity of voting supplies to enable the colony to oppose the invasion of the French and Indians. In order to obviate the difficulty of the royal order, Hamilton was willing to assent to a law creating bills of credit without the suspending clause provided the assembly would strike a sum sufficient simply for the occasion and established a fund to sink the notes within five years.[85] This was done by Governor Thomas in 1746 and permitted by the English statute of 1751. The assembly, opposed to war, left the request unanswered till May. It then presented a bill to create £30,000 based on an extension of the excise tax for ten years and granting but one-third of the amount to the king's use.[86] The governor amended the bill by cutting down the time of the excise tax to four years. The house promptly rejected the amendment and informed the governor that " the Representatives of the People have an Undoubted Right to judge and determine not only the sum to be raised for the Use of the Crown but of the manner of raising it.'' Hamilton, worn in health and weary with the endless bickerings, resigned his post. He was succeeded by Robert H. Morris.

The same controversy waged on and nothing was done by the province as a principal or in conjunction with Virginia to drive the invaders from the soil of Pennsylvania. In December, 1754, Governor Morris refused his assent to a bill of £20,000 for the king's use on the ground that it did not contain the suspending clause. To show that he

85 *Pa. Votes of Assembly*, IV, 284.
86 *Ibid.*, 311, 312.

did not rely on his own discretion, he laid before the assembly the opinion of Sir Dudley Ryder, late attorney-general and the present chief justice of England. This opinion was in answer to a query whether the governor could legally or safely, without a breach of his bond and duty to the crown, pass a currency bill without the suspending clause. Ryder offered the opinion that " it is by no means safe, advisable, or Consistent with his Duty to pass such bills without a Suspending Clause." [87] The house refused to recognize this opinion as valid, insisting that the royal charter gave the freemen of the colony legislative independence in all cases whatever and that the crown, even upon an address of Parliament, could not resume this power or add further limitations than what the charter provided. Therefore, said the assembly, although the crown may issue instructions to royal governors, in Pennsylvania such orders have no force.[88] Pownall, ex-governor of Massachusetts, wrote, "the suspending clause is universally rejected in principle because such suspension disfranchises the inherent full power of legislation which they claim by their rights to the British liberties or by the special declarations of such in their charters." [89] This is a clear statement of the situation. Complete political independence was the ideal of the colonial representative bodies and they had no mind to be limited either by royal or proprietary instructions which hedged about their legislative independence. In the chartered colonies there was no doubt of the right of the crown

87 Pa. Votes of Assembly, IV, 343-347.
88 Ibid., 350-352.
89 Pownall, Adm. of Cols., (ed. 1768), 73-74. William Bollan, agent for Mass., declared before the Board of Trade in 1761, " that the Government of Massachusetts Bay, having by their Charter a free and unrestrained Power of Legislation, they would never consent to the inserting suspending Clauses in any Acts to be passed by them and had never done it in any one Instance . . . "
B. T. Jour., LXIX, 250. Cf. Chalmers, Introd. to Revolt of Cols., II, 135-138.

to issue instructions to the governors for putting into execution the acts of trade. The governors were made the administrators of the acts of trade and they took the oaths and gave security to bind them to a faithful performance of the instructions of the crown pursuant to those acts. The question arises, could the crown once having granted away full legislative powers by charter, instruct the governors on matters not provided for by English law? In 1752, the Board of Trade, doubtful on this point, submitted the question to the crown lawyers, but the records reveal no response.[90] The opinion of Ryder seems to indicate that the crown had this right, but it must be remembered that the order of 1740 was based on an address of the House of Commons and there was no doubt of the legal supremacy of Parliament in all cases over both the realm and colonies. In spite of this fact the assembly even denied the force of a royal order so based because it was contrary to the charter.

Looking at the question solely from the point of view of expediency, and waiving the question of legality, it would appear that the royal instruction of 1740 placed peculiar hardships on the colony. The critical posture of affairs in the colony absolutely demanded the prompt raising of supplies for the sake of defense, yet a strict adherence to the order meant that the only form of money, bills of credit, would not be available till the law was approved by a far distant government. The law of 1751, which pertained only to New England, made provision for such sudden emergencies by permitting the issue of treasury notes to be redeemed at the end of a short period. Recognizing the serious situation, Governor Morris, like his predecessor, expressed a willingness to assent to an issue of currency on the basis of this law.[91] In December,

[90] B. T. Paps., Props., XVIII, V 101; Entry Bk. I, ff. 2-12; Jour., LX, 105.

[91] Pa. Votes of Assembly, IV, 354-356; Pa. Col. Recs., VI, 39-44, 192.

1754, the house presented to him a bill to issue £20,000 for the " king's use " and to continue in circulation for twelve years. Morris cut the time down to five years, as provided by the law of 1751.[92] The assembly refused to allow any amendment, the governor refused to recede from his position and the frontier of the province was left defenseless. The house then became thoroughly convinced that the governor was hindered by proprietary instructions. The contention then centered upon the right of the proprietors to instruct their governor. The house declared that proprietary orders were " void in themselves " and an " Infringement upon the Privileges granted by charter to the People of the Province."[93] The assembly not only denied the right of the proprietors to veto laws of the colony, but also the right to instruct their governor. Seeing no way out of the difficulty the assembly resolved to appeal to the crown in protest against proprietary orders. In January, 1755, an address was drawn up and sent to the colonial agent to lay before the king.[94] It was stated that the repeated efforts of the assembly to vote money for defenses had been thwarted by the action of the governor acting under proprietary instructions and prayed that if the crown on consideration found such orders dangerous to the interests of the Empire and contrary to the charter, relief should be afforded. The Board of Trade granted a hearing on this memorial to the Penns and the agent of the assembly with their respective counsel. Counsel for the proprietors denied that the governor was limited in this matter by instructions and in justification of the governor's conduct submitted the royal order of 1740, the opinion of Sir Dudley Ryder, and the English statute of 1751. The board reported to the Privy

[92] *Pa. Col. Recs.*, VI, 206, 210, 212.
[93] *Ibid.*, VI, 221, 228, 230, 236.
[94] *Pa. Votes of Assembly*, IV, 379; *B. T. Paps., Props.*, XIX, V 137, 144, 145, 146; *Penn Mss., Official Corres.*, VII, Board of Trade to Thos. Penn, Apr. 25, 1755.

Council that there was no proof nor the least foundation for the suggestion that the governor was hindered by proprietary orders and recommended that the address of the assembly should be rejected.[95] Although the Penns were victors in this matter, the end of the struggle was not yet. One fact is certain, that the proprietors, deprived of the right of final assent to colonial laws and denied the power to instruct their governor, could rely upon the support of the English government to safeguard their landed and governmental interests against the hostile action of the assembly.

Meanwhile during the years 1754-1755 the government did little indeed to protect the province against the invasion of the French. Because of the dead-lock nothing was done to aid Virginia check French encroachments and Washington marched on to his defeat at Fort Necessity in 1754 unsupported by Pennsylvania.[96] Again in 1755 Braddock's expedition against Fort Duquesne received little aid from this province.[97] The assembly threw the whole blame upon the shoulders of the governor, the latter laid it at the door of the assembly; it was shifted from one side to the other with such ingenuity and under such plausible appearances, that it is hard to judge where the censure ought to rest. The fact remains that while the governor and assembly were wrangling on in the east free from the horrors of war, the defenseless inhabitants on the frontier were left to the fate of the tomahawk and firebrand. It is fair to assume that had they laid aside their disputes in this hour of trial and energetically supported Washington and Braddock, the French might have been driven from the province and the lives and property of the people saved the horrors of savage warfare which fol-

[95] *Pa. Statutes at Large*, V, 513-521; *B. T. Jour.*, LXIII, 159, 165, 177, 178; *Penn Mss., Sup. Proc.*, 85, Thos. Penn to Gov. Morris, May 10, 1755.

[96] See page 296.

[97] See page 304.

lowed in the wake of French victory. Thomas Penn wrote
that a member of the assembly remarked " that they had
rather the French should conquer them than they should
give up their privileges to the proprietors."[98] Governor
Morris wrote that the assembly " seem'd determined to
take advantage of their Country's distress to get the whole
powers of Government into their own hands."[99] And in
fact, the assembly confessed that " Those who would give
up essential Liberty to purchase a Little Temporary safety
deserve neither Liberty nor safety."[100] The refusal of
the assembly to accept the amendment of the governor
limiting the £20,000 to a term of five years lends color to
the charge that the house, made up mostly of Quaker pacificists, had no intention of providing any defenses for the
province.[101] The ideal which the popular branch sought
to attain was complete independence in provincial politics
and it seemed inclined to reach this position at any sacrifice.

After the defeat of Braddock, the savages carried their
horrible work of burning and killing over the frontier
and forced the pioneer people to evacuate their homes for
places of safety. The situation called urgently for prompt
and generous aid from the government. After the event
the assembly presented to the governor a bill to create
£60,000 in bills of credit secured by a tax on all property,
real and personal, for two years. The governor promptly
amended the bill to exclude the estates of the Penns.[102]
With this the contest over royal and proprietary instructions fell into abeyance and a prolonged and acrimonious
struggle ensued over the taxation of the proprietary estates. This dispute persisted through the French war and

[98] *Penn Mss., Letter Bk.*, IV, 63, Thos. Penn to Gov. Morris,
Feb. 26, 1755.
[99] *Pa. Col. Recs.*, VI, 518, 544, 564.
[100] *Ibid.*, VI, 695, VII, 255.
[101] *Ibid.*, VI, 720, 739.
[102] *Ibid.*, II, 396.

the conspiracy of Pontiac when the critical situation of affairs demanded the sinking of all differences and the uniting of all interests in the general security of the frontier. Because of the contention over this question the people of the west were not accorded adequate protection. This dispute so embittered the defenseless inhabitants of the frontier that it led to armed protests against the assembly. It engendered bitter feeling in the assembly against the proprietors and led to the effort to overthrow proprietary rule in the interest of royal control. It hampered and delayed the military operations of the English government in the south and forced the English commanders to interfere in provincial politics. A similar struggle was in process in the neighboring province of Maryland to the prejudice of local and general defense. It was the offensive and dilatory action of these colonies which is largely responsible for the Stamp Act.

Two questions are involved in this struggle between the governor and assembly, the one of justice and the other of power. The assembly was convinced that it was eminently unjust that the people alone should " undergo the Weight of this Uncommon Tax, and even expose their Persons for the defense of his Estate, who by virtue of his Power only, and without even a Colour of Right, should refuse to bear the least share of the Burthen though to receive so great a benefit." It was contended that the Penns by " giving a part to save the whole and not only to save it but render it of double and treble value . . . could hardly be called hurting and encumbering an Estate." [103] To throw upon the people the whole burden of defending their own estates as well as those of the proprietors seemed to the assembly contrary to all the principles of justice. On the other hand the proprietors expressed a willingness to bear a share of the burden, but to them it appeared equally unjust to subject all their estates to taxation.

[103] *Pa. Col. Recs.*, VI, 527, 532, 695; VIII, 105.

They were ready to have those estates which yielded an income taxed in common with the property of the people, but to impose a tax on the vast areas of unlocated and unsurveyed lands which were productive of no returns appeared to them subversive of the principles of right. Moreover, they held it to be unfair to deny them a share in the selection of the assessors of the value of their estates, a right which the smallest property holder in the province enjoyed.[104] In point of power it was the aim of the assembly, as charged by Governor Morris, to render itself " independent and assume a Superiority over your Proprietaries and governors, a plan which you would not fail to carry into execution were your power equal to your Inclination." [105] The house quickly repudiated the imputation of any " Scheme of future Independency " but insisted upon the sole right of judging the propriety and necessity of all laws without any direction whatever from either the Penns or their governor. The house denied the proprietors the right to instruct the governor,[106] denied the governor the right to amend money bills and left him only the power to accept or reject them as offered according to the practice of the Commons in England. The house insisted upon the power to dispose of all public money, leaving the governor but scant control in this respect, and upon the power to appoint all officials in any way concerned with the revenue. " In short, the Powers of Government are almost all taken out of the Hands of the Governor, and lodged in the Assembly; as to what little remains, scarce a bill comes up without an attempt to lessen them." [107] These are the words of a member of the provincial council in 1757. It is good evidence that the assembly was more concerned with what its members considered their rights and privileges as Englishmen than

[104] *Pa. Col. Recs.*, VII, 396; VIII, 73.
[105] *Ibid.*, VI, 387, 544, 564.
[106] *Ibid.*, VI, 390; VII, 255.
[107] *Ibid.*, VII, 449, 528, 708.

in the question of local and imperial defense. It is unmistakable indication of the development toward complete autonomy and responsible government.

The controversy was laid at rest momentarily by a gift of £5000 from the proprietors toward the charges of defense.[108] The law of November, 1755, granted £60,000 to the king's use in bills of credit and exempted the proprietary estates from taxation.[109] The gift brought but a temporary allayment of the trouble. The plan of the imperial government to carry into operation an effective campaign against the French made large demands upon the colonies for men and money. In 1756, after a long debate over the taxation of proprietary estates, the matter was compromised by an issue of £30,000 in bills of credit based on an extension of the excise tax for ten years.[110] To these laws the Board of Trade could have no objection since the money was demanded by the needs of the situation and the bills were to continue in circulation for but a short period. They were accordingly confirmed by the crown. In 1757 and 1758 the assembly voted £200,000 in bills of credit on a land tax to meet the expenses of military operations.[111] But each year the old struggle over the taxation of the estates of the Penns rose up to delay the campaign, to hamper the English generals and to cause distress to the frontier people. In these years the proprietary estates were not taxed, but only after Generals Abercromby, Amherst and Stanwix had interfered to allay the strife.[112] But the assembly abated not a bit in its position. It was resolved to appeal to the proprietors.

In February, 1757, Benjamin Franklin left for England,

108 *Penn Mss., Official Corres.*, VII, 121, Proprietors to Gov. Morris, Oct. 5, 1755.
109 *Pa. Statutes at Large*, V, 201.
110 *Ibid.*, V, 243.
111 *Ibid.*, V, 295, 303, 337.
112 *Pa. Col. Recs.*, VII, 453; VIII, 78, 331; *Pa. Archives*, 1st. ser., III, 118, 715; Kimball, *Corres. Wm. Pitt*, I, 41, II, 88, 130.

as the agent of the assembly, to lay before the proprietors a statement of grievances.[113] In November, 1758, the Penns, through their counsel, replied that they were willing to have the income from their estates inquired into and stood ready to contribute, whatever the former gift lacked, a proportion of the tax levied by the previous laws.[114] But it was stipulated that this tax should be imposed only on that part of their estate " that is in its nature taxable " and insisted upon having a voice in the choice of assessors of the value. In consequence the assembly submitted to the governor a bill to create £100,000 in bills of credit for the campaign of 1759 based on a tax on all property, including that of the Penns.[115] Moreover, it made provision that the proprietors should pay a proportionate share of former taxes, crediting the gift of £5000. The governor amended the bill to exclude all estates of the proprietors except the quit-rents and appropriated tracts and to give the Penns a voice in the selection of assessors.[116] The house would hearken to no amendments, holding that the governor had no power to change money bills.[117] The pressing need of money to set on foot the military operations forced General Amherst to labor with the assembly to yield but to no effect. Amherst then turned to Governor Denny and persuaded him to waive his instructions from the proprietors.[118] Under stress of the exigencies of the occasion and under the influence of Amherst, Denny yielded and was rewarded by the assembly with a vote of £1000.[119] At once the cry was raised that the governor was bribed. If it was corruption it was

---

113 Franklin, *Works*, (Smyth ed.) III, 370-377; *Pa. Votes of Assembly*, IV, 697; *Pa. Col. Recs.*, VIII, 278.

114 *Pa. Col. Recs.*, VIII, 281.

115 *Ibid.*, VIII, 301.

116 *Ibid.*, VIII, 302, 303, 319, 320, 325-329.

117 *Ibid.*, VIII, 304, 323-325, 331.

118 *Ibid.*, VIII, 331-332; Kimball, *Corres. of Wm. Pitt*, II, 88.

119 *Pa. Col. Recs.*, VIII, 333; *Pa. Statutes at Large*, V, 379.

a charge which may be fastened upon many another provincial governor. The position of a governor was most precarious. On the one hand Denny was under a bond of £5000 to the proprietors to obey their orders and on the other he was dependent upon the assembly for his support and the charges of government. A violation of his instructions carried with it a forfeiture of his security and loss of office, a refusal to bend to the will of the assembly contrary to his orders meant no salary, no supplies, and a serious hindrance to military operations. Under the stress of circumstances the governor was no doubt justified in waiving his instructions, but he is open to censure for accepting the vote of money from the house. Moreover, in violation of his instructions Denny assented to a bill to reissue for a period of sixteen years the £80,000 put in circulation by the law of 1746.[120] To this law was attached a rider granting to Colonel Hunter, the financial agent of the crown, a loan of £50,000 for one year without interest to enable him to liquidate the expenses of a former campaign pending the arrival of funds from England. The only redress of the proprietors was to put Denny's bond in suit and to appeal to the crown to veto the laws. The first was rendered ineffectual by the decision of the assembly to indemnify Denny should the Penns take action against the bond.[121] Denny was dismissed from office and an appeal against the laws was made to the crown.

In March, 1760, the proprietors laid before the king a memorial protesting against the confirmation of eleven acts which in one way or another violated their territorial and governmental rights under the charter.[122] The paper was turned over to the Board of Trade. Before it appeared the proprietors and the agents of the assembly with

---

120 Kimball, *Corres. of Wm. Pitt*, II, 130; *Pa. Col. Recs.*, VIII, 358, 362; *Pa. Statutes at Large*, V, 427, 456.

121 *Pa. Votes of Assembly*, V, 68.

122 *Pa. Statutes at Large*, V, 661-663, 689.

their respective counsel.[123]   The Penns were represented
by the crown lawyers, Attorney-General Charles Pratt,
and Solicitor General Charles Yorke.[124]   The fact that
they were able to secure the services of these officials seems
to indicate the close sympathy between crown and proprietary government.   Indeed, the crown faced practically
the same problems in the royal provinces and identity of
interests led to the support of the Penns by the crown.
The agents of the assembly, Benjamin Franklin and
Robert Charles, employed as counsel, Sir William de Grey,
later attorney-general and chief justice of England, and
Richard Jackson, later counsel to the Board of Trade.[125]
It was to be a battle of the highest legal talent in the realm.
Four hearings were held before the board during May and
June.[126]   The chief law in debate was the land tax bill of
1759.   The attorney-general opened the case by stating
" the general Tendency and Disposition of the House of
Assembly of the Province at all times to encroach upon the
Rights of the Proprietaries, the Prerogative of the Crown,
and the Sovereign Government of the Mother Country, by
their asserting that the Lieutenant Governor was not the
Governor of the Crown; — by their almost rebellious Declarations with respect to the Instruction concerning Paper
Currency founded upon an Address of Parliament; — by
denying the Right of the Proprietaries to instruct their
Govr and other Acts of avowed Democracy."   He then
proceeded to discuss the objections to the law; the arbitrary taxation of proprietary estates which yielded no
revenue, making bills of credit a legal tender in payment
of the proprietary quit-rents, and leaving the money
granted to the public service to the sole disposition of a

[123] *Pa. Statutes at Large*, V, 690.
[124] *Ibid.*, V, 692.
[125] *Ibid.*, V, 692.
[126] *Ibid.*, V, 691-697; *B. T. Jour.*, LXVIII, 106, 108, 118, 129,
133, 135, 136-143, 143-148, 148-149, 151-153.

committee of the assembly.[127] Mr. de Grey characterized
the charges against his constituents as "ornaments of
speech unsupported by any evidence whatever" and insisted that the conduct of the assembly during the war
was "particularly meritorious."[128] A very unique point
was raised by de Grey. He contended that the laws before them were regularly passed and laid before the crown
in conformity with the charter and the only question then
to be decided was whether the laws were consistent with
the sovereignty and prerogatives of the crown. This argument was based on the clause of the charter which reserved to the king the power of veto in these respects, but
that the clause which required all laws to be consonant
to equity and not repugnant to English statutes conferred
no veto power on the crown. Moreover, de Grey contended
that the interests of the proprietors could not be considered in this matter nor had they any right to rely upon
the crown for redress. This argument was based on the
fact that the governors were under bond to the proprietors to obey their instructions and any violation of the obligation was entirely a private matter. At the close of
the hearing the board sat two days to consider the laws
and on June 24 sent its report to the Plantation Committee of the Council.[129]

The whole tenor of the report is eminently favorable to
the proprietors. In the first place considerable space was
given in refutation of the curious argument of de Grey.[130]
The board maintained the right of the crown to veto all
laws of the province whether inconsistent with the royal
prerogative or contrary to equity and English law and
that such had ever been the practice. Furthermore, the
proprietors were in no ways excluded from the right of
all English subjects to appeal to the throne for redress,

127 *Pa. Statutes at Large*, V, 692-693.
128 *Ibid.*, V, 694-695.
129 *Ibid.*, V, 697.
130 *Ibid.*, V, 699-703; *Pa. Col. Recs.*, VIII, 525-529.

neither could the latter be excluded from securing all information necessary to the proper exercise of the veto power. The appeal of the Penns in this case was deemed especially proper because of the injury done to them by the assembly which used the public purse first to corrupt the governor and then to take away the means by which he could be punished. The act to issue £100,000 was offered for disapproval on the same objections as made by the attorney-general.[131] The fact that the currency was already in circulation and that the veto of the law would impair its credit and injure innocent holders was duly considered, but the injustice to the proprietors overshadowed all else and demanded the veto. The law to reissue the £80,000 for sixteen years and its supplement were reported for disapproval because the period of circulation was too long and the amount was not needed by reason of the large amount of currency put in circulation during the war.[132] The board held that although the act of 1751, which limited the issue of notes for emergencies to five years and those for circulation to three years, extended only to New England, yet the restrictions were valid for all colonies and that therefore Pennsylvania should be kept up to that standard. These laws were also open to the same objections as urged against the land tax act; the proprietors were forced to receive their rents in currency and the governor was allowed no voice in the disposal of the money. Moreover, the board objected to the blending in one act two totally different matters, the reissue of the currency and the loan to Colonel Hunter. This device subjected the governor and crown to the alternative of approving an objectionable measure or of rejecting one quite necessary to the public service. That this was the conscious intention of the assembly there is little doubt.

131 *Pa. Statutes at Large*, V, 704-711; *Pa. Col. Recs.*, VIII, 529-535.

132 *Pa. Statutes at Large*, V, 711-716; *Pa. Col. Recs.*, VIII, 535-538.

This practice was forbidden in the royal provinces by standing instructions forbidding the governors to assent to riders,[133] but over the executives of the chartered colonies the crown enjoyed no such control. As the money from the English treasury was then on its way to Colonel Hunter and would probably anticipate the notice of the veto it was thought that no harm would be done to the holders of the currency by reason of the disallowance of the law.

The agents for the assembly were not content to allow the matter to rest there but carried it on appeal to the Plantation Committee of the Council. In the last of August the committee granted both sides two hearings.[134] As a result the law to reissue £80,000 with its supplement was vetoed but on the land tax law a compromise was reached. This was accomplished through the mediation of Lord Mansfield. The committee was of the opinion that the act was "fundamentally unjust and wrong," but on condition that the law be altered by the assembly to meet the objections, it was reported for approval. The agreement, solemnly subscribed to by the agents for the assembly, stipulated that the law should be changed to exclude from taxation the unsurveyed waste lands of the proprietors, to tax their located unimproved lands no higher than the lowest rate at which similiar lands of the people were taxed, to give the governor a voice in the disposal of the money raised by the law, and to make provision for the payment of proprietary quit-rents according to the terms of the contracts.[135] The ideal condition would have been not to confirm the law until the assembly had seen fit to honor the agreement of its agents. This was not possible under the charter which required that all laws not acted upon within six months after delivery to the council stood

133 Greene, *Provincial Governor*, 164.

134 *Pa. Statutes at Large*, V, 654; *Pa. Col. Recs.*, VIII, 553.

135 *Pa. Statutes at Large*, V, 655-657, 659; *Pa. Col. Recs.*, VIII, 554, 555, 557.

confirmed by the lapse of time. In a royal province the crown was able to suspend action on a law indefinitely but this was precluded by the clause of the charter. The law could not be altered except by trusting to the good faith of the assembly to fulfill the pledge or by an appeal to the sovereign power of Parliament. The fact of the matter is that the assembly showed little inclination to honor the agreement.

In January, 1761, the governor called upon the assembly to alter the act of 1759 in accordance with the pledge.[136] The assembly replied that no part of the proprietors' unsurveyed waste lands was taxed, that in some cases their located uncultivated lands were not taxed at all and in others not assessed higher than similar lands of the inhabitants, and that there was no intention to impair the contracts of the Penns by obliging them to receive their quit-rents in currency.[137] Although these statements may have been sincere, the principles of good faith required the redemption of the pledge of the agents by altering the law. Although this was urged time and again by the governor the house consistently refused to do so. The conduct of the assembly practically amounted to a repudiation of the agreement. Not only did it refuse to alter the law but it had the temerity to offer to the governor for his assent other supply bills containing several of the very features objected to at home, such as giving the governor no share in the disposal of the money, making no provision for the payment of proprietary rents according to contract, and tacking on riders. The house persisted in its refusal to allow the governor to amend money bills and the governor steadfastly refused to accept the bills unless in accordance with the agreement and the sentiments as expressed by the Board of Trade in 1760.[138] The deadlock

136 *Pa. Col. Recs.*, VIII, 559, 563, 579.
137 *Ibid.*, VIII, 584-585.
138 *Ibid.*, VIII, 606-609, 611, 693, 695-697, 716-719; IX, 10-11, 19, 20, 21, 53.

was particularly aggravating coming at the time of the wide-spread Indian uprising under the leadership of Pontiac. The frontier was left open to the Indian warfare and the military operations of the English commanders were delayed. The attitude of the assembly called forth a severe censure from General Amherst.[139] Under the press of circumstances the assembly finally yielded to the demands of the governor in the supply bill of 1764.[140] It was at this time that the Paxton Boys from the frontier, left defenseless, took matters into their own hands by killing the peaceful Indians seated on Conestoga Manor and with arms in their hands marched on Philadelphia to force the assembly to grant them defenses and redress their grievances. It was at this time that the assembly, embittered against the proprietors, petitioned the crown to grant the province royal government.[141]

It was no doubt with a sigh of relief that Thomas Penn wrote from London in December, 1763, to Governor John Penn, "our disputes with the assembly about paper money will soon be at an end, as a bill is to be brought into parliament to put the colonies in that respect on the same footing with New England."[142]

During the war the merchants of London, Liverpool and Glasgow trading to Virginia complained of the pernicious effects of a legal tender paper currency in this province. The vast charges of the war forced Virginia for the first time to resort to a paper currency.[143] Likewise Pennsylvania was driven to greater issues to meet the heavy burdens of defense. The latter province created between 1755 and 1760 £485,000 in bills of credit for this purpose,[144] in addition to the £80,000 put in circulation

139 *Pa. Col. Recs.*, IX, 62, 114.
140 *Ibid.*, IX, 174-178, 180-188; *Pa. Statutes at Large*, VI, 344.
141 Lincoln, *Revolutionary Movement in Pa.*, 98-113.
142 *Penn Mss., Letter Bk.*, VIII, 14, Thos. Penn to John Penn, Dec. 10, 1763.
143 Beer, *British Col. Pol., 1754-1765*, 185-188.
144 *B. T. Paps., Pl. Gen.*, XXI, ff. 83-87.

by the act of 1746. The colonies south of New England
had not been included in the act of 1751 which forbade
the issue of paper as a legal tender currency, because they
had kept within the bounds of moderation in issuing bills
of credit and not because the " reasonings and principles " upon which the act of 1751 was based were not applicable to all the colonies.[145] But the vast issues in Pennsylvania and Virginia brought about the same difficulties
which English merchants had experienced before in New
England. In 1763, at the close of the war, the English
merchants renewed their protests. In February, 1763,
after hearing the arguments of the merchants and agents
for Virginia, the Board of Trade came to the conclusion
that the issue of paper currency with the legal tender
quality was " destructive of the publick Credit of those
colonies, injurious to the Commerce of Great Britain, inconsistent with the interest of the Crown, and contrary
to the sense of the Parliament " as expressed in the Act
of 1751 pertaining to New England.[146] No further action
was taken till the beginning of the next year. In January, 1764, the board took into consideration the condition
of the currency in the colonies not under the law of 1751
and notified the merchants and colonial agents to appear
before it. Several hearings were granted to both sides
on the question of the advisability of extending the act of
1751 to all the colonies.[147] The board then availed itself
of the information of colonial proprietors and others conversant with the actual conditions in America. At the
meeting of February 2, there was present two governors,
five former governors, the proprietors of Pennsylvania, as
also the agent, Richard Jackson, and the chief justice of
the latter province.[148] It was agreed unanimously that

145 *N. J. Archives*, IX, 409-410.
146 *B. T. Jour.*, LXXI, 39, 41-45.
147 *Ibid.*, LXXII, 11, 16, 23.
148 *Ibid.*, LXXII, 42, 54.

to check by act of Parliament all further issues of paper money as a legal tender and to forbid the currency in circulation to be a legal tender after the period fixed for redemption was "highly expedient and proper."[149] Thomas Penn and Richard Jackson asked that action should be deferred till the next session of Parliament in order to allow the colonies time to express their sentiments on the subject. The next day the agents for six colonies asked the same favor. The board was impatient of delay and asked the agents for a categorical answer whether they would or would not oppose the bill.[150] Granted a few days for consultation, they replied that they could not agree to the bill. They gave it as their undivided opinion that a certain quantity of legal tender paper money was needed in each colony for strictly local purposes and craved time for the colonies to consider the matter and report the quantum necessary.[151] The board was not disposed to hearken to the request and on February 9 reported to the Privy Council the necessity of an act of Parliament to check the issue of legal tender bills of credit.[152]

The board claimed that "this means of declaring bills of Credit to be a legal Tender, was false in it's principles, unjust in it's foundation, and manifestly fraudulent in it's operation." It claimed also that paper currency tended to drive specie, the fittest materials for a medium of exchange, out of circulation; that the quantity issued was all out of proportion to the actual needs, and that a sufficient foundation for securing the paper was not provided whereby the bills of credit had greatly depreciated and fluctuated in value, and worked injustice to colonial creditors and brought loss and suffering to the English merchants trading to the colonies. The baneful influences which a depreciated currency cast upon the

[149] *B. T. Jour.*, LXXII, 57-58.
[150] *Ibid.*, 59-60.
[151] *Ibid.*, 70-71, 80.
[152] *N. J. Archives*, IX, 405-414.

morals of the people did not escape the attention of the Board. The charge was brought that debtors in the colonial assemblies urged the creation of new issues with fraudulent intentions. Since the act of 1751 had corrected the evils of a paper currency as a legal tender in New England, the board urged that the beneficial restrictions of this act should be extended to all the colonies. The efforts of the board resulted in the passage of the statute of 1764 which forbade the issue of bills of credit as a legal tender or the continuance of the bills then current beyond the period fixed for redemption.[153] In view of the facts in the case, there is little doubt of the necessity and propriety of this action.

The passage of the currency act of 1764 was doubtless one of the factors which promoted in the colonies discontent with English rule. Franklin, before the bar of the House of Commons in 1766, specified the currency act as one of the five causes which tended to lessen the respect of the colonies for the authority of Parliament.[154] It was the hostility of the English government to the financial schemes of Virginia which caused Patrick Henry to exclaim in the Parson's Cause that the king "from being the father of his people, degenerated into a Tyrant, and forfeits all rights to his Subjects' obedience." The subsequent popularity of Henry attests to the prevalence of a spirit of discontent with English interference.[155] The currency act drew strong remonstrances from the pens of John Dickinson [156] and Benjamin Franklin [157] who summed up the colonial side of the currency question. They contended that the chronic lack of specie was not due to the

[153] 4 George III, c. 34.
[154] Franklin, *Works*, (Smyth ed.) IV, 420.
[155] Beer, *British Col. Pol., 1754-1765*, 185-186.
[156] *The Late Regulations Respecting the British Colonies Considered*, 1765, *Works*, I, 218-221.
[157] *Remarks and Facts concerning American Paper Money*, 1766, *Works*, (Smyth ed.) V, 1-14.

deleterious effect of an unsound paper currency, but to the unfavorable balance of trade which drained the gold and silver to England. Franklin admitted that specie formed the best medium of exchange, but claimed that the lack of mines and the unfavorable balance of trade forced the colonies to the expediency of paper currency. Under the circumstances, he said, a paper currency, kept within proper bounds, was necessary. It aided settlement, increased production, and in the long run inured to the benefit of England by creating an increased demand for home manufactures.[158] These were the arguments of the colonists and the truth of them cannot be easily gainsaid. But the fact remains that the over-issue of notes all out of proportion to the needs of domestic economy and the consequent depreciation undoubtedly helped to drive specie out of the colonies and worked injustice to English as well as colonial creditors. It was contended that the English merchants suffered no losses since their debts were paid according to the rate of exchange between the colony and London.[159] But the chief difficulty here lay in the fact that this rate fluctuated violently between the time of contract and payment. In 1723, when Pennsylvania first entered upon a paper currency policy, the exchange between Philadelphia and London was 50 per cent., it rose to 70 per cent. in 1741, then fell violently to 50, and during the French and Indian war fluctuated between 55 and 72½ per cent.[160] The rise in exchange had the effect of impairing contract obligations entered into at a time when the exchange was lower. Pownall said, "Parliament very properly interposed, by applying the only adequate and

[158] See the opinions of Gov. Burnet of N. Y., 1724; and Gov. Montgomerie of N. J., *N. Y. Col. Docs.*, V, 738, 832. Also the opinions of the governors of Pa., *B. T. Paps., Props.*, XI, R 42, 47, 78.

[159] Dickinson, *Late Regulations, Works*, I, 218; Franklin, *Remarks and Facts, Works*, (Smyth ed.) V, 5; Beer, *British Col. Pol., 1754-1765*, 180-182.

[160] *B. T. Paps., Props.*, XIV, T 25, 47, 48; *Pl. Gen.*, XXI, ff. 83-87.

efficient remedy, namely, by prohibiting these colony legislatures from being able to make the paper currency a *legal
tender.*" [161] But the colonial contention was summed up
in the words of Franklin, " It seems hard therefore to
draw all their real Money from them, and then refuse
them the poor Privilege of using Paper instead of it." [162]
In fact, the action of the English government in this case
receives ample justification when one remembers the evil
influences of a paper currency, as typified in Shay's Rebellion, after the colonies had gained their independence.
The critical situation of the period after 1776 forced the
framers of the constitution of 1789 to provide that no
state shall emit bills of credit, make anything but gold and
silver a tender in payment of debts, or pass any law to
impair the obligations of contracts.

The refusal of the assembly to honor the royal proclamation of 1704 and the act of Parliament of 1708 fixing
the rate of foreign coin current in the colonies; its declaration against the right of the crown to instruct the governor even upon an address of Parliament, and the repudiation of the agreement of 1760 entered into by its agents
with the home government are conclusive evidence of the
strained relations between the two parts of the Empire.

[161] Pownall, *Administration of Cols.* (ed. 1768), 188.
[162] Franklin, *Works,* (Smyth ed.), V, 7.

CHAPTER EIGHT

THE QUAKER AND ANGLICAN

The Quaker movement to America, like that of the Puritans, was the result of religious persecution and political oppression at home. Penn wrote, " we in New England . . . New Jersey and Pennsylvania went thither, by ample grants from the crown, to make and keep ourselves easy and safe in our civil and religious privileges, . . . it was to be free of the church's power and out of her reach that we went so far, and not to make colonies for her but from her, for ourselves.'' [1] The Quakers and Puritans were out of sympathy with the ideas dominant in church and state in England and they betook themselves to America where they might be able to work out their own peculiar conceptions in religion and politics untrammeled by the state or church at home. It was Archbishop Laud's policy of Thorough in the time of Charles I which drove the Puritans to America; it was the Clarendon Code of the Restoration which led the Quakers to found colonies in New Jersey and Pennsylvania.

Driven to seek shelter in the settled colonies of the new world, the Quakers meet with the same spirit of persecution. In Puritan New England the newcomers met with stripes, banishment, and even death on the gallows. In Anglican Virginia they were unwelcome, and in most colonies they were visited with civil and religious disabilities.[2] Without political influence in most of the colonies, lacking unity and cohesion of life by reason of their broadly scattered settlements, it was highly desirable that the Quakers

[1] *Duke of Portland Mss.*, IV, 80, Hist. Mss. Com., *Report* 15, pt. 4.
[2] Osgood, *Amer. Cols. in 17th. Cent.*, I, 269-287; Bruce, *Institutional Hist. of Va.*, I, 222-251.

should found a colony for themselves, where, free from the oppression of other faiths, they would be able to establish a government of their own device and see the working into practice of their own peculiar conceptions in matters of religion. Such was the purpose which actuated Penn to secure a grant of land in America.[3]

While both the Puritans and the Quakers became colonists for religious reasons, their ideas in politics and religion were diametrically opposed to each other. The Puritans went to America to found a colony of their own faith exclusively. Penn said that he went '' thither to lay the foundation for a free colony for all mankind that should go thither, more especially those of my own profession, not that I would lessen the civil liberties of others because of their persuasion, but screen and defend our own from any infringement on that account.''[4] In Penn's religious philosophy there was no place for intolerance. It was in this spirit that Penn and the Quakers drew up a law in England before their departure, later ratified by an assembly of the freemen of the colony in 1682, granting religious liberty to '' all persons living in this province, who confess one almighty and eternal God, to be the creator, upholder and ruler of the world, . . . and live peaceably and justly in civil society . . .''; and bestowed political privileges upon all '' such as profess faith in Jesus Christ.'' Thus freedom of worship was granted to all Deists and civil liberties to all Christians.[5]

The path which led to a realization of Penn's ''Holy Experiment'' was beset with many and serious difficulties. It must be borne in mind that Penn's dominion was not an independent state invested with sovereign power, but was a dependency subject to the control of the English government. In the first place, the royal charter contained

[3] Andrews, *Colonial Self-Government*, 162-168; Sharpless, *A Quaker Experiment in Government*, 7-20.
[4] *Penn-Logan Corres.*, I, 373.
[5] *Pa. Col. Recs.*, I, 40, 41.

provisions which made it possible for an Anglican government at home to interfere in the religious regulations of a dissenting colony. Then again, by the charter as well by the clause of the act of 1696, it was stipulated that the laws of the province should be consonant to reason and equity and agreeable as far as circumstances would allow to English law.[6] But the court which decided upon these questions was the English government. The Quakers, according to English law, were dissenters and hence their legislation, which gave expression to their dissenting views, was liable to be declared null and void as contrary to English law. The Quaker law which granted freedom of worship to all believers in God was contrary to the Toleration Act of 1689 which excluded Catholics, Jews and Socinians.[7] The law of the colony allowed Quakers to use the affirmation in all cases whatsoever, but the English law of 1696 allowed the Quakers to affirm in all public proceedings except in giving evidence in criminal cases, in serving on juries, or holding a place of public trust.[8] The position of the Friends was most uncomfortable. If they kept faith with their religious tenets, as men having the courage of their convictions will ever do, they violated their charter and rendered it liable to forfeiture and their laws to be declared null. If they kept faith with their charter they would prove false to their ideals. Finally, by the charter the ecclesiastical jurisdiction of the bishop of London in the colony was expressly provided for in the clause which allowed him to appoint ministers for congregations of not less than twenty upon application to him.[9] This provision was inserted at the instigation of Henry Compton, bishop of London, who watched over the interests

---

[6] Poore, *Charters and Consts.*, (2d. ed.) II, 1511; 7 and 8 Wm. III, c. 22, sec. 8.

[7] I William and Mary, c. 18.

[8] 7 and 8 William III, c. 34.

[9] Poore, *Charters and Consts.*, II, 1515.

of the infant church in America with a zealous eye.[10] It is quite probable that the refusal of the Puritan government in Massachusetts to open their narrow franchise to persons of other persuasions is responsible for this provision in Penn's charter. Of course this stipulation accorded well with Penn's principles as to freedom of worship, but later we shall see that Penn had cause to regret the intense opposition of this active prelate to the Quaker doctrines.

For the first decade of the life of the colony the Quakers experienced no difficulty in putting into effect their religious doctrines. The two cardinal tenets of the Quakers, which were to cause them great anxiety and vexation, were the sinfulness of an oath and the wrongfulness of all war, whether defensive or offensive. To them the biblical injunctions from the Sermon on the Mount, '' Swear not at all; . . . But let your communication be, Yea, Yea; Nay, Nay,'' and '' Resist not evil '' formed the basis of the Quaker beliefs.[11] Since the Quakers were dominant in the colony it was but natural that their ideas on the questions of the oath and war should be reflected in their legislation. By the law of 1682 it was specified that the solemn promise of the witness to speak the truth, the whole truth and nothing but the truth to the matter or thing in question was sufficient to qualify him. Had this state of freedom from interference persisted the oath would have disappeared, all Christians would have been honored with political privileges, all Deists with freedom of worship, and the colony would have played no part in wars. But this utopian state was not to exist. In 1689 began the long series of wars between England and France which involved the colonies. Unfortunately for the Quakers who disbelieved in all war, they were called upon to coöperate

10 Cal. State Paps., Col., 1681-1685, 3, 13; B. T. Jour., III, 253.
11 Sharpless, A Quaker Experiment in Government, 12-15; Trevelyan, England under the Stuarts, 312-315.

with the other colonies in the defense of the frontier. Despite royal orders, the Quaker assembly refused to put the colony in a state of defense or to aid New York to defend her frontier. The refusal led the crown in 1692 to deprive Penn of his powers of government and to place the province under the control of the royal governor of New York.[12] This was a premonition of the difficulties the Quakers were to suffer at the hands of the English government because of their religious principles. The institution of royal control paved the way for the undoing of Penn's cherished views as to political privileges. The royal commission to Fletcher, as governor of Pennsylvania, directed him to call an assembly whose members before taking their seats should subscribe to the provisions of the Toleration Act of 1689.[13] By this action a test of office now for the first time appeared in the province, and destroyed Penn's plan with respect to political privileges, for thereby Catholics, Jews, and Socinians were excluded from the assembly. It is curious to note that the Toleration Act, which in England was designed to grant freedom of worship to favored dissenting sects, was subverted to a political use in the colony. It is also noteworthy that this act, applicable only to England because the colonies were not mentioned therein, was extended to the colony by force of a royal order. In effect it was legislating for the colony by royal prerogative. To the imposition of this political test the members of the assembly made no protest, but the Quaker contingent objected to taking the oaths required by it. To meet this objection, fourteen Quakers by the grace and favor of Governor Fletcher were allowed '' for conscience sake '' to make the affirmation instead.[14] In 1694 Penn's powers of government were restored to him on his promise to see that the assembly obeyed the orders

12 See page 262.
13 *N. Y. Col. Docs.*, III, 856.
14 *Pa. Col. Recs.*, I, 398.

from. the crown as to defense. In the Frame of Government of 1696, drawn up by the colonists without Penn's consent, the English Toleration Act was made a test of office in the province.[15] This action together with the fact that no objection was made to the imposition of the Toleration Act as a test in 1693 makes plain that Penn's co-religionists did not share his advanced and enlightened views as to civil liberties. They wished a government by Protestant Christians only. In 1699, on Penn's return to the province, the old order was restored. By the Charter of Privileges of 1701 the principles of freedom of worship to all believers in one God and civil privileges to all Christions were reasserted and received further sanction in the laws of that year.[16] These acts still had to run the gauntlet of the home government.

The latter years of the reign of William III and the time of Queen Anne was a period of anxiety to the Quakers. The reasons for this are simple and clear. In the closing years of the reign of William III there developed reactionary tendencies against the stand taken in the Toleration Act. This movement reached its culmination in the reign of Queen Anne, when a wave of High Church feeling set in against toleration and dissent. Queen Anne was favorable to the High Church Tory party, and encouraged by royal support, the party sought to put into effect its policy against non-conformity. After several unsuccessful attempts, the Tories were able to secure the passage of two laws in the last years of Queen Anne's reign. These were the Occasional Conformity Act of 1711 and the Schism Act of 1714; the former designed to check the evasion of the test act by dissenters, the latter intended to place the education of children of dissenting parents in the hands of the Church.[17] It was under the influence

---

[15] Pa. Col. Recs., I, 50; Charters and Laws, 247-249.

[16] Pa. Col. Recs., II, 57; Pa. Statutes at Large, II, 3.

[17] Lecky, History of England, I, 55-105; Trevelyan, England under the Stuarts, 475-476, 485-486, 503-517.

of this reactionary movement at home that the Church became militant and aggressive in the colonies. Its reflex influence is seen in the establishment by law of the Anglican Church in Maryland and the Carolinas and of the growth of Anglicanism in other colonies.[18] The efforts of Penn and the Quakers to obtain the consummation of their ideals fell upon unpleasant times. In the sphere of politics the period is also marked by the institution of a closer control of the colonies as evidenced by the act of 1696, the creation of the Board of Trade, the establishment of admiralty courts and an orderly customs service in the colonies, and the efforts to vacate the colonial charters. Then for the first time the Board of Trade demanded obedience to that provision of the charter which required that the laws of the province be submitted to the royal review. The board frequently called into consultation the bishop of London on laws affecting the interests of Churchmen in the colonies, and under his influence many such laws were disallowed. Henry Compton, the bishop of London at this period, was most active in his zeal and care for the Church in America over which his episcopal jurisdiction extended. Moreover, Pennsylvania was to become acquainted for the first time with royal officials in the admiralty and customs service, all of whom were zealous Churchmen as well as active agents of imperial control. Such were the influences at work bringing the Anglican state-church system into conflict with the Quaker government and religion. It seems that the Church, from which the Quakers had hoped to flee, followed them into their new home.

Had the colony been peopled solely by the followers of Penn, or by those like the German Pietists, whose religious views were similar to those held by Quakers, or by those who were entirely indifferent on religious questions, there would have been slight cause for the home government to interfere with many of the Quaker ideals.

[18] Osgood, *Amer. Cols. in 17th. Cent.*, II, 325-332.

But this condition of affairs seldom existed. Within the province itself the Quakers were to meet with the sturdiest sort of opposition by the coming in of others who differed fundamentally from them on religious matters,. As those of the Anglican faith found their way into Pennsylvania, formed their congregations, erected their churches, and gained some influence in the community, there was bound to be a revival in the colony of the traditional enmity between Anglican and Quaker. In 1695 there was organized in Philadelphia, Christ Church, the first Anglican church in the colony.[19] It became the center of a strong and aggressive Anglican minority against the Quaker government on the tender questions of the oath and war. From this time on there always existed two parties in the province, the Quaker party and the Church party. From the very nature of the case a conflict was inevitable between those who believed in the ecclesiastical laws of England and those who fled to America to be out of reach of the Church's power; between those who were desirous of defending their homes and lives against the assaults of the French and Indians and those who believed all war was iniquitous. The Quakers, who formed the dominant party in provincial politics, were able to carry into actual practice their peculiar views; while the Anglicans could rely upon the support of the home government and the mother Church to safeguard their interests. The contest was violent and bitter.

The Episcopalians were weak in numbers but several circumstances combined to give them an influence all out of proportion to their numbers and position. They could look for support to the English government and the bishop of London. Then again there was established in 1701 by royal charter the Society for the Propagation of the Gospel in Foreign Parts.[20] It was organized by the English

[19] Watson, *Annals of Phila.*, (1877), I, 378.

[20] Humphries, *Historical Account of the Society for the Propagation of the Gospel*, 4-24.

bishops and other Churchmen, both lay and clerical, and the object was to provide "learned and orthodox ministers" to preach the gospel and administer the sacraments in America and to bring the colonists back into the arms of the historic church. In 1702, the Society sent out itinerant ministers, George Keith and John Talbot. They traveled from Massachusetts to the Carolinas preaching and organizing the scattered members of the Church into congregations. Great efforts were put forth especially in New Jersey and Pennsylvania, the strongholds of Quaker power.[21] Keith especially was very bitter in his attitude toward the Quakers and very active in his work among them on behalf of the Church. This bitterness is explained by the fact that he had been turned out of the Quaker fold in Pennsylvania. He took orders in the Episcopal Church and returned to America fired with zeal for the church of his new adoption. In the Quaker provinces he was able to win over quite a few Keithian Quakers. to the Anglican communion.[22] As a result of the work of the Society and its missionaries, the Church grew in New Jersey and Pennsylvania. Christ Church, Philadelphia, increased in membership, churches were organized at Chester and Radnor and other places in the province, and several in Delaware.[23] The Society supplied ministers and their salaries, while the English government contributed the passage money.[24] These churches became the centers of the keenest sort of enmity to the Quakers. The hatred of the missionaries toward the Quakers is evidenced by the fact that they classified Quakerism with heathenism, atheism, paganism, and, as one wrote, "God knows what." They were referred to as "pests" and

---

[21] Humphries, *op. cit.*, 31-36; Hills, *History of the Church in Burlington*, 18-23; *passim.*

[22] Hills, *op. cit.* 29-30, 45, 48-50, 52.

[23] Humphries, *op. cit.*, 27-28, 35, 60-72.

[24] Andrews and Davenport, *Guide to the Materials in British Archives*, 398.

their doctrines as "poisonous lyes." Talbot wrote that
Penn in his writings appeared to be a "greater Anti-
Christ than Julian the Apostate."[25] Such was the character of the feeling displayed by the Churchmen toward
the Quakers whose colony they had invaded. The Anglican position and influence was further strengthened by
the activity of the royal officials. Prior to 1697 there were
few agents of the crown in the colony or neighboring colonies, but with the establishment of a revenue service and
admiralty courts, Pennsylvania as well as other chartered
colonies for the first time became acquainted with men
who were not only active in enforcing imperial laws but
equally zealous on behalf of the Church. Moreover, the
hostility of the central government to the colonial charters
resulted in Maryland's becoming a royal province in 1690
and New Jersey in 1702.[26] The efforts of the royal agents
in Pennsylvania and the neighboring provinces, the work
of the Society and its missionaries, the activity of the
bishop of London and the central government, all combined to threaten and overthrow the "Holy Experiment."
Governors Cornbury of New Jersey and Nicholson of Maryland, Quary and Moore, royal officers in Pennsylvania,
were actively engaged in support of the Church, not only
in their respective colonies, but also in the near-by provinces.[27] Hence when we consider the strength and activity of all these various agents on behalf of Anglicanism
we are able to appreciate the lamentation of the Quakers

[25] Hills, 41, 43, 83, 115; Perry, *Hist. Collections rel. to the Amer. Col. Church*, II, 68, 69, 163.

[26] Mereness, *Maryland as a Proprietary Province*, 437 ff., Tanner, *Province of New Jersey*, (Columbia College Studies, XXX), 579-601.

[27] Nicholson, Quary, Basse and other royal agents contributed in money and material toward the churches in N. J. and Pa. Nichol-son was called the "Prime Benefactor and Founder in chief of all." Hills, 28, 37, 39, 41, 45, 59, 129, *passim;* Dorr, *History of Christ Church*, 37, 39. Queen Anne sent gifts to the churches at Phila. and Burlington, Hills, 132; Dorr, 37.

that they were being made dissenters in their own colony.
The difficulty of working out their own religious ideas
while remaining a dependency of England is well illustrated in several cases. The colonial law of 1700 legalized
the naming or writing of the days and months "as in
Scripture and not by heathen names." In place of the
calendar names for the days and months they were given
a numerical nomenclature.[28] This is indicative of the
Quaker scorn of pomp and love of simplicity. The home
government disallowed this law on the ground that a man
was privileged to call the names and days what he pleased,
and the Board of Trade characterized the law " as in-
significant and not fit to remain in force." [29] Such interference to say the least was unwarranted. By this law
the Quakers did not at all interfere with the calendar arrangement nor seek to impose their peculiar views on
others, but simply sought to legalize their own custom.
But the disallowance in this case as in many others did
not accomplish its design, for future laws legalized the
naming of the days and months according to the Quaker
custom. The whole situation is further illustrated in the
case of the Quaker law imposing penalties upon those
guilty of introducing stage-plays, masques, revels, bull
baiting, cock-fighting, or guilty of playing at cards, dice,
lottery and such like enticing games.[30] This act of 1700
was disallowed by the crown because " some innocent
sports are thereby prohibited without reason." [31] Twice
the law was reënacted although twice rejected by the
crown on the same ground.[32] The disallowance finally had
its effect, but it may be said that such unwarranted interference in the internal polity of the colony served to create
only disrespect for the will of the central government rather

[28] *Pa. Statutes at Large*, II, 19.
[29] *Ibid.*, 480.
[30] *Ibid.*, 4.
[31] *Ibid.*, 490.
[32] *Ibid.*, 186, 360, 525, 529, 543, 550.

than a proper regard for its authority. This lack of sympathy with colonial ideas simply illustrates the great weakness in the old British colonial system and it was without doubt one of the factors which tended to create discord and friction rather than a spirit of good-will between the two parts of the Empire.

As regards the principle of freedom of worship it will be remembered that the law of 1700 granted religious liberty to all believers in one God. This was not in accordance with the Toleration Act which granted religious liberty to all except Catholics, Jews and Socinians. When the colonial statute came before Attorney-General Northey for examination in 1705 he reported that it was not fit to be sanctioned because it showed no regard for the Christian religion nor for the Toleration Act, which obliged people to renounce the Papacy and to believe in the Blessed Trinity and in the inspiration of the Old and New Testaments, and he concluded his report with the words, '' none can tell what conscientious practices allowed by this act may extend to.'' [33]   The crown vetoed the law.[34]   But it is quite clear that at this time as in the time of Fletcher the Quakers did not share the enlightened views of Penn, which were too advanced for that narrow age. Upon notice of the objections and even before the act was vetoed, the assembly reënacted the law to obviate the objections, thus placing religious toleration on the basis of the English law.[35]   The Quaker assembly went further and fell away from their great leaders' high ideals with regard to political privileges, which by the law of 1700 were bestowed upon all Christians. The law of 1706 took the same stand as in Fletcher's time and made the Toleration Act a test of office.[36]   Although the excluded sects, Catholics, Jews and Socinians, formed no appreciable part of the popula-

[33] Pa. Statutes at Large, II, 489.
[34] Ibid., 450.
[35] Ibid., 171.
[36] Ibid., 219.

tion, yet the fact remains that the Quaker province down to 1776 denied religious and political liberty to those of the above faiths. On these questions there could be no conflict between the Quaker and the Churchman for the former acquiesced in the ideals of the latter. But it is interesting to note that the initiative on these points came from the English government by the exercise of its authority.

The real quarrel between Quaker and Anglican came over the oath and war. Of the latter question we shall treat in subsequent pages; it will be enough to say here that the refusal of the Quaker assembly to defend the province and to coöperate in the defense of the colonies against the French led to the downfall of Quaker power in politics. On the question of the oath there could be no compromise between those who believed in the sinfulness of the oath and those who held that the affirmation was detrimental to good government. The law of 1700 allowed those who for conscience's sake scrupled to take the oath to affirm in all cases whatever.[37] There was no intention to make the affirmation absolute to the entire exclusion of the oath; what the Quakers desired was simply to legalize their own ideas and not to force them upon others. Hence the law provided that a magistrate who scrupled not to administer the oath should be free to tender it to one who was free to take it, but the administration thereof was to be recorded as the act of the jurant magistrate only, although declared to be just as valid as if done in the name of the court. The difficulties of this position were serious. In the first place, while to the Quaker the affirmation was a sufficient obligation, by the Anglican it was considered to be deficient in binding force and not of the strength necessary to elicit the truth and accuracy of a statement or to qualify a person for office. Then again, it is essential to remember that a Quaker could neither tender nor re-

37 *Pa. Statutes at Large,* II, 39.

ceive an oath. This fact created a serious dilemma. It would happen that in cases cognizable before a single Quaker justice, or before a bench composed entirely of Quakers, if the oath was demanded the oath could not be given and a failure of justice would ensue. To this extent the law imposed the Quaker view on those who believed just as sincerely in the oath as did the Quaker in the affirmation. Moreover, this condition of affairs would allow an unscrupulous culprit to cheat justice by insisting upon an oath. Then again, this law was repugnant to the English statute of 1696 which forbade the use of the affirmation in giving evidence in criminal cases, in serving on juries, and in qualifying for an office of trust in the government. Although this statute did not extend to the colonies, it was but natural that the Churchmen in the province would claim the benefits of it.

The passage of the affirmation act of 1700 aroused a storm of protest from the members of Christ Church. In January, 1701, the vestry directed a complaint to the Board of Trade praying for a disallowance of the act and saying that the law infringed their religious rights as Churchmen guaranteed to them by the charter; that their lives, liberty and property were put in jeopardy contrary to English statute and common law by judges and juries not under oath; and that though burdened with taxes the Quaker government would provide no military defenses whatever.[38] Similar petitions were also directed to the archbishop of Canterbury and the bishop of London.[39] In October the vestry again addressed the Board of Trade praying for royal government in the province.[40] At this time they were especially desirous that the bill in Parliament to vacate the colonial charters should pass. It was felt that the charters stood in the way of the progress of the Church.

[38] *B. T. Paps., Props.*, VI, pt. 1, G 13; *Jour.*, XIV, 16.
[39] *Ibid., Props.*, VI, pt. 1, G 13.
[40] *Ibid., Props.*, VI, pt. 2, I 2.

Apprehension was felt lest the return of Penn to England to defend his charter should prejudice the passage of the bill. The vestry charged that the Quakers voted funds to Penn to aid in the charter's defense on his assurance that he would keep the Churchmen out of the province and the government in the hands of the Quakers. In order to show the need of royal government the memorial retailed several instances of gross irregularities alleged to have been committed in the province during Penn's sojourn there, 1699-1701. In one case involving a capital offense the grand jury refused to take the oath, and in another a Quaker guilty of a heinous offense was freed by trickery. The memorial concluded by saying that "if the records of this country be searched they will furnish a picture that will surfeit the world with Quaker tenets and practices." Other petitions were directed to the English prelates narrating instances of gross immoralities and irregularities too hideous to be disclosed.[41]   Penn felt very bitterly because of these unfair aspersions cast upon the fair name of the Quakers and his colony.   He laid his troubles to the activity of Quary with his " artful letters," helped by the bishop of London and Governor Nicholson of Maryland. Penn wrote, " Church is their Cry and to disturb us their Merit, whose labors have made this place; they misrepresent all we doe & would make us Dissenters in our own Countrey," and that although the Churchmen enjoyed many places of trust in the government " they must have all; and what they do not attempt in State, they do boldly in the pulpit."[42]   Penn wrote to Robert Harley, " They will have no office in the government unless they swear, and have power to swear others, because they know our government is under attests only, as may be easily thought, and then complain they cannot be admitted into the gov-

[41] " Some remarkable passages relating to ye Governt. of Pennsilva. from 1694 to 1701." *Clarendon Mss.*, (Bodleian Lib.) 102, ff. 24-32.

[42] *Pa. Archives*, 1st. ser., I, 141.

ernment because they are churchmen; a most abusive treatment of us "[43] Penn said further, "The spring of this in good measure had been from Colonel Nicholson of Virginia, a line from anybody to him, and from the Bishop to Dr. Bray his suffragan in Maryland, might quench this." It was not to be expected, as Penn wrote, that the Quakers would be "so self-denying as to let those who had no part of the heat of the day, not one-third of the number, and not one-fourth of the estate, and not one-tenth of the trouble and labor, should give laws to us, and make us dissenters, and worse than that in our own country."[44] These few statements show the nature as well as the bitterness of the struggle between those whose views on the question of the oath were so radically different.

The Anglicans came to the conclusion that the only way by which the interests of the Church might be advanced was through royal government in the province. Randolph, Nicholson, Quary, and Cornbury repeatedly urged the vacation of the charters not only for the sake of increased administrative efficiency in imperial concerns, but also because the charters stood as obstacles to the progress of the Church. This movement naturally was supported by the Anglicans, both lay and clerical, in the province. As early as 1697 Governor Markham charged Nicholson with stirring up a cabal against the Quaker government, with collecting evidence and affidavits in order to fasten calumny upon the chartered colonies, especially Pennsylvania; and with saying that "rebellion would not be treason" in order to bring about royal control.[45] Penn as well as Winthrop of Connecticut twice appeared before the Board of Trade to complain of the "imperious and arbitrary conduct of Col. Nicholson."[46] It has already been stated that

[43] *Duke of Portland Mss.*, IV, 32, Hist. Mss. Com. *Report* 15, pt. 4.
[44] *Ibid.*, 32, 80.
[45] *B. T. Paps., Props.*, II, B 3. 16.
[46] *B. T. Jour.*, IX, 276, 401. Cf. the charges against Nicholson by the council of Virginia. *Va. Magazine of History*, III, 373-382.

the vestry of Christ Church in 1701 appealed to the home government for royal protection. Likewise the people of Delaware asked for royal government chiefly because the Quaker assembly would provide no defense for the colony and territories.[47]

After the failure of the bill of 1701 in Parliament, Quary, then in England, laid before the Board of Trade a list of charges against the province. He came armed with addresses from the members of the assembly from Delaware asking for royal government, with letters from Christ Church, and various affidavits and depositions to show the prevalence of corrupt government under Quaker rule.[48] In April, 1702, Quary laid before the board this list of charges, a curious mixture of fact and fancy.[49] He asserted that a Quaker jury had come to a decision by flipping a coin, and instanced three other cases of partial and shoddy justice. Penn replied by saying that the jury had been punished and offered extenuating circumstances in explanation of the three cases.[50] On the whole the charges were very shallow indeed, and from a survey of the complaints one comes to the conclusion that the enemies of the Quakers in their zeal to advance the cause of the Church and royal government stooped to means which were devoid of justice and fair-play. It is manifestly unfair to seize upon chance irregularities which are bound to appear in any community, no matter how well ordered, and to dress them up to represent the true condition of affairs. It seems that this is what Quary and his followers were guilty of doing. Not only this. Churchmen sought to create disturbances in the province in order to be able to represent to the home government that anarchy prevailed there.[51] The purpose of such low measures was to

[47] B. T. Paps., Props., VI, pt. 2, I 6.
[48] Ibid., Jour., XIV, 389-391.
[49] Ibid., Props., VI, pt. 2, I 17; VII, M 21.
[50] Ibid., VI, pt. 2, I 19.
[51] James Logan wrote to Penn, 1702, "We are really unhappily

heap odium on the Quaker government in hopes of securing royal control.[52]

The Board of Trade lent a willing ear to Quary's charges. In May, it directed a letter to Penn requesting him to answer whether all officials in the colony take the oath as directed by English law or in lieu thereof the affirmation allowed to Quakers, and whether all persons are allowed to take the oath who are obliged and willing to do so.[53] Penn replied that the people engaged with him in founding the colony were chiefly Quakers and that the constitution and laws were made to meet their peculiar views; hence the solemn affirmation was the usual way of pledging faith to the crown and proprietor and in giving evidence, but that no attempt was made to force an attest on any one who desired the oath.[54] In January, 1703, the board reported to the Privy Council that it was absolutely necessary for the king's service and quite agreeable to the charter that the following measures should be enforced in the province. First, that all persons before entering upon office should take the oath enjoined by the laws of England or in lieu thereof the affirmation allowed to Quakers; second, that all who in England were obliged and willing to take the oath in any public or judicial proceeding should be permitted to do so in the province, and in case of default or refusal the proceedings should be

engaged here by lying exposed to such malicious spies, whose sedulity to serve a dishonest cause keeps their thoughts constantly on the tenters, and dresses up each trivial passage in their secret cabals into a monstrous shape of malfeasance, the real subject of which is so slight where acted, that the persons concerned in it scarce ever think of it more till they hear it roar from some mighty court or committee there, and made an argument for invading others' rights, though in itself scarce worthy of one thought of a man of business." *Penn-Logan Corres.*, I, 85-86.

[52] *Penn-Logan Corres.*, I, 218, 230, 343.

[53] *B. T. Paps., Props.*, Entry Bk. C, f. 475; Entry Bk. D, ff. 55, 170-172; *Jour.*, XV, 37.

[54] *Ibid.*, Entry Bk. D, ff. 258-260; *Props.*, VII, L 3.

deemed null and void.[55]   The council approved the report the same day and copies were dispatched to Quary, Nicholson and Cornbury whose hostility to the Quakers was a sufficient guarantee of its enforcement.[56]   Penn at once protested against the royal order on both religious and constitutional grounds.[57]   On religious grounds he declared that the enforcement of this order would practically render incapable of holding office the best and wealthiest of the Quakers who would then have nothing but their labor for their pains in founding the colony.   On constitutional grounds he held that the crown had no power to extend to the colonies by force of the prerogative a law of England wherein the colonies were not mentioned.   This, he held, was in effect legislating for the province by royal order contrary to the charter which granted the proprietor and the freemen of the colony power to make laws.   Penn said that the laws of the colony could be augumented only by the imperial Parliament or the provincial assembly, and he asked that the order be put in the form of an instruction, but to this the board would not listen.[58]

Armed with the royal order Quary appeared before the provincial council in May, 1703, to demand compliance.[59]   To the first part of the order which demanded that all persons before entering upon office should take the oath directed by the law of England, or in lieu thereof the affirmation allowed to Quakers, no objection was made since the Quakers were already in sympathy with the Toleration Act as a test of office.   But the last clause was sure to make trouble, for it meant that a failure of justice would follow in the case of an Anglican litigant and a Quaker court.   The situation is best explained in the words of the provincial council.   '' It will be very difficult, in Bucks

[55] B. T. Paps., Props., Entry Bk. D, ff. 285-288.
[56] Ibid., ff. 291-292, 306; Props., VII, L 22, 26.
[57] Ibid., Props., VII, L 18.
[58] B. T. Jour., XV, 396.
[59] Pa. Col. Recs., II, 89, 90, 97, 98.

almost impossible, to find a sufficient number of fit persons to make a quorum of justices, that will take or administer an oath; it will be a very great hardship to have none on the bench but such as can swear; for our Friends can no more be concerned in administering an oath than they can take one; and in all actions where the case pinches either party, if they can, from any corner of the government bring in an evidence that demands an oath, the cause must either drop, or a fit number of persons must be there always, to administer it, though only perhaps, on account of such an evidence."[60] In Philadelphia, after the court proceeded to business, when oaths came to be demanded the Quaker justices withdrew from the bench and left the administration of justice in the hands of those who could administer the oath.[61] The Quakers quite naturally complained that by such measures, they, who by toil and hardship had settled the colony, were "thrust out of all business."

It is evident that Quary and Moore, both royal officials, and other Churchmen, used this order as well as other means to cast discredit upon the government and to cause hardship to the Quakers.[62] This is evidenced by two cases. In March, 1703, Governor Hamilton died and according to law the government devolved upon the council *ad interim*. It became necessary then to administer to the council the oath enjoined by the acts of trade. The royal commission empowered six persons named to administer the oath. In June Quary appeared before the council to perform the obligation, but as a majority of the council were Quakers they asked that the affirmation be allowed

[60] *B. T. Paps., Props.*, VII, M 19; *Penn-Logan Corres.*, I, 215, 229, 239, 244.

[61] *Penn-Logan Corres.*, I, 236, 238.

[62] In 1703 Logan wrote to Penn, that Quary and John Moore, "his vice-regent in mischief as well as other offices," had laid plots to create confusion and have cause for complaints home. *Ibid.*, I, 238.

them instead. This request was denied on the ground that the commission did not warrant the administration of the affirmation. The council then fell back upon the alternative and John Bewley, the collector, was enjoined to appear and qualify the council. Bewley at first refused under pressure of Quary's threats, but after earnest solicitation on the part of the council, he acquiesced and administered the oath to two and the affirmation to the rest of the council.[63] In another case Governor Hamilton had issued a special commission of oyer and terminer directed only to such justices as could tender the oath. Hamilton deemed it best that capital offenses should be tried under oath, especially at this time when the Churchmen bitterly complained that persons were deprived of life, liberty, and property by courts not under oath.[64] The court opened and only such as could take the oath were summoned to jury duty, but when the oath was tendered to them " some refused for one reason, some for another and not one would act." The Quakers charged that the refusal of the jurors to be sworn was due to the intrigues of Quary and Moore. The latter held that the trial of these cases belonged properly to the regular provincial court and not to a special commission, and that the commission issued by Hamilton was in itself invalid because the governor had not received the crown's approbation as required by the law of 1696.[65] To the Quakers the action of Quary and Moore appeared to be simply a plot to create trouble and confusion in the province in order to urge upon the crown the necessity of establishing royal government. The cases were then tried by the regular court composed of Quaker justices and by jurors and witnesses under affirmation. One was condemned to be burnt in the hand for manslaughter and a woman was sentenced to death for the crime of infanti-

63 *Penn-Logan Corres.*, I, 215-216, 239; *B. T. Paps., Props.*, VII, M 19, 20.

64 *Penn-Logan Corres.*, I, 193-196, 217.

65 *B. T. Paps., Props.*, VII, L 50.

cide.[66] Quary immediately wrote to the Board of Trade
giving an account of the whole affair, saying that great
excitement prevailed in the province because the court had
not acted under oath and expressing amazement that the
court would take such action when it knew that there were
pending before the Board of Trade several complaints that
subjects were executed without the use of the oath.[67]
Cornbury of New Jersey likewise sent home a complaint.[68]
On receipt of these letters the board wrote to Penn directing him to instruct his governor to stop such proceedings.[69] Penn replied rather indignantly asking what right
Cornbury had to interfere in the province.[70]

The law of 1700 allowing the Quakers to affirm in all
cases did not come up for final consideration till 1705.
The Board of Trade objected that the affirmation was " not
sufficient."[71] Penn replied that he could see no reason
" to oust a people that made it a country from the government of it for their tenderness about an oath, that went
thither to avoid it with other things."[72] The plea availed
nothing and the law was disallowed by royal order of February, 1706.[73] Would the Quakers honor the royal order
of 1703 and the veto of 1706 by passing a law prejudicial
to themselves? or would they cast to the winds royal authority and reënact the law? The necessity of keeping
the government in their own hands and of protecting their
own interests led them to take the latter course. On notice of the board's objections and even before the law was
vetoed the assembly framed a bill of the same tenor as the
former. Governor Evans objected to it as contrary to the
royal order of 1703. This contention was correct, for as

66 Penn-Logan Corres., I, 195.
67 N. Y. Col. Docs., IV, 1045.
68 B. T. Jour., XVI, 187; Penn-Logan Corres., I, 205.
69 B. T. Paps., Props., Entry Bk. D, ff. 358, 360.
70 Ibid.; Props., VII, L 45; Entry Bk. D. f. 360.
71 Pa. Statutes at Large, II, 465.
72 Ibid., 468.
73 Ibid., 451.

the bill stood it meant that one who was obliged and willing to take an oath would be forced to take the affirmation before a court composed of Quakers. According to the construction placed upon the royal order by the assembly the bill was not contrary to it. The assembly admitted that there would be a failure of justice if no jurant magistrate was present on the bench, but held that the Queen did not intend that there should be a stoppage of justice or that the Quakers should be excluded from the government which would inevitably follow if the Quakers were compelled to administer the oath. This argument was hardly warranted by the terms of the royal order but the Quakers were driven to it by force of circumstances. The govenor held otherwise and not wishing to violate the royal order he requested the assembly either to draw up a bill consonant to the order, or else insert a suspending clause. The house yielded by inserting a clause to suspend the force of the law for a short period. In justification of his assent to the law the governor wrote to the Board of Trade declaring that the country would not be satisfied or the assembly content with any other sort of measure.[74]

At once the Church party was aroused to action. Quary wrote to the Board of Trade '' of that daring insolent Act . . . which directly struck at the Queens Prerogative by disowning her orders and Instructions . . .,'' and suggested that '' whenever the Government is in the Crown, all these confusions will be at end, provided the Quakers are excluded from having the administration of government in their hands.''[75] To the bishop of London the vestry of St. Paul's, Chester, addressed a memorial asking him to use his influence to secure the disallowance of the act and stating that the assembly raised money both on Quakers and non-Quakers in order to secure the crown's

[74] *B. T. Paps., Props.*, VIII, pt. 2, O 66, 67, 68; *Pa. Statutes at Large*, II, 507-511; *Pa. Col. Recs.*, II, 225-230; 236.

[75] *N. Y. Col. Docs.*, V, 17, 18, 19, 20.

approval of the law. The vestry held that there was no
danger of a failure of justice, as the Quakers alleged,
since in all the counties there existed sufficient persons
fitted to administer the oath if authorized to do so, but that
the real object of the Quakers was to exclude the Churchmen from the government.[76] The bishop laid this paper
before the Board of Trade with a letter in which he stig-
matized the law as a " new instance of Mr. Penns inso-
lence," and added " I presume the next fit of conscience
will be not to allow the sight or conservation upon their
holy ground (of those) that can take an oath or has already defiled himself with it." [77]   Christ Church, Philadelphia, employed George Willcocks, Quary's London
agent, to prevent the approval of the law and to secure
a renewal of the order of 1703.[78]   The plea of Christ
Church, like that of St. Paul's, was to the effect that the
Quakers desired to keep other persuasions from a share in
the government.   In July, 1706, the attorney-general reported favorably on the law.   Although, he said, the law
was contrary to the act of Parliament which forbade the use
of the affirmation in qualifying for public office, in serving
on juries, and in giving evidence in criminal cases, yet as
that statute did not extend to the province a law might
be made in the colony to allow the affirmation in such
cases " because the greatest part of the inhabitants are
Quakers."   His sole objection was to the clause which allowed a deposition in writing as good evidence in criminal
cases, which was considered " too hard." [79]   After a review of the report of the crown lawyer and the letter of
the bishop of London, the board decided to report the law
for disallowance unless Penn gave assurance that the assembly would modify it so that no court should sit to try

[76] B. T. Paps., Props., VIII, pt. 2, O 77.
[77] Ibid., Jour., XVIII, 353.
[78] Ibid., Props., VIII, pt. 2, O 82; Penn-Logan Cor., II, 235, 253.
[79] B. T. Paps., Props., VIII, pt. 2, O 78; Pa. Statutes at Large,
II, 513.

cases, either civil or criminal, unless there was always present on the bench a jurant magistrate, that those who refused to take the oath should be obliged to declare that they did so upon a " conscientious scruple " before admitted to take the affirmation, and that evidence in writing should be restricted solely to civil causes.[80]   The records disclose no response of Penn's to these conditions.   In November Willcocks presented to the board a paper of objections against the law.[81]   In summary, his chief objection was that the law tended to establish the Quakers in the government to the total exclusion of other sects and to the detriment of the Church, that it was contrary to the act of Parliament, that an affirmation was not of sufficient validity or solemnity to insure truth and justice in judicial proceedings or to bind a person to a faithful execution of a public office, and that a deposition in writing was unjust in criminal causes.   The board was slow to take action and in January, 1707, Willcocks urged a report.[82]   In July the board granted a hearing to Willcocks and Penn and the objections were given to Penn to answer in writing.[83]   In October Penn replied in a paper which characterized the charges as " frivolous, not to say malicious, to our persuasion," and declared that the object of the Churchmen was to disqualify the Quakers from a share in their own government. " Is it not very hard," said Penn, " that these Gentlemen Should make us Dissenters in our own Country? and effect themselves our Lords and Masters of life, Liberty and Property." [84]   Both sides claimed that it was the intention of the one to exclude the other from participating in the government.   Whatever the intention of each party may

---

80 *Pa. Statutes at Large*, II, 513-514; *B. T. Jour.* XVIII, 354.

81 *B. T. Jour.*, XVIII, 394; *Props.*, VIII, pt. 2, O 81; *Pa. Statutes at Large*, II, 514-518.

82 *Pa. Statutes at Large*, II, 520; *B. T. Jour.*, XIX, 26, 286.

83 *B. T. Jour.*, XIX, 293, 307, 310.

84 *B. T. Paps.*, *Props.*, IX, P 11; for rejoinder of Willcox, *ibid.*, P 15; *Jour.*, XIX, 335, 387, 402.

have been the fact remains that the diverse views of the two sects on the question of the oath or affirmation which allowed of no compromise meant that either one or the other must be excluded in part from sharing in government. Had the English law, for which the Churchmen contended, been enforced in the province, the Quakers would have been compelled either to withdraw from politics or give up their cherished views on the affirmation. On the other hand had the Quakers forced the Churchmen to take the affirmation when an oath could not properly be administered, the latter would have been excluded from government. The final outcome of the whole affair in England was that the board reported the law for disapproval, and this was done by the royal order of June, 1708.[85] But it is interesting to note that the law was condemned by the board not on the ground of the affirmation but solely on the objection of the crown lawyer that paper evidence should not be allowed in criminal causes.[86] It seems evident that the home government did not support the contentions of the Churchmen and the bishop of London, but were inclined to allow the Quakers to affirm in all cases. This favorable attitude of the board is probably due to the fact that in 1707 the Tory membership was replaced by Whigs who were lenient to dissent.

Some of the Quakers recognized the inconsistency of their position on the question of the oath. Isaac Norris, an eminent Quaker, wrote to Penn, '' We say, our principles are not destructive to or repugnant to Civill Government, and will admit of liberty of conscience to all; Yet it appears, according to the best scheme I can form, from the opinion of many Friends, to be concerned in Government and hold them, we must either be independent and by ourselves; or, if mixed, partial to our own opinion, and not allow liberty to others, who make conscience they say,

[85] *B. T. Paps., Props.*, Entry Bk. F, ff. 22-23, 26; *Pa. Statutes at Large*, II, 506.
[86] *Pa. Statutes at Large*, II, 523.

to have an oath, we desire from them; or be as thou used
to express it, ' Dissenters in our own country.' '' [87]   The
Quakers did not believe in any connection whatsoever between church and state, yet in their effort to support and
defend their religious principles by law they made themselves guilty of forcing their views on others who held opposite opinions.   This is true not only on the question of
the oath but also in relation to war.   The Quaker assembly
refused to establish a militia or to provide military supplies and defenses against the French and therefore they
were acting not on behalf of the people who desired military protection but only for the Quaker sect which was
principled against war.   The inconsistency of their position led men like Isaac Norris and James Logan to advise
Penn to surrender his powers of government to the
crown.[88]   This fact together with the hostility of the home
government to colonial charters led Penn in 1703 to make
proposals to the crown looking to a surrender of his governmental powers.   The negotiations dragged on till 1712
when a deed of surrender was on the point of being consummated only to fail by reason of Penn's serious illness
which incapacitated him from further business.[89]

Upon notice of the veto of the law of 1706 the assembly
set to work to frame another of the same tenor, thus showing slight regard for the royal will in their determination
to safeguard their interests.   Governor Gookin, himself a
Churchman, refused his consent.   The next assembly submitted a bill more conformable to the governor's wishes
and it was passed into law.   Comparing the act of February, 1711,[90] with its predecessors we notice that whereas
the former laws obliged one who desired the oath to take
an affirmation when the court was composed wholly of
Quakers, the present law provided that nothing therein

[87] *Penn-Logan Corres.*, II, 431.
[88] *Ibid.*, I, 226, II, 119, 138-139, 167-168, 190, 225, 239-240, 423.
[89] See page 364.
[90] *Pa. Statutes at Large*, II, 355.

should hinder a magistrate or proper officer from administering the oath to one who had no scruples against taking it. No attempt was made to impose the affirmation upon those who were willing and desirous to take the oath. This is significant, for it shows that the Quakers were yielding under the stress of opposition. Curiously enough protest against the approval of this law came not from the Churchmen in the colony, but from the vestry of St. Mary's, Burlington, in New Jersey. This church was the center of Anglicanism in West Jersey. The minister and vestry of Christ Church, Philadelphia, notified their brethren across the river of the passage of the law.[91] St. Mary's drew up a petition to the Queen praying for the royal disapproval of the act.[92] Addresses were also sent to the bishop of London and the Earl of Clarendon, the former Lord Cornbury, to solicit their influence against the offending law.[93] This action was taken because the Churchmen feared that the passage of the Pennsylvania law would influence the New Jersey assembly to enact a similiar law. In fact such a bill passed the lower house in that province in 1710 only to fail in the council. The petition to the Queen opens with the statement that the admission of the Quakers to public offices retarded the royal service, obstructed the peace of the province and was a damp to the " best of Churches the Church of England." It expressed great fear for the ruin of both the church and state if the Quakers were allowed to govern the colony and to administer justice without oaths, so contrary to English law. The specific objection to the law was that it provided for an affirmation which omitted the name of God. This omission was contrary to the affirmation provided by English law which specified the following attest: " I, A. B., do declare in the presence of Almighty God the witness of the

[91] Hills, *History of the Church in Burlington*, 134.
[92] *B. T. Paps., Props.*, IX, Q.17; *Acts of Privy Council, Col.*, II, 654; *Pa. Statutes at Large*, II, 536-538.
[93] Hills, *op. cit.*, 135.

truth of what I say.'' The Quakers held that the use of the divine name in an affirmation approximated an oath. The petition was turned over to the Board of Trade. Twice Penn attended the board to support the law,[94] but in spite of all, it was reported to the Privy Council for disallowance on the ground that it was contrary to the act of Parliament which required the name of God in the affirmation and forbade the use of the attest in criminal causes.[95] It is significant to note that the report of the board was signed by the bishop of London, a thing rarely done, and is indicative of the activity of this prelate in the interests of the Church in America. The law was vetoed by order in council of December, 1711.[96]

The royal veto availed nothing for in June, 1712, a new act was placed on the statute book which in effect was similar to the one just negative.[97] To this law the solicitor-general made the very same objections as did the board on the previous measure.[98] The law was disallowed in February, 1714.[99] In the next year the assembly enacted two laws in the hopes that one would escape annulment. The one provided an affirmation with the name of God inserted for those who could take the attest in this form, the other omitted the divine name to ease the consciences of those who objected to taking the affirmation in the other form.[100] These acts did not reach the board till 1718 and it was charged in an unsigned letter to that body that the laws were withheld in order to escape the royal disallowance.[101] This is not a true statement of the reasons for delay. The records show that the laws were trans-

[94] *B. T. Jour.*, XXII, 446, XXIII, 23, 33; *Pa. Statutes at Large*, II, 538, 539.

[95] *Pa. Statutes at Large*, II, 540.

[96] *Ibid.*, 535; *B. T. Paps., Props.*, IX, Q 29.

[97] *Pa. Statutes at Large*, II, 425.

[98] *Ibid.*, 549-550; *Pa. Archives* 1st. ser., I, 157ff.

[99] *Pa. Statutes at Large*, II, 543.

[100] *Ibid.*, III, 39, 58.

[101] *Ibid.*, II, 441; *B. T. Paps., Props.*, X, Q 150.

mitted to England in 1716 and failed to be submitted to the board in consequence of Penn's serious illness. In 1718 Joshua Gee, a mortgagee of the province, promptly submitted the laws to the Board of Trade when notified of the delay.[102] The law which inserted the name of God in the affirmation received the royal approbation in July, 1719, but the other omitting the name was again vetoed.[103]

Meanwhile another question arose to cause perplexity in the province. In 1715 Parliament extended to the colonies the act of 1696 which forbade the use of the affirmation in qualifying for public office, in serving on juries, and in giving evidence in criminal causes.[104] On the other hand the colonial laws of 1715 allowed the use of the affirmation in such cases and although the home government had not yet acted upon them they were undoubtedly null and void as contrary to the English statute. But the assembly did not think so. In October, 1716, the assembly asked the judges of the provincial court why justice in several criminal causes was so long delayed. They replied that the governor, from whose power their commissions were derived, held that the colonial laws were abrogated by the recent statute of Parliament, and hence they thought it imprudent to act in defiance of this opinion.[105] The assembly then passed a resolution that the laws of the province were valid till vetoed by the crown, and since the laws of 1715 had not been so vetoed they were in force in spite of the recent act of Parliament.[106] The position of the assembly was hardly tenable, for there is little doubt that an English statute, passed after the enactment of a colonial law and before the latter was acted upon at home,

---

[102] *B. T. Paps., Props.*, X, Q 155; *Pa. Statutes at Large*, II, 443-445.

[103] *B. T. Paps., Props.*, X, Q 170; *Pa. Statutes at Large*, II, 440, 458, 465.

[104] I George I, c. 6.

[105] *Pa. Votes of Assembly*, II, 194.

[106] *Ibid.*, 195.

took precedence over it.   The question was not settled for
several years; but as the crown did not act upon the laws
of 1715 till 1719 and as there was need of setting the
wheels of justice in motion to prevent crime and relieve
the prisoners languishing in jail, the colony sought to
remedy matters by the law of May, 1718.[107]   This law provided that in all cases whatsoever, civil as well as criminal,
judges, jurors, and witnesses could qualify according to
their religious views, by taking either the oath or affirmation prescribed by English law.   The new law was just
as repugnant to the English statute as were the laws of
1715.   Why then did Governor Keith assent to it and declare the former acts void?   Probably because the prevalence of crime necessitated the administration of justice.
The assembly drew up an address to the crown and appropriated £150 to employ an agent to solicit the royal
confirmation.   Thomas Beake, assisted by Joshua Gee and
Henry Gouldney, two of the mortgagees of the province,
acted as agent for the law.[108]   Richard West, counsel to
the Board of Trade, reported that the law was proper to
be confirmed.[109]   In turn the board represented to the
Privy Council that the law granted the Quakers greater
privileges than allowed them in England, but in consideration of the fact that without this concession the administration of justice in the province would be difficult, the law
was worthy of the crown's approval.[110]   In May, 1719, the
law was confirmed by royal order,[111] and two months later

107 *Pa. Statutes at Large*, III, 199.
108 *Pa. Votes of Assembly*, II, 235-236, 240, 242, 272.
109 *B. T. Paps., Props.*, Entry Bk. G, ff. 162, 163; *Props.*, X, pt. 2,
Q 169.
110 *Ibid.*, Entry Bk. G, f. 172; *Props.*, X, pt. 2, Q 170; *Pa. Statutes
at Large*, III, 438.
111 *Pa. Statutes at Large*, III, 437; *B. T. Paps., Props.*, Entry Bk.
G, f. 204; *Props.*, X, pt. 2, Q 180.   At this point the question arises
as to what authority the crown could take upon itself the power to
confirm a colonial law contrary to an act of Parliament which
mentioned the colonies.   The crown had the power to issue orders

similar action was taken on one of the laws of 1715. Thus at last after twenty years of trial and vexation the Quakers won the right to use the affirmation in all cases whatever. In one particular, however, the Quaker contentions were not yet realized. One of the laws of 1715, that which provided an affirmation with the name of God omitted, had been vetoed in 1719. Three years later the Quaker conscience on this question was eased by the action of Parliament itself. The English statute of 1722 granted greater indulgences to the Quakers by providing new forms of attestation which omitted the name of God.[112] In 1724 the assembly passed a law specifying the new forms [113] and Joshua Gee was employed to obtain the royal confirmation.[114] No objections were made at home and the law was sanctioned by the crown in March, 1725.[115] Great was the rejoicing of the Quakers when the glad tidings were received. The assembly and the Yearly Meeting of the Friends sent addresses to the crown offering thanks and expressing a sense of obligation to George I for his gracious favor to the Quakers.[116]

With the accession of George I the spirit of England toward dissent had changed. The advent of the House of Hanover and the rise to power of the Whig classes, favorable to dissent, saw the repeal of the Schism Act and the Occasional Conformity Act, the work of the Tory reactionaries. Likewise, greater indulgence was granted to

in accordance with acts of Parliament or where the legislature gave it discretionary power, but it is not clear by what authority the crown could exercise a right to dispense with the provisions of an act of Parliament. This question, as many others, simply illustrates the loose constitutional relations which existed between England and the colonies.

[112] 8 George I, c. 6.
[113] Pa. Statutes at Large, III, 427.
[114] Ibid., 516; B. T. Jour., XXXIV, 321.
[115] Pa. Statutes at Large, III, 514, 516, 517; B. T. Paps., Props., XI, R 50, 56, 57.
[116] Pa. Bundle, Amer. and W. I., 28, (P. R. O.) XXIV, 10, 11; Sharpless, A Quaker Experiment in Gov't., 145-146.

dissent, as seen in the law of 1722 favorable to Quaker interests.[117] The Church became less aggressive in the colonies. The Society for the Propagation of the Gospel was less active. Henry Compton, the zealous bishop of London, was now dead, as was Quary the leader of the opposition of the Churchmen to the Quakers in Pennsylvania. The year 1713 saw the close of the first half of the war against France and for twenty-six years the Quakers were freed from anxiety on account of defense. Still such was the opposition of the colonial Churchmen, supported by the government and prelacy at home, that the Quakers were not able to obtain the full realization of their ideals. They sought to legalize their principles on the question of the affirmation but in so doing they perforce imposed the affirmation in some cases on those who believed just as sincerely in the validity of the oath. In this particular they were forced finally to yield under the persistent attacks of the Churchmen, and after 1711 to allow an oath where an oath was required. But as Sharpless says, "the two systems did not work side by side without friction."[118] The Quakers could not administer oaths in any way whatever and were consequently excluded from any office which demanded the administration of the oath. Under these circumstances the Quakers either withdrew from such positions in government or else retained office and violated their religious principles.[119]

Considering the whole situation from the standpoint of the imperial relations, one is impressed with the meddlesome attitude of the royal officials, such as Quary, Moore, Nicholson, Cornbury, Basse and others, not only in their official capacity, but also as supporters of the Church. Their tendency, as Penn expressed it, was "to do us all despite they can in the name of the church and the revenue

[117] Lecky, *History of England*, I, 274 ff.
[118] Sharpless, *op. cit.*, 146.
[119] *Ibid.*, 146-149.

. . . to serve every turn of advantage or revenge.''[120]
Such conduct served rather to weaken than to strengthen
the ties which bound the colonies to the mother country.
One is also impressed with the unwarranted interference
of the Board of Trade and Privy Council in the internal
affairs of the colony in such cases as the disallowance of
laws legalizing the Quaker customs with regard to the
calendar nomenclature and forbidding certain sports and
games. But on the question of the affirmation, the attitude
of the crown was neither unjust or arbitrary. In fact, the
crown was not inclined to grant the wishes of colonial
Churchmen that the oath should be imposed according to
English statute, but showed a decided willingness to grant
the Quakers the right to use the affirmation in all cases.
But when the Quakers sought to impose an affirmation on
those who desired the oath, the disallowance of such laws
was justified in order to prevent a miscarriage of justice.
In brief, the crown simply upheld the principle of religious
toleration, in which the Quakers themselves professed belief but failed to practice consistently. In this respect,
the veto was effective and salutary, and the Quakers were
forced to yield.

The vexations of the Quakers had not yet come to an end.
The colony as part of the Empire became involved in the
long series of wars between England and France for the
mastery of North America. The question of local and imperial defense against the French and Indians drew into
the vortex of controversy the religious principles of the
Quakers who believed that all war was wrong. The next
chapters concern themselves with this phase of the relations between the province and the home government.

[120] *Duke of Portland Mss.*, IV, 80, Hist. Mss. Com., *Report* 15,
pt. 4.

CHAPTER NINE

IMPERIAL DEFENSE, 1689-1748.

Few questions arose in the history of the Empire to create greater perplexity than the serious problem of defense. It was a problem so impossible of solution that it not only caused the overthrow of Quaker political power in the province, but of far greater import, it '' was the rock upon which the old Empire was shattered.''

From the days of Hawkins and Drake to the close of the last French war in 1763, the Empire was almost continually at war with the rival powers of France and Spain for supremacy of trade and dominion in the new world. The indeterminate boundary lines which marked the respective territorial claims of these rival nationalties laid deep the foundations of bitter wars. The struggle of European powers for commercial and colonial supremacy brought on a long series of international wars. The whole situation from the standpoint of the colonies as well as the Empire was fraught with serious problems. In 1760 Franklin stated the case thus: '' Our North American colonies are to be considered as the frontier of the British Empire on that side. The frontier of any dominion being attack'd, it becomes not merely the ' cause ' of the people affected, (the inhabitants of that frontier) but properly the ' cause ' of the whole body.'' [1] The problem then presented itself: what share of the cost of defending the Empire in America should be borne by the colonists and what share should fall to the lot of the English tax-payer.[2] The problem of

[1] Franklin, *Works* (Smyth ed.), IV, 50.
[2] Beer, *British Col. Policy, 1754-1765*, 6-15.

protection had both a military and naval aspect. The
coastal defense of the colonies in time of war, the system
of convoys to protect merchantmen plying to and fro between the mother country and America,[3] and protection on
the high seas in that age of keen international rivalry was
a burden placed entirely upon the English sea power and
a charge supported entirely by the English treasury. It
was also recognized that at a time when the Empire was
at peace in Europe, the burden of defense against a purely
local enemy, such as the Indians, should fall upon the
colony or colonies involved. But at a time when the Empire was at war, the problem of distributing the burden
was not so easy of solution. The home government did
not tax the colonists directly or indirectly in order to
create a revenue to support the charges of war. It was
content to rely upon a system of requisitions, merely calling upon the colonies to vote men and money to coöperate
with other colonies and the home government in military
operations. Such a system left it entirely to the local
legislatures to comply with the royal orders or to refuse
to comply. In this chapter and the next we shall endeavor
to describe the operations of this system.

As far as the province of Pennsylvania was concerned
this problem was complicated by the peculiar views of the
Quakers upon the subject of war. One of the cardinal
tenets of this sect was the belief in the iniquity of all war.
Briefly stated, military non-resistance in its most extreme
form, except for local police protection, was the accepted
belief.[4] The biblical injunction '' Resist not evil '' was
accepted as literally as the command '' Swear not at all.''
But the efforts of the Quakers to work out in actual practice this utopian view fell upon an unfortunate age.
Hardly had the province been founded when the Empire

---

[3] For Convoys, see *Acts of the Privy Council, Col.*, II, index under
convoys.
[4] Sharpless, *A Quaker Experiment in Gov't.*, ch. 7.

became involved with France in a long series of wars for mastery in North America. The colony as part of the Empire found itself concerned not only in the question of local defense against the encroachments of the French, but also in the duty of coöperating with neighboring colonies and England in a cause which was of common concern. Would the Quakers, dominant in the assembly, belie their doctrines and enter heartily into the war, or would they remain true to their convictions and refuse to honor the royal requisitions?

In April, 1689, the colonies were notified of the declaration of war against France, known in colonial annals as King William's War.[5] A few days later the Lords of Trade recommended to the Privy Council that as the proprietary governments of Pennsylvania, Maryland, and the Carolinas were not under immediate royal control, they should be directed by royal order to put their dominions in a state of defense.[6] Governor Blackwell of Pennsylvania placed this order before the provincial council and requested that a militia be established. The replies of the Quaker councilors are significant. Said one, ''I see no danger, but from the Bears and Wolves ''; said another, '' the raising of arms would arouse the Indians ''; and a third replied that the English king knew full well '' the judgment of the Quakers in this case before Governor Penn had his patent.''[7] These words were simply a premonition of the arguments to be used by the Quakers to evade compliance with the royal requisitions. Blackwell threatened to report the matter to the king and to Penn, but whether he did or not is a matter of conjecture.[8] It is certain, however, that in this instance the Quaker assembly made no provision for the defense of the colony.

But the situation involved more than putting the colony

5 *B. T. Jour.*, VI, 207.
6 *Ibid.*, VI, 211; *Pa. Col. Recs.*, I, 302.
7 *Pa. Col. Recs.*, I, 306.
8 *Ibid.*, I, 311.

itself into a posture of defense. It involved coöperation in the common undertaking of securing the protection of all. In the earlier days the crucial point was the St. Lawrence Valley. This territory was of prime importance to both England and France as the natural highway leading to the Great West beyond. With the explorations of Lasalle, Marquette, and Joliet, and the building of forts and trading posts along the great lakes under the able administration of Governor Frontenac, France had taken determined steps to establish her claim, not only to the region drained by the St. Lawrence, but also to the wide expanses of the Mississippi Valley. French activity threatened English claims to the interior of the continent. The control of the situation was in the hands of the Iroquois Indians who had their home in the St. Lawrence Valley. This strong confederacy could be used by either side to check the expansion of the other westward and it became the policy of the rival nations to secure the friendship and aid of the savages.[9] With these facts clearly in mind we are able to understand why the defense of the New York frontier and the establishment of friendly relations with the Indians were objects of common concern and not burdens which were to be borne solely by the colony of New York and the home government.

In 1689 the storm broke along the whole northern frontier and the French and their savage allies carried death and destruction into the English settlements. In July, 1691, Governor Sloughter of New York called upon all the colonies north of Carolina for aid.[10] After stating the designs of the French and the consequent danger to all the colonies, he asked from each a quota of one hundred and fifty men for the defense of the frontier and the dispatch of a commissioner to meet with the governor of

[9] Channing, *Hist. of U. S.*, I, ch. 5; Osgood, *Amer. Cols. in 17th. Cent.*, II, 426.

[10] *Cal. State Paps., Col.*, 1689-1692, 503; *N. Y. Col. Docs.*, III, 184.

New York to concert measures for common defense and to agree upon the raising of a common fund for the support of the military operations. The responses illustrate well the lack of a community of interests and the prevalence of a spirit of particularism and jealousy among the colonies. The New England colonies claimed that they had their own frontiers to defend and were consequently unable to send aid to New York.[11] Maryland sent a small sum and a complaint that it was unfair to ask her to contribute as much as Pennsylvania and Virginia whose population and trade were more considerable.[12] Pennsylvania responded that she was unable to comply with the request because of the poverty of the province.[13] None of the colonies sent commissioners to New York.

New York was unable to bear the burden alone by reason of her meager population and resources. It was not just that an obligation which was of vital concern to all should be borne by only one colony and New York in her distress carried the case to the English government. In 1692 frequent petitions reached the crown from this colony asking that the power of the home government be used to compel the other colonies to aid in the defense of the New York frontier.[14] These petitions stated that people were leaving the province for other colonies in order to escape the expenses and burdens of war whereby the trade of New York was decayed, her strength diminished, and her revenue lessened and that the colony by its own exertions was unequal to the burden of defending Albany, the key to the situation. In consequence of these pleas, in October, 1692, royal letters were directed to the colonial governors

11 *Cal. State Paps., Col.*, 1689-1692, 475, 477, 508, 531; *N. Y. Col. Docs.*, III, 786.

12 *Cal. State Paps., Col.*, 1689-1692, 515, 669; *N. Y. Col. Docs.*, III, 788.

13 *Cal. State Paps., Col.*, 1689-1692, 513, 514, 525; *N. Y. Col. Docs.*, III, 789, 791.

14 *Cal. State Paps., Col.*, 1689-1692, 700.

north of Carolina to assist New York with men and money
when called upon and to appoint representatives to meet
and agree upon the quotas.[15]
But the action of the central government went further.
Frequent complaints assailed the ears of the home authorities as to the irregularities committed in the chartered
colonies, free from royal control.[16] They were accused
of harboring pirates and fugitives from justice, of disobedience to the acts of trade, and by refusing to aid in war
measures drew into their bounds people who wished to escape this burden in the frontier colonies. Time and again
royal appointees in the colonies had urged the vacation of
the charters and the substitution of royal control as the
only solution of the problem. In order to increase the
strength of the province the government of New York
urged either the restoration of the original boundaries
under the patent to the Duke of York, which would have
included Connecticut west of the Connecticut River and
New Jersey, and in addition the colonies of Pennsylvania
and Delaware; or else the revival of the old Dominion of
New England as it existed under the administration of Andros.[17] In June, 1691, Governor Nicholson of Virginia,
wrote to the Lords of Trade that as long as the charters
remained in force these colonies would be in a state of
anarchy.[18] As to Pennsylvania he said, since the Quaker
government refused to provide defenses of any sort, the
province offered itself an easy prey to the conquest of the
French, especially if the people are of " Penn's pernicious
principles they may hold correspondence with the French
and Indians by land and the French by sea." This was
not the only charge that the sympathy of Penn for the
exiled Stuarts, whose cause was now championed by Louis

15 *Cal. State Paps., Col.*, 1689-1692, 717, 718.
16 *Ibid.*, 473-474, 602, 703-704.
17 *Ibid.*, 513, 514, 520; *N. Y. Col. Docs.*, III, 789, 791, 796, 812,
833, 836.
18 *Cal. State Paps., Col.*, 1689-1692, 473-474.

XIV, would probably lead to the acquisition of his province by the French.[19] The receipt of this letter brought the Lords of Trade to the resolution to recommend to the Privy Council that the province should be taken under royal control and annexed to some adjoining royal province.[20] No action was taken at the time but the frequency of the complaints led to the granting of the royal commission to Benjamin Fletcher in May, 1692, creating him governor of New York and Pennsylvania.[21] There is no doubt that this grant was a war measure induced by the exigencies of the struggle with France. Penn wrote that the usurpation of his powers of government was due to the misrepresentations of the neighboring colonies that because of the Quakers the French would make their way into the colony.[22] In the case of Connecticut the powers of government were not taken away from the corporation, but the command of her militia was transferred by royal commission to Fletcher.[23] This transfer of the government of one colony and the command of the militia of another met in part the request of New York for greater resources, but it was not a true solution of the problem. The root of the trouble lay in the fact that each colony was a distinct unit, organized with its separate machinery of government, and able thereby to thwart the commands of the English government.

In May, 1693, Fletcher met the assembly of Pennsyl-

[19] *Cal. State Paps., Col.*, 1689-1692, 200, 704; 1693-1696, 126. Among the Stuart papers there is a proposal of Thomas Willis, of April, 1716, in which he devises a scheme to collect money to effect a restoration of the Stuarts. It was proposed that several of the collectors should be from " such of the Quakers as are called Pennites, many of them being men of consideration and as ready to contribute to a restoration as any." *Stuart Papers*, IV, 28, in Hist. Mss. Com. *Reports*. See also Bruce, *Institutional Hist. of Va.*, I, 247-248.

[20] *Cal. State Paps., Col.*, 1689-1692, 551.

[21] *Ibid.*, 602, 624, 629, 638, 661, 725.

[22] *Ibid.*, 744.

[23] *N. Y. Col. Docs.*, IV, 29.

vania and presented the royal order calling for assistance
to New York on demand. At first he received a refusal,
but a threat to dissolve the assembly was sufficient to elicit
a grant of money on the express condition that it should
not be " dipt in blood," but used " to feed the hungrie
and clothe the naked " savage.[24] Thus the Quakers did
not go on record as absolutely refusing the demand of the
home government, but in order to stand by their principles
and to ward off censure from the English authorities,
granted assistance provided it should not be employed directly in war-like measures. Fletcher made continual
complaints to the home government that nothing could be
expected from this colony as long as the government was
in the hands of the Quakers.[25] But Pennsylvania with
her Quaker régime offered no more trouble than did the
other colonies. Connecticut considered the royal commission to command her militia contrary to her charter and in
consequence Fletcher was compelled to depart in disappoint-
ment from that colony as he had from Pennsylvania.[26]
Moreover, the royal order of 1692 to other colonies met with
little compliance. Phips of Massachusetts held that the
transfer of the command of the militia of Connecticut and
Pennsylvania made it less reasonable for New York to ask
aid from other colonies.[27] Three colonies sent money, one
sent a few troops, and only one a representative to New
York.[28] Since the colonies would not unite through commissioners to agree upon the quotas of men and money to be
furnished by each one, it became necessary for the central
government to intervene. As a result, in August, 1694, the
English government fixed the number to be supplied by
each colony for the defense of New York.[29]

[24] Pa. Col. Recs., I, 399, 400.
[25] Cal. State Paps., Col., 1693-1696, 171, 235.
[26] Ibid., 192-199; N. Y. Col. Docs., IV, 69-71.
[27] Cal. State Paps., Col., 1693-1696, 157, 164.
[28] Ibid., 89, 112, 154, 164, 169, 171, 172, 191.
[29] Ibid., 299, 315, 316, 335-336.

In the same year Penn's powers of government were restored on condition that he at once return to his province, take over the government, provide for the safety of the colony, and transmit to the council and assembly all royal orders to that end.[30] Penn expressed his opinion that the assembly would '' dutifully comply and yield obedience '' to all royal requisitions, but accepted the stipulation that if the orders were not obeyed the government was to be handed back to Fletcher. Despite Penn's belief the royal order was ignored in the colony, Penn was unable to return at once to America, nothing was done to put the colony in a state of defense, and the government was not restored to Fletcher. The quota to be supplied by Pennsylvania for New York was the small number of eighty men. In May, 1695, Governor Markham laid the requisition before the house and met with a refusal.[31] Finally in October of the next year £300 was granted for the relief of the distressed Indians of New York.[32] Little more was done by the other colonies in response to the royal order of 1694. Some of them claimed that they were too poor, others that they had their own problems of defense to solve and therefore could send no assistance to New York.[33] Virginia, Maryland, and Massachusetts appealed to the home government to exempt them from the royal order for the reasons just stated.[34] Virginia voted £500 and Maryland £200, and the crown instructed Fletcher to accept this money in lieu of personal service.[35] The money was a welcome addition to the resources of New York, but it did not supply the military forces of which the province stood so

[30] Cal. State Paps., Col., 1693-1696, 245, 308, 310, 316, 317, 321, 335. Cf. Sharpless, A Quaker Experiment in Gov't., 193.

[31] Pa. Col. Recs., I, 486-487.

[32] Ibid., 492-495; Charter and Laws, 255; B. T. Paps., Props., II, B 3, 19, 20.

[33] Cal. State Paps., Col., 1693-1696, 361, 385, 477, 540, 560, 584, 593, 597.

[34] Ibid., 383, 390, 493, 499, 635.

[35] Ibid., 635, 636; Acts of Privy Council, Col., II, 227, 228.

badly in need. New York appealed to England for troops
and in response four companies were dispatched from home
to the frontier of the colony in 1695.[36] The particularism
of the colonies threw the burden upon the English government and a precedent was set which was followed to the
close of the last French war in 1763.

With the opening of the struggle with France the problem of uniting the colonies for common defense became
of paramount importance. Farseeing colonists were impressed with the need of a colonial union in order to make
an effective stand against the French. The French were
inferior to the English in point of numbers and compact-
ness of settlement, but vastly superior in point of
organization. Their centralized system of control,
which gave the direction of all affairs into the
hands of one man, was superior from a military point
of view to the decentralized system prevailing in the English colonies, where control was scattered among a number
of petty governments, each with its own policy and jealousies. It was felt that the encroachments of France were
dictated by the lack of concert among the English colonies. Peter de la Noy stated the case well in a letter to
Penn in 1695: "The French assume a boldness purely
from divisions into separate bodyes and the piques that
are so common amongst the several governrs. of which the
French don't want a constant intelligence."[37] It was

36 *Cal. State Paps., Col.*, 1693-1696, 221, 231-232; *Acts of Privy
Council, Col.*, II, 261. See the report of the Lords of Trade to the
Privy Council, September 30, 1696, for a good summary of the
whole situation. *Cal. State Paps., Col.*, 1693-1696, 165-166.

37 *N. Y. Col. Docs.*, IV, 224. The memorial of John Nelson of
New York to the Board of Trade in 1696 states that the greatest
defect in the colonial system was "the number and independency
of so many small governments, whereby our strength is not only
reduced but weakened." He suggested that if New England and
New York were placed under one government "we should at least
be fifteen to one against the French in Canada, and instead of a
bare defense might with ships from England, make an entire conquest of the place." *Cal. State Paps., Col.*, 1696-1697, 136.

a fear which received repeated expression.[38] The lack of union, the working at cross purposes of the colonies, each doing as it seemed best without regard for the interests of all, simply invited hostile attack. Frequent petitions were presented to the crown praying for the establishment of a definite union.

An imperfect union was established when the command of the troops of Connecticut and the powers of government in Pennsylvania were invested in the governor of New York. But such a temporary union did not solve the problem. The assemblies of these colonies resisted all Fletcher's demands. A system which made the English government dependent upon the will of the local assemblies was a failure.[39] Furthermore, the colonies knew that the crown had no authority to march the militia outside the boundary of any colony without the consent of the men or by act of the assembly of that colony. Any league composed of a number of colonies, each organized with its own government and given the power to judge of the propriety of royal orders, had the means to thwart the will of the crown and render imperial interests subservient to local convenience.[40] The radical defect in the whole system was the policy of acting upon the colonists through a number of distinct governments rather upon the individual by some supreme authority. The mischief could be remedied by resorting to the power of the imperial legislature either to tax the colonists in order to create a revenue to support

[38] *Cal. State Paps., Col.*, 1693-1696, 160-161; 1696-1697, 338.

[39] Fletcher wrote to the Lords of Trade, Nov., 1694, "My Commissions for Pennsylvania and Connecticut cannot meet the malady, whereas if all were united under one government, all would be subject to the same laws and duties." *Cal. State Paps., Col.*, 1693-1696, 402.

[40] Fletcher wrote to the secretary of state, Dec., 1693, "Nothing is so weakening to Their Majesties service and interest in this part of the Empire as those Governments which act by separate interest from the Crown, make their own laws and exercise sovereign power without appeal." *Ibid.*, 217.

the charges of defense and to vest the command of the militia in the crown, or else to centralize control in the colonies. The former measure was not resorted to till 1765. On the other hand an efficient colonial union demanded that the charters be vacated and the colonies combined into larger administrative units. Such a policy was urged by royal appointees and others in the colonies, particularly by the officials of New York when they asked that either the original boundaries of the province be restored and Pennsylvania and Delaware be added, or else that a union similar to that under Andros be established. In 1695 a committee of the Privy Council proposed the revival of such a dominion for the purpose of defense [41] and the same scheme was urged upon the home government in various memorials from the colonies.[42] On the other hand the major part of the colonists resisted such a scheme. Jealous of their charters, closely wedded to their peculiar institutions, and particularistic in their tendencies, all they wished was a loose military confederation. They asked that the royal governor of New York should be appointed governor also of the royal provinces of Massachusetts and New Hampshire and captain-general of the forces of these provinces and of the chartered colonies of Rhode Island, Connecticut, and New Jersey, and that " no breach be made on any of the Grants and Privileges of the several provinces in their Civil affairs."[43] The plan of union offered by William Penn in 1697 likewise contemplated a loose confederation of the colonies much like that of the old New England confederation. When called upon by the Board of Trade to see that his province paid obedience to the royal order of 1694, Penn complained that his colony was over-rated

[41] *Cal. State Paps., Col.*, 1693-1696, 541.
[42] *Ibid.*, 1696-1697, 136, 189, 435. Kellogg, *Amer. Col. Charter*, Amer. Hist. Assoc., *Report*, 1903, I, 280-281.
[43] *Cal. State Paps., Col.*, 1696-1697, 338, 352; *N. Y. Col. Docs.*, IV, 224.

in comparison with other colonies.[44] He declared to the board that the quotas could best be fixed by a congress of colonial deputies.[45] The board asked him to present his ideas in writing and he drew up his " Briefe and Plaine Scheme."[46] This scheme provided for a congress of two deputies from each colony to meet biennially in time of peace and annually or oftener in time of war. The business of this body was to adjust inter-colonial differences and to concert measures for the common defense. In this way Penn thought that quotas of men and money levied upon the colonies could be more equitably apportioned than by the English government, for the simple reason that the colonists were more conversant with local conditions. Penn's scheme did not offer a true solution of the problem of creating an effective union for defense. The failure of the old New England Confederation and of the Articles of Confederation of a later period show conclusively the futility of placing any dependence upon a requisition system. Finally, in February, 1697, the Board of Trade reported to the Privy Council that because of the charters no other than a military union was practicable and recommended that it should be adopted.[47] This recommendation was carried out in the same year when the Earl of Bellomont was commissioned royal governor of New York, Massachusetts, and New Hampshire and captain-general of all the forces of New England, New York, and New Jersey.[48] But Connecticut and Rhode Island resisted all of Bello-

[44] B. T. Paps., Props., Entry Bk. A, ff. 36, 37, 52.

[45] B. T. Jour., IX, 276, 394, 400-401, 403.

[46] B. T. Paps., Pl. Gen., IV, pt. 1, A 40; N. Y. Col. Docs., IV, 296-297.

[47] Cal. State Paps., Col., 1696-1697, 384; N. Y. Col. Docs., IV, 259. The board wrote " The importance and advantages of a Union for mutual defense and common security are by all sides agreed on; but the objections against the methods proposed for putting it into execution are various, according to the different interests of those by whom they are made."

[48] N. Y. Col. Docs., IV, 261, 262, 266-273, 284-292, 302.

mont's attempts to command their troops, considering his
appointment a breach of their royal charters.[49] The problem was not yet solved.

King William's War was ended by the treaty of Ryswick
of 1697. This treaty met few of the difficulties which confronted the two nations in America. The boundary question on the north was by no means decided. In view of the
likelihood of renewed hostilities the home government took
steps to fortify the New York frontier. In 1700 the Board
of Trade proposed that the colonies should contribute
£5000 toward the charges of erecting fortifications in
northern New York.[50] The English government consented
to contribute two-fifths of the sum and the rest was to be
apportioned among the colonies.[51] This proposal shows
clearly that England was willing to bear its share of imperial defense. The sum which fell to the lot of Pennsylvania was £350. The governor of New York was instructed to call upon the colonies for their respective
quotas. In August, 1701, Penn laid the requisition before
the assembly but it refused to comply on the plea that the
province was too poor, and, with the proverbial spirit of
jealousy, pointed out that the neighboring colonies under
royal control had done nothing.[52] Thus the deficiencies
of some furnished the pretext for refusal on the part of
others. The next month Penn again urged the assembly
to comply, but a resolution to vote the money was rejected
with unanimity.[53]

[49] The agents of New York pointed out to the Board of Trade that
the scheme would not work because it was still possible for the
legislatures to thwart the royal commission to command their
militia. It was suggested that no obedience could be expected until
Parliament passed an act uniting all the forces of the colonies and
vesting the military power in the crown during war. *Cal State
Paps., Col.*, 1696-1697, 352-353.

[50] *N. Y. Col. Docs.*, IV, 706.

[51] *Ibid.*, 832, 839.

[52] *Pa. Votes of Assembly*, I, 140-142.

[53] *Ibid.*, I, 143, 146; *Pa. Col. Recs.*, II, 78, 79.

In 1702 England declared war against France and Spain. In September the Board of Trade directed Penn to put his province in a state of defense and in case of danger on the New York frontier to send the assistance as required by the order of 1700.[54] Governor Cornbury of New York called upon the colonies for the requisitions. Governor Hamilton of Pennsylvania urged the assembly to comply, as also to erect fortifications and to establish a militia.[55] The assembly would do nothing. The responses of other colonies to the call of Cornbury were of a similiar character. Cornbury and Quary frequently informed the Board of Trade that the royal orders were not of sufficient force either to elicit compliance with the directions to aid New York or to provide internal defenses.[56] Both suggested that the only way to control the wayward colonies was to make use of the power of Parliament. Quary wrote, '' Nothing will do but a short act of Parliament '' which would '' open the Peoples eyes to see their own interest, and make them more ready to comply with other of Her Majesty's just commands, and cure them of that sour temper which hath already possessed them in Opposition to Government.'' This remedy was suggested time and again and the logic of events finally forced Parliament to this step in 1765. In 1703 the board gave Penn strict orders to see that his assembly granted the money for New York defenses and to report promptly his success in the matter.[57] The house simply replied with the plea that the expense of securing its own frontier and maintaining friendly relations with the Indians of the province prevented the raising of a supply for New York.[58] This reply is characteristic of the other colonies also. The respective

[54] B. T. Paps., Props., VI, pt. 2, I 24.
[55] Pa. Votes of Assembly, I, Appendix, xx.
[56] N. Y. Col. Docs., IV, 1052-1053, 1060-1061, 1070, 1084.
[57] B. T. Paps., Props., Entry Bk. D, f. 316.
[58] Pa. Votes of Assembly, I, pt. 2, 18; Pa. Col. Recs., II, 142, 155, 165.

colonies simply considered the conformity of the royal requisitions to their immediate needs without regard to the general welfare. Particularism was especially strong in those colonies whose frontiers were not subject to the immediate assaults of the French and Indians. But it was only a question of time till the middle colonies became a prey to the horrors of savage warfare and foreign invasion which was now the lot of the border colonies. Though freed from attacks by land, Pennsylvania suffered in common with all from the depredations of hostile privateers upon colonial commerce.

The thriving trade of the colonies, the basis of their prosperity, offered a vulnerable point of attack for the privateers of France and Spain. The activity of the privateers put a temporary check upon the trade of Pennsylvania to her chief markets in the West Indies. The attacks were not confined to the high seas, but reached also the shipping and settlements of Delaware Bay.[59] The merchants appealed to the assembly for protection. The Quaker assembly turned a deaf ear to the entreaties, contending that the erection of fortifications would cost more than the impoverished condition of the province could bear, and that after all the city of Philadelphia, the only port of the colony, was in no danger of attack by reason of its distance from the seas.[60] Furthermore, the house took the stand that it was incumbent upon the English government to afford protection by sea. The heavy losses of 1708 again lead the governor to implore the house to take action.[61] It replied that the attacks were due to the neglect of the royal navy, for the Queen had given " the High Adml. and his Deputies, ample authority to scour the Coast of such Robbers, and secure the Navigation of this as well as the rest of her Colonies, and protect the Mer-

59 *Penn-Logan Corres.*, I, 240, 289, 301; II, 123, 275, 348.
60 *Pa. Col. Recs.*, II, 249, 250.
61 *Ibid.*, 413-414, 417-420.

chants in their Lawful Trade.''[62]   According to the interpretation of the house its legislative power under the charter was bounded by the limits of the province, hence it had no authority to fit out vessels of war or commission privateers to serve beyond these boundaries, and that under these conditions the merchants must appeal for protection to Lord Cornbury, whose vice-admiralty commission gave him authority over the river and bay and high-seas.[63]   The appeal to Cornbury availed nothing for the two ships stationed at New York were then at sea.[64]   Likewise Governor Seymour of Maryland could give no assistance.[65]   In 1709 Governor Gookin informed the assembly of an attack upon Lewes and asked that some provision be made for fortifications.[66]   The house replied that the admiralty had ordered the ship of war *Garland* to cruise between the Delaware Capes and Hatteras and that the coast would soon be cleared of privateers.[67]   But the governor said that he knew of no orders received by the *Garland* regarding Pennsylvania.[68]   The Quakers, as James Logan expressed it, '' threw the whole burden of defense upon the Lord High Admiral by sea and the Queen by land.''[69]

In the earlier part of the war the colonists, left to themselves, had failed in their attacks upon Canada. It was therefore decided to enlist the support of the combined colonies and to secure the aid of the English government. Colonel Samuel Vetch and Governor Nicholson were the prime movers in this enterprise. In March, 1709, the crown sent letters to the colonies north of Maryland announcing a campaign against Canada and requiring the

62 *Pa. Col. Recs.*, II, 415-416.
63 *Ibid.*, 421-422.
64 *Ibid.*, 418; *Penn-Logan Corres.*, II, 281.
65 *Pa. Col. Recs.*, II, 417.
66 *Ibid.*, 472; *Pa. Votes of Assembly*, II, 43.
67 *Pa. Col. Recs.*, II, 475; *Pa. Votes of Assembly*, II, 44.
68 *Pa. Col. Recs.*, II, 476; *Pa. Votes of Assembly*, II, 45.
69 *Penn-Logan Corres.*, II, 344.

governors to assist the undertaking and to obey the orders of Colonel Vetch.[70] The plan of operation was two-fold. The troops of Rhode Island and Massachusetts in conjunction with five regiments of British regulars were to attack Quebec; while the troops of New York, Connecticut, New Jersey, and Pennsylvania were to operate against Montreal. Pennsylvania was called upon for a quota of one hundred and fifty men. The governor, urging that the enthusiasm of New England be emulated, said that if the house would appropriate £4000 necessary to raise and equip the men, he would provide recruits.[71] Out of respect for the Quaker principles he did not ask the assembly to pass a militia law but simply to vote money. The house decided that because of their principles no money could be raised for the expedition, but that a present might be granted to the Queen, and accordingly a gift of £500 was voted.[72] Even this sum was placed in safe hands till the Quaker could be sure it would not be used for war-like purposes. But the campaign amounted to nothing. After the northern colonies had made all preparations the English forces failed to appear and the operations had to be given up.[73] The colonists on their own initiative in 1710 captured Port Royal. Nicholson went to England to urge a renewal of the previous plan and in consequence the English government directed the governors to the same effect as before. In June, 1711, the New England governors met in conference at New London to discuss the plan of operations and to fix the quotas to be contributed by the colonies.[74] Pennsylvania's levy was fixed at two hundred and forty men to be at Albany by the first days of July. The assembly, after complaining that the colony was rated too

[70] N. Y. Col. Docs., V, 70-74.

[71] Pa. Votes of Assembly, II, 34, 35.

[72] Ibid., 41; Penn-Logan Corres., II, 351; Perry, Church Papers, II, 51-52.

[73] Parkman, Half Century of Conflict, I, 137-140.

[74] N. Y. Col. Docs., V, 257.

high and that the expense of maintaining friendship with
its own Indians was all it could bear, expressed a willingness
to pay tribute to Caesar as far as their religious principles
would permit. Accordingly £2000 was voted to the
"Queen's Use."[75] Strange to say the men were never
raised and the money was never used as intended. The
expedition of 1711 proved a sorry fiasco, due chiefly to the
utter incompetence of the British commanders.[76] In 1712,
the Tory party, then dominant in English politics, favored
a policy of peace, and hostilities were suspended in Europe.
The war was formally closed by the Treaty of Utrecht,
1713. This brought no final determination of the conflicting territorial claims of England and France in North
America. The struggle was simply laid aside till some future time.

It is clear that Quaker principles and the interests of
the Empire seriously clashed. Two essential functions of
government are the protection of life and property from
domestic violence and the preservation of the dominions
from external danger. In the first case there was no inconsistency between Quaker principles and government
and the actual conditions of life. Constables, sheriffs, and
a judicial system were provided for local police protection.
In the second case the Quaker principles were in no way
related to actual conditions, but were based upon *a priori*
theories. The Quakers pleaded, as expressed by James
Logan, "we are a peaceable people, had wholly renounced
war, and the spirit of it; that we were willing to trust
ourselves to the protection of God alone, in an assurance
that the sword can neither be drawn nor sheathed but by
his direction."[77] Had this principle been universally established, arms and the art of war would have wholly dis-

---

[75] *N. Y. Col. Docs.*, V, 262; *Penn-Logan Corres.*, II, 436; *Pa. Votes of Assembly*, II, 97, 99.

[76] Greene, *Provincial America*, 159-160.

[77] *Penn-Logan Corres.*, I, 288.

appeared, but the plea of the Quaker, noble though it was, found no support in the conditions prevailing in the eighteenth century. The ideals of the Quakers did not conform to the needs of the imperial authorities or of those in the province who demanded protection.[78] The refusal of the Quaker assembly to comply with the demands of the home government drew upon this sect the charge that their principles were inconsistent with good government; that a legislature dominated by Quakers representing but one sect and not the whole people, was contrary to all the known principles of popular government.[79] The fear was frequently expressed that the province would fall an easy prey to the French because of the Quaker dominance. It was this charge chiefly which brought about the institution of royal government in 1692. In order to secure proper protection two remedies were proposed; that the Quakers should be excluded from government [80] and that royal control be established. In 1694 the Lords of Trade agreed to represent to the Privy Council the great increase of Quakers in Pennsylvania and other colonies and their refusal to aid in defense whereby the safety of some of the dominions were seriously endangered.[81] Royal agents, such as Quary and Randolph, were never weary of calling the attention of the home authorities to the lack of defenses in Pennsylvania and urging the vacation of the charter. But such complaints were not confined to this colony. Repeated were the complaints of Bellomont, governor of New York, that Rhode Island and Connecticut refused to recognize his right to command their militia and neglected to provide

[78] Logan wrote, that the combatants in the colonies replied to the Quaker peace arguments, that should the Quakers lose their lives only "it would be little to the crown, seeing 'tis our doing, but others are involved with us, and should the enemy make themselves master of the country it would too sensibly touch England in the rest of her colonies." *Penn-Logan Corres.*, I, 228.

[79] *Ibid.*, II, 125, 345.

[80] *N. Y. Col. Docs.*, V, 32-33, 81.

[81] *Acts of Privy Council, Col.*, II, 265.

defenses. These charges form one of the most serious items urged in support of the bill of 1701 in Parliament to vacate the charters.

Especially active in support of the agitation to vacate the charter of Pennsylvania and to secure the benefits of royal control was the Church party. The Churchmen were desirous of crown government not only for the sake of adequate protection in time of war, but for the advance of the interests of the Anglican church. The vestry of Christ Church and the assemblymen of Delaware represented to the king that all were taxed, Quaker and non-Quaker alike, for the support of government, yet the legislature refused to afford them any protection.[82] The petition for royal government was doubtless justified, but the tactics used in some cases to effect this end were beyond justification. In 1702, when the assembly refused to establish a militia, Governor Hamilton exercised his authority as captain-general to raise troops. He commissioned officers with power to levy and command a militia. Opposition to the militia came not from the Quakers, but from some of the Church party, although loudest in their complaints against the Quaker government for refusing to afford protection. Hamilton wrote to Penn " of the ungentlemanly conduct of those who call themselves Churchmen " who discouraged the enlistment of men with the purpose of discrediting the Quaker government in the eyes of the home authorities by representing the lack of defenses.[83] This charge is substantiated by the evidence of Evans, Hamilton's successor, and of James Logan.[84] Such conduct was due to the petty treachery of small minds like Quary and a few others, who apparently left nothing undone to find a pretext for the establishment of royal control.[85]

[82] B. T. Paps., Props., VI, pt. 1, G 13; pt. 2, I, 2, 6, 7.
[83] Ibid., VII, L 10.
[84] Pa. Col. Recs., II, 162; Penn-Logan Corres., I, 124, 128.
[85] See page 238.

In 1702 Quary, then in England, laid before the Board of Trade a series of charges against the province. Numbered among them was the complaint of the entire lack of defenses, although the French had advanced within four days' journey of Newcastle.[86] Penn with effect pointed out that Virginia and Maryland, although governed immediately by the crown, had provided no defenses.[87] It was sufficient proof, as Penn no doubt meant to imply, that royal government was not a panacea for the ills of indirect control. The truth is that the assemblies of the royal colonies were just as particularistic in their attitude toward the problem of defense as the chartered colonies. Penn well indicated this spirit of particularism when he said that there was no need of defenses for several reasons. In the first place he held that it was impossible to defend widely scattered settlements. Then again, that the province by reason of its geographical location was immune from attack both by sea and by land. Philadelphia, the chief port, was situated one hundred and sixty miles from the sea and navigation was quite dangerous because of the numerous shoals. By land the chief source of danger was the Indians, and not the French, and the kindly treatment accorded the savages freed the province from that danger. But such arguments did not at all justify the refusal of the Quaker government to contribute to the aid of New York when the security of all the colonies depended upon the defense of the northern frontier. Perhaps the real purpose of the Quakers is revealed in the reply of the assembly to Quary's charges.[88] It said that the crown was fully aware of the Quaker principles regarding war when the charter was granted and that hence no expectation of the crown on this point had been disappointed. It declared that the Quakers had left the mother country to

86 B. T. Paps., Props., VI, pt. 2, I 17; VII, M 21.
87 Ibid., VI, pt. 2, I, 19, 20.
88 Ibid., VII, M 18.

escape all war-like preparations and that the province was
better off without defenses. Moreover, the Quakers said
that those who complained most had the least to lose, and
since before coming into the province the Quaker principles were known to them, they were free to depart if not
contented.

A few of the most prominent among the Quakers fully
realized the weakness of their position. They saw the inconsistency of their ethical principles as compared with actual conditions.[89] They were aware that they had not adhered to their high intentions to grant civil and religious liberty to all since the Quakers dominant in government represented only their views on the question of war and not
the views of a majority of the colonists who demanded
protection. Isaac Norris and James Logan earnestly advised Penn to surrender his powers of government to the
crown.[90] On the other hand it may be said that the Quaker
assembly did not place itself in a position of absolute refusal to grant aid. It granted money during King William's War to relieve the distressed Indians in New York,
and during Queen Anne's War it voted a sum for the
"Queen's Use." Fully realizing that this was only a
specious device to evade a direct grant for military purposes, some justification was found necessary. The
Quakers said, "we did not see it inconsistent with our principles to give the Queen money, notwithstanding the use
she might put it to, *that* being not our part, but hers."[91]

[89] *Penn-Logan Corres.*, II, 276. Logan to Penn, "This place
under such dangers, lying so naked and exposed, gives occasions
for great murmurs, and Friends themselves, finding their principles utterly unqualify them for the discharge of some duties of
government, and which that of land now reckons indispensably necessary, are quite tired of it, and wish themselves free of the load
which follows it."

[90] See page 355.

[91] *Penn-Logan Corres.*, II, 436. Isaac Norris wrote, "The argument in this case is, that our friends in England pay all taxes,
and never scruple that which is expressly declared to be for carrying
on a vigorous war against France." *Ibid.*, II, 348.

Responsibility was shifted to the shoulders of others. They held that tribute was due to the powers which God had set over them as far as their religious principles would allow. The position was not consistent and their motives lacked the element of the heroic, but they probably acted on the theory that in a complicated moral situation a sacrifice of a part of ethical principles is necessary to safeguard ideals. By voting money for the use of the crown, the Quakers saved themselves from the charge of an absolute refusal and warded off the censure of the home government. By such means they escaped direct taxes for war, enabled the governor to raise troops without the passage of a law to establish a militia, and kept themselves in power in the government.[92]   In the long run it was the geographical position of the province which permitted the continuance of this policy. When French invasions and Indian warfare reached the soil of Pennsylvania, then the Quakers were forced to yield the government into other hands.

For twenty-six years after the Treaty of Utrecht the Empire enjoyed all the advantages of a long peace. This was due to the policy of the great premier, Robert Walpole, who realized that only under conditions of peace could he succeed in his policy of building up the trade and industry of England. But the keen international commercial rivalry was at length to break out into open warfare. The clashing of the English and Spanish merchants for supremacy of trade in the West Indies and South America, led England to declare war upon her rival in 1739. Two months before the ultimatum of war was issued, John Penn wrote from London to Governor Thomas advising him to make an effort to secure the establishment of a provincial militia in view of the impending conflict.[93]   Thomas called

92 Sharpless, *A Quaker Experiment in Gov't.*, 204-208.
93 *Penn Mss., Letter Bk.*, I, 306-307, John Penn to Gov. Thomas, Aug. 2, 1739; *ibid.*, 308, John Penn to Thos. Penn, Aug. 2, 1739.

the attention of the assembly to the gathering clouds of war in Europe and recommended it to place the colony in a position of defense before it was too late.[94] The house admitted the dark aspect of affairs abroad but refused to do aught except to revert to the well-worn arguments.[95] It asserted that to establish a militia by compelling some to serve and exempting non-combatants would be not only unfair to the latter class but also inconsistent with Quaker principles; that the governor had power by the charter to raise troops without the aid of the assembly; and finally that there was no need of defenses because of the fortunate geographical position of the colony by sea and land.

The battle-ground of the war with Spain was the West Indies. England anticipated the struggle by despatching a fleet under Admiral Vernon to ravage the Spanish main three months before the formal declaration of war. Early in 1740 the colonies were instructed to raise troops for a West Indian expedition. By recruiting forces in the colonies the English government saved the expense and delay of raising men at home and of transporting them to the field. The requisition only required the colonies to raise troops and furnish provisions and transports till their arrival in the West Indies, when men and transports would be cared for by the English government. When in June the governor of Pennsylvania asked the assembly to grant

---

[94] *Pa. Votes of Assembly*, III, 353.

[95] *Ibid.*, III, 361, 367. *Penn Mss., Off. Corres.*, III, 89, Gov. Thomas to John Penn, Nov. 5, 1739. William Allen wrote to John Penn that "at present the House of Assembly consists of almost all Quakers, who I believe will do nothing but Trust in the Lord." *Penn Mss. Off. Corres.*, Nov. 17, 1739. Gov. Thomas also wrote to the Penns expressing disgust "with the mistaken zeal & folly of the Quakers in thrusting themselves into the Assembly at this critical Juncture, when they might have saved appearances & allowed others to do what is so absolutely necessary for their Protection. They who profess Conscience, will not allow others to act agreeable to theirs, that is, to make use of the Strength & Courage God has given them to defend all that can be dear to a man in this world." *Ibid.*, III, Nov. 5, 1739.

supplies to enable him to carry out the requisition, the house expressed regret that it could do nothing.[96] The governor relying on his own powers then began to act with energy. By July he had raised and officered seven companies of troops. Again he asked the assembly to grant money for provisions and transports.[97] The Quaker house simply harped on the subject of its religious principles and further complained of the governor's action in enlisting indentured servants without securing the consent of their masters or of offering the latter any compensation. The merchants of Philadelphia appealed to the assembly to consider itself the representatives of the whole province and not of a Quaker minority alone, and not to act contrary to the royal order thereby drawing upon the colony the censure of the home government.[98] The petition had the effect of eliciting a vote of £3000 to the " king's use," but with the proviso that payment should be withheld till the enlisted servants were released and the governor promised not to enroll any more.[99] This the governor refused to do, holding that the servants had enrolled themselves voluntarily, and that in the opinion of able lawyers the crown had a right to their service; hence to discharge them would not only violate the royal right but cause mutiny.[100] Since no assistance could be expected from the assembly the proprietors and merchants came to the governor's relief by subscribing £6600, while others offered their ships as transports on the condition of being reimbursed by the home government.[101] In pursuance of secret instructions Gov-

[96] *Pa. Votes of Assembly*, III, 389, 390-391, 392, 395; Gov. Thomas to Duke of Newcastle, July 21, 1740, *Amer. and West Indies*, (P. R. O.), 28, Pa., XXIV, ff. 36-39.

[97] *Amer. and W. I.*, 28, Pa. XXIV, ff. 40-42, Thomas to Newcastle, Aug. 29, 1740.

[98] *Pa. Votes of Assembly*, III, 402.

[99] *Ibid.*, III, 409.

[100] *Amer. and W. I.*, 28, Pa., XXIV, ff. 40-42, Thomas to Newcastle, Aug. 29, 1740.

[101] *Ibid.*, ff. 74-75, Thomas to Newcastle, Oct. 2, 1740.

ernor Thomas drew upon the Commissioners of the Navy to liquidate the amounts due to the subscribers and ship-owners.[102] The assembly retaliated by stopping the governor's salary and threatening to appeal home against him.[103] To anticipate this action Thomas wrote to the secretary of state and the Board of Trade giving a statement of the whole situation and taking the Quakers severely to task for their obstructing tactics.[104] He accused the Quakers of exerting their whole strength to secure the return of an assembly opposed to all war measures, and asserted that this purpose was realized only by an appeal to the German inhabitants who were persuaded to support the Quakers in power on the plea that a militia would bring them under as severe bondage to the proprietors as they were formerly under to their princes in Germany, that the expense would impoverish them, and that their liberties would be best safeguarded by a Quaker assembly. As a parting word Thomas wrote, " I am too well acquainted with the narrow, bigoted views of this governing sect here not to be convinced that it is impossible for me to serve his Majesty faithfully and please them under the present circumstances of affairs," and he expressed a wish to resign.[105] Richard Partridge, the London agent of the assembly, secured from the office of the Board of Trade by surreptitious means a copy of this letter which he forwarded to the colony where it was used to inflame the wrath of the Quakers against the governor. The board called upon Partridge to explain how he secured the copy and on his refusal to answer he was forbidden to act before that body for any colony until he made satisfaction.[106]

102 *A. and W. I.*, 28, f. 77, Thomas to Newcastle, Oct. 27, 1740.

103 *Penn Mss., Letter Bk.*, I, 339, John and Richard Penn to Thos. Penn, Nov., 20, 1740.

104 *Pa. Statutes at Large*, IV, 468-477; *Amer and W. I.*, 28, Pa., XXIV, f. 97, Thomas to Newcastle, Nov. 26, 1741.

105 *Pa. Statutes at Large*, IV, 477.

106 *B. T. Paps., Props.*, Entry Bk. H, f. 146.

The expedition against Cartagena in March, 1740, proved a disgraceful failure. Like the expedition against Quebec in 1711, the fiasco was due to the incompetence and wrangling of the English commanders.[107] In August came a call for recruits to fill up the sadly depleted ranks of the colonial troops. In response Thomas acted with energy but the horrible mortality of the troops in the West Indies and the persistent exaggeration of this circumstance by the Quakers caused great discontent and made enlistments very difficult.[108] In spite of these obstacles, Thomas raised about one hundred and seventy recruits who were despatched to the south. He was compelled to advance from his own pockets a bounty of £4 to each man, drawing upon the Paymaster-General for reimbursement and upon the Commissioners of the Navy for provision and transport money.[109] The clash between Quaker principles and the interests of the Empire precluded expectation of little assistance from the Quaker assembly and the share of the province in the enterprise was thrown upon the English exchequer.

Moreover, on the question of internal defenses the assembly remained just as obstinate. During the Spanish war the commerce of the province suffered severely from the depredations of hostile privateers which infested the coast. Repeatedly the governor implored the assembly to provide fortifications. A petition signed by eighty-five merchants prayed for the protection of trade upon which the prosperity of the province depended.[110] The house simply replied that no vessels of the colony had been taken since the war began, that no certain information existed that the coast was annoyed by Spanish privateers, and moreover,

107 Fortescue, *Hist. of British Army*, II, 59-79.
108 *Amer. and W. I.*, 28, Pa., XXIV, f. 97, Thomas to Newcastle, Nov. 26, 1741.
109 *Ibid.*, ff. 100, 102, 104, Thomas to Newcastle, May 22, Sept. 30, Nov. 24, 1742.
110 *Pa. Votes of Assembly*, III, 432, 433.

that shipping was protected by the English navy without expense to the province. Finally, the assembly voted £3000 to purchase bills of exchange to pay into the royal exchequer.[111] By such means the Quakers sought to evade the charge that they refused to pay nothing toward defense and at the same time to avoid any direct compromise with their principles. Governor Thomas wrote that the province would never be adequately protected until the Quakers were excluded from the legislature by the imposition of the oath.[112] With this suggestion Thomas Penn agreed.[113] In 1742 two hundred and sixty-five prominent men of the province petitioned the crown for protection.[114] Despairing of assistance from the assembly, recourse to the home government was the only practical alternative. The petition set forth that the colony lacked fortifications, munitions of war, and a militia whereby the province lay exposed to the attacks of the French by land and privateers by sea; that the earnest efforts of the governor and proprietors to secure defense were rendered ineffectual by the Quakers in the assembly, who, though not a third of the population, refused to act because of religious principles, and that the civil power without a militia established by law was too feeble to repel the insurrection of slaves should they rise as in the neighboring colony. The petition was referred to the Board of Trade before which a hearing was granted in April to the counsel for the petitioners and assembly.[115] Meanwhile some forty London Quakers espoused the cause of their colonial brethren and presented

111 *Pa. Votes of Assembly*, III, 432; *Cal. Treas. Papers*, 1742-1745, 276.

112 *Penn Mass., Official Corres.*, III, 169; Gov. Thomas to F. J. Paris, May 14, 1741.

113 *Ibid., Off. Corres.*, III, 141, Thos. Penn to Paris, March 27, 1741; *ibid, Letter Bk.*, I, 372, John Penn to John Kinsey, March 3, 1742. See also the letter of Gov. Morris of New Jersey recommending the same idea. N. J. Hist. Soc., *Collections*, IV, 187.

114 *B. T. Paps., Props.*, XV, T 57.

115 *B. T. Jour.*, LI, 27, 32, 34.

a counter-petition.[116] It stated that the colonial Quakers had been unfairly attacked and asked that a reasonable time be allowed the latter to reply, not doubting that upon a fair hearing they would be able to acquit themselves of the insinuations and show their allegiance to the crown and their regard for the welfare of the province. The hearings were postponed in order to give the London Quakers time to lay their petition regularly before the Privy Council.[117] Paris, solicitor for the petition, urged the board to take action before the counter-petition was received from the council. In the latter part of June two hearings were granted by the board at which appeared Paris, solicitor, and Bathurst, counsel, for the petitioners, and Sharpe, solicitor, and Hume Campbell, counsel, for the assembly.[118] For the assembly it was argued that by the Charter of Privileges of 1701 and the law of 1705 granting liberty of conscience the Quakers were exempt from military service; that the colony was in no need of armaments because of its peaceful policy toward the Indians, and that by the royal charter, which empowered the proprietors to raise and command the people, the Penns were obliged to defend the colony in time of sudden invasion. On the other side it was held that the grant of liberty of conscience pertained to matters purely religious and made no exemptions from military service. The Quaker contentions were to say the least weak and were refuted by the board in its report of July to the Privy Council.[119] This report pointed out that an inspection of the laws of the province and the evidence of the letter of Governor Thomas clearly proved that the assembly had done nothing to provide for the security of the colony, although from the nature of society and government and by charter it was obliged to perform

---

[116] B. T. Paps., Props., XV, T 60.

[117] B. T. Jour., LI, 36.

[118] Ibid., 52, 53, 63, 65, 66, 68.

[119] B. T. Paps., Props., Entry Bk. H, ff. 210-217; Acts of Privy Council, Col., III, 710-712.

this essential function. The report declared that there was
no more reason to exempt one colony than another from
this obligation, especially since no law existed to exempt
the Quakers from military service, and that the proprietors were no more obliged to defend the colony in time of
war than was the governor of a royal province. In conclusion, it proposed that the crown should instruct the governor of Pennsylvania to report what was necessary to
place the colony in a position of security. Counsel for the
assembly carried the case to the Privy Council, where, after
a hearing, the report of the Board of Trade was upheld.
The board was not directed to send the instruction to the
governor till June, 1743, because of the unsettled condition
of politics in England following the resignation of Robert
Walpole.[120] In March, 1744, Governor Thomas replied
saying that it was necessary to build forts and mount cannon at suitable places along the Delaware River for the
protection of the three hundred vessels which traded yearly
to the province.[121] For the frontier he suggested that one
or two forts should be built to protect the traders and to
secure the colony from the incursions of the French and
Indians. Finally, he stated that a quantity of stores of
war should be supplied and a law enacted obliging the inhabitants to do military service as in other colonies. These
suggestions were undoubtedly warranted by the situation
in the colony, but the dominance of Quaker power precluded a better order of affairs along this line. The governor's letter was referred to the Board of Trade for consideration. There the question arose as to how best to
carry these recommendations into effect; could it be done
by order in council, or did it require the passage of an act
of Parliament? The board sent the charter of Pennsyl-

120 *Penn Mss., Letter Bk.,* I, 371, John Penn to Gov. Thomas,
March 1, 1742; *B. T. Paps., Props.,* XVI, V 2, 3; Entry Bk. H, ff.
218-219.

121 *B. T. Paps., Props.,* XVI, V 10; *B. T. Jour.,* LII, 112.

vania to the crown lawyers, asking an opinion as to how
the colony could be compelled to provide for its own security.[122] They replied that in point of prudence and expediency the colony was obliged to take all precautions necessary for its defense, but in point of law the colonial as
sembly was the sole judge of the methods to be taken for
that purpose and could not be forced to do more than it
saw fit " unless by the force of an act of parliament here,
which alone can prescribe certain rules for their Conduct."[123] This opinion is important in several respects.
In the first place, it showed conclusively that nothing was
to be expected from the assembly as long as the Quakers
held control. Even before this opinion was received by
the board, Thomas Penn wrote from London that " some
of the Ministers, conferring among themselves, are of the
opinion nothing will do but an act of parliament and I
think they cannot do the business without one."[124] The
object of such an act was to exclude the Quakers from the
legislature by imposing the oath upon all. No parliamentary action was taken at that time because, as Thomas Penn
informs us, the Privy Council was too greatly pressed with
other business. In the second place, the opinion of the
crown lawyers was significant of the political change taking place in England in the direction of parliamentary supremacy over the colonies.[125] The logic of the whole situation, in other colonies as well as in Pennsylvania, was to
force the English ministry to resort to parliamentary power
twenty years later to obtain a proper defense of the colonies.

The conflict with Spain was now merged in the broader

[122] *B. T. Paps., Props.,* Entry Bk. H, f. 220; *B. T. Jour.,* LII, 121.
[123] *B. T. Paps., Props.,* XVI, V 12; Entry Bk. H, ff. 221-222.
[124] *Penn Mss., Letter Bk.,* II, 102, 118, Thos. Penn to Gov. Thomas
Sept. 4, 1744, March 7, 1745.
[125] The same question arose a little earlier in the case of the
Connecticut Intestacy Law. C. M. Andrews, *Yale Review,* Nov.,
1894, 288-291.

war of the Austrian Succession, or King George's War of
colonial history. England declared war against France and
Spain in March, 1744. Anticipating the outbreak of hostilities, the crown instructed the colonial governors in the
previous year to put their respective colonies into a position of defense.[126] Governor Thomas laid the royal order
before the assembly of Pennsylvania, which answered that
it was willing to give proof of its loyalty when the occasion
demanded, but that recent information showed that war
was less likely now than when the order was issued.[127] In
July, 1744, the governor published the declaration of war
and the house had occasion to exhibit the loyalty professed.[128] When the governor entreated the house to provide fortifications and a militia, it replied that he was well
aware of its sentiments on the question of war and that no
further explanation was necessary. Moreover, it stated
that as the governor had raised troops before without a
militia bill, he could do so again.[129] The same spirit was
shown with regard to intercolonial military plans.

The constant and irritating attacks on colonial commerce
by French privateers exasperated the New Englanders.
The source of this trouble was the strong French fortress
at Louisburg, "the Dunkirk of America," on Cape Breton
Island. New England, especially Massachusetts under the
activity of Governor Shirley, laid plans to capture the place
and invited the colonies north of Maryland to coöperate
in the enterprise. In February, 1745, Governor Thomas
explained to the assembly of Pennsylvania that the capture
of Louisburg, the only French harbor of strength in America, would put an end to the depredations on colonial commerce and asked support for the undertaking.[130] The success of the enterprise meant as much to Pennsylvania as to

126 *Pa. Votes of Assembly*, III, 537.
127 *Ibid.*, 544.
128 *Ibid.*, 553-554.
129 *Ibid.*, 557.
130 *Ibid.*, IV, 6.

New England, but the assembly held a different opinion. In a narrow spirit of selfishness and jealousy it replied that " if Massachusetts expects aid from us it is reasonable we should have been consulted, as it is a matter which concerns Massachusetts alone." [131] Similar evasive arguments were used: that the enterprise was too hazardous; that aid from the other colonies would arrive too late; that the English government had not directed the undertaking and hence it might interfere with royal plans; and that support from England was too uncertain. In May, the New England forces in conjunction with an English fleet under Commodore Warren laid siege to Louisburg without the aid of Pennsylvania. Shirley and Warren appealed to the province for assistance in the purchase of provisions and clothing, the lack of which rendered half the besieging forces unfit for duty.[132] The assembly replied that since the enterprise was solely a private concern in which Massachusetts did not see fit to consult other colonies and that since the success of the undertaking would inure to the benefit of New England alone, that section had no right to involve Pennsylvania in the expense.[133] After the fall of Louisburg, Governor Thomas laid before the assembly in July a letter from Warren asking the province to contribute eighty men, provisioned and armed for eight months, to aid in the preservation of the conquest, and a letter from the secretary of state directing the governor to assist Warren in case of application for men, provisions, and ships.[134] The house replied that its pacific principles did not permit it to join in direct military measures, " yet we have ever held it Our Duty to render Tribute to Caesar," and voted £4000 to purchase provisions for the garrison at Louisburg.[135] Further appeals simply elicited the re-

131 *Pa. Votes of Assembly*, IV, 7.
132 *Ibid.*, 11.
133 *Ibid.*, 12.
134 *Ibid.*, 12.
135 *Ibid.*, 14.

sponse that the money already granted should excuse the house from any further aid.[136]

In 1746 a general campaign against Canada was planned along lines similar to that of 1709 and 1711. The New England troops acting in conjunction with British regulars and fleet were to attack Quebec, while the middle and southern colonies, except the Carolinas, were to operate against Montreal. In May Governor Thomas submitted to the assembly the requisition from the secretary of state.[137] The troops were to enter into the royal pay on enlistment, arms and clothing were to be provided by the colony, but General St. Clair, financial agent of the crown, was authorized " to make a reasonable allowance for defraying that Expence." It is clear that the charges of these undertakings was thrown largely upon the English treasury. The governor asked the house to furnish arms and clothing pending the arrival of St. Clair and suggested that a bounty should be offered to encourage enlistments. In response £5000 was voted to the " king's use." [138] This sum was expended in bounties and furnishing provisions for four companies of troops, while the governor provided arms and clothing on his own credit, and deferred drawing on the paymaster-general for reimbursement in expectation of the arrival of St. Clair.[139] Seven colonies raised forces for the campaign, but as in 1709 the English troops failed to arrive and the proposed operations came to naught. Meanwhile the provincials lay idle at Albany awaiting orders from England, the pay of the men was badly in arrears, and there were grave fears of mutiny. In August Governor Thomas asked the assembly to advance a sum of money sufficient to pay the arrears of the Pennsylvania troops and to support them at Albany till the English fleet

---

[136] *Pa. Votes of Assembly*, IV, 18, 19-20, 23, 27, 30-31.
[137] *Ibid.*, 37.
[138] *Ibid.*, 38, 40, 41.
[139] *Amer. and W. I.*, 28, Pa., XXIV, Thomas to Newcastle, Sept. 10, 1746.

arrived.[140] The assembly would do nothing and Governor
Clinton of New York was forced to supply the Pennsylvania troops with blankets on the credit of their government to prevent desertion. In 1747 the assembly was informed that the failure of orders from England placed
the care of the troops of the colony upon the local government.[141] The house replied that it was evident the English government had given up the enterprise and hence
there was no need of holding the troops together, but if
Governor Clinton felt justified in doing so he was to hold
himself responsible for their subsistence. The troops were
discharged in November, 1747, and there was due the men
and officers of Pennsylvania the sum of £2750. Twice
Governor Thomas appealed to the house to advance a sum
sufficient to liquidate the debt and to submit the account
to England for reimbursement, but the assembly pleaded
poverty and held that in consideration of the desertions
and the pay granted by Clinton, and the expectation of
payment by Parliament, the men had no reason to complain.[142] Whether Parliament made provision for the
troops is a matter of conjecture. Governor Thomas was
reimbursed for the sum of £3821 advanced on his own
credit for arms and clothing by drawing upon the paymaster-general.[143] Altogether the assembly contributed
£6213 for support of the expedition.[144]

During the summer of 1747, Spanish and French privateers made attacks upon the Delaware coast and seized a
number of merchant vessels. Fearing for the safety of
the city and the destruction of trade, the provincial council and the merchants appealed to the assembly for protec-

140 *Pa. Votes of Assembly*, IV, 43, 45, 49.

141 *Ibid.*, 50; Franklin, *Works*, (Smyth ed.), IV, 82-83; Fortescue,
Hist. of British Army, II, 259.

142 *Pa. Votes of Assembly*, IV, 68, 70, 72.

143 *B. T. Paps., Pl. Gen.*, XIV, O 15; Entry Bk. G, ff. 213-214,
331-332.

144 *Pa. Votes of Assembly*, IV, 69.

tion, but in vain.[145]   The house replied that the length
of the coast line and the scattered condition of settlement
made it impracticable to prevent these depredations.[146]
As to the outrages on the Delaware coast that was a matter, said the house, which should be brought to the attention of the government of Delaware.   The refusal of the
assembly forced the merchants to appeal to the neighboring
colonies for cannon and to the Lords of the Admiralty in
England for an armed vessel to be stationed at the Delaware Capes.[147]   New York sent cannon and the admiralty
board ordered the sloop *Otter* to service in Delaware
Bay.[148]   At the same time the citizens organized voluntary militia companies, and without aid from the assembly,
arms were provided and batteries erected upon the river.[149]

Hostilities were ended in 1748 by the Peace of Aix-la-
Chapelle.   But it was realized that this treaty, like those
of Ryswick and Utrecht before, brought no solution of the
fundamental issues between England and France in North
America.   The boundary line of Nova Scotia and the St.
Lawrence Valley was still a matter of dispute, but of far
greater importance both from the standpoint of the Empire as well as the province of Pennsylvania was the impending struggle for mastery of the trans-Alleghany west.
Then for the first time the colony found itself subject to
the sufferings and charges of war which had befallen the
border colonies to the north and south long before.   French
encroachments had at last reached the soil of Pennsylvania,
what was to be her response?

[145] *Pa. Votes of Assembly,* IV, 58, 66, 68; *Pa. Col. Recs.,* V, 234,
260.
[146] *Pa. Votes of Assembly,* IV, 60, 67; *Pa. Col. Recs.,* V, 236-237.
[147] *Pa. Col. Recs.,* V, 229, 231-232.
[148] *Ibid.,* 239, 241-243.
[149] *Ibid.,* 172, 174; *Pa. Archives,* 2d. ser., II, 501; *Pa. Votes of
Assembly,* IV, 72.

CHAPTER TEN

THE FRENCH AND INDIAN WAR

Until the middle of the eighteenth century, Maryland, Pennsylvania, and Virginia, by virtue of their geographical situation, had been largely free from the sufferings and expenses entailed by French invasions and Indian attacks. New York and New England on the north and Georgia and South Carolina on the south had borne nearly the entire burden of military defense. These border colonies were compelled to act under the ever present menace of invasions by the French and Spaniards and their savage allies, while the middle colonies rested in comparative peace and security. These facts help to explain the lack of interest displayed by the middle group in the concerns of the border colonies. But irresistible forces were at work bringing the two nations together in a final struggle for supremacy in the Great West and involving the middle colonies in the burdens of war which long since had befallen the northern and southern colonies. Under the treaties of Ryswick, Utrecht, and Aix-la-Chapelle the French laid claim to all the territory drained by the Ohio and its tributaries. By their sea-to-sea charters the English claimed the same region. Both sides were strengthening their respective positions by actual colonization and the erection of forts. Gradually the French drew their cordon of forts closer and closer around the English colonies till the middle of the century saw them passing the portages from Lake Erie to the Scioto, Muskingum, and Alleghany and thence to the Ohio. In 1749 the French governor sent an expedition under Celeron de Bienville to lay claim to the Ohio Valley and to warn off English settlers and traders from the dominions of the king of France.[1]   By 1753 the French had built Fort le Bouef on French Creek, a tributary of Alleghany River, and had seized the English trading post at Fort Venango at the junction of the river and creek.[2] Meanwhile English traders and settlers were creeping westward over the barriers of the Alleghanies in search of new fields to exploit.   In 1744 at a great council at Lancaster, the English wheedled the Iroquois into granting to them control of the Ohio country north of the river.[3]   In 1749 the crown granted to the Ohio Company, composed of prominent Virginians, a large area of land along the river for purposes of trade and colonization.[4]   Time and again the colonial governors and others had urged upon the English government the need of forts in the Ohio Valley to protect the traders and settlers and to prevent the encroachments of the French, but just as often these entreaties had remained unanswered at home.[5]   It was left for the colonists themselves to demonstrate the validity of English claims to the trans-Alleghany west.

In November, 1753, Dinwiddie, the able and energetic governor of Virginia, sent young Washington to Fort le Bouef to protest against the French occupation of a region " so notoriously known to be the property of the Crown of Great Britain."   The French commandant refused to vacate unless ordered to do so by his superior, Governor Duquesne.   In August, 1753, the Earl of Holdernesse, secretary of state, directed letters to the colonial governors stating that the crown had received knowledge of a hostile invasion of English soil by a force of French and Indians, and instructed them to secure the withdrawal of the enemy by warnings, and if peaceful methods failed, to resort to

---

[1] Parkman, *Montcalm and Wolfe*, I, chs. i, ii.

[2] *Ibid.*, I, ch. v.

[3] Detailed report in *Pa. Col. Recs.*, IV, 598-737.

[4] Carter, *Illinois Country, 1763-1774*, 103.

[5] *B. T. Paps.*, *Props.*, X, pt. 2, Q 179; XI, R 6; XIII, S 17; XVIII, V 84.

the use of the force.[6] Since England and France were at peace in Europe the governors were cautioned not to employ violence until they were assured that the incursion was within the undoubted limits of English territorial claims. This precaution was taken in order not to put England in the light of an aggressor in time of peace. The assembly of Virginia granted Governor Dinwiddie £10,000 to enable him to drive back the invaders.[7] He called upon the neighboring colonies to support the Virginia enterprise. Governor Hamilton of Pennsylvania in submitting the secretary's letter and Washington's report that English territory had been invaded, entreated the house not to delay in the granting of ample support for Virginia.[8] The assembly refused to comply on the ground that the undoubted limits of the province were not invaded.[9] The jurisdiction of the Ohio region was a matter in dispute between Virginia and Pennsylvania, and the assembly, therefore, did not consider itself qualified to fix the western limits of the province or to vote supplies contrary to the secretary's letter.[10] The conduct of the assembly was reprehensible in view of the fact that the secretary directed the colonies to act in mutual assistance. Granting that the province of Pennsylvania was not invaded, the dominions of England were and Virginia should have been supported. Early in March Hamilton again declared to the assembly that he had actual proof that the soil of the colony was invaded, but if it thought otherwise, he plead for support on behalf of Virginia.[11] The assembly adjourned without response. In April Hamilton again called the legislature in session in response to an urgent

[6] Pa. Votes of Assembly, IV, 278-279; Pa. Col. Recs., V, 689-690.
[7] Dinwiddie Corres, I, 60-69, 79-82.
[8] Pa. Votes of Assembly, IV, 278-279; Pa. Col. Recs., V, 719-722.
[9] Pa. Votes of Assembly, IV, 286; Pa. Col. Recs., V, 748.
[10] Shepherd, Proprietary Gov't. in Pa., 161-162; Dinwiddie Corres., I, 93-94, 354.
[11] Pa. Votes of Assembly, IV, 294-296, 300; Pa. Col. Recs., V, 753-755, 759 ff.

plea for aid from Dinwiddie.[12] The house reluctantly voted £10,000 in paper currency but on such conditions that the governor could not assent to the issue without a breach of the royal order of 1740.[13] The Virginia forces under Washington set out for the frontier in the last of March unsupported by the neighboring colonies. The regulars from New York and South Carolina arrived too late to be of service, while Pennsylvania and Maryland, so vitally concerned, did practically nothing.[14] Washington pressed on to repel the invaders from Fort Duquesne but in the early days of July he was attacked at Fort Necessity and forced to surrender to a superior body of French.

In August Hamilton informed the house of Washington's defeat and urged that the province should act on its own initiative until the plans of Virginia were known.[15] The assembly voted £15,000 in paper currency for the " king's use " which the governor refused to confirm without the insertion of the suspending clause pursuant to the royal order of 1740.[16] Realizing the desperate needs of the situation, Hamilton agreed to assent to an issue of a sum of fiat money necessary for the occasion provided funds were established for sinking the same within five years as allowed by the act of 1751.[17] The house drew up a bill to create £20,000 in paper money to continue current for twelve years, the governor cut down the time to five years, each side remained firm and a deadlock ensued. The assembly refused to acknowledge the binding force of a royal instruction or to allow the governor the right to amend money bills.[18] The obstinacy of the house called

---

[12] *Pa. Votes of Assembly*, IV, 302; *Pa. Col. Recs.*, VI, 5, 7, 22.
[13] *Pa. Votes of Assembly*, IV, 304, 306, 309; *Pa. Statutes at Large*, V, 517-521.
[14] *Dinwiddie Corres.*, I, 204, 206, 232.
[15] *Pa. Votes of Assembly*, IV, 318; *Pa. Col. Recs.*, VI, 133-135.
[16] *Pa. Votes of Assembly*, IV, 322, 324.
[17] See page 200.
[18] See page 201.

forth the just censure of the secretary of state.[19] He expressed surprise that the province had failed to aid Virginia and laid the success of the French to the refusal of the colonies to coöperate. He demanded for the future that the province should act vigorously not only in defense of its own domain but in coöperation with other colonies. The assembly threw the blame on the governor, he shifted it to the assembly, but wherever condemnation rests the fact remains that the province was partly responsible for Washington's defeat. The interpretation put upon the secretary's letter of 1753 as to the undoubted limits of the English claim and the refusal to create a sum of money in accordance with the act of 1751 lends color to the charge that the Quaker pacificists, who dominated the assembly, were simply evading the summons to participate in the war. But the root of the matter lay deeper; an important constitutional principle was at stake. The Quaker assembly voted money for the "king's use," but in so doing insisted upon the sole right to judge for itself as well as the people of the utility and propriety of all laws without any outside direction from the crown or proprietors. The assembly was firmly convinced that subjection to the will of the crown or the Penns in fiscal matters meant the destruction of free institutions. Indeed, the assembly held the constitutional issue of far more importance than the security of the province or the welfare of the Empire. The attachment to the principle of self-control very largely accounts for the failure of the province to act with energy in the war.

With the impending struggle between England and France for the mastery of the Great West, the problem of uniting the colonies again became a subject of very real importance. Two factors largely contributed to the agitation for a colonial union; the want of a concert of action among the colonies against the French, and the lack of

[19] *Pa. Col. Recs.*, VI, 177.

uniformity in the relations of the colonies to the Indians. It was thoroughly believed by farsighted colonists and royal officials that the decentralized system of defense among the colonies simply invited contempt and outrage on the part of the French.[20] Dinwiddie, Clinton of New York, Franklin and Hamilton of Pennsylvania, and others repeatedly urged the formation of a colonial union.[21] With regard to the Indian question, each colony was left free to control the political and commercial relations between its settlers and the Indians within its boundaries. These relations were far from satisfactory, for the savages continually complained of the unjust encroachments of the English on their lands and of the unscrupulous conduct of colonial traders.   The lack of uniform and just dealings with the Indians was weakening their attachment to the English cause at this critical juncture and driving them to the side of the French.   In 1750 Richard Peters wrote to the Penns, that the bad state of the relations of the English to the Indians '' may bring on an Indian War and what will the event of that is altogether uncertain. The Assembly of this Province is unwilling to have anything to do with the New Yorkers as they are to join with us, and indeed all the colonies manage miserably and instead of strengthening his Majesties Interest they wilfully and foolishly break it into pieces, and in the End will destroy it.'' [22] Peter's prophecy was fulfilled in 1763.

[20] Dinwiddie wrote to the secretary of state, that "The French too justly observe the want of connection in the Colonies, and from thence conclude . . . that altho' we are vastly superiour to them in Numbers, yet they can take and secure the Co't'y before we can agree to hinder them." *Dinwiddie Corres.*, I, 203; see also II, 230, 265. Governor Clinton expressed the same view in a letter of October, 1750, addressed to Governor Hamilton of Pa. *Pa. Col. Recs.*, V, 480.

[21] Franklin, *Works* (Smyth ed.), III, 40-43; *Dinwiddie Corres.*, I, 285, 406-407; *Penn Mss., Official Corres.*, V, Clinton to Hamilton, Oct. 8, 1750; Hamilton to Thos. Penn, April 30, 1751; *Pa. Col. Recs.*, V, 480.

[22] *Penn Mss., Official Corres.*, V, Richard Peters to proprietors, Oct. 15, 23, 1750.

As hostilities became more imminent the English government laid plans to redress the complaints of the Indians and to secure their wavering friendship. With this purpose in view the Board of Trade in September, 1753, instructed the governors north of the Carolinas, except Rhode Island and Connecticut, to hold a joint conference with the Iroquois.[23] Commissioners from eight colonies met at Albany in the summer of 1754 and seized the occasion to work out a scheme of colonial union.[24] The conference decided unanimously upon two resolutions; " That a union of the colonies was absolutely necessary for their preservation "; and " That it was necessary the Union should be established by act of Parliament." It is needless to recount the reasons which prompted the first resolution.[25] The necessity of doing away with the old requisition system had been proven beyond the shadow of doubt. The need of replacing the pernicious decentralized system of regulating Indian affairs by substituting a uniform policy was of vital concern. As to the second resolution it was deemed necessary to call upon the sovereignty of the imperial legislature to make the union binding and preclude the possibility of nullification and secession on the part of any colony or colonies " till the whole crumbled into its original parts." In the Albany Plan of Union the essential feature was a central authority with jurisdiction over all Indian affairs and with power to raise and pay troops, build forts, and equip vessels. In order to carry

23 *Pa. Votes of Assembly*, IV, 278-279.

24 Franklin, *Works* (Smyth ed.), III, 203-226; *Pa. Col. Recs.*, VI, 65-68, 71, 78, 105-109.

25 Franklin wrote that from one or other of several causes, " the Assemblies of six out of seven colonies applied to, had granted no assistance to Virginia, when lately invaded by the French, though purposely convened, and the importance of the occasion earnestly urged upon them;—considering moreover, that one principal encouragement to the French, in insulting and invading the British American dominions, was their knowledge of our disunited state, and of our weakness arising from such want of union." Franklin, *Works* (Smyth ed.), III, 203-204.

into effect these powers it was authorized to make laws and to levy taxes and duties. Here was a proper solution of a most serious problem; a supreme authority with power to act directly upon the individual in matters of general interest. The only solution was either the scheme devised at Albany or else the exercise of the central and sovereign powers of Parliament. The former had the virtue of allowing the colonists to make laws and levy taxes through their own representatives. Franklin and others realized that taxation by Parliament in which the colonists had no representatives would give "extreme dissatisfaction." [26] The commissioners at Albany were without power to give a final assent to the plan and it was submitted to the colonial legislatures for ratification. But with the same spirit of unanimity in which the nationalists at Albany adopted the plan, the assemblies either failed to act or positively rejected it.[27] Franklin wrote " Every Body cries a Union is absolutely necessary; but when they come to the Manner and Form of the Union, their weak Noddles are perfectly distracted." [28] The rejection is hardly a matter of surprise when one remembers the strength of local prejudices and the tendencies of the colonies toward complete autonomy. Parliament was finally forced to tax the colonies for the support of an American army, but the attempts to reconcile the apparently inconsistent claims of imperial sovereignty with colonial self-government led to the severance of the Empire. When left to form their own imperial government the Americans established only a " league of friendship " which guaranteed local rights. It required all the anarchy of the Critical Period and the herculean efforts of such nationalists as Hamilton, Madison, and Wilson to overcome the particularism of the states and to bring about the adoption and ratification of the

26 Franklin, *Works* (Smyth ed.), III, 232-237.
27 Beer, *British Col. Pol., 1754-1765*, 21-22.
28 Franklin, *Works* (Smyth ed.), III, 242.

federal constitution of 1789. In view of these facts the adoption of the Albany Plan of Union is hardly conceivable. The English conception of a union differed widely from the American idea as framed at Albany.[29] In the same month that the commissioners met at Albany, Sir Thomas Robinson, secretary of state, directed the Board of Trade to prepare " a plan of general concert to be entered into by the American colonies for their mutual defense."[30] English statesmen also saw clearly the need of a colonial union. In August the board presented a plan which contemplated merely a military union.[31] It provided for a congress of one commissioner from each colony to agree upon a military establishment and to proportion the quotas of men and money among the colonies. The colonial as also the English troops should be under the command of an officer appointed by the crown and who should also act as general superintendent of Indian affairs. This scheme kept intact the old unworkable requisition system and was therefore an inadequate solution of the problem of imperial defense. This defect was realized by the board. In presenting its report the board said that in case a colony refused to send a commissioner to the congress or to raise the required quotas, then " no other method can be taken, but that of an application for an interposition of the Authority of Parliament." Franklin likewise realized that " if ever there be an Union, it must be form'd at home by the Ministry and Parliament."[32] But any imposition of a plan by act of Parliament would have tended rather to alienate the colonies than to bind them together, the chief object in view. The plan of the board required the consent of

29 Gov. Morris wrote in Nov., 1755, "The plan formed at Albany, was upon such Republican Principles, that I do not wonder it was not relished at home, as it seemed calculated to unite the Colonys in such a manner, as to give the Crown little or no influence in their Councils." *Pa. Archives*, 1st. ser., II, 499.

30 *B. T. Paps.*, *Pl. Gen.*, XV, O 125.

31 Beer, *British Col. Pol.*, *1754-1765*, 27.

32 Franklin, *Works* (Smyth ed.), III, 267, 276, 242.

the colonies while the exigencies of the occasion demanded prompt action. Therefore, the board recommended that the crown should appoint immediately a commander-in-chief of all the forces in America and a general superintendent of Indian affairs. In view of these facts the home government was forced to fall back upon the requisition system.

In the latter part of 1754, after the defeat of the Virginia forces, Dinwiddie repeatedly called upon the home government for troops and stores of war.[33] This plea for aid was in line with the recommendation of the Board of Trade. In 1755 General Braddock was sent to the colonies as commander-in-chief, supported by two regiments of British troops. Parliament made provision for this force and for two regiments to be recruited in the colonies. In October, 1754, the secretary of state instructed the colonial governors to raise troops to join Braddock's forces on arrival, to make ready provisions for them, to furnish English officers with means of travel within the colony, to obey Braddock's orders with respect to the quartering of troops, impressment of carriages, and necessaries for the troops raised in the colony.[34] Since these expenses were deemed of a "local and peculiar nature" the charges were to be borne by the colony itself. In addition each colony was required to contribute to a common fund for objects of a "more general concern." In Pennsylvania a bitter debate between the governor and assembly over the validity of royal instructions prevented compliance with the requisition. In January, 1755, General St. Clair, quarter-master to the English forces, asked Governor Morris by letter how far the assembly had complied with the requisition.[35] Morris replied, "such is the Infatuation and Obstinacy of the People, I have to deal with, or at least their Representatives, that tho' their Country is

33 *Dinwiddie Corres.*, I, 280, 281, 364-365.
34 *Pa. Votes of Assembly*, IV, 242-243; *Pa. Col. Recs.*, VI, 200-203.
35 *Pa. Col. Recs.*, VI, 298-299.

invaded, and everything they enjoy depends upon removing the French from their borders, yet I could not persuade them to act with vigor at this Juncture, or even to grant Supplies expected by the Crown and recommended by the Secretary of State." [36] This drew from Braddock a letter to Morris " expressing the greatest surprise to find such pusillanimous and improper Behavior in your Assembly, and to hear of Faction and Opposition where Liberty and Property are invaded." [37] He threatened to employ " unpleasant methods " if the assembly did not act a part more becoming.

Thus matters stood when Morris went to join the conference of governors called by Braddock to meet at his camp at Alexandria. Here a plan of campaign was agreed upon.[38] With respect to the common fund the governors frankly confessed to Braddock that applications to their assemblies for that purpose proved futile and gave it as their unanimous opinion that such a fund " can never be established without the aid of Parliament." They suggested that the English ministry should be urged to find a method to compel the colonies to contribute. Braddock was assured by the governors that they would leave nothing undone to persuade their assemblies to honor the requisition but they expressed a fear that the " present expedition must be at a stand unless the General shall think proper to make Use of the Credit upon the Government at home to defray the Expense of all the operations under his direction." The governors returned to their respective colonies to do what they could.

Morris of Pennsylvania could accomplish little. The contest between him and the assembly over royal instruction continued to prevent the province from fulfilling its proper

36 *Pa. Col. Recs.*, VI, 299-300.
37 *Ibid.*, 307, 331, 332.
38 *Ibid.*, 365-368. The governors present were: Shirley of Mass., Delancey of N. Y., Morris of Pa., Sharpe of Md., and Dinwiddie of Va.

share in the military operations. The assembly was willing
to grant assistance but only on its own terms. On its own
credit, the house issued £15,000 in treasury notes, one-
third of which was expended in securing provisions for the
troops, in clearing roads, and maintaining an express,
while the remainder was given to Massachusetts for the
support of Shirley's expedition.[39] A great measure of
praise is due Governor Morris and Benjamin Franklin for
assistance afforded to Braddock in the expedition to drive
the French from Fort Duquesne.[40]

It is needless to relate the well-known story of the disastrous defeat of the expedition. The British regiments
marched on to defeat unsupported except by the Virginia
militia. In July the governor informed the assembly of
the failure at Fort Duquesne and of the retreat of the English forces which affected none so much as Pennsylvania
whose soil was now left exposed to the insults of the French
and Indians.[41] He exhorted the house to establish a militia
and to grant supplies for the purchase of arms and ammunition. On August 4 the assembly submitted to the
governor a bill to create £50,000 in bills of credit to be discharged by a tax on all property, real and personal.
The governor amended it to exempt the estates of the
Penns.[42] Again a deadlock ensued which lasted all summer while the inhabitants on the frontier were left unpro-
tected against the horrors of tomahawk and fire-brand.
The situation in the interior was pitiful. The success of
the French let loose the savages to burn and kill to their
hearts' content. The back-country folk, without arms,
ammunition or military organization, were forced to evacuate their homes and flee to the east for protection.[43] The

[39] Pa. Votes of Assembly, IV, 391.
[40] Pa. Archives, 1st. ser., II, 294 ff., 311, 335, 372.
[41] Pa. Votes of Assembly, IV, 415-416.
[42] Ibid., 419, 421-422.
[43] Pa. Col. Recs., VI, 645, 646, 671, 766-768; Pa. Votes of Assembly, IV, 493.

situation was aggravated when Colonel Dunbar, instead
of remaining with the English forces to check the Indians,
marched on to safety at Philadelphia. From every quarter petitions came to the assembly pleading earnestly that
all disputes be laid aside in this time of trial and that
prompt measures be taken to protect the lives and property of the people.[44] So embittered were the frontier people at the refractory attitude of the Quaker assembly that
threats of violence were made against it. In the counties
of Bucks, Chester, and Lancaster the people threatened
to march to Philadelphia and with arms in their hands to
force the assembly to afford them protection.[45] On the
other hand it was charged that the Quakers, free from attacks in the east, took " uncommon pains " to persuade
the people from taking up arms, and so great is their influence, wrote Governor Morris, upon the " People and even
upon the Assembly, a great Majority of which are Quakers,
that the inhabitants seem as unconcerned as ever." [46] In
particular the Quakers were charged with appealing to the
German Pietists, whose religious principles were similar
to those of the Quakers, to support the latter in power on
the plea that the Penns designed to abridge them of their
rights and reduce them to slavery.[47]

Despairing of any assistance from the assembly, the governor appealed to Shirley, now commander-in-chief, and to
the other colonies for aid. Shirley replied that he could
do nothing.[48] Governor Belcher of New Jersey responded
that if the populous and wealthy province of Pennsylvania
would not protect itself it was unreasonable to ask his prov-

[44] *Pa. Col. Recs.*, VI, 550, 647, 734; *Pa. Votes of Assembly*, IV,
493, 495, 502; *Pa. Archives*, 1st. ser., II, 385, 448, 449, 450.

[45] *Pa. Col. Recs.*, VI, 667, 729; VII, 87. Edward Biddle wrote
from Reading that " The people exclaim against the Quakers, &
some are scarce restrained from burning the Houses of those few
who are in This Town." *Ibid.*, VI, 705.

[46] *Ibid.*, VI, 563.

[47] *Ibid.*, 599, 604, 621.

[48] *Pa. Archives*, 1st. ser., II, 450, 469, 493-495.

ınce to send aid and leave its own frontiers exposed.[49]
Virginia had only sufficient arms to supply her own militia.[50] Nothing could be expected from Maryland where
the same controversy was in progress which rendered Pennsylvania helpless. Governor Morris appealed to the receiver-general of the Penns for a loan of £1000 to purchase
arms but he replied that he had neither money or authority
to comply.[51] In fact, the attitude of the assembly of Pennsylvania had rather the effect of deferring other colonies
from action than of eliciting a prompt response to the call
for support. The assembly of Maryland in the struggle
with its proprietor closely watched the trend of affairs in
Pennsylvania and resorted to the same tactics.[52] Belcher
wrote to Morris that his assembly would do nothing for
the common defense '' taking for their Example, the bad
one given by your Assembly, and that of Maryland.'' [53]
Dinwiddie declared that the obstinacy of Maryland and
Pennsylvania made the Virginia assembly backward in voting supplies.[54] Herein we have a good illustration of common political aspirations and community of interests among
the colonies.

The controversy in Pennsylvania aroused anew the enemies of the Quakers and of the proprietary government.
The enemies of the former urged that the Quakers should
be excluded from the government because their pacific
principles were injurious to the welfare of the province.
This idea had been suggested repeatedly during the eight-

[49] *Pa. Archives*, 1st. ser., II, 471.

[50] *Ibid.*, II, 482.

[51] *Ibid.*, II, 475, 476.

[52] Black, *Maryland's Attitude in the Struggle for Canada, Johns
Hopkins Studies*, X, 359-365.

[53] *Pa. Archives*, 1st. ser., II, 269. Belcher wrote that his province was well spirited, "altho Pennsylvania sets them so vile an
Example." *N. J. Archives*, VIII, pt. 2, 169.

[54] *Dinwiddie Corres.*, II, 52. Dinwiddie wrote that the example
of Pa. and Md. make application to his assembly for aid "an
Up-hill Work." *Ibid.*, II, 192.

eenth century and it was now urged by Governor Morris and others.[55] In fact, Thomas Penn wrote from London in March, 1755, that the English ministry had hinted to the London Quakers that if they could not persuade their colonial brethren to act more rationally " they will not be suffered to continue in Station to perplex the Governors."[56] Those hostile to proprietary government urged that the charters of Pennsylvania and Maryland should be vacated and direct control by the crown be established. Dinwiddie especially urged this remedy upon the English officials.[57] He wrote " we shall continue in distress'd and distracted Condit'n till H.M'y takes the Proprietary Gov'ts into his own Hands." In fact, the English ministry had approached the Penns several times with offers to purchase the powers of government.[58] Both of these recommendations were wise but neither reached the root of the situation. Other colonies were not hampered by Quaker principles and were governed directly by the crown, yet the assemblies proved to be just as refractory as that of Pennsylvania. Shirley, Dinwiddie, Morris, Belcher, Sharpe of Maryland, and Braddock saw with clear judgment that the only solution was parliamentary interference. The real difficulty was the requisition system.

The dispute over the taxation of proprietary estates was temporarily allayed by a free gift from the Penns of £5000 for defense. A supply bill was passed granting £60,000 in paper currency to the king's use.[59] Although

55 *Pa. Archives*, 1st. ser., II, 281, 528, 531.

56 *Penn Mss.*, *Saunders Coates*, Thos. Penn to Richard Peters, March 26, 1755; *Letter Bk.*, IV, Thos. Penn to Peters, July 7, 1756.

57 *Dinwiddie Corres.*, II, 414-415, 418. Belcher of N. J. also advised such action. *Pa. Archives*, 1st. ser., II, 478.

58 Thos. Penn wrote to Richard Peters, May 8, 1756, " . . . there is no question but the Administration would very gladly get the Proprietary Governments into their own hands, and some of them have told me so but not without the free consent of the Proprietors, and paying a full consideration for the value of them." *Penn Mss.*, *Letter Bk.* IV.

59 *Pa. Statutes at Large*, V, 201-212.

the estates of the proprietors were freed from taxation it
is significant to note that the Quaker assembly took precaution that the money should not be employed for direct
warlike purposes. It stipulated that the funds should be
expended in maintaining friendly relations with the Indians, in relief of distressed settlers and " other purposes
for the king's Service." " Other purposes " meant nothing when it is remembered that the disbursement of the
funds was placed in the hands of a committee named by
the assembly principled against war. At the same time
a militia bill was passed which Dinwiddie characterized
as a " joke on all military affairs," and which Governor
Morris declared " was intended to answer no purpose but
to amuse the people." [60] Out of regard for Quaker principles the bill provided for voluntary enlistments. Moreover, it provided that officers should be elected by the
troops, and that the forces should not be led more than
three days' journey from the inhabited parts of the province or serve more than three weeks in garrison duty without their consent. One may readily gather from the terms
of these bills to what an extent the assembly had encroached
upon the proper powers of the executive. In a crisis which
demanded the concentration of military power, the governor was denied authority to employ the troops to the best
advantage, to appoint the most efficient officers, and to dispose of the funds at his discretion. With the aid of these
laws a cordon of forts and blockhouses were erected along
the frontier at strategic points and garrisoned by provincial troops. Both Governor Morris and Benjamin
Franklin deserve praise for their untiring efforts at this
time.[61]

Wearied with the repeated refusals of the Quaker assembly to respond to the demands for protection, over a

[60] *Dinwiddie Corres.*, II, 313; *Pa. Archives*, 1st. ser., II, 508,
526, 531.

[61] *Pa. Archives*, 1st. ser., II, 535-575 *passim;* Franklin, *Works*,
(Smyth ed.), III, 292-293, 304-305, 325-326.

hundred men of prominence in the province signed a petition to the king picturing the distressed condition of the people and praying for royal aid.[62] The memorial stated that the attitude of the assembly was doubly injurious to the province, cooling the ardor of other colonies on behalf of the common cause and alienating the friendly Indians. It declared that no redress was possible as long as the assembly was composed of Quakers who studiously avoided all military measures by spinning out the time in unreasonable disputes. In February, 1756, the petition was referred to the Board of Trade where a hearing was granted to the petitioners and the assembly through their respective solicitors and counsel.[63] As the address was presumably drawn up before the passage of the military and supply bills no mention was made of them. Hence counsel for the assembly branded as false the charge that the Quakers made no provision for defense.[64] The real object, said he, was to oust the Quakers from the government. He pointed out that the assembly had repeatedly offered the governor supply bills only to have them rejected by the arbitrary instructions of the proprietors. He held it to be gross injustice that the Penns should contribute nothing either to the maintenance of friendly relations with the Indians or to the cost of defense, although the proprietors reaped immense advantages from both. As to the Indian barbarities, he argued, they were not perpetrated by the allies of the French but by a small band of Delawares and Shawonese, long in amity with the province,

---

[62] B. T. Paps., Props., XIX, V 152; William Smith, Brief State of the Province of Pa., 1755, (Sabin Reprint).

[63] B. T. Jour., LXIV, 78, 90, 97-98. The petitioners were represented by F. J. Paris, solicitor, Yorke and Forester, counsel; the assembly by Joshua Sharpe, solicitor, Henley and Pratt, counsel, Richard Partridge and Robert Charles, agents.

[64] The argument for the assembly may be found in Add. Mss. (British Museum), 15489, ff. 47-50, (Transcript in the Lib. of Cong.); and for the petitioners, Pa. Mag. of Hist., Oct., 1886, X, 294-315.

and he intimated broadly that these Indians were roused to vengeance by the unjust dealing of the Penns with them concerning land. In answer to the aspersion that the Quakers, principled against war, should thrust themselves into the assembly at this critical time, the counsel for the house declared that the election of representatives was annual, by ballot, and without corruption, hence, if the Quakers continued to be the choice of the people under these conditions, it was good evidence of the " faith and confidence wch. the whole Community place in that Denomination of Men and of the Belief that they will not betray nor give up the essential Liberties and advantages of this Constitution to purchase a little temporary Safety." But this statement was not sound. The Quakers did not represent the whole community.[65] The three eastern counties returned twenty-six representatives to the legislature, while the five western counties, equal in population, sent only ten. It is nearer the truth to say that the assembly represented the interests of the Quaker and conservative classes of the east, who feared the growing democracy of the west. The dominance of the Quakers was also made possible by the high suffrage franchise, according to which only one in fifty in the city of Philadelphia cast a ballot. The large body of Scotch-Irish and Germans on the frontier and the large unenfranchised class in the east, all of whom demanded adequate protection against the enemy, were denied the means to make their sentiments felt. The report of the Board of Trade of March 3 to the Privy Council was favorable to the petitioners.[66] The report severely criticized the supply bill because it did not specify military services among the objects of expenditure and it said that the " other things " stipulated in the bill was rendered nugatory because the commissioners empowered to dispose of the funds were named by a Quaker

65 Lincoln, *Revolutionary Movement in Pa.*, 40-52.
66 *Pa. Votes of Assembly*, IV, 628-630.

assembly. It further declared that the military bill was intended rather to exempt persons from service than to encourage enlistments and that the restrictive features rendered the law quite impracticable. The report expressed the opinion that the measures taken for defense were " improper, inadequate and ineffectual " and that there was no hope for a better order of affairs as long as the Quakers remained in power. In conclusion, the board recommended that the Quakers should be excluded from the assembly by the imposition of an oath on all representatives by act of Parliament. A bill to this end was introduced but action upon it was forestalled by the London Quakers who promised to persuade their colonial co-religionists not to stand at the next election in the province.[67]

In 1756 several events of importance occurred. In May England formally declared war against France.[68] Until this time the Empire was nominally at peace although hostilities had begun between the subjects of the two nations in America. It was the final struggle between England and France for supremacy of trade and dominion, not only in North America, but in the West Indies, East India, and Africa. In December William Pitt was created secretary of state and under the masterful guidance of this great imperialist, English arms eventually emerged triumphant in all quarters of the globe. In Pennsylvania the power of the Quakers was broken. In the assembly which convened in the fall of the year few Quakers remained : some had declined a reëlection and others had resigned. An act of Parliament was not needed to exclude them.[69] At last when the struggle had reached the borders of the province, the Quakers, whose principles stood out of touch with the stern condition of affairs, were forced to yield the

[67] Sharpless, A Quaker Experiment in Gov't., 252; Penn Mss., Letter Bk. IV, Thos. Penn to Richard Peters, July 7, 1756; Thos. Penn to Isaac Norris, Feb. 14, 1756.

[68] Pa. Archives, 1st. ser., II, 659, 735.

[69] Pa. Votes of Assembly, IV. 627.

powers of government to others. The "Holy Experiment" of the founder and his followers had fallen indeed upon evil times. But, as Franklin said, "We shall soon see if matters will be better managed by a majority of different religious persuasions."[70]

Pitt promptly made preparations for executing a vigorous offensive campaign against the French. The colonies were divided into two military districts; the northern consisting of New England, New York, and New Jersey, the southern of Pennsylvania and the colonies south. In February, 1757, Pitt sent letters to the governors informing them of the dispatch of troops and a fleet from England to operate against the French.[71] The governors were instructed to call upon their assemblies to raise as large a force as possible for the general campaign, under the command of the Earl of Loudoun. This number was exclusive of the forces necessary for the immediate defense of the province. Each colony was required to raise, pay, and clothe its quota of men, while arms, stores of war, and provision were to be furnished at the expense of the crown. Pitt expressed the hope that the colonies would act zealously and "not clogg the Enlistments of Men, or the raising of Money for their Pay &c with such Limitations as have been hitherto found to render the service difficult and ineffectual." Was the hope realized?

In March Loudoun met the governors of the southern district at Philadelphia when a plan of campaign was agreed upon and the quotas to be supplied by each province were fixed.[72] Five thousand troops were named as necessary for the defense of the south,—twelve hundred English troops and thirty-eight hundred provincials.

[70] Franklin, *Works* (Smyth ed.), III, 345.

[71] *Pa. Archives*, 1st. ser., II, 657, 718; III, 95; Kimball, *Pitt Corres.*, I, 1, 5-6, 9.

[72] *Pa. Col. Recs.*, VII, 470-471; Kimball, *Pitt Corres.*, I, 6, note 40. The governors present were Denny of Pa., Sharpe of Md., Dinwiddie of Va., and Dobbs of No. Car.

Pennsylvania's quota was fourteen hundred men, of which two hundred were to be sent south for the defense of South Carolina and Georgia and the rest to be employed in the protection of the province itself. The governors, on parting, promised Loudoun, as they had assured Braddock before, that they would make every effort to persuade their assemblies to fulfill the plans.

Although the departure of the Quakers from the assembly of Pennsylvania wrought a change of attitude on the question of war, the position of a house of different religious persuasions remained the same on the constitutional question. The old quarrel between the governor and assembly prevented the province from carrying out its full share in the operations planned. This serious hindrance to military operations necessitated the personal interference of Loudoun.[73] He first appealed to the leaders of the assembly but to no avail. Then in consultation with Dinwiddie it was agreed that under the circumstances the only alternative was to advise the governor to waive his instructions from the proprietors. Loudoun wrote to Pitt that this was of supreme necessity, " for had the (supply) bill been rejected the whole of their troops would have been disbanded immediately, and that Province laid open to be a Prey to the Enemy, or I had been obliged to have left more troops for its defence than could be spared from the other plans of operation for this campaign." The governor was placed on the horns of a dilemma; he was forced either to violate the instructions from the Penns or else hinder the campaign. The former was the lesser evil and Governor Denny yielded. Although the proprietary estates were exempted from taxation, yet the funds were placed in the control of a committee named by the assembly.[74] The bill provided for the raising of fourteen hundred men, three hundred for garrison duty and the rest

[73] Kimball, *Pitt Corres.*, I, 41; *Pa. Col. Rec.*, VII, 453-454.
[74] *Pa. Statutes at Large*, V, 294, 303, 309.

for offensive operations on the frontier of the province. No provision was made for the dispatch of two hundred men to South Carolina. Again it is obvious to what an extent the assembly had encroached on the powers which belonged properly to the executive or the commander-in-chief. Loudoun wrote to Pitt, " Their whole Attention seems to be, to usurp every part of the Prerogative, into the hands of the Assembly, and to disappoint every Plan of the Government." [75] Such dictation by the popular branch of the government was by no means peculiar to Pennsylvania; it was a condition which faced every provincial governor.[76]

The troubles of Loudoun and Governor Denny were not at an end. In June the latter informed the assembly that it was not within his power to comply with the agreement to send troops to South Carolina, that the term of enlistment of the troops was near expiration, their pay was badly in arrears, and many had deserted whereby the frontier was left inadequately protected.[77] The house refused to frame a militia bill such as the governor could properly sign or to raise an additional force of five hundred men called for by Loudoun. In July Loudoun wrote Pitt that the southern provinces " behaved very Ill; Pennsylvania have not now raised near the Number of Men agreed upon; and have not sent their 200 Men to South Carolina. They have no Militia Law, and have refused to raise the Additional Number I desired of them." [78] While the colonies of the north, New Jersey excepted, acted with a fair show of energy in response to Loudoun's requisitions, the same cannot be said of the south.[79] No support could be expected from Maryland where the strug-

75 Kimball, *Pitt Corres.*, I, 77.
76 Greene, *Provincial Governor*, 100-105.
77 *Pa. Col. Recs.*, VII, 563.
78 Kimball, *Pitt Corres.*, I, 76-77.
79 As to the response of the colonies of the northern dep't., see Kimball, *Pitt Corres.*, I, 26, 58, 61-62.

gle over the taxation of the estates of Lord Baltimore could not be compromised. In New Jersey Loudoun was obliged to exert his personal influence in order to secure even one-half the quota of troops levied upon the province.[80] Under such a condition of affairs, the commander was unable to devote his undivided attention to the operations of the campaign itself. Loudoun informed Pitt, that there were " so many difficulties to remove in this country in order to set things in Motion, that being on the spot was necessary at present." [81] Such were the evils which flowed from the requisition system. Loudoun's expedition against Louisburg proved a dismal failure and the French captured Fort William Henry, a point of great strategic importance.

In 1758 Pitt made a fresh start. The incompetent Loudoun was replaced by James Abercromby.[82] It was the determination of the crown, wrote Pitt to the governors, " to repair the Losses and Disappointments of the last inactive campaign & by the most vigorous and Extensive Efforts to avert the dangers impending in North America." [83] The plan of campaign was three-fold: an attack upon the center of Canada by way of Crown Point, and upon the flanks of French power at Louisburg and Fort Duquesne. The northern colonies were required to raise, pay, and clothe twenty thousand men. On similar terms the southern provinces were called upon to raise " a body of several thousand Men to join the king's Forces in those parts." Abercromby placed the quota of Virginia, Maryland, and Pennsylvania at six thousand men.[84] The campaign in the south was put under the command of General John Forbes.[85] In March the assembly of Pennsylvania

---

[80] Kimball, *Pitt Corres.*, I, 41, 43, 63.

[81] *Ibid.*, 54-55.

[82] *Ibid.*, I, 133-134; *Pa. Col. Recs.*, VIII, 26.

[83] Kimball, *Pitt Corres.*, I, 140-43; *Pa. Col. Recs.*, VIII, 27-28.

[84] Kimball, *Pitt Corres.*, I, 215; *Pa. Col. Recs.*, VIII, 37-38.

[85] Kimball, *Pitt Corres.*, I, 146; *Pa. Archives*, 1st. ser., III, 321.

promptly responded with a resolve to raise, pay, and clothe twenty-seven hundred and fifty men, offered a bounty of £5 to encourage enlistments, and presented the governor with a bill to create £100,000 in paper currency to cover the expenses.[86] The members of the house professed to be animated by great zeal and exhorted the governor to make every effort to have the troops ready by May 1, the time set by the requisition. Prompt action was again blocked by the revival of the old conflict over the taxation of the Penns' estates. After a month's delay Governor Denny signed a supply bill of the same tenor as the year before. The northern colonies evinced a lively spirit in the military operations,[87] but the south was half-hearted.[88] On May 19 Forbes wrote to Pitt picturing the obstacles which confronted him.[89] Of the sum voted by Pennsylvania only one-half was available for the campaign, the remainder was consumed in liquidating the arrearages of the former enterprise. The delay in voting the money and printing the bills of credit seriously retarded the operations. Forbes said he had hopes of securing a thousand men by June 1, " but when the rest will be got I can scarce say." From Virginia he hardly expected more than an equal number at the same time. Support from Maryland was out of the question.[90] Governor Sharpe of Maryland raised two hundred men on his own credit for the expedition against Fort Duquesne, while Governor Dobbs sent the same number at the expense of the crown.[91]

[86] Pa. Votes of Assembly, IV, 797, 799-800, 801, 804-805, 806, 813, 814-815.

[87] The colonies of the northern division were called upon to raise 20,000 men, but the forces raised numbered only 17,480. Kimball, Pitt. Corres., I, 135, 208, 213, 222, 226, 227; Beer, British Col. Pol., 1754-1765, 60-61.

[88] Kimball, Pitt Corres., I, 185, 210, 229, 230, 237, 240, 243.

[89] Ibid., I, 245-246.

[90] Forbes took into the pay of the crown a small force of Md. troops, for which the assembly refused to make provision. Ibid., I, 243, 279, 329.

[91] Ibid., I, 241.

The provincials, according to Forbes, were not only seriously deficient in numbers, but also in quality.[92] Like Loudoun before him, Forbes was also seriously handicapped by the short term of enlistments. The troops of Pennsylvania and Virginia were engaged only to the first of December. In October, after Fort Duquesne had fallen, Forbes asked the governors of Pennsylvania, Maryland, and Virginia what number of provincials they could furnish for garrison duty for the winter, since he had not sufficient regulars at his command to undertake the task.[93] The Virginia assembly responded by instructing the governor to recall the forces on December 1, assistance from Maryland could not be expected, and the assembly of Pennsylvania replied that Forbes could not reasonably ask the province to bear this additional expense in view of the large aids granted to the crown, especially since the frontier was so far distant from the inhabited part of the province and that garrison duty was usually performed by the regulars in other colonies.[94] The same narrow spirit was shown by the assembly on several other occasions. Forbes wrote to Pitt that the assembly would do nothing to forward the service " that they did not think themselves compelled to do by the words of your letter to them." [95] The following evidence in support of this statement may be offered. At the outset of the expedition Forbes was without camp necessaries by reason of their failure to arrive

[92] Forbes said of the Pa. and Va. forces that " a few of their principal Officers excepted, all the rest are an extream bad Collection of broken Innkeepers, Horse Jockeys, & Indian traders, and that the Men under them, are a direct copy of their Officers, nor can it well be otherwise, as they are a gathering from the scum of the worst people in every Country, who have wrought themselves up, into a panick at the very name of Indians." *Ibid.*, I, 242.

[93] Pa. *Votes of Assembly*, V, 2-3; *Pa. Col. Recs.*, VIII, 224, 227, 233; Kimball, *Pitt Corres.*, I, 374.

[94] Kimball, *Pitt Corres.*, I, 407-408; *Pa. Col. Recs.*, VIII, 229, 240; *Pa. Votes of Assembly*, V, 6.

[95] Kimball, *Pitt Corres.*, I, 338.

from England. He applied to the assembly for them and received a frank refusal. The house declared that according to the requisition such impedimenta were to be furnished by the crown, that the province had fulfilled all required of it, and that Forbes had authority according to his orders to supply these things.[96] Still another proof. Admiral Craven asked the assembly to provide him with thirty recruits for the fleet and in return promised to station a ship of war at Philadelphia.[97] The assembly replied that it was not expected that the colony should recruit the fleet at its own expense, neither was it able to bear this additional charge in view of the large number of troops raised and supported.[98] Such conduct shows up in a most unfavorable light compared with that of Massachusetts. The latter not only raised and supported seven thousand men for the general service, but equipped and manned two vessels to act with the English fleet and supplied the necessary recruits.[99]

The successes at Louisburg and Fort Duquesne in 1758 left the center of Canada still under French control. The undertakings of the next two years were devoted chiefly to the conquest of Montreal and Quebec. In the south the purpose was to fortify Fort Duquesne and to protect the long frontier.[100] To recount in detail the conduct of the southern provinces during these two years would be needless and wearisome. The English commanders were confronted with the same condition of affairs as had perplexed Braddock, Loudoun, and Forbes. Each year Pitt made requisition for the same number of men on the same terms.[101] Maryland and the Carolinas did practically nothing for the general service. Each year the assembly of

96 *Pa. Col. Recs.*, VIII, 112; *Pa. Votes of Assembly*, IV, 831-832.
97 *Pa. Votes of Assembly*, IV, 832.
98 *Ibid.*, 833, 835.
99 Kimball, *Pitt Corres.*, I, 361-363; II, 253-254.
100 *Ibid.*, I, 440; II, 12-13.
101 *Ibid.*, I, 417; II, 15, 234; *Pa. Col. Recs.*, VIII, 272, 315, 451.

Pennsylvania voted to raise its quota of men but each time the same weary quarrel over the taxation of the proprietary estates arose to hinder and delay military operations. In 1759 General Amherst hurried to the province at the solicitation of Colonel Stanwix, to break by personal influence the deadlock between the executive and assembly.[102] His appeal to the leading men of the house failed. He appealed to the assembly itself, pointing out that a refusal to yield meant the dismissal " of all thoughts of carrying on the intended Offensive Operations, and Building a Fort, but the house remained Deaf to all kinds of Remonstrances." Recourse to the governor was the only alternative. The assembly considered the principle at stake of more vital concern than the success of the campaign. Governor Denny, under pressure of Amherst's advice and a judicious bribe from the assembly, waived his instructions and the proprietary estates were taxed for the first time. Again in 1761 Morris, Denny's successor, likewise violated his instructions at the request of Amherst. In order to justify his acquiescence, Morris wrote to Pitt that the assembly would do nothing for the general service " but at the price of obtaining the most unjust advantages over their proprietaries, with whom they are contending. And to which nothing could have induced me to submit, but my Zeal for the General Service, and my fears of depriving the King of so considerable aid at this most critical juncture." [103] It is clear that the assembly played upon the exigencies of the occasion to make itself the supreme power in the provincial constitution. Each year the number of troops available reached but half the number voted.[104]

[102] Kimball, *Pitt Corres.*, II, 88, 131; *Pa. Col. Recs.*, VIII, 331-332.

[103] Kimball, *Pitt Corres.*, II, 276; *Pa. Archives*, 1st. ser., III, 715; *Pa. Col. Recs.*, VIII, 331-332.

[104] Amherst and Stanwix agreed that Pa., Md., Va., and No. Car. should raise a body of 6400 men, but the latter said that he never expected any forces at all from Md. and No. Car., and only about

Each year the controversy over the supply bill retarded operations. The funds voted for one campaign were spent in paying off the debts due for the previous campaign.[105] The pay of the troops was usually in arrears, murmurings of mutiny were frequent, and desertions were many. The short enlistments precluded the employment of the provincials in winter garrison duty. In December, 1759, the assembly ordered the governor to disband all the troops except one hundred and fifty for garrison duty. This action was based on the plea of poverty and the claim that there was little need of troops to lie inactive during the winter season, since Quebec had fallen and Stanwix had made a treaty with the Indians.[106] The governor as well as Amherst and Stanwix strongly protested.[107] They urged that the outcome of the conference with the Indians was uncertain, that Canada had not yet been wholly conquered, and that there were not sufficient regulars to man the frontier garrisons. But the assembly saw no reason to alter its determination.[108] In the next year General Monckton experienced the same difficulty. It was only after Amherst was forced to withdraw Colonel Vaughan's regiment from the province that the assembly voted to keep three hundred men in garrison duty till November or until the conclusion of peace.[109] These evils were not confined to Pennsylvania; all the southern colonies exhibited the same refractory attitude. On the other hand,

2700 from Pa. and Va. Kimball, *Pitt Corres.*, II, 132. For the campaign of 1760, Md. and the Cars. sent no forces., Pa. voted 2700 but raised only 1350, and Va. alone raised 1000, the number voted. *Pa. Col. Recs.*, IX, 48.

105 Kimball, *Pitt Corres.*, II, 130.

106 *Pa. Votes of Assembly*, V. 92.

107 *Ibid.*, 93; *Pa. Col. Recs.*, VIII, 426, 437; *Pa. Archives*, 1st. ser., III, 695.

108 *Pa. Votes of Assembly*, V. 98; *Pa. Col. Recs.*, VIII, 428; Kimball, *Pitt Corres.*, II, 265-266.

109 *Pa. Votes of Assembly*, V, 117, 118, 128, 130; *Pa. Col. Recs.*, VIII, 495-596, 509-511; *Pa. Statutes at Large*, VI, 92.

the northern colonies acted a more becoming part, although the fall of Quebec in 1759 and the rumors of peace in 1760 caused a slight decrease in the number of men raised there.[110]

With the fall of Quebec and the conquest of Montreal, Canada became practically a British possession. For the operations of 1761 and 1762, the colonies were required to raise only two-thirds of the former levies.[111] In May, 1761, Amherst informed Pitt that " nothing is to be expected from Pennsylvania."[112] This sums up the situation for both years. The assembly refused to honor the requisitions except on the terms of the supply bills of the two previous years. The Privy Council had censured the supply bill of 1759 as " fundamentally wrong and unjust," but confirmed it on condition that the assembly would alter it in the objectionable features. The house refused to abide by the agreement made between its agents and the crown, the governor refused to accept any grants except on the conditions stipulated by the Privy Council, both sides remained steadfastly firm in their positions and all expectation of aid from Pennsylvania for the general service vanished into thin air. In 1761 the governor informed Pitt that the assembly " never did intend, from the beginning, to comply with his Majesty's requisitions in the smallest degree, but at the price of obtaining for themselves Powers and Advantages, which must have rendered the Government so weak and impotent, as to be unable, at any future time, to contend with them, however necessary it might be . . ."[113] All the governor was able to secure from the house was a grant of £23,500, out of the Parliamentary fund, to provide forts and troops

[110] Beer, *British Col. Pol.*, 64-67; Kimball, *Pitt Corres.*, II, 307-308, 461.

[111] Kimball, *Pitt Corres.*, II, 367; *Pa. Col. Recs.*, VIII, 588, 678.

[112] Kimball, *Pitt Corres.*, II, 426.

[113] *Ibid.*, II, 432-434; *Pa. Archives*, 1st. ser., IV, 47.

for the defense of Philadelphia and to negotiate a treaty with the Indians.[114]

We have now passed in review, perhaps with too much emphasis on details, the administrative and political aspects of the problem of imperial defense from the beginning of the wars between England and France for mastery in North America to the triumph of the former in 1763. From the facts deduced we are pressed to the conclusion that the requisition system was vicious and inadequate in practice and inherently wrong in conception. It would be needless to recount the evils of the system; they have already been laid bare. The dissatisfaction and jealousy created by unfair apportionment of quotas, the habit of one colony waiting to see what its neighbor would do for the general service, the conflict between the governors and assemblies, the influence of the assemblies in the direction of the troops and the expenditure of the funds, the short-term enlistments, the scanty levies of men in some cases, the fluctuations in the number of men available, all conspired to impair the efficiency of the army, to delay operations, to limit the scope of the activity of the troops, to hamper the English commanders by forcing them to consume their time and energy in local politics, and to harm the general interests and security of the Empire. The lack of unity and concert exerted a double influence for evil; it encouraged French attacks, and injured and alienated the friendship of the Indians. The system was unfair whether viewed from the standpoint of the colonies or England. In the colonies the burden of defense was very inequitably distributed. Galloway said in 1774 " You all know there were Colonies which at some times granted liberal aids, and at others nothing; Other Colonies gave nothing during the war; none gave equitably in proportion to their wealth, and all that did give were actuated

114 *Pa. Statutes at Large*, VI, 226-229.

THE FRENCH AND INDIAN WAR

by partial and self-interested motives, and gave only in proportion to the approach or remoteness of the danger." [115] It is estimated that the three colonies of Massachusetts, New York, and Connecticut, although they numbered but one-third of the total white population in the mainland colonies, supplied seventh-tenths of the colonial forces.[116] A system which threw the chief burden upon a few energetic colonies and permitted others to escape their due share in the common responsibilities was not only fundamentally wrong and unjust, but created intercolonial discontent and jealousy. But the system created greater dissatisfaction at home. At the close of the war with France it appeared unjust to the English tax-payer that he should be compelled to bear not only the whole cost of naval protection, but also a large share of military defense.[117] Even in times of peace the home government kept garrisons on the frontiers of New York, South Carolina, and Georgia.[118] These military posts were necessary to guard the boundaries of the colonies, to protect the traders and prevent sudden incursions by the Indians stirred up to revenge by the French and Spaniards. Although this was a burden properly belonging to the colonies, their refusal to assume the responsibility forced it upon the home government. In the time of the imperial wars, England not only sent troops to coöperate with the colonial forces, but reimbursed the colonies for a portion of their outlay. This policy was followed chiefly in the last French war. For the campaign of 1755 the colonies expended about £170,000, and Parliament compensated them, except Pennsylvania and Maryland which did practically nothing, to the extent of £165,000. For the campaigns of 1758-1762,

[115] Ford, *Journals of Continental Congress*, I, 45.
[116] Beer, *British Col. Pol.*, 68.
[117] Franklin, *Works* (Smyth ed.), V, 41-42; Beer, *British Col. Pol.*, 272.
[118] Beer, *British Col. Pol.*, 11-13.

Parliament voted the colonies £866,666.[119] This was in addition to the charges borne by the English treasury in furnishing arms, ammunition, provisions, tents, and artillery to the colonial troops. Franklin estimated that the parliamentary grants reimbursed the colonies for two-fifths of their outlay in raising clothing, and paying their troops.[120] In the case of Pennsylvania, the province was reimbursed to the extent of thirty-five per cent. of her expenditures for the campaigns of 1758-1760.[121] For the years 1761-1762 Pennsylvania did nothing and received nothing from Parliament. The purpose of these grants was partly to encourage the colonies to zealous and prompt action,[122] but chiefly to secure as large a force as possible in the colonies in order to obviate the difficulties and expense of recruiting troops at home and transporting them to America.[123]

By the Treaty of Paris of 1763, Canada and the territory east of the Mississippi River passed from French to Eng-

[119] Beer, *British Col. Pol., 1754-1765*, 53-57.

[120] Franklin, *Works* (Smyth ed.), IV, 402.

[121] For the three years Pa. issued £300,000 in bills of credit, or £193,548 sterling computed at 55 per cent. discount, the rate of exchange between London and Phila., and received from the parliamentary funds £68,859 sterling. *Pa. Statutes at Large*, V, 460; VI, 114, 329, 487.

[122] In 1757 Pitt wrote to the governors saying, " that no Encouragement may be wanting to this great and salutary Attempt," recommendations would be made to Parliament at the next session to compensate each colony for its outlay, according " as the active Vigour and strenuous Efforts of the respective Provinces shall justly appear to merit." Kimball, *Pitt Corres.*, I, 139. This plan was followed each year. Governor Pownall of Mass. informed Pitt that " not only the Preservation of the Countrey by this Province being able to continue its Efforts, but the Preservation of the Government of this province itself depends upon that Recompence." *Ibid.*, I, 363. Likewise, Gov. Fitch of Conn., wrote that his colony was enabled to continue its efforts for the general service by " relying on the gracious Assurance of a Compensation." *Ibid.*, II, 85, 141.

[123] Beer, *British Col. Pol.*, 57 and note 4; Fortescue, *Hist. of British Army*, II, 578.

lish control. The acquisition of a large conquered area
to the Empire necessitated a readjustment of the colonial
policy, which involved deeply the problem of defense.
The problem now became of great importance because of
the control over a number of French and western Indians,
both unfriendly to the English. It was chiefly the Indian
question which arose to vex the Empire. As early as 1760,
when Canada was practically an English possession, English troops replaced the French garrisons in many of the
posts in the new territory.[124] These posts were necessary
to prevent reconquest by the French and to check the hostility of the Indians. The feeling of discontent among the
savages was very evident by 1761. This was due to several
causes.[125] " The fur trade under the French had been
well regulated," says Carter, " but its condition under the
English from 1760-1763 was deplorable." Then again, the
Indians feared that their lands, heretofore left practically
untouched by the French, would be appropriated by the
English bent on permanent settlement. The spirit of discontent among the Indians was kept alive by the French
who filled the hearts of the savages with fear of the English. Even before the conquest of Canada, as we have
seen, colonial and English statesmen thoroughly appreciated the bad effects of the decentralized system of Indian
control. In 1754 the Albany Conference and the Board of
Trade sought to centralize the regulation of Indian affairs.
The failure of these plans led the English government to
appoint Indian commissioners for the northern and southern colonies respectively, with power over the political relations with the Indians only.[126] After 1760 the discontent of the western Indians brought the problem of centralization again to the front. The Board of Trade advised the crown of the danger of allowing settlement in

124 Carter, *The Illinois Country*, 27.
125 *Ibid.*, 28-29, 77-80; Beer, *British Col. Pol.*, 252-254.
126 Carter, *The Ill. Country*, 80-81; Beer, *British Col. Pol.*, 254-256.

the new territory before the claims of the Indians were adjusted. In 1761, on the basis of this report, the purchase of Indian lands was taken out of the control of the colonies and placed in the hands of the English government.[127] This action foreshadowed the Proclamation of 1763 which forbade settlement west of the sources of the rivers emptying into the Atlantic and required traders with the Indians to take out licenses from the colonial governors.[128] But before the policy could be applied, the western Indians, under the able leadership of Pontiac, rose in rebellion.

In May, 1763, the storm broke on the frontier. Colonel Bouquet informed the governor of Pennsylvania that the forts at Le Bouef, Presquisle, and Venango had fallen with their garrisons, and that Forts Pitt and Ligonier alone had withstood attacks.[129] Amherst informed Governor Hamilton that he had dispatched two companies of regulars to the province, but could spare no more, and urged the assembly promptly to raise troops to protect the frontier.[130] In July the house resolved to take into the pay of the province " any number of back inhabitants and others," not exceeding seven hundred men, to be employed on the frontier " within the purchased parts of the said Province during the time of Harvest or until the next meeting of the House."[131] It is evident that a large majority of the members of the assembly, who lived in the east free from Indian attacks, were alive only to their own security and felt a gross indifference to the needs of the people of the west. In September Governor Hamilton informed the house that the harvest was garnered, the term of the troops was about to expire, and urged the extreme necessity of continuing the forces.[132] The assembly made

127 *N. Y. Col. Docs.*, VII, 473, 478.
128 Beer, *British Col. Pol.*, 256-257.
129 *Pa. Col., Recs.*, IX, 31, 32, 35.
130 *Ibid.*, IX, 34.
131 *Ibid.*, 36.
132 *Ibid.*, 42.

no immediate response. This drew from General Amherst and the Earl of Egremont, secretary of state, just and severe censures.[133] In the last of October the assembly responded by voting £24,000 to employ eight hundred and twenty-five men "in the most effectual manner for the defense and protection of the province till the First of February next."[134]

By this time the insurrection had assumed such a serious aspect that the Earl of Halifax, secretary of state, instructed Amherst to call upon the colonies for assistance.[135] In November Amherst levied requisitions upon New York, New Jersey, Pennsylvania, and Virginia as the colonies most intimately concerned.[136] New York held it to be unreasonable not to include the New England colonies, and made assistance from them a condition of her own contribution.[137] New Jersey followed the lead of New York.[138] In December General Gage, who succeeded Amherst, levied requisitions upon the New England colonies.[139] After considerable difficulty he was able to secure a small force from Connecticut, one-half the number required from New York and New Jersey, and Virginia alone acted with spirit. What was the attitude of Pennsylvania whose territory was so vitally concerned? On

---

[133] Amherst wrote to Gov. Hamilton of his surprise "at the infatuation of the People in your Province, who tamely look on while their Brethren are butchered by the Savages, when, without doubt, it is in their Power by exerting a proper Spirit, not only to protect the Settlements, but to punish any Indians that are hardy enough to disturb them." *Pa. Col. Recs.*, IX, 62. For the censure of Halifax, see *ibid.*, 114. Thos. Penn wrote to Gov. Hamilton, "As you apprehended I find General Amherst has made loud complaints of Pennsylvania." *Penn Mss., Letter Bk.*, VIII, Nov. 11, 1763.

[134] *Pa. Statutes at Large*, VI, 311-319.

[135] Beer, *British Col. Pol.*, 262-263.

[136] *Pa. Col. Recs.*, IX, 74-75; *Pa. Archives*, 4th. ser., III, 249-251.

[137] Beer, *British Col. Pol.*, 263.

[138] *N. J. Archives*, IX, 398-399, 401, 428-429, 431-432.

[139] *Pa. Col. Recs.*, IX, 90; Beer, *British Col. Pol.*, 263-264.

December 24 the assembly resolved to raise, pay and clothe one thousand men and presented the governor with a bill to create £55,000 in paper currency to cover the charges.[140] Governor John Penn refused his consent to the supply bill on the ground that it contained clauses in violation of the agreement made in 1760 between the crown and the agents of the assembly concerning the taxation of proprietary lands.[141] The house held a different view, and for five months in the midst of distress on the frontier the deadlock persisted. In the last of May the house, under the pressure of '' publick necessities and the distresses of war,'' was compelled to yield in the contest, but in so doing informed the governor that it had '' waved very important Rights.'' [142] Intensely angered at the arbitrary conduct of the proprietors and their governor, the assembly sent Benjamin Franklin to England bearing a petition to the crown praying for royal government. In order to preserve the liberties of the people it was felt necessary '' to fly from petty tyrants to the throne.'' On the other hand, the people of the back country, provoked to wrath at the indifference of the assembly to the protection of the frontier, took arms in their hands, killed certain Indians taken under the protection of the province, and then marched upon Philadelphia to secure a redress of grievances.[143] But looking at the whole matter from the standpoint of the Empire, the events of Pontiac's Conspiracy made clear, what the former wars had shown conclusively, that the requisition system was a failure whether applied in time of local or imperial wars.

The Treaty of Paris of 1763 added to the Empire immense areas of new territory and as a result the imperial government was confronted, as we have seen, with the serious task of readjusting her colonial system to meet the

140 *Pa. Col. Recs.*, IX, 98, 148.
141 *Ibid.*, 152, 153-154.
142 *Ibid.*, 188.
143 *Ibid.*, 94-96, 100, 138-145.

new conditions. Not the least of the problems awaiting
solution was that of maintaining the conquered region from
French intrigues and the incursions of hostile savages.
It was felt at home that since the mother country had borne
a heavy financial burden to save the colonists from foreign
conquest, therefore, " the colonists, now firmly secured
from foreign enemies, should be somehow induced to contribute to the exigencies of state in future." To secure
colonial contributions to general purposes two courses were
open to the English ministry; either to continue the requisition system, relying upon the fidelity of the colonies to
grant aids through their own assemblies, or else to resort
to the latent powers of the imperial legislature. The
harmful influence and the refractory attitude of the assemblies in the matter of protection had created a feeling
on both sides of the Atlantic that some central authority
was necessary to over-rule colonial particularism. Far-
sighted colonial statesmen at Albany took steps to remedy
this great fault. But the failure of the colonies to adopt
the Albany Plan of Union made it clear that the only
alternative was the exercise of the powers of the British
Parliament.[144] Parliamentary taxation was a remedy suggested repeatedly by colonial officials, such as Clinton,
Shirley, Sharpe, and Dinwiddie among the the governors,[145]

[144] Franklin wrote in 1789 that if the Albany Plan of Union had
been adopted and carried into execution " the subsequent Separation of the Colonies from the Mother Country might not so soon
have happened, . . . For the Colonies, so united, would have
really been, as they then thought themselves, sufficient to their own
Defence, and being trusted with it, . . . an Army from Britain,
for that purpose would have been unnecessary; The Pretences for
framing the Stamp Act would then not have existed, nor the other
Projects for drawing a Revenue from America to Britain by Act of
Parliament, which were the causes of the Breach & attended with
such terrible Expense of Blood and Treasure." *Works* (Smyth ed),
III, 226-227.

[145] *N. Y. Col. Docs.*, VI, 939; *Dinwiddie Corres.*, I, 204, 207, 241,
246, 250, 251, 329, 345; *Sharpe Corres.*, I, 99; Beer, *British Col.
Pol.*, ch. iii.

and by Braddock and Loudoun among the commanders.[146]
The logic of events forced the English ministry to this
course at the close of the war.[147] As a result two statutes
were passed, the Sugar Act of 1764 and the Stamp Act of
1765, whose express purpose was, as run the preambles,
to create a revenue "in your Majesty's said dominions
in America, for defraying the expenses of defending, protecting, and securing the same."[148] It was estimated that
the operation of these acts would yield a revenue of
£105,000 to £145,000 a year, which would cover from a
third to a half of the cost of supporting an army of ten
thousand men in America.[149] But the extension of the
powers of Parliament in the field of colonial taxation for
revenue purposes involved a tremendous change in the colonial policy. The idea of creating a revenue by the authority of Parliament was a distinct innovation in the imperial system of administration. It was perfectly clear to
English statesmen that such a tax in the light of recent
events was perfectly justifiable, and they never questioned
the legal right of Parliament to exercise this latent power.
But on the other hand, it is very evident that in so doing
they had no conception whatever of the serious consequences involved in this step. The protests of the colonial assemblies and their agents against the passage of the
stamp bill were looked upon simply as a strong popular
outcry against new taxes and the bill found its way into
law with practically no opposition in Parliament.[150] The

---

[146] Kimball, *Pitt Corres.*, I, 44; Beer, *British Col. Pol.*, 45, note 6.
[147] In May, 1763, the secretary of state instructed the Board of
Trade to report "in what Mode, least Burthensome & most palatable
to the Colonies, can they contribute towards the Support of the
Additional Expence" which is necessary to the protection of the
new territory. *B. T. Paps., Pl. Gen.*, XVII, Q 31; *B. T. Jour.*,
LXXI 256; Fitzmaurice, *Life of Shelburne*, I, 249.
[148] 4 George III, ch. 15; 5 George III, ch. 12.
[149] Beer, *British Col. Pol.*, 285-286.
[150] *Ibid.*, 284-285. Even Franklin did not appreciate the consequences involved in this action. In 1764 he wrote that Par⁻

English ministry and Parliament were entirely ignorant of the temper and character of the colonists and of the nature of their political institutions.

Former pages have set forth the character of the opposition in the colonies to the Sugar Act of 1764. Colonial discontent was fanned into a flame orf the passage of the Stamp Act. The orders of the crown or of proprietors to their governors could be thwarted by the assemblies in control of the financial situation. Acts of Parliament could only be nullified by popular resistance. The officials appointed to distribute the stamps were forced to resign their positions either through fear or persuasion.[151] Threats were made against those who dared to use the stamps, in some cases trade was resumed without the use of stamps, and the power of the English Parliament was successfully defied and its statute nullified. What was the basis of this violent opposition? Various factors contributed to this end. In the first place, the colonists objected to the mode of taxation. It was felt with substantial unity in America that the very existence of free institutions was threatened by parliamentary taxation. As we have seen it was the devotion to the principle of self-government which provoked the bitter contests in Pennsylvania and Maryland between the assemblies and the proprietors over the control of the fiscal policy; it was the attachment to this principle that led the colonies to reject the Albany Plan of Union. It was unreasonable to expect that the colonists would permit Parliament to exercise a power to tax them when they had unanimously refused to

liament may find it necessary to establish an army in America to defend Canada and levy a tax on colonial commerce to create a revenue to support the troops, and he thought that in a few years the colonists would be well satisfied with the system. After the passage of the Stamp Act he wrote that the tax would probably be borne by the colonists. *Works* (Smyth ed.), IV, 237, 390.

151 Howard, *Preliminaries of the Revolution*, ch. viii.

yield this function to a central government in which they
were to be represented.   The political instincts of the colonists were outraged when Parliament assumed an authority which violated the relations which had always existed
between the two parts of the Empire.   The whole controversy brought into the realm of discussion the nature of
the relations between the two parts of the Empire.   The
colonists held that it was essential to freedom and the undoubted right of all Englishmen that " no Taxes be imposed on them but with their own consent, given personally,
or through their representatives," and as the colonies were
not, and under the circumstances, could not be represented
in Parliament, no taxes could be levied upon them " con-
stitutionally " but by their respective legislatures.   This
familiar doctrine was enunciated in the resolves of a congress of colonial delegates, and found repeated expression
in pamphlet literature, in newspapers, and in the resolves
of colonial assemblies and public gatherings of various
sorts.   No matter how illogical and unscientific this doctrine may be from the standpoint of law and political
science, it was in accordance with the political growth of
the colonies and was necessary to the continued existence of
their systems of independent self-government.

Furthermore, the colonists held that they were already
sufficiently taxed in return for English protection.   This
feeling was well expressed by Alexander Hamilton when
he wrote, " The principle profits of our trade center in
Great Britain; . . .   are not these principle profits a
sufficient recompense for protecting it ? " [152]   The colonists

[152] Hamilton, *Works* (Lodge ed.), I, 65, 110, 112, 113, 118-119;
John Adams, *Works* (C. F. Adams ed.), IV, 46-47; Samuel Adams,
Writings (Cushing ed.), I, 42-43, 49-53; Dickinson, *Writings* I,
237-239; Franklin, *Works* (Smyth ed.), IV, 402.   The Stamp Act
Congress resolved " that as the profits of the trade of these colonies
ultimately center in Great Britain, to pay for the manufactures
which they are obliged to take from thence, they eventually contribute very largely to all the supplies granted there to the crown."

expressed a willingness that the mother country should regulate their commerce to her own exclusive advantage, but felt that this was a sufficient tribute for protection, and that further grants of aid to imperial purposes should be left to the fidelity of the assemblies. The colonists looked upon the war against France in the nature of a conquest to advance the interests of the mother country. They felt that they had already borne a burden even beyond their abilities, as evidenced by the fact that Parliament reimbursed them for a portion of their outlay, and that therefore it was unreasonable to ask them to bear an additional burden for the protection of a territory from which the metropolis and not the colonies reaped the advantages.[153] Opposed to this view was that of the English statesmen who held that it was a war for the protection of the colonies, and that therefore now secured from foreign attacks, the colonists should help to share the expense of defending the new territory. The whole controversy revealed not only the divergent views held on opposite sides of the Atlantic as to the political nature of the Empire, but also brought out clearly the conflict between the provincialism of the colonies and the needs and policies of the Empire.

The intense opposition to the Stamp Act cannot be accounted for solely by an excessive attachment of the colonists to principles of political and constitutional rights; the protest was as much economic as political. It must be remembered that the Stamp Act came as a sequel to the Currency and Sugar Acts of the previous year. These new regulations were considered especially burdensome in several respects. The colonies had always experienced a lack of specie because the balance of trade was against them, the Sugar Act now placed prohibitions upon the trade of the colonies to the foreign West Indies from whence they se-

153 Dickinson, *Writings*, I, 239-240; Franklin, *Works*, IV, 436-437; Samuel Adams, *Writings*, I, 41.

cured the coin drained off at once to England, the Currency Act abolished paper money, and now in a condition of economic depression and financial stringency, the duties of the Stamp and Sugar Acts were made payable in specie.[154] The Stamp Act Congress resolved that " from the scarcity of specie, the payment of them was absolutely impracticable." Then again, the scattered condition of settlements, the inadequacy of postal facilities, and the heavy postage charges would create delay, expense and inconvenience in securing the stamps, which would be felt especially in the interior.[155] Moreover, the stamp tax was considered very unequal in incidence. Franklin and Dickinson contended that it would fall most heavily upon those least able to bear it.[156] Colonial taxation was usually proportioned to the abilities of the inhabitants, the taxes were small and justified by the simple needs of the local government.[157] Hence they opposed the payment of taxes for the protection of Canada which brought no especial benefit to them. Franklin said before the bar of the House of Commons in 1766, that the people of America would never submit to pay the stamp duty, even if moderated, " unless compelled by force of arms."[158]

[154] Dickinson, *Writings*, I, 217-218. Franklin said in the House of Commons in 1766 that "there was not gold and silver enough in the Colonies to pay the stamp duty for one year." *Works*, IV, 415.

[155] Franklin, *Works*, IV, 414.

[156] Dickinson, *Writings*, I, 229-232; Franklin, *Works*, IV, 414.

[157] Dinwiddie wrote in 1756 that the people would be angry if they heard of his proposals to levy a parliamentary tax upon them, for "they are averse to all Taxes." *Corres.*, II, 340-341. Loudoun wrote that the "Taxes which the People pay in this Country, are really so trifling, that they do not deserve the Name." Kimball, *Pitt Corres.*, I, 44. Cf. Callender, *Economic Hist. of U. S.*, 123, 137-140, which brings out the fact that social conditions in America were unfavorable to direct taxation.

[158] Franklin, *Works*, IV, 418.

CHAPTER ELEVEN

IMPERIAL CENTRALIZATION

In 1701 the Board of Trade represented to the king and to Parliament that the chartered colonies " have no ways answered the chief design for which such large Tracts of Land and such Privileges and Immunities were granted by the Crown " and recommended that the powers of government should be " reassumed to the Crown." The policy of centralizing and regulating colonial administration took definite shape shortly after the passage of the acts of trade and navigation. Great praise and credit is due to individual and corporate enterprise for planting and developing English colonies in America, but with the formulation of a definite colonial policy, English statesmen began to realize that a system of indirect control under the charters no longer answered the purpose for which colonization was undertaken. Indirect control constituted the chief defect in the system of chartered colonies. Instead of acting upon the colonists through its own agents, the crown was forced to rely upon officials practically outside the reach of royal authority. As Professor Osgood says, " In the face of such a situation and for the attainment of genuine imperial objects the English government was as helpless as would be the human body without arms or hands."[1] Hence, in order to make the Empire more cohesive, and to secure efficiency and uniformity in colonial administration, it was necessary for the English government to resume the powers of government granted to proprietors and corporations. It is the purpose of this chap-

[1] Osgood, *Amer. Cols.*, III, 22-24, 518-519.

ter to set forth the needs and the methods which led to the transition from private enterprise to state control.

The policy of vacating the charters and establishing direct control originated about 1676, when Edward Randolph was sent to New England to investigate the conduct of the colonies.[2] He found by bitter experience that Massachusetts ordered her own affairs without regard for the acts of trade or royal commands.[3] As a result the English courts in 1677 denied the claim of Massachusetts to the territory of New Hampshire and the latter was erected into a royal province. The refractory conduct of Massachusetts led to the vacation of her charter by summary judicial proceedings in 1684.[4] The policy of the later Stuarts was broad in its scope, including not only the vacation of the charters, but the consolidation of the colonies into larger administrative units in imitation of the French system in Canada.[5] In 1685 New York became a royal province by the accession of the duke of York to the throne as James II. Charges were found against the colonies of Rhode Island, Connecticut, and the Jerseys, and menaced with the loss of their charters, they voluntarily submitted to royal authority.[6] In 1686 the colonies of New England, New York, and New Jersey were erected into the Dominion of New England under the rule of one man, Sir Edmund Andros, invested with all the powers of government. The consummation of this policy was fraught with immense difficulties. There is little doubt of the justification of these measures viewed from the standpoint of imperial interests. The advisers of James II saw clearly the anomalous position of the chartered colonies in the Empire. Unrestricted individualism and the idea of an un-

[2] Osgood, *Amer. Cols.*, III, 310-313.
[3] *Ibid.*, 228-239.
[4] *Ibid.*, ch. x.
[5] Kellogg, *Amer. Col. Charter*, in Amer. Hist. Assoc., *Reports*, 1903, I, 223-224.
[6] Osgood, *Amer. Cols.*, III, 395-397.

controllable power in each colony meant the destruction of the English colonial system. But on the other hand, the Andros régime, imposed from without, stood unrelated to the political and social institutions which the colonists had fashioned for themselves in the course of fifty years, untrammeled by English interference. Local and imperial interests and ideals were radically opposed to each other and their adjustment was beyond the region of probability. The news of the English revolution of 1688 fanned into a flame the smoldering discontent in New England and the Andros government was swept away.[7] The upheaval of 1689 in New England was simply a premonition of what was to occur several generations later when the English government again found it necessary to restrict colonial freedom of action, but the result was far more disastrous.

The accession of William III witnessed no change in the policy initiated by the later Stuarts. The return to a settled condition of internal affairs at home brought a renewal of interest in the colonies similar to that which followed the Restoration. The reasons for this are clear. The beginning of the long series of wars with France for colonial and commercial supremacy made the question of imperial defense of paramount importance. The mercantile interests, growing in power and influence, demanded a more vigorous administration of the acts of trade. The problems of defense and trade brought the colonies into sharp relief. To solve the problems the policy of vacating the charters and consolidating the colonies was still to be followed. In April, 1689, the Lords of Trade recommended to the Privy Council the reëstablishment of a government in New England similar to the Andros rule for the sake of defense against French attacks.[8] In the next month the Lords of Trade offered the opinion that a consideration of the relations which existed between the proprietary colonies and

[7] Osgood, *Amer. Cols.*, III, ch. xiv.
[8] *Cal. State Paps.*, *Col.*, 1689-1692, 34.

the crown was a matter worthy the attention of Parliament in order to bring them " under the nearer dependence on the crown, as his majesties revenue in the plantations is very much concerned therein."[9]   But parliamentary action was not resorted to till a few years later and the centralization of colonial control was left to the crown.

Taking advantage of the overthrow of the rule of Lord Baltimore in Maryland, the crown established royal government in 1691.[10] Despite the efforts of the agents of Massachusetts to secure a restoration of the old charter, a new instrument was granted which consolidated Massachusetts, Plymouth, and Maine into one province, and which provided for a royal governor and made a reservation of a veto power and appellate jurisdiction to the crown.[11]   In 1692 William III deprived Penn of his powers of government because of the necessities of war.[12] By royal commission the command of the militia of Rhode Island and Connecticut was placed in the hands of the royal governors of Massachusetts and New York respectively.[13] From the colonists themselves came appeals to the crown praying for royal control and consolidation. Far-sighted colonials saw that unity of action against the French and Indians was out of the question until the particular jealousies and interests of the colonies were overcome.[14] The governor and council of New York repeatedly entreated the home government to restore the original boundaries of

[9] *Cal. State Paps., Col.*, 1689-1692, 39.

[10] Osgood, *Amer. Cols.*, III, 503-506.

[11] *Ibid.*, 424-440.

[12] See page 262.

[13] See page 262.

[14] See page 265. In 1696 Stephen Sewall wrote that he wished the crown would reduce all the colonies to three administrative districts, each under the rule of a royal governor. *Cal. State Paps., Col.*, 1696-1697, 189. Such also was the plan of Robert Livingstone, 1701. *N. Y. Col. Docs.*, IV, 874. John Nelson, in a memorial to the Board of Trade, also suggested the formation of the northern colonies into one government. *Cal. State Paps., Col.*, 1696-1697, 136.

the province or else reëstablish the Dominion of New England as it existed not long since under Andros. The Privy Council concurred in the latter suggestion in 1695.[15] But to such a scheme the agents of the chartered colonies offered strong protests and the crown had to content itself by appointing in 1697 a governor of the royal colonies of New Hampshire, Massachusetts, and New York, and investing him with the command of the militia of Rhode Island, Connecticut, and New Jersey.[16] But as we have seen such a personal union did not solve effectively the serious problem of securing centralization of control and coöperation of intercolonial forces.

Prior to 1696 Parliament was not called upon to assist in this task. By a combination of executive and judicial action the Stuarts established royal control. William III not only continued the colonial policy of his predecessors but like them resorted to the exercise of the royal prerogative to carry the programme into operation. The law officers of the crown repeatedly gave the opinion that the king by virtue of his " prerogative and Soverainty over those Colonies " had a right to assume the powers of government delegated by charters and, as we have seen, William III did not hesitate to exercise this right.[17] The chief objection, however, to executive action was that the charters were never legally vacated.[18] The annulment of the charters could be accomplished only by the action of the courts or by Parliament. Judicial procedure was a cumbersome

15 See page 267.
16 See page 268.
17 *N. Y. Col. Docs.*, IV, 1; *Cal. State Paps., Col.*, 1693-1696, 20; *R. I. Col. Recs.*, IV, 16; Chalmers, *Opinions of Eminent Lawyers* (ed. 1858), 66-67; Greene, *Provincial Governor*, 18-19.
18 In 1694, the crown lawyers held in the case of Pennsylvania that the king had a right to assume the powers of government in case of necessity but when the reasons for which the government was taken from the proprietor ceased to hold good, the control again properly belonged to Penn. *Cal. State Paps., Col.*, 1693-1696, 308. See Channing, *Hist. of U. S.*, II, 225.

method because of the tedious delays incident to the great
distance of the colonies from the courts at Westminster
and to the fact that separate action would be required in
the case of each charter. Parliamentary action would be
more effective because more comprehensive in character.
After the Revolution of 1689 there was a decided tendency
to look to Parliament to regulate colonial administration.
This is evidenced by the act of 1696, chiefly administrative
in character, and the efforts to establish a parliamentary
council of trade, both of which are significant, not only of
the assertion of the right of the legislature to deal with the
colonial management, but of the tendency to encroach upon
the royal prerogative. This tendency in the direction of
legislative interference in colonial business was fraught
with great possibilities for the future.

Parliamentary interest in the colonies is further evidenced by the appointment of a large committee in the
House of Lords in February, 1697, to investigate the state
of the trade of the kingdom.[19] Before this committee the
ever faithful Randolph appeared to prefer serious charges
against the chartered colonies. At great length he detailed the abuses practiced in these colonies prejudicial
to the authority of the crown and the welfare of the Empire.[20] Pennsylvania and Delaware were especially singled out as the objects of Randolph's enmity and for special investigation by the committee.[21] Randolph expressed
a grave fear that in view of the passage of the late Scotch
Act incorporating a West India Company and the prevalence of an illegal trade with Scotland and Holland,
Penn's dominions would in a short time become a staple
for Scotch and European goods. Randolph charged that
Governor Markham connived at piracy and illegal trade

[19] *House of Lords Jour.*, XVI, 94; *House of Lords Mss.*, n.s.,
II, 410.
[20] *House of Lords Mss.*, n.s., II, 440-444.
[21] *Ibid.*, 411.

and accused the provincial courts of denying justice where the acts of trade were concerned. To substantiate the statements, Randolph not only brought evidence from the letters and records of the customs officials, but produced several witnesses.[22] As a solution of the problem he recommended that the charters should be vacated and royal control established instead.[23] With respect to Delaware, Randolph suggested that it should be annexed to the royal province of Maryland, holding that Penn had no legal claim to the powers of government of that territory under the deeds of the duke of York.[24] Five times William Penn attended the committee in his own defense. In refutation of the charges, he held that the contraband trade was due to the negligence of the royal officials and that they should be held responsible for it and not his government.[25] The committee, impressed with the extent of illegal trade, asked Penn " what objections he can make to the putting of the government of the Proprietors' Plantations into the King's hands." [26] Penn made answer that the moment he lost his government the country was worth nothing to him, for without it he could not sell an acre of land. To meet this hostile feeling Penn proposed that his governor should be approved by the crown and give security for his good behavior. The committee adopted this suggestion and directed the crown to carry it out.[27] In conclusion Penn was told that if further complaints were made " Parliament may possibly take another course in the matter, which

22 *House of Lords Mss.*, n.s., II, 462-466.
23 *Ibid.*, 444.
24 Professor Osgood had discussed in an able manner the important question whether the proprietors of New Jersey possessed a legal right to governmental powers under the sub-grants to them from the duke of York. *Amer. Cols.*, II, 169-172. See also the case of *Bellomont vs. Basse, Harvard Law Review*, XVIII, 483.
25 *House of Lords Mss.*, n.s., II, 412, 456-457.
26 *Ibid.*, 413.
27 See page 50.

will be less pleasing " to the proprietors.[28] That Penn
feared Parliament would take away his charter is evidenced by his letter of January, 1699, to Robery Harley,
an influential member of the House of Commons.[29] Penn
wrote prior to his departure for America, saying, " Pray
be a friend to the absent, and without vanity, the meritorious . . . Let us be treated like Englishmen, and
not loose our domestick advantages for cultivating of wil-
dernesses, so much to the honour and wealth of the crown.''
Penn was right in this feeling, for in 1701, during his absence in Pennsylvania, the first bill was introduced in Parliament to sweep away the charters.

This action was based on the frequent complaints of the
royal agents in the colonies, — Randolph, Quary, Nicholson, Basse, and others. They found by experience that the
act of 1696 did not have the desired effect in promoting a
more efficient administration of the acts of trade in the
chartered colonies. In former pages we have been made
familiar with the sturdy opposition to the vice-admiralty
courts, with the obstacles placed in the way of the customs
officials, with the refusal or neglect of the governors to
secure royal confirmation or to give security, and with the
prevalence of illegal trade and piracy. We have seen that
they refused to obey the royal requisitions for men and
money for the defense of the New York frontier, and that
they refused to honor the royal commissions to command
their troops, and they denied appeals to the Privy Council.
These charges form a partial catalogue of the reprehensible
conduct of the chartered colonies, gleaned from the letters
of the royal appointees. Therefore, with great frequency
they urged the English government to vacate the charters
and to substitute royal government.[30] And it cannot be

---

[28] *House of Lords Mss.*, n.s., II, 414.

[29] *Duke of Portland Mss.*, III, 601-602, in Hist. Mss. Com., *Report*, 14, pt. 2.

[30] *B. T. Paps., Pl. Gen.*, IV, pt. 1, A 11; IV, pt. 2, B 40, C 18;
V, pt. 2, D 48; *No. Car. Col. Recs.*, I, 527.

gainsaid that the evidence in support of these charges is strong and convincing. It seemed absolutely necessary that the home government should be given the powers adequate to control the affairs of the colonies in the interest of the Empire.

In 1700 Randolph was back in London acting energetically with the Board of Trade in order to secure the annulment of the colonial charters. In February and March, 1701, he laid before the board two long papers charging high crimes and misdemeanors upon the governors of the chartered colonies, whether on the mainland or islands.[31] An examination of these papers simply reveal the old charges made time and again in the numerous letters of the royal officials. Upon the basis of Randolph's statements, the Board of Trade represented the matter in a full and able document to the king on March 26, 1701.[32] Three days later the same report was submitted to the consideration of the House of Commons.[33] A review of this report exhibits in clear relief the evils which flowed from an indirect and decentralized system of imperial control. It is needless to recount the charges made in the board's report, for in large part they simply reëcho the familiar complaints. But one point demands consideration. The report pointed out clearly the injury worked to the royal provinces by the chartered colonies. By raising and lowering the rate of coin to their particular advantage,[34] by exempting their inhabitants from taxes to which those of the royal colonies were subject, by harboring fugitives from justice and servitude,[35] the report held

31 *B. T. Paps., Props.*, V, F 69; VI, pt. 2, G 3; *No. Car. Col. Recs.*, I, 545-547; *N. J. Archives*, II, 358; Toppan, *Edward Randolph*, V, 263-273.

32 *B. T. Paps., Props.*, Entry Bk. C, 12-17; *No. Car. Col. Recs.*, I, 535.

33 *House of Commons Jour.*, XIII, 399, 446-449.

34 See page 183 ff.

35 For the complaints of Fletcher, Nicholson, and Cornbury as to

that the chartered colonies undermined " the Trade and Welfare of the other Plantations, and seduce and draw away the People thereof; by which Diminution of Hands the rest of the Colonies more beneficial to England do very much suff[r]." The evils of a mixed system of direct and indirect control are very evident. In the royal colonies the crown by its hold on the governors and its power over legislation was able to secure uniformity in administration, while the chartered colonies, shielded by their royal patents from royal control, were enabled to order their affairs without much regard for the interests of the Empire or the colonies. In conclusion the report recommended that the powers of government delegated to proprietors and corporations by charter should be reunited to the crown, without prejudice to the territorial rights of the patentees. " Which being no otherwise so well to be effected as by the Legislative power of this Kingdome " were the final words of the report. On April 24, in response to an order of the House of Commons, the board submitted a full account of the charges against the chartered colonies, and on the same day a bill was introduced into the House of Lords to vacate the charters.[36] The bill simply provided for an annulment of those clauses in the charters which delegated powers of government to the patentees, leaving the latter in possession of their rights to the soil. It is also noteworthy that restrictions were placed on crown control by the stipulation that the king should govern in accordance with the laws in force in the colonies, and with such other laws as shall be passed by the colonial assemblies,

desertion see: *N. Y. Col. Docs.*, IV, 159, 160, 189, 1059, 1099; *Cal. State Paps., Col.*, 1693-1696, 511, 630; 1696-1697, 420, 421, 511, 546.
[36] *House of Commons Jour.*, XIII, 465, 502-505; *House of Lords Jour.*, XVI, 659; *B. T. Jour.*, XIV, 1, 3; *House of Lords Mss.*, n.s., IV, 314. For the bill in full, consult *House of Lords Mss.*, IV, 314-315; *B. T. Paps., Props.*, VI, pt. 2, I 16; Entry Bk. C, 426-430. The bill included the charters of Rhode Island, Conn., N. J., Pa., Del., Md., Cars., Bahamas, and Mass.

so far as they were agreeable to the statutes of England. Thus Parliament, which stood as the embodiment of representative government in the English state, sought to vouchsafe to the colonists the same institution. With the introduction of the bill, Randolph and the Board of Trade set to work in earnest to secure its passage. Randolph showed the same lively interest at this time as on earlier occasions. The board employed him to lobby for the bill and provided him with funds for that service.[37] He secured witnesses in support of the charges, among whom were Joseph Dudley, Jeremiah Basse, and Jahleel Brenton, royal officials in the colonial service and arch-conspirators with Randolph against the chartered governments.[38] The board employed as counsel for the bill, Montagu and Darnell, who together with Randolph, Brenton, and Basse, concerted measures to effect its enactment.[39] The House of Lords called upon the Boards of Trade, Customs, and Admiralty to submit all papers in their respective offices which concerned the colonies involved.[40] It is curious that the letters submitted by the customs and admiralty departments consisted only of those from Quary which detailed the opposition to the admiralty courts and the prevalence of illegal trade in Pennsylvania.[41] The whole procedure was planned without notice whatever to the interests of the proprietors or

[37] B. T. Jour., XIV, 7; Toppan, Edward Randolph, V, 273, 274; No. Car. Col Recs., I, 538.

[38] House of Lords Jour., XVI, 666. Randolph spent about £96 in lobbying for the bill, and he said he met "with nothing but trouble in Soliciting the said Bill." Most of the money was spent for witnesses, "keeping them together in the old palace yard, 5sh., 8d.; dining them the same dayes, £2, 8sh., 12d.; keeping witnesses together, 8sh., 6d., etc." B. T. Paps., Props., VI, pt. 1, G 20.

[39] B. T. Jour., XIV, 21, 22-23, 25, 27.

[40] House of Lords Jour., XVI, 668, 670, 671; House of Lords Mss., n.s., IV, 318-355; B. T. Jour., XIV, 17, 26; B. T. Paps., Props., VI, pt. 1, G 16; Entry Bk. C, 63, 64, 66.

[41] House of Lords Mss., n.s., IV, 317, 342-353; House of Lords Jour., XVI, 671.

corporations. The first intimation they received of the danger to their charters came through the introduction of the bill. The proceedings savored rather of Star Chamber methods than a just, open, and full hearing of both sides. At once William Penn Jr., in the absence of his father, petitioned the Lords to be heard against the measure which was designed to deprive his father of an estate purchased from the crown upon a valuable consideration.[42] Sir Henry Ashurst, agent for Rhode Island, the Earl of Bath on behalf of the proprietors of the Carolinas and Bahamas, and Lord Baltimore also petitioned to be heard.[43] The burden of defense fell chiefly upon the shoulders of Penn Jr., and Ashurst. Four times they appeared with their counsel, Dodd and Phipps, before the Lords in defense of the charters.[44] Penn protested Randolph as an improper witness, but whether the objection was sustained is not disclosed.[45] Against Randolph's accusations, counsel for Penn produced in evidence several papers to show that the colony had taken action against illegal trade and piracy, and he expressed the hope that " the papers read will justify Mr. Penn " and " sufficiently expose Mr. Randall in what he has said."[46] Randolph did not rely upon his own testimony, but produced several witnesses among whom was one, Captain Street, who testified that he was present at a trial in Pennsylvania where the court condemned a man to be hung and yet neither judges, jurors, or witnesses were under oath.[47] Darnell, counsel for the

[42] *House of Lords Mss.*, n.s., IV, 317; *House of Lords Jour.*, XVI, 660.

[43] *House of Lords Mss.*, n.s., IV, 317, 342; *House of Lords Jour.*, XVI, 666, 670.

[44] *House of Lords Mss.*, n.s., IV, 315-316; *House of Lords Jour.*, XVI, 679, 680, 688.

[45] *House of Lords Mss.*, n.s., IV, 316. Randolph complained to the Lords that he had been threatened with arrest, whereupon he was given the protection of the house pending the passage of the bill. *House of Lords Jour.*, XVI, 687.

[46] *House of Lords Mss.*, n.s., IV, 316.

[47] *Ibid.*, IV, 316.

bill, accused Penn of making temporary laws to evade the royal veto and of allowing justice to be administered without the oath.[48] The Lords proceeded to a second reading of the bill on May 23, and after a consideration of the bill was postponed four times, the measure was dropped altogether.[49] Randolph informed the board on the day of the last postponement that there was no hope of its enactment this session.[50] The board wrote to Nicholson that " the bill, by reason of the shortness of time and the multiplicity of other affairs " precluded final action.[51] The greater interest of the Lords in the impeachment trial of Whig leaders and the early dissolution of Parliament worked against its enactment. Then again it is very probable that the influence of Ashurst,[52] Lord Baltimore, and the Earl of Bath was sufficiently strong to stay the hand of the Lords against the measure.

The Board of Trade was in no way downcast in its initial failure. A determination to persist is clearly evident. It wrote Nicholson that the bill would be renewed next session, to which he replied " I hope in God it will this Session." [53] Ashurst informed his colony to be prepared for another attempt, as " Insolent Randall & D. & another nameless friend was and are very active gentlemen against all proprietary governments." [54] Indeed such was the case. Randolph, preparatory to a second attempt, proceeded to take the affidavits of such witnesses as were unable to be present at the next session.[55] The board, on the recommendation of Basse, instructed the royal governors to investigate and report on the conduct of the char-

[48] *House of Lords Mss.*, n.s., IV, 316.
[49] *Ibid.*, 316-317; *House of Lords Jour.*, XVI, 688, 697, 717, 722, 726, 736.
[50] *B. T. Jour.*, XIV, 55; Toppan, *Edward Randolph*, V, 274.
[51] *No. Car. Col. Recs.*, I, 539.
[52] *Mass. Hist. Soc., Coll.*, sixth ser., III, 75.
[53] *No. Car. Col. Recs.*, I, 539-541.
[54] *Mass. Hist. Soc., Coll.*, sixth ser., III, 85.
[55] *B. T. Jour.*, XIV, 55; Toppan, *Edward Randolph*, V, 274.

tered colonies.[56] On the other hand, the representatives
of chartered interests, now fully aware of the enmity to
their charters, made active preparations for defense.
When Penn in his province heard of the attack he summoned his council and informed it of the necessity of
hastening to England. An assembly was promptly called
which voted him £2000 and the proprietor hurried
home.[57] However, just before his departure, Penn wrote
to Robert Harley and to the Board of Trade in a spirit
of just indignation at the falsity of the charges, the biased
character of the witnesses, and the arbitrary manner in
which the charters were considered.[58] To Penn it seemed
a "great trifling with honour and property, when men
must be forfeited in both, unheard." Penn said "let
our faults be proved, first the facts, next the malice or intention; but not behind our backs; . . . a Bill to
punish us before tried is worse than one of attainder."
And there is much to be said in favor of Penn's contention.
The board acted with perfect confidence in the veracity
and accuracy of the statements of Randolph, Basse, Dudley, and others, proceeded in the dark without a full hearing of the proprietors or colonial agents, and without regard for the rights of those concerned. Penn wrote to
the board in full refutation of the charges against his
province and from a general survey of the evidence available it appears that they were simply shreds and patches
of the truth. Penn wrote that it seemed "as if all the
old known Rules of Justice were to be read backward"
when the charges of "persons gaping for Preferments

56 *B. T. Jour.*, XIV, 107; *B. T. Paps., Props.*, VI, pt. 1, G 22.
Cornbury and Dudley for New England; Blackiston, Randolph, and
Andros for the other chartered colonies, were authorized to investigate and report on conditions. As they were all royal agents
and hostile to the chartered colonies it may not be said that this
was a non-partisan method of investigation.

57 *Pa. Col. Recs.*, II, 32, 35, 51.

58 *Duke of Portland Mss.*, IV, 19-21 in Hist. Mss. Com., *Report*,
15, pt. 4; *B. T. Paps., Props.*, VI, pt. 1, G 39.

under the Specious pretence of Serving the King's Interest . . . should be countenanced & encouraged and all their Representations without further Inquiry Credited, and made the bottom for the Ruine of the rather meritorious than culpable.'' Moreover, the whole procedure savored of confiscation when it is remembered that no monetary consideration was to be granted to the corporations or proprietors in return for the great expenditure of capital, blood, and brawn to plant colonies which yielded so considerable a profit to the metropolis. Penn said, " I have sunk my fortune and family £20,000 above my gains by land, to make and succeed this enterprise, which the loss of government will make one to me, and never count upon the money owing from the Crown to my father, that was at the bottom the consideration of the grant.'' And it does appear a gross violation of property and ingratitude to private initiative and capital for the state to step in and deprive the patentees, on *ex parte* evidence, of the rights of government without proper compensation.[59] It is true the bill to vacate the charters guaranteed to the patentees the rights to the land, but they held that the land was worth naught to them without governmental powers. The whole matter serves to illustrate the want of a proper appreciation and consideration of colonial interests which characterized so much of imperial administration during the eighteenth century, and which contributed in no small degree to the severing of the Empire.

On Penn's arrival in England he laid before the Earl of Manchester, secretary of state, some proposals to be

59 Jeremiah Dummer wrote in 1715 at the time of an attack on the charters; "It seems therefore a Severity without a Precedent that a People who have the misfortune of being a Thousand Leagues distant from their Sovereign, . . . should Unsummon'd, unheard, in one day be deprived of all their valuable Privileges, which they and their Fathers have enjoy'd for near a Hundred Years." *Defence of the Charters* (London, 1721).

framed into a bill designed to give the English government those powers necessary to carry out imperial measures.[60] He proposed that the military powers in the charters should be reunited to the crown, that the commander-in-chief appointed by royal authority should be empowered to superintend the customs service and vice-admiralty courts, that judicial proceedings should run in the king's name, and that the crown should enjoy a veto power on all colonial legislation and the right to hear appeals in all causes involving the sum of £300 or over. Such a measure would have imposed serious limitations on the powers of government delegated by the charters, but it had the virtue of saving to the colonies the rights of government in distinctly local affairs. This was probably the point Penn had in mind in view of the bitter hostility of the Board of Trade to the charters. But the board rejected the proposals as in no way contributing to the end of conserving the interests of the Empire and held that the former bill was the only proper measure.[61] In February, 1702, Henry Baker was directed by the secretary of state to act as solicitor for the second bill about to be brought into the House of Commons for vacating the charters.[62] Into his hands were given all the papers in the office of the Board of Trade relating to the irregularities committed in the chartered colonies. The untimely death of William III in March prevented further action and thus ended the parliamentary attacks on the charters for a few years.

The troubles of Penn were not yet ended. In January, 1702, he wrote from England to James Logan that '' Col.

[60] B. T. Paps., Props., VI, pt. 1, H 13; Penn Mss., Penn-Forbes Coll., II, 68.

[61] B. T. Jour., XIV, 335, 336; B. T. Paps., Props., Entry Bk. C, 381, 383.

[62] B. T. Jour., XIV, 338. In Nov., 1702, another effort was made to introduce into Parliament a bill to vacate the charters. Ibid., XV, 288, 292-293; B. T. Paps., Props., VII, L 2.

Quary comes on purpose to do us mischief, (sent for hence by the party), as well as to himself what good he can."[63] Quary, responsible for so much vexation to Penn and the Quakers in the province, now hurried to England to press his complaints before the Board of Trade. In October, 1701, Quary wrote to the board informing it of his intention to sail shortly for home to present matters of importance with regard to Penn's dominions.[64] Wishing to anticipate Penn's influence, Quary asked that no action should be taken relative to Pennsylvania until he arrived. The board was complaisant.[65] Quary came armed with complaints, petitions, affidavits, and other papers which he submitted to the board on March 31, 1702.[66] At the board's request these charges were abstracted in two memorials of April 16 and 20 and sent to Penn for answer.[67] After Penn's replies were at hand, several hearings were granted to both sides when the whole series of charges were threshed out.[68] It is interesting to note that at these hearings Randolph, Basse, and Byfield, the persistent enemies of the charters, were present at Quary's request to substantiate his complaints.[69] These memorials consisted of a curious *pot-pourri* of complaints, a mixture of strength and weakness; a few of them of considerable truth, the rest were a gross misrepresentation of the facts in the case. Many of the charges we have already discussed in treating of the vice-admiralty courts, the affirmation, and defense. It seemed that Quary was guilty of seizing upon every chance irregularity and distorting it

[63] *Penn-Logan Corres.*, I, 69.
[64] *B. T. Paps., Props.*, VI, pt. 1, H 2.
[65] *B. T. Jour.*, XIV, 288.
[66] *Ibid.*, XIV, 389-391.
[67] *B. T. Paps., Props.*, VII, M 21; VI, pt. 2, I 17; Entry Bk. C, 402, 403, 432-435.
[68] *B. T. Jour.*, XIV, 396, 403-404, 447-448; XV, 15, 27, 29-35, 53-59, 66-69, 75-80. For Penn's replies see *B. T. Paps., Props.*, VI, pt. 2, I 19, 20.
[69] *B. T. Jour.*, XIV, 419-420; XV, 26.

into a serious charge against the government of the province. He accused Penn of restoring to office Anthony Morris, who had issued a writ to seize some goods out of the hands of the marshal of the admiralty court, but on the other hand Penn pointed out that Quary had deputized as judge of the court, David Lloyd, at whose instigation the writ was issued. To Quary it appeared that Penn's action was reprehensible, while his own was proper. Penn stood accused of invading the jurisdiction of the admiralty court by appointing water-bailiffs, but Penn was able to show that he was forced to do this because of the necessity of preserving peace during Quary's absence on a trading expedition when no one was left to exercise the powers of the admiralty court. Furthermore, Penn's right to issue such commissions was upheld by the crown lawyers. Quary charged Penn with the dangerous practice of inviting foreigners and hostile Indians to come to the province for the exclusive trading purposes of the proprietor. Penn replied that he had discouraged Frenchmen employed by Quary from trading with the Indians. Other charges of a similar absurd character were made but in many cases Penn was able to show them to be misrepresentations. With respect to the question of defense, Quary was on much stronger ground. That the provincial government had established no militia, provided no fortifications and stores of war, and had refused to honor the royal requisitions were charges strongly entrenched in fact. Penn's reply that there was no need of defenses by sea because of the inland position of the province, or by land because of the kindly policy toward the savages did not meet the needs of the general interests which required each colony to look to its own defense and to assist those in immediate danger from foreign invasion and Indian outrage.

At the close of the hearing on Quary's charges, Randolph came forward to take up the wager of battle against

Penn.[70] He again attacked Penn's claim to Delaware as illegal. He charged that Pennsylvania had levied a tonnage duty prejudicial to English shipping; that a large illicit trade with Scotland was allowed; that during Penn's second visit to his colony, laws were passed repugnant to the acts of trade; that Penn and his deputy-governor, Markham, had appropriated to their own use the king's share of seizures and forfeitures, and that Markham had illegally imprisoned Randolph until he gave up several forfeited bonds. Then came the complaint of Gabriel Thomas, a tool in Quary's hands, that he had been reduced to poverty by the unjust conduct of Penn in a land transaction and craved the aid of the board in securing satisfaction.[71] When called upon for an answer, Penn characterized Thomas as a base and beggarly man upon whom he was sorry to waste any time.[72] Although Thomas pressed his complaint several times the board ignored it.[73] Convinced of the partiality of the board in entertaining these unjust accusations, Penn resolved to carry his case to higher authorities.[74] On June 26 the Privy Council requested the board to wait upon it in regard to matters submitted by Penn.[75] The board attended and was informed of the charges made against it by Penn. He complained that the board had shown great partiality to Quary, had recommended his expenses to the treasury for reimbursement and

---

[70] *B. T. Jour.*, XV, 90.

[71] *B. T. Paps., Props.*, VI, pt. 2, K 33. Thomas confessed that he was under a bond of £1000 to appear on behalf of Quary against Penn before the Board of Trade; and he also said that Penn had threatened him with imprisonment unless he testified that Quary's accusation were false.

[72] *Ibid.*, K 37, 46.

[73] *Ibid.*, VII, L 1, 4; *B. T. Jour.*, XV, 307, 308.

[74] In August, 1702, Penn wrote that he had decided to appeal to the Privy Council where he thought his affairs more properly lay than with the Board of Trade " after the Partiality those Gentlemen but too plainly exprest in favor of the common enemy of our poor country." *Amer. and W. I.*, 599 (Public Record Office, London).

[75] *B. T. Jour.*, XV, 106-107.

in other ways supported and favored him. Penn asked that Quary should be stopped in his return to the province until he had answered charges of a serious character against him.[76] On the other hand, the board accused Penn of causing unnecessary delays in the hearing although frequently requested to be prompt because of the need of Quary's immediate return to his duties in the province.[77] The charges brought by Penn against his arch-enemy have been treated at length elsewhere.[78] Using his office for personal advantage, lack of a knowledge of the civil law of which he was judge, and arbitrary conduct were charged against Quary. Some he denied, to others he confessed and Penn was able to secure his dismissal as judge of the admiralty court and the appointment of his own nominee. Penn's victory was empty, for in a few months the board secured not only Quary's restoration to the court but his promotion to the post of surveyor-general left vacant by the death of Randolph in 1703. This recognition of Quary certainly implied a confidence in his integrity and his faithfulness on the part of the Board of Trade. It may hardly be said with truth that the partisan and partial methods followed by the home government in dealing with colonial affairs was well suited to the ordering of an Empire.

Beset on all sides by a sea of difficulties, Penn sought to end his trials by giving up his powers of government.

[76] Quary petitioned the board for the reimbursement of his expenses, amounting to £300, incurred by his visit to England; that Penn'a. and Del. should be given royal government; and that care should be taken to guard him in the discharge of his duties from the threats and malice of Penn. The board wrote to the secretary of state asking that Quary's expenses should be reimbursed from the exchequer, that he be granted a royal letter of favor, and be appointed a member of the royal councils in N. Y., Va., and Md. *B. T. Paps., Props.*, VI, pt. 2, K 3; Entry Bk. D, 53.

[77] The hearings had been postponed several times because of Penn's illness, but finally the board resolved to proceed without him if he did not appear when summoned. *B. T. Jour.*, XV, 40, 43, 44.

[78] See page 112.

To this conclusion he was forced, not only by the enmity of the English officials, but by vexations in the province. Quary, Basse, Nicholson and others, backed by the Board of Trade, left no stone unturned to force an entrance for royal government. The intrigues of Basse in the Jerseys led the proprietors to surrender their powers of government to the crown in April, 1702.[79] Penn wrote to James Logan, " the Jersey surrender is an ugly preface; however there is a higher hand to which I look."[80] In the province the Church party, under the leadership of Quary and Moore, were bitter in their opposition to the Quaker government on the questions of defense and the affirmation. From Christ Church and Delaware came petitions to the crown complaining of the lack of protection and praying for royal control. The quarrel between the democratic assembly, under the leadership of David Lloyd, and the proprietary officials over questions of popular power and private interests bred keen factional feeling among Penn's own people. Logan wrote, " Thy dispute at home, the war without defense here, with the example of the Jersey's surrendering, make this government too precarious to be called one . . . our circumstances are uneasy and require a speedy redress."[81] Logan counseled Penn to extricate himself from his difficulties by yielding his powers of government to the crown. Even the Quakers, who sympathized with Penn, were indifferent on the question of surrender because they saw " government so ill-fitted to their principles "; all they asked was that " they might not fall a spoil to such base hands that now seek our ruin."[82] There is little wonder that Penn wished to seek relief from the difficulties which threatened to engulf him. In May, 1703, he wrote to the Board of Trade, that observing " your bent is extreamly strong to bring all pro-

79 Kellogg, *Amer. Col. Charter*, 235-239.
80 *Penn-Logan Corres.*, I, 78.
81 *Ibid.*, I, 87, 121.
82 *Ibid.*, 147, 233-234.

prietary Governments more immediately under the disposition of the Crown. . . . I thought it fit to let you know that upon a just regard for me and the people in our civil rights . . . I shall upon satisfaction resigne to the Crowne the Government thereof." [83]   After the Queen had signified her willingness to treat with Penn, he presented to the board in June the conditions on which he would surrender his governmental powers.[84]   He asked that Pennsylvania and Delaware should continue as distinct provinces; that a patent should be granted to him and his heirs for the territory of Delaware; that the rights to the soil of Pennsylvania and the powers incident thereto should be guaranteed to him and his heirs; that the crown should confirm the laws and constitutions of the province; that no appeals involving under the sum of £200 should lie to the crown; and that he and his heirs should have the privilege of nominating two or more persons for governor from whom the crown should appoint one. The latter was asked for the purpose of safeguarding the interests of the Quakers and to distinguish the Penn family as founders of the province. As a monetary consideration Penn asked £30,000 and a revenue of one-half penny a pound on all tobacco raised in the province, which he " hoped would not be thought hard " considering that he had spent £10,500 at the first settlement and twice as much since in supporting the government of a colony which now yielded so great a benefit to England. Penn estimated that, besides the exportation to England of many products needed there, the province had purchased English goods on which the customs revenue had increased from £1500 to £10,000 a year since the founding of the colony. Penn held that the government was the best part of the consideration in lieu of the royal debt to his

[83] B. T. Paps., Props., VII, L 28; B. T. Jour., XVI, 104.
[84] B. T. Paps., Props., VII, L 29, 35, 36; Entry Bk. D, 314, 320, 321, 338; B. T. Jour., XVI, 119.

father, since he had purchased the lands from the Indians. Early in July the board took these conditions into consideration and held them to be exorbitant.[85] To reserve to himself the right to nominate the governor was in effect to retain in his own hands the power of government. Penn, not unmindful of his co-religionists, insisted that a reservation of this power was necessary to guard the Quakers, who hazarded their lives and fortunes to settle the province, against the possible hardships which might otherwise be visited upon them because of their peculiar views on religion.[86] The board held that to require as a condition the royal confirmation of the colonial laws took from the crown the power which it now possessed under the charter of vetoing or confirming them. Looking at the matter from the standpoint of Penn and the Quakers the conditions do not seem unfair. It was but natural that Penn, who had sunk his fortune in the colony without any countervailing returns,[87] and that the Quakers, who had risked their all to establish a home for themselves, should seek to secure a proper safeguard of their interests. It was but proper that the English government should offer due compensation to Penn and the Quakers for planting a colony which proved to be so advantageous to the commerce of the metropolis. The failure to agree on conditions brought a suspension of negotiations.

[85] *B. T. Jour.*, XVI, 170-171. The board reported to Parliament in 1703 that Penn's proposals were " esteemed very unreasonable, and thereupon pressed him to come to more moderate Terms." *Bulletin N. Y. Public Lib.*, Oct., 1907, XI, no. 10, 472.

[86] Logan wrote, " . . . remember the people thou brought hither from their native land," to which Penn made answer, " Fear not my bargain with the Crown, for it shall never be made without a security to the inhabitants, according to the constitution and laws of the country." *Penn-Logan Corres.*, I, 245, 263.

[87] Penn probably felt as Camden wrote of the failure of Humphrey Gilbert, " that it is a difficulter thing to carry colonies into remote Countreys upon private mens Purses, than he and others in an erroneous Credulity had persuaded themselves, to their own Cost and Detriment." Camden, *Hist. of Elizabeth*, 287.

In January, 1705, Penn reopened the question of surrender. Penn became hopelessly involved in debt through
the treachery of his stewards, the Fords.[88] The province
continued to be rent by the factional struggles of the
Quaker and Church parties and by the proprietary and
anti-proprietary parties. The hostility of the Board of
Trade and the royal officials in the colonies had not abated.
The Churchmen of the province besought Lord Cornbury,
governor of New York, to use his good offices to secure
royal control.[89] Chiefly because of Penn's load of debts
and the insurgency in politics in the colony, Logan continued to advise his chief to surrender his government.[90] In
December, 1704, Penn personally acquainted the board with
his desire to renew the negotiations and expressed a willingness to waive his former demand to nominate the governor.[91] In the next month, at the board's request, Penn
submitted new proposals in writing.[92] They embodied
much the same conditions as before, except that Penn
now omitted any mention of the power to name the governor, but asked that he and his heirs should be exempt
from "troublesome office and the Public Taxes" in the
province. After some debate and correspondence the
board apparently considered the conditions too high and
took no further action.[93] Early in March Penn asked the
board what it was he was expected to surrender. To this
came the reply demanding an unconditional surrender of
his powers of government, and the reservation to himself
and heirs the rights to the soil and the powers and privi-

[88] Shepherd, *Proprietary Gov't. in Pa.*, 183-190; *Penn-Logan Corres.*, I, 280, 351, 354; II, 19-20, 71, 95-96.

[89] *Penn-Logan Corres.*, I, 223.

[90] *Ibid.*, I, 350, 362; II, 2-3, 25, 41.

[91] *B. T. Jour.*, XVII, 221.

[92] *B. T. Paps., Props.*, VIII, pt. 1, N 1.

[93] *Ibid.*, N 1, nos. 2, 3; Entry Bk. E, 87, 89-90; *B. T. Jour.*, XVII,
223, 230, 233.

leges incident thereto.[94] In April the proprietor presented new conditions upon which he was willing to surrender his government.[95] These were laid before the board in a formal statement in May.[96] He asked the royal approval for the laws of the province which guaranteed to the inhabitiants a representative assembly elected annually, with power to make laws, levy taxes, and sit on its own adjournments; a guarantee that it shall not be in the power of the governor and assembly at any future time to abridge the law granting liberty of conscience or to subject the Quakers to any fines or forfeitures by reason of their peculiar dress or carriage or to compel them to serve in the militia or to contribute to warlike charges. For himself and heirs he asked that the county of Bucks should be erected into a palatinate with all the powers and regalities exercised at any time in the County Palatine of Durham, that his rights to the soil of Pennsylvania and Delaware should be guaranteed, and that he and his family should be exempt from provincial taxes. After sitting twice in consideration of these conditions the board replied that it could not concur in them.[97] It said that Delaware could not be considered in the negotiations as it formed no part of the province under the charter; that the palatinate of Bucks would give to the proprietor greater powers than he now enjoyed by the royal charter; and that it could not agree to the stipulations with regard to liberty of conscience or to the confirmation of the laws until each one was considered in particular. When Penn pointed out that liberty of conscience was already provided for by the law of the colony, the board decided to examine at once into the laws before proceeding further in the mat-

[94] *B. T. Paps., Props.*, Entry Bk. E, 131, 132; *B. T. Jour.*, XVII, 318.
[95] *B. T. Jour.*, XVII, 370.
[96] *Ibid.*, 373, 386, 388; *B. T. Paps., Props.*, VIII, pt. 1, N 30.
[97] *B. T. Jour.*, XVII, 392, 398, 401.

ter of surrender. Although Penn entreated the board to proceed in the business of surrender and laid before it several new papers of conditions, no further action was taken.[98] The board was again busily engaged in preparation for another attack upon the charters. As a result not only were the laws granting freedom of worship and the use of the affirmation by the Quakers disallowed by the crown,[99] but the charters were again put in jeopardy by Parliament.

Cornbury and Dudley, governors of New York and Massachusetts respectively, were now the aggressors against the charters. Especially singled out for attack were the colonies of Rhode Island and Connecticut. Opposition to the admiralty courts, refusal to allow appeals to the Privy Council, illegal trade, piracy, lack of defenses, refusal to obey the royal requisitions for war, opposition to the royal commissions to command their militia, and a general tendency to independence, formed the list of familiar accusations.[100] With implicit confidence in these charges the Tory ministry and board again decided on parliamentary action.[101] In February, 1706, Blathwayt, a member of the board and patron of Dudley, introduced into the House of Commons, at the direction of the crown, a bill to vest the powers of government in the chartered colonies in the crown.[102] The measure did not pass beyond the first reading. Whig influence in Parliament was now in the ascendant and Whig regard for property and vested interests probably accounts in part for the failure to overthrow

[98] B. T. Jour., XVII, 414; XVIII, 40, 53, 57, 93, 97, 99-100, 106; B. T. Paps., Props., VIII, pt. 1, N 32, 42.

[99] See pages 233, 243.

[100] B. T. Paps., Props., VIII, pt. 1, N 23, O 9-12, 19; VIII, pt. 2, O 38-47; N. Y. Col. Docs., IV, 1058, 1061, 1070, 1079.

[101] B. T. Paps., Props., Entry Bk. E, 238; B. T. Jour., XVIII, 160, 163, 165; No. Car. Col. Recs., I, 630-633; R. I. Col. Recs., IV, 12-15.

[102] B. T. Paps., Props., VIII, pt. 2, O 30; Entry Bk. E, 324; B. T. Jour., XVIII, 219; House of Commons Jour., XV, 168.

the charters. Then again the influence of the proprietors and colonial agents, especially Ashurst, agent for Connecticut and a prominent Whig, was sufficient to check final action.[103] In 1707 the membership of the Board of Trade was changed from a Tory to a Whig personnel and the charters were in no further danger till the Tories returned to power in 1710.

Meanwhile, Penn's difficulties increased, his load of debts grew heavier, the factional struggles grew more bitter, and Logan urged the proprietor to resume negotiations for surrender.[104] In January, 1707, Penn besought the Board of Trade to proceed upon his proposals.[105] The conditions of 1705 were submitted as a basis. In February the board reported on them to the Earl of Sutherland, secretary of state.[106] The report pointed out the advantages of royal control; it would conduce to the support of the royal prerogative, a more impartial administration of justice where so many different religious sects were concerned, and would afford the crown a better opportunity to administer the laws of trade and provide for defense. But as to the conditions of surrender the report gave the opinion that it should be absolute and unconditional, including a renunciation of all claims to the powers of government in Pennsylvania and Delaware. But out of regard for Penn's claim upon the crown by reason of the royal debt to his father, and in consideration of the proprietor's vast outlay in founding a colony which yielded him no profitable returns, but proved so advantageous to the revenue and commerce of the metropolis, the report recommended that Penn

103 Ashurst wrote to his government, " . . . I made such interest against it with some of the leading men of the House so that it was thrown out at the first reading. I have the vanity to say that if you had not employed me you would have been in a sad condition this day." Mass. Hist. Soc., *Coll.*, sixth ser., III, 384,
104 *Penn-Logan Corres.*, II, 139, 146, 156, 167, 179.
105 *B. T. Jour.*, XIX, 53; *B. T. Paps., Props.*, VIII, pt. 2, O 87.
106 *B. T. Jour.*, XIX, 55, 57; *B. T. Paps., Props.*, Entry Bk. E, 439-442.

should receive an equitable compensation.[107] The report
was referred to the Lords of the Treasury to fix upon the
quantum.[108] The treasury board referred the report back
to the Board of Trade to agree upon the compensation, on
the ground that the board's knowledge of conditions made
it a better judge of the matter. From the nature of the
queries sent to Penn by the board it is evident that the
crown did not wish to assume the power of government
without counting the costs of supporting it. Penn was
asked to state not only what amount he expended in founding the colony and what compensation he expected, but also
what revenue the land yielded, what the charges of government were, and what revenue was settled for its support.[109]
Penn replied indignantly that his profits from the land
had nothing to do with the case, since his government was
the only matter in consideration. In regard to the charges
of government he could not give the exact amount, but
stated that by the law of 1706 the assembly made provision for its support for three years. As to compensation,
Penn now asked £20,000.[110] But the negotiations went
no further for several years.

Penn's cup of sadness was now filled to overflowing.
The Fords sued Penn for debt, the court cast the verdict
against him and the doors of a debtor's prison closed about
the great Quaker.[111] In October, 1708, Penn mortgaged

107 For the period 1698-1704, imports of English and foreign
goods to the colony amounted to £79,657; and exports to England
equaled £23,043. B. T. Paps., Props., VIII, pt. 2, O 99, 100.

108 B. T. Jour.. XIX, 109; B. T. Paps., Props., Entry Bk. E, 439,
460.

109 B. T. Jour., XIX, 155; B. T. Paps., Props., Entry Bk. F, 472.

110 B. T. Jour., XIX, 290; B. T. Paps., Props., IX, P 8; Entry
Bk. F, 10-12.

111 Shepherd, Proprietary Gov't. in Pa., 194-195; Penn-Logan
Corres., II, 237, 251, 255. For an account of Penn's financial
perplexities with the Fords see the statements in Clarendon Mss.,
102, f. 160; Rawlinson Mss., D, 923, f. 276. (Bodleian Lib.,
Oxford).

his province and liquidated the Ford debt.[112] Although eased in finances, his difficulties in the province increased. Outrages in Delaware on the part of Maryland were numerous. The people of Delaware, impatient of proprietary rule, questioned Penn's right to the government, complained of the lack of defenses, and threatened to appeal to the crown.[113] The turbulent democracy under Lloyd tried to throw the province into confusion in order to secure royal control.[114] The refusal of the Quaker assembly to aid in the expedition against Canada and to provide protection against the French and Spanish privateers brought upon it the bitter invectives of those who demanded defense.[115] Isaac Norris wrote to Penn that the lack of defense " will give the government a severe jostle, if not quite cost it," and expressed a fear that " it must be a governor immediately from the Crown that must set us to rights." [116] In July, 1710, Penn renewed his proposals.[117] The Board of Trade again examined into the matter and made its report in February, 1711, expressing the same opinions as made in the representation of 1707.[118] In February, 1712, Penn's proposals were subject to the examination of the attorney-general.[119] Before him Penn appeared and made out his title to Delaware and a deed of surrender was drawn up. The question of compensation was referred to the Lord High Treasurer. When Penn had satisfied him that the assembly had made suitable provision for the support of the government, it was agreed that the

112 Shepherd, *op. cit.* 196-198; *B. T. Paps., Props.*, X, pt. 2, Q 207.
113 Shepherd, *op cit.* 131; *Penn-Logan Corres.*, II, 303, 311, 324-325, 326, 334.
114 *Penn-Logan Corres.*, II, 337.
115 *Ibid.*, 347.
116 *Ibid.*, 348, 351, 356, 357, 421, 423, 435.
117 *B. T. Jour.*, XXII, 89, 93; *B. T. Paps., Props.*, IX, P 100; Entry Bk. F, 225-229.
118 *B. T. Jour.*, XXII, 216, 222; *B. T. Paps., Props.*, Entry Bk. F, 254-261.
119 *B. T. Paps., Props.*, Entry Bk. F, 466-468.

proprietor should receive £12,000 payable in four years.[120] The deed of surrender stipulated that Penn, his heirs, and assigns should yield to the crown all title to the government, civil and military, reserving to himself and heirs all rights to the soil and the jurisdictions incident thereto provided in the charter, and that nothing in the deed should be construed to abridge the laws or acts of the government passed prior to the consummation of the surrender and not disallowed by the crown.[121] On March 12, 1712, Penn received from the treasury £1000 on account before the deed was formally executed.[122] Soon after this Penn was stricken down with apoplexy which rendered him incapable of further business and thus through accident alone did the province of Pennsylvania remain a chartered colony.[123] In 1714 the crown made an effort to perfect the deed by act of Parliament, but no action was taken because of the unsettled differences between the mortgagees of the province and the Penn heirs.[124]

The Tories returned to power in 1710 and again the representatives of the chartered colonies were alarmed. In July, 1712, Penn informed Logan that " you will find all the charters and proprietary governments annexed to the Crown by act of Parliament next session." [125] It was the purpose of Henry St. John, secretary of state, to place all the colonies under a uniform system of control by the home government.[126] In 1713 Jeremiah Dummer, agent for Connecticut, informed the governor of designs upon the charter. Alarmed by this news, the Connecticut government resolved to coöperate with Rhode Island and Massa-

120 *Cal. Treas. Paps.*, 1708-1714, 360; *B. T. Paps., Props.*, X, pt. 1, Q 53.

121 *Penn Mss., Penn-Forbes Coll.*, I, ff. 13-14.

122 *Cal. Treas. Paps.*, 1708-1714, 360, 428; 1720-1728, 14; *B. T. Paps., Props.*, X, pt. 2, Q 208.

123 Janney, *Life of Penn*, 538-542.

124 See page 142 ff.

125 Janney, *Life of Penn*, 538.

126 *N. Y. Col. Docs.*, V, 255-256.

chusetts in defense of their patents,— a premonition of the method used by the colonies in 1765 to defend their rights of self-government against English interference.[127] The Tory ministry remained inactive in this policy and the accession of the Whigs to power in 1714 under the House of Hanover freed the charters from serious danger.

It is evident from the foregoing account that the policy of vacating the charters and of strengthening English authority came from a small group of active men in the colonial service,— Randolph, Nicholson, Quary, Basse, Cornbury, Dudley, and a number of lesser lights. These men, backed by the Board of Trade, originated much of the colonial policy of the period of 1696-1714. One is impressed, as the records make clear, with the unwearied efforts of these officials, not only to support royal authority and imperial interests, but also to advance the cause of the English Church in the colonies. Randolph, the chief of them, said " 'tis my only design in this, and all other my publick services, that His Majesties interests and the Acts of Trade be inviolably maintained and supported in His Majesties plantations, by all persons concerned." His career as a royal customs official to the year of his death bears ample witness to the truth of this spirit. In the colonies he left nothing undone and spared no pains to secure a proper administration of the acts of trade. At home it was his official experience, his evidence, and untiring efforts which were largely responsible for the attacks on the charters and the policy of centralizing colonial control. Of much the same type, but in some cases of inferior ability, were the rest of this group. At home they were relied upon as faithful officials, frequently consulted by the Board of Trade, the Commissioners of the Customs, and Parliament, full credence given to their reports, and indeed much of the official action of the English government was based upon their recommendations. But in the colonies they

127 R. I. Col. Recs., IV, 410, 414.

were regarded with feelings of intense hatred. Their ceaseless hostility to the charters, their meddlesome activity in internal affairs embittered the hearts of the colonists against them. Their devoted support of the Anglican Church brought upon them the denunciations of the dissenters, Puritans and Quakers. There is much evidence to justify the attitude of the colonists toward them. The records indicate that they were ofttimes arbitrary in their dealings with the people, void of tact, over-zealous in the enforcement of their royal powers, and wanting in a proper appreciation of the needs and circumstances of the colonists. The enforcement and adjustment of an economic and administrative system which was not of the colonists, own choosing nor the resultant of colonial needs and desires called for the highest and best type of official. Many of England's agents in all branches of the colonial service during this period in no way measured up to this standard. Too often they were merely placemen, dependent upon the pickings of office for support, defective in character, of a narrow cast of mind, and too often led by a blind devotion to the imperial system into arbitrary and unwarranted assumptions of power. Randolph was accused by the agents of Massachusetts and Pennsylvania and by Sir Lionel Copley, governor of royal Maryland, of arbitrary conduct toward the local magistrates, of prosecuting alleged illegal traders on insufficient evidence, and of corrupt practices.[128] In former pages we have dealt at length with the career of Robert Quary in Pennsylvania, and his "vice-regent in mischief," John Moore. They confessed

[128] B. T. Paps., Props., II, B 18; Cal. State Paps., Col., 1689-1692, 287-288. Copley and the council of Md. wrote that Randolph prosecuted vessels for illegal trade "on the bare account of what he calls New England rogues and pitiful damned Scotch pedlars," and by his arbitrary actions "has done here what he has done elsewhere—made the country weary of him." Cal. State Paps., Col., 1689-1692, 679, 750; see also, ibid., 1693-1696, 80, 110. See Osgood's characterization of Randolph, Amer. Cols., III, 379-380; also Channing, Hist. of U. S., II, 259-262.

to an ignorance of the civil law which they were called upon to administer, they used their offices for personal advantage, they espoused the cause of Delaware in the controversy with Pennsylvania, and under their leadership the Churchmen of the province sought to discredit the Quaker government in the hope of securing royal control. Basse, who played the role of intriguer in New Jersey, was of the same arbitrary character.[129] By the use of unfair means he stirred up confusion in the Jerseys and forced the proprietors to surrender their governmental powers to the crown, and his later career as a royal official attests to the same sort of conduct.[130] The profligate career of Lord Cornbury, royal governor of New York and New Jersey, stands as a severe indictment of the English civil service.[131] Even Nicholson stood charged with serious offenses by the royal council of Virginia, and with insolent behavior toward some of the chartered governments.[132] Such in general was the character of the men on whose word and evidence the home government was content to rely with confidence. The frequent and voluminous letters of these royal appointees to the home government fail to reveal but little sympathy with the colonists and but little evidence of a proper understanding of colo-

[129] Hunter, governor of N. J., wrote to the Board of Trade in 1711, saying that "Mr. Bass, the present Secretary being so obnoxious a man and indeed infamous that I cannot believe her Majty. will be induct to keep him there after the representations I have made agt. him." *N. Y. Col. Docs.*, V, 256. See also *N. J. Archives*, IV, 139, 172, 209 for further complaints against Basse. Bellomont, gov. of N. Y. characterized Basse as a man "puff'd up and exalted with vanity, that he was unsupportable to everybody," accused him of being a greater liar than Fletcher, a cormorant in eating and drinking, and by his meanness and immorality made the people of N. J. tired of him. Bellomont to Penn, June 21, 1698, *Penn Mss., Penn-Forbes Coll.*, II.

[130] Kellogg, *Amer. Col. Charter*, 238-239; Tanner, *Province of N. J., Columbia College Studies*, XXX, 93, 170, 176, 190, *passim*.

[131] Tanner, *op. cit.*, 140-141, 168-180; Spencer, *Phases of Royal Gov't. in N. Y.*, 10, 12-13.

[132] See page 237.

nial conditions. On the one hand, such a type of official was not of the proper sort to adjust the imperial system to colonial needs or to strengthen the ties which held the mother country and dependencies together. On the other hand, the reliance of the central authorities on the biased evidence of the colonial officials did not conduce to a wise and rational management of colonial business.[133]   The failure of the imperial government to appoint to the colonial service men of merit and to organize the colonial office at home with the purpose of securing an intelligent administration of colonial affairs goes far to account for the development of inharmonious relations between the two parts of the Empire.

The accession of the House of Hanover in 1714 witnessed a change in the attitude toward the charters and to colonial concerns in general. During the previous period the colonists found themselves on the defensive because of the attempts to centralize control. In the next period this policy was less persistently followed and the charters were freed from pressure. Several factors combined to effect this change of attitude. Not the least of these was the passing of the royal officials of the earlier period from the scene of activity. The careers of Randolph and Quary had been stayed by the hand of death. The profligate conduct of Cornbury brought about his dismissal as governor. The influence of Nicholson and Dudley was on the wane. Then again, the former active Board of Trade had grown lax in its duties and had deteriorated in personnel under the baneful influence of the corrupt patronage system in English politics of the era of Walpole and Newcastle. Furthermore, in the province of war and religion the colonists found themselves free from vexation. The

---

[133] To support a list of charges against Rhode Island, Dudley sent home the affidavits of four men; Paul, his son, Nathaniel Byfield, and James Menzies, royal agents and tools of Dudley, and Nathaniel Coddington, a man with a grievance against the colony. *B. T. Paps., Props.,* VIII, pt. 2, O 10-12.

Treaty of Utrecht of 1713 brought twenty-five years of peace
and the problem of defense had fallen into the background.
Henry Compton, the zealous bishop of London, was dead,
the Society for the Propagation of the Gospel was less
active, the Whig régime was favorable to dissent, and the
Puritans and Quakers were freed from the pressure of the
English Church. It was during this period of freedom
from rigorous imperial control that the colonists became the
aggressors and made rapid strides in curtailing and ab-
sorbing the powers of the proprietary and royal officials.
Yet it must not be presumed that the English authorities
both at home and in the colonies were oblivious to the defects in the system of colonial administration. We have
seen that they tried to reorganize the Board of Trade in
order to give it greater powers and to centralize colonial
management at home. As far as the colonies were concerned they continued to point out the necessity of vacating
the charters. In 1715 the conditions of anarchy in the
Carolinas, due to the inefficient administration of the board
of proprietors, led to the bill in Parliament to vacate all
the charters, but the influence of the proprietary interests
checked the measure.[134] But in 1720 the crown took action in the case of South Carolina by establishing royal
government.[135] In 1719 the Board of Trade, aroused by
the irregular way in which Pennsylvania submitted its
laws to the home government, urged the Privy Council
to vacate the charters. Again in the oft-quoted report of
1721 the board detailed fully the abuses practiced in the
chartered colonies and advised that the powers of government should be reunited to the crown.[136] This plan not
only contemplated the vacation of the charters, but went
further in proposing the appointment of a governor-gen-

[134] Kellogg, *Amer. Col. Charter*, 308-310.
[135] Smith, *So. Car. as a Royal Province*, 11-14; McCrady, *So.
Car. under Royal Gov't.*, chs. i, ii.
[136] *N. Y. Col. Docs.*, V, 591-629; *B. T. Paps., Pl. Gen.*, Entry Bk.
E, 286 ff.

eral over all the colonies,— an approximation of the French system in Canada or the old Andros régime. This plan was supported by the Earl of Stair and by Martin Bladen, an active member of the Board of Trade.[137] The board continued to take advantage of every opportunity to urge upon the ministry or Parliament the necessity of curtailing the powers of the chartered colonies. In 1723, at the sanction of the crown, the board sought to induce the colonies of Rhode Island and Connecticut to submit voluntarily to royal government, but in plain terms they refused to yield to the suggestion.[138] In the case of the Carolinas the crown was more fortunate. In 1729 the proprietors, weary with the expense and trouble of governing turbulent colonies, sold their interests to the crown for £25,000.[139] In 1731 the board suggested to the crown that Connecticut should receive an explanatory charter placing it in the relations which Massachusetts held to the crown. The colony turned a deaf ear to the proposal.[140] Neither Connecticut or the proprietors of Pennsylvania would willingly permit their affairs to be brought to the attention of Parliament for fear that such a step would endanger their charters.[141] They had reason to feel apprehension.[142]

[137] *No. Car. Col. Recs.*, II, 625 ff.; *King's Mss.*, 205, f. 972 (British Museum), quoted in full in Carson, *Anniv. Hist. of Const. of U. S.*, II, 460-464. Colden of N. Y. is authority for the statement that the English ministry in 1723 planned to send the Earl of Stair to America as governor-general over all the colonies, but that the want of a monetary support prevented ʼthe execution of the scheme. Franklin, *Works* (Smyth ed.), III, 201.

[138] Kellogg, *Amer. Col. Charter*, 313-314; *Acts of Privy Council, Col.*, III, 11.

[139] Kellogg, *op. cit.*, 246-250.

[140] *Talcott Papers*, Conn. Hist. Soc., *Coll.*, I, 175-176; 232; II, 435-436; Andrews, *Conn. Intestacy Law, Yale Review*, Nov., 1894, 288-292.

[141] See page 134.

[142] Partridge, agent for Rhode Island, wrote to his government in 1732, " . . . the Lords of Trade I doubt not are glad of any opportunity to lay hold of an advantage against the Charter Governmᵗˢ. that if possible they may be resumed to the Crown, for I

The reports of 1732 and 1734 from the board to Parliament complained that Connecticut and Rhode Island sent no laws to the crown and that Pennsylvania and Massachusetts submitted theirs very irregularly.[143] This led to the bill of 1734 which proposed that each colony should submit its laws to the crown within a year after enactment and that no law, except in extreme cases, should become operative till the royal sanction was given. In 1744 and 1748, because of disobedience to royal orders, it was proposed to give royal instructions the force of law. But just as often as these measures were recommended, so often Parliament failed to act upon them. The fact is that Parliament proved to be a better friend of the colonies than the Board of Trade. Yet this period, especially after 1730, marks the beginning of a more active parliamentary influence in colonial management. The régime of Walpole and Newcastle witnessed the gradual transfer of colonial administration from the king in council to Parliament acting through various administrative boards. This is seen in the several addresses to the crown calling for reports on colonial laws, trade, finances and manufactures. Positive action was taken in the interests of the English industrial and trading classes; such as the Hat Act of 1732 and the Iron Act of 1750, the Molasses Act of 1733, the address of 1740 to the crown forbidding colonial governors to assent to the issue of bills of credit without the suspending clause, the act of 1741 against the Massachusetts Land Bank, the Currency Act of 1751, and the act of 1732 to protect English merchants in the collection of colonial debts. This increased display of interest and activity of the imperial legislature in colonial concerns foreshadowed the action of that body after 1763 which

don't take them to be Friends to our Northern Colonies." Kimball, *Corres. of Govs. of R. I.*, I, 30.

[143] For the report of 1734, see *Talcott Papers*, Conn. Hist. Soc., *Coll.*, II, 445-462.

raised the fundamental question of the relations between Parliament and the colonies and caused the disruption of the Empire.

On the other hand much of the pressure against the charters came from the colonists themselves. Those who attacked the charters in the interest of royal government were actuated by various motives. The Churchmen in Pennsylvania and other chartered colonies desired crown government in the interests of the English Church.[144] Others petitioned for a change of government because of the inefficiency of proprietary rule. The conditions of confusion in the Jerseys led the people to ask for royal government, and the proprietors yielded in 1702.[145] The people of South Carolina, a prey to incompetent proprietary rule, overthrew the government which led to crown control in 1720. Still another group protested against what they considered the arbitrary character of proprietary government. In 1689 a body of Protestant insurgents, out of sympathy with the narrow Catholic official system in Maryland, destroyed the government of Lord Baltimore and offered the province to the crown.[146] In Pennsylvania during the eighteenth century the assembly, which reflected democratic sentiments and which stood for self-government, found itself hedged about by proprietary authority Hardly had the province been settled when there developed a bitter conflict between the assembly and the proprietary officials over questions of finance and government. Autonomous government was out of the question if the will of the assembly could be thwarted by the governor acting under proprietary instructions and caring rather for the landed interests of the Penns than the welfare of the people. The struggle waged about the questions of paper currency and the taxation of the Penn estates. Each dispute

[144] Kellogg, *Amer. Col. Charter*, 291-298.
[145] *N. J. Archives*, II, 322-327, 380-384, 394.
[146] Osgood, *Amer. Cols.*, III, 495-499.

involved the question of political power. If the proprietors could determine by instructions the financial policy of the province, the assembly was reduced to a subordinate position. Such was not the case in the corporate colonies where by charter the assembly was the central and controlling organ of government. It was this position which the assemblies of the provinces sought to attain. Ofttimes the proprietary governor was forced to submit to the will of the assembly in contravention of his instructions, but when this method failed a threat was made to appeal to the crown for a redress of grievances. The first concerted effort to overthrow proprietary rule came in 1728-9. Sir William Keith, a political adventurer, took advantage of the quarrel between the governor and assembly over the issue of bills of credit to promote disturbance in order to secure royal interference and government.[147] Keith was probably actuated by a desire to secure a royal appointment,[148] but his plot was frustrated when the governor yielded to the wishes of the assembly. Again in 1741-2 Governor Thomas and the assembly quarreled over a grant of supplies for the West Indian expedition. Thomas informed John Penn that the assembly " publickly avow their design to throw the Government into the hands of the Crown " and sought to create confusion " as the most probable way of bringing it about." [149] John Penn wrote that he was " under no uneasiness about the Success of

[147] *Penn Mss., Official Corres.*, III, Gov. Gordon to proprietors, Oct. 6, 1728; to John Penn, May 16, 1728.

[148] Keith, while governor of Pa., with singular duplicity, wrote to the Board of Trade in 1717 pointing out the advantages of consolidating the colonies of Pa., Del., and West Jersey into one government. *B. T. Paps., Props.*, X, pt. 1, Q 140. In 1724 he suggested to the duke of Newcastle the advisability of perfecting the agreement with the Penn heirs in order to put the colony under royal government. *Amer. and W. I.*, 28, f. 8. In 1736, Keith applied for the post of lieutenant-governor of N. J. *N. J. Archives*, V, 446.

[149] *Penn Mss., Official Corres.*, III, Gov. Thomas to John Penn, Nov. 4, 1740; March 25, 1741; June 4, 1742.

their petition.'' [150]   The fact is that the refusal of the asembly to honor the royal requisition did not place it in a favorable position before the home government. The dispute between the two branches of government reached a crisis at the time of the French and Indian war over the question of taxing the Penn estates. Unable to compel the governor to break his instructions forbidding the taxation of the proprietary lands, the assembly sent Franklin to England in 1757 to secure a redress of grievances. The time seemed propitious for a change of government. Pennsylvania and Maryland were not in good repute because of their inactivity during the war. Dinwiddie of Virginia repeatedly urged that these charters should be vacated.[151] Richard Partridge, agent for Rhode Island, wrote to the governor informing him of the '' satirical expressions '' hurled against the charters at the last session of Parliament, and added that it was not the first time '' harsh Things have been vehemently uttered before the Lords -of Trade as well as in the House of Commons.'' [152] Such was the time when Franklin wrote from England to Isaac Norris suggesting that petitions from the people of Pennsylvania and Maryland expressing dislike for proprietary rule and praying for royal government would be favorably received.[153] Franklin was not above the arts of the intriguer. He said '' Tumults and Insurrections, that might prove the Proprietary government unable to preserve order, or show the People to be ungovernable, would do the business immediately.'' Such were the reprehensible means employed by Basse and Keith. Although the ministry had several times mentioned the question of a change of government to the Penns, yet there was

150 *Penn Mss., Letter Bk.*, I, John Penn to Gov. Thomas, Aug. 16, 1742; *Official Corres.*, III, Thos. Penn to Paris, April 24, 1741.
151 *Dinwiddie Corres.*, I, 142; II, 414-415, 418.
152 Kimball, *Corres. of Govs. of R. I.*, II, 140-141.
153 Franklin, *Works* (Smyth ed.), III, 455, 472.

no thought of forcing them.[154]   The attitude of the home government had changed from one of hostility in the earlier period to one of support now.   In 1760 the crown, at the recommendation of the Board of Trade, disallowed six laws protested by the Penns as prejudicial to their powers of government and landed interests.   In concluding this report, the board said that steps must be taken to curb the exorbitant demands of the assembly and uphold the royal prerogative vested in the proprietors by charter.[155]

The climax was reached in 1764 when Franklin again left for England bearing a petition from the assembly to the crown asking for royal government.   In that year the assembly was forced to yield to the governor in a supply bill under stress of the Indian insurrection.   In yielding, the assembly informed Governor John Penn that it had given up important rights and hoped that an " equitable government . . . is not far distant " when the arbitrary conduct of proprietary rule would be ended.[156]   In seeking a change of government, the members of the assembly, under the leadership of Franklin and Joseph Galloway, were not actuated by motives of zeal for the royal prerogative or imperial interests, but by the hope that royal government would free them from the evils of proprietary rule.   This is evidenced by the introduction of the international dispute.   When the assembly learned of the passage of the Sugar Act and the intention to levy a stamp tax, the house was inclined to proceed more cautiously in the matter.   The aim of the assembly was freedom from any outside direction or interference whatever.   Hence

---

[154] *Penn Mss., Letter Bk.*, V, Thos. Penn to Gov. Hamilton, July 7, 1757; to Logan, June 21, 1757; VI, to Gov. Hamilton, June 6, 1760.

[155] See page 156.

[156] *Pa. Col. Recs.*, IX, 188; Franklin, *Cool Thoughts on the Present Situation, Works* (Smyth ed.), IV, 226-240; Lincoln, *Revolutionary Movement in Pa.*, 101-102; Shepherd, *Proprietary Gov't. in Pa.*, 555-559, 562-564.

the agent was instructed not to present the petition if upon careful inquiry and advice he had reason to fear that a change of government would mean the loss of the " inestimable Privileges, Civil and Religious," which the people enjoyed under the present laws and constitution.[157] On the other hand, John Dickinson, a man of conservative temperament and sound judgment, pointed out the weakness in the position of the assembly.[158]   He was aware of the evils of proprietary government, but held it was better to bear those ills " than fly to others we know not of." He pointed out in the first place, that the province was now under the ban of " royal and ministerial displeasure " because of its course during the late war; a feeling which will be greatly heightened when the ministry learns of its " obstinacy and inactivity " during Pontiac's Conspiracy. In the second place, he said it was absurd to think that the crown would be disposed to grant the request for a change of government which proceeded from the refusal of the assembly to abide by the agreement made between the crown and the agents of the assembly in 1760. Then again, he argued that it was better to preserve those privileges, civil and religious, which the people now enjoy, than to have them " consumed in a blaze of royal authority," especially at a time when the home government were designing the " strictest reformations " in the colonies. Finally, Dickinson showed that royal government was not a " security for that tranquility and happiness we promise ourselves from a change," by pointing out the frequent and violent quarrels which have occurred between the royal governors and their assemblies. But no arguments could move the assembly and Franklin left for England with the petition

[157] Lincoln, *op. cit.*, 129-130; Shepherd, *op. cit.*, 567; *Votes of Assembly*, V, 361; *Penn Mss., Official Corres.*, IX, Wm. Allen to Thos. Penn, Sept. 25, 1764.

[158] Dickinson, *Writings* (Ford ed.), 21-60.

in November, 1764. He did not present the application till a year later, because the colonial agents were busily engaged in trying to check the passage of the stamp bill.[159] Dickinson was right when he said that instead of granting greater privileges the home government was bent on diminishing those the colonists possessed. In spite of the vigorous protests the Stamp Act was passed. With its enactment the opposition to proprietary rule was gradually hushed.[160] All factions united to protect the powers of self-government against the aggressions of the mother country. The levy of a direct tax by Parliament was a far more serious matter in the minds of the people of Pennsylvania than the vexations of proprietary rule.

[159] *Penn Mss., Letter Bk.*, VIII, Thos. Penn to Peters, Nov. 15, 1765; to John Penn, Nov. 9, 1765; to Wm. Allen, March 8, Feb. 9, 1765; to Wm. Peters, Feb., 1765; to Chew, Feb. 7, 1765. Thos. Penn wrote to John Penn, Nov. 30, 1765, "The petitions have been considered by the King in Council, and resolved not to be proper for further consideration, but by his Majesty's order postponed, sine die, that is (to use my Lord President's own expression) forever and ever, . . . we shall not have any further trouble about them, not any of the Council thought them proper to be referred to a Committee, as they prayed for a thing not in the King's power to grant nor in the least in his will, not giving any good reasons for their request." *Penn Mss., Letter Bk.*, VIII, Thos. Penn wrote to Wm. Allen, Dec. 15, 1765, that not one of the council would consider the petition "for they were sure our fault was yielding too much to the Assembly." *Letter Bk.*, VIII.

[160] John Penn wrote that "the People seem to have forgot former differences and are all united against the Stamp Act, that we shall not hear of their revival (i. e. of faction), especially as the petition for change of Government is laid aside." *Penn Mss., Letter Bk.*, VIII, Thos. Penn to John Penn, Feb. 26, 1766; to Dr. Smith, April 1, 1766.

CHAPTER TWELVE

CONCLUSION

In this work the relations between an individual colony and the dominant government have been closely examined with the purpose of elucidating the character of British colonial administration in the seventy years prior to 1765; it is now fitting to summarize the results of this inquiry.

The central fact in the history of the imperial relation, running like a thread through the period, was the conflict between the interests and purposes of the imperial government and the colonists. The English theory of empire was primarily economic. A colonial policy was adopted, embodied in the acts of trade and navigation, which regulated the economic and political life of the colonies in the interest of a self-sufficient commercial empire. The enforcement of this policy required that the colonies should be strictly subordinate to the law and sovereignty of the mother country. The success of the policy implied a large measure of political and social unity between the province and metropolis, and a sense of pride in the empire on the part of the colonists. They did not exist. The motives which impelled William Penn and the Quakers to colonize in America were not imperial and commercial in character. They hoped to found a state based upon principles of religious and political liberty which were not accepted by the dominant classes in England. Self-control and not English control was the chief desire of the colonists. This pronounced spirit of separatism and individualism was in turn fostered by the leveling influences of a primitive frontier life which made for democracy and self-reliance. Moreover, the isolation of the province bred provincialism, and the thousand leagues of ocean which lay between the colony and the center of authority and the difficult means of communication created a mutual failure of colonists and Englishmen at home to understand the needs and desires of each other, weakened the force of sovereign commands, and placed insuperable obstacles in the path of imperial administration. In brief, differences in purpose, in economic needs, in social structure, and the consequent institutional divergences produced an antagonism between the colony and the mother country which constitutes the key-note of the imperial relation. Fundamentally, the question at issue was that of reconciling " two very difficult points, superiority in the presiding state, and freedom in the subordinate." The English colonial policy, based upon abstract and general principles from the point of view of the temper and genius of the colonist and his environment, was in the nature of an experiment.

Colonial and commercial expansion was not undertaken directly by the state, but was the result of private initiative. The instruments of empire building were the trading corporation and the proprietorship or fief, fashioned upon models hitherto limited in scope to England itself, but now adapted to new uses. By royal charter the crown granted to William Penn and his heirs liberal powers of government which they were required to exercise in harmony with the law and sovereignty of England. But a feudal and provincial system did not harmonize with the desires of the people. In a series of constitutional conflicts between the popular and prerogative elements in the constitution of the province, the government experienced a democratic transformation. The chief contests between the assembly, which stood for popular interests and power, and the governor, who represented the private interests and the prerogatives of the proprietors, surged about the question of taxation and expenditure of public funds, the regulation of the judiciary, the appointment of judges and other officers, the issue of paper currency, and proprietary instructions, each of which involved the question of sovereignty. The triumph of the assembly was facilitated by the liberal spirit of the first proprietor who identified himself in a large measure with colonial tendencies. To a greater extent it was due to the isolated position of the Penns. Endowed with royal power, but possessed of none of the dignities of a king, they were compelled to yield in an unequal struggle to the superior strength of the forces of democracy. By the time of the Stamp Act Pennsylvania was *de facto* a self-governing colony of the modern type, in which the assembly enjoyed a position of political supremacy, controlling to a large degree the policy of the colony through its own laws and committees. In fact, within its sphere the legislature was scarcely less powerful than the British Parliament, claiming the same privileges which Parliament possessed and considering itself as clothed with a similar power and authority. The most convenient and effective weapon to effect this transformation was the popular control of the finances, a control which formed the basis of autonomy and hence was guarded with unfaltering resolution against any outside interference, proprietary or imperial. In this contest for the mastery of government, the people insisted upon the principles of English common and statute law which guaranteed the liberty and rights of the subject against the arbitrary exercise of royal' power.

This advance toward independence involved also the power and authority of the central government and the interests of the Empire. It was found by experience that the power of government placed in the hands of private individuals was insufficient to check the forces of particularism and to uphold imperial policies. The charters erected institutional barriers against an effective exercise of the sovereign will. The assembly availed itself of the incomplete provisions of the charter to disregard the royal disallowance and it showed no hesitation in doing so when bent upon upholding the religious principles of the Quakers, the privileges of freemen, the regulation of the judiciary, and the issue of bills of credit. Moreover, by act of assembly and by process familiar to common law, the people thwarted the power and limited the jurisdiction of the royal vice-admiralty courts. Oaths, bonds, and royal confirmation required of the governors appointed by the proprietors did not insure a more effective enforcement of the acts of trade. From the standpoint of imperial control the chartered colony was an anomaly and in the judgment of colonial administrators the substitution of direct royal control was eminently necessary. In the two decades after 1696 several serious attempts were made to sweep away the charters by act of Parliament, but such measures failed to pass chiefly through the influence of the representatives of chartered interests.

The charters answered neither the purposes of the central government, nor met the demands of the colonists. The disparity of interests between the proprietors and the colonists provoked many protests against proprietary government. Loyalty to the charters was strong in the corporate colonies where the people possessed a system of complete self-government which harmonized with their desires. In the provinces much of the pressure against the charters came from the colonists themselves. In Maryland and South Carolina the people overthrew proprietary government and in response to popular appeals, royal government was established. The proprietors of New Jersey surrendered their powers under pressure of popular discontent and English hostility. In Pennsylvania, Churchmen petitioned for royal government to protect their interests against Quaker domination and to advance the interests of the English Church, non-Quakers appealed for royal protection when military defenses were denied them by a Quaker assembly principled against war, and the assembly itself, hampered in its contest for self-control by proprietary orders, appealed to the throne for redress. The Quakers themselves, finding that their principles were ill-suited to government, expressed a willingness to yield. Factional differences, financial distress, and the enmity of the home government to the charters, led Penn in 1703 to offer to surrender his powers of government to the crown. His demands of a monetary consideration and a guarantee of religious liberty to the Quakers proved too high, but under the stress of increasing difficulties they were abated and a treaty of surrender was drawn in 1712, only to fail of execution through the untimely physical disabilities of the great Quaker. In subsequent years colonial administrators continued to direct the attention of Parliament to the ills of chartered government, but that body remained a friend of the charters till 1774. The assembly, on the other hand, continued to threaten to appeal to the crown for royal government, not out of regard for the interests of the Empire, but in the hope that thereby the colony would be freed from the ills of proprietary rule, but the crown reversed its former policy and showed a decided inclination to uphold the proprietors in their powers of government.

The eighteenth century was preëminently the period of the royal province.[1] The question naturally arises, was the substitution of the responsible agents of the crown for the officials of corporations and proprietors sufficient to check the forces of independence and insure greater administrative efficiency. The history of the royal provinces

[1] Royal government was established ultimately in all the colonies except Rhode Island, Connecticut, Maryland, and Pennsylvania. Maryland was administered as a royal province from 1691 to 1715, when the government was restored to the Protestant heir. Georgia was established as a chartered colony in 1732, but in 1754, according to the terms of the charter, the government reverted to the crown.

warrants the conclusion that direct crown control did not check violations of the laws of trade[2] and attacks upon the vice-admiralty courts, nor elicit greater obedience to the commands of the crown. With the vacation of the charters institutional barriers had been overcome, but natural and social barriers remained to thwart the will of the imperial government. Distance, difficulties of communication, the isolation, strange environment, and individualism of the colonists precluded the possibility of adjusting to the colonies a system of government not their own. But these factors do not account in full for the failure to enforce imperial policies. The evils of a corrupt patronage system, a low sense of public duty, and the vicissitudes of party and factional politics at home combined to impair the efficiency of colonial administration. These faults characterized not only colonial administration, but the entire English governmental system, particularly in the age of Walpole and Newcastle. In the selection of colonial administrators too frequently family and political influence were the chief considerations. Absenteeism in the customs service contributed to a lax enforcement of the acts of trade, lack of leadership accounts in large part for the failure of the expeditions against Quebec in 1711 and Cartagena in 1740, and incompetency characterized appointments to other branches of the colonial service. In some cases the royal agents were unfaithful, using their powers for personal advantage. In other cases they were deficient in tact and a knowledge of colonial conditions and hence were inclined to be arbitrary in the exercise of

---

[2] In 1701, Penn wrote "that being King's governments, the end proposed to prevent false trade, will not do it, and if so, the hardship is imposed in vain"; and he pointed out that in spite of the vigilance and activity of the royal officials, "Maryland since a King's government was twenty times a greater sinner" than Pennsylvania under proprietary rule. *Duke of Portland Mss.*, IV, 19-20, Hist. Mss., Com. *Report* 15, pt. 4.

their functions. The failure of the crown to appoint uniformly to the colonial service men of integrity, breadth of view, and experience goes far to account for the discontent with English rule.[3]

After all the fault was not so much with the men as the system they were called upon to administer. The neglect of the central government to create a permanent revenue to support the civil and military establishments in America invested the particularistic assemblies with the power to judge of the propriety and convenience of royal commands. The legislative control of the finances enabled the colonists to encroach upon the power of the royal agents and force them to submit to popular dictation.[4] The failure to define with certainty the power and jurisdiction of the vice-admiralty courts left them subject to humiliating attack by the colonists. The convenience of the American coast-line made it impossible for customs officers to check illegal trade without the assistance of revenue cutters. The vicious fee system and the inadequate compensation granted to customs and admiralty officials tempted them either to collude with illicit traders

---

[3] Franklin justified the dependence of royal governors upon the assemblies for financial support on the ground that "they are generally strangers to the Provinces they are sent to govern, have no estate, natural connexion, or relation there; that they come only to make money as fast as they can; are sometimes men of vicious characters and broken fortunes, sent by a Minister to get them out of the way." *Works* (Smyth ed.), V, 83. Cf. Greene, *Provincial Governor*, 46-47, 172, 175, and Spencer, *Constitutional Conflict in Mass.*, 78.

[4] Colden of New York wrote that the "unreasonable increase of popular power by which the Ballance of power essential to the English Constitution is destroy'd in the Colonies is wholly owing to the Governours having no subsistence but from the Assembly. I can give several instances . . . where Governours have for several years stood firm to the Kings Instructions in Support of his prerogative & . . . after all were obliged to comply with the humours of the Assembly or starve or be sunk in debt." Keys, *Cadwallader Colden*, 235. Cf. *N. Y. Col. Docs.*, IV, 1050; V, 805, 844, 887.

or to act arbitrarily against fair traders. Repeatedly and earnestly royal officials called the attention of the home government to these imperfections in the system of administration,[5] but Parliament and the ministry seemed unwilling to adopt a policy of coercion.[6] In the face of the determined resistance of the colonists to the authority of the imperial government, royal agents without support from home found it impossible to enforce their powers. Moreover, the lack of centralization and coördination in the system of administration at home and the subordinate position of the Board of Trade, the chief office concerned with colonial business, created delay, confusion, and friction in imperial administration. Here again the crown was advised repeatedly to raise the Board of Trade to a position of ministerial executive authority in order to give American affairs the prompt and undivided attention demanded by their importance and the remoteness of the colonies from London. Again the advice fell upon unheeding ears. Moreover, the lack of an expert knowledge of colonial conditions and institutions on the part of Parliament and administrators at home, the long drawn out delays in the transaction of colonial business, and the expense and labor connected therewith made the colonies reluctant to submit their affairs to the judgment of the

[5] Royal officials through the eighteenth century proposed with frequency the levy of a tax upon the colonists in order to support the charges of royal government. Beer, *British Colonial Policy, 1754-1765*, 38-48; *N. Y. Col. Docs.*, VI, 268-269; *No. Car. Col. Recs.*, II, 635. Quary wrote, " A Governor ought to have his support as well as dependence from the Crown, though at the same time the fund should come from the people, but by such means as ought first to settle it in the Crown." *N. Y. Col. Docs.*, IV, 1050.

[6] When the assemblies refused to grant the governors permanent salaries in response to royal commands, threats were usually made to appeal to Parliament to tax them, but such a policy was not resorted to till after 1763. Spencer, *Constitutional Conflict in Mass.*, 70, 71, 75, 79, 84, 88; Beer, *British Col. Policy, 1754-1765*, 37-38.

imperial government. The ignorance of colonial desires
and tendencies made the action of a far distant government
and its agents seem arbitrary and autocratic, and in consequence the colonists adopted an attitude of resentment
toward English control.

On the other hand, judged from the history of one
colony it may be said in general that English control was
not harsh or oppressive. In the consideration of the laws
of the colony the Board of Trade did not act in an arbitrary manner, but threw every safeguard about them and
showed a desire to consult the convenience of the colony
in most cases. For example, when the crown disallowed
colonial laws granting the Quakers the privilege of using
the affirmation in all cases, it was done not out of hostility
to the Quakers, but in the interest of religious liberty and
to prevent a miscarriage of justice. When such laws were
modified to meet the objections, the Quakers were allowed
the full use of the affirmation, although contrary to English statute. Furthermore, the assembly was left in control of the internal affairs of the colony and of taxation
both for local and imperial purposes. This political freedom was due partly to the charter and the defects in the
system of colonial administration, and in part to the for-
bearance of the home government. Parliament and the
ministry were undoubtedly cognizant of the determined
resistance of the colonies to the law and commands of the
home government, but they were unwilling to interfere in
colonial matters in the direction of greater centralization.
Fortunately for the colonists the lack of vigor in English
control, the cumbersome system of administration, and
distance left them to develop their institutions in a normal
and natural fashion and thereby royal and proprietary
government was brought into harmony with actual conditions.

In the matter of imperial defense the colonies fell far
short of their duty. It is true that their trade was regu-

lated by imperial statute primarily in the interest of the
wealth and strength of the mother country, but in return
the colonists enjoyed many compensating advantages, not
the least of which was protection. Protection on the high
seas in that age of piracy and frequent international conflict was borne entirely by the home government without
expense to the colonies. Naval protection was absolutely
necessary for the security of colonial commerce upon which
their prosperity was founded. In addition, in time of
war in Europe English troops and money were employed
to coöperate with the colonies in attacks upon French and
Spanish strongholds in America. In the protection of the
long and vulnerable frontier of the Empire the conduct
of many of the colonies was deficient. In this respect the
attitude of Pennsylvania was particularly offensive. The
assembly, dominated by Quaker pacificists, failed to assume one of the most essential functions of government
and hence was delinquent in duty, not only to the people
of the colony, but to the neighboring colonies. Other colonies proved to be equally lacking in public spirit, although
they were not vexed with Quaker domination. Distance,
primitive methods of travel, and the little intercourse between the colonies narrowed their experience and range of
vision and made them indifferent to the remote dangers
on the frontier. This was particularly true of the colonies
between New York and the Carolinas whose frontiers were
not immediately subject to the invasions of foreign troops
and their savage allies. Moreover, the system of crown
requisitions which called upon the colonies for men and
supplies in time of war enabled the assembly to judge of
the propriety of imperial measures according to local convenience. In fact, the distribution of authority among co-
ordinate bodies impaired the effectiveness of frontier defense. Between the colonies, planted at different times
and working on separate lines, there was little community
of interest, and in consequence disunion encouraged the

French to attack the colonies.[7]   The frontier problem created a desire for a union, but the intense antipathies cherished by one colony against another and their strong attachment to principles of self-government precluded the
possibility of establishing a supreme and central authority
demanded by the exigencies of defense.   The indifference
of the colonies and their failure to coöperate for defense
led imperialists to propose that a union and taxation
should be imposed by act of Parliament, but the home government was unwilling to interfere.   As a result many of
the colonies fell far short of their abilities in time of imperial war, and in time of peace forced the home government to garrison the frontier and thereby assume a responsibility properly belonging to the local governments.

The fifth decade of the century saw the beginning of a
stricter control over the colonies and the renewal of war
after a long period of peace and *laissez-faire* administration.   Under the presidency of Halifax the Board of Trade
exhibited a new vigor and colonial administration was in
some degree centralized in this office.   Parliament restrained the issue of bills of credit in New England and
regulated their issue in other colonies in order to protect
property and commerce against the evils of an unsound
financial policy.   The efforts to give royal instructions the
force of law and to look to Parliament to curb the independence of the colonies are significant, not only of the
helplessness of the royal prerogative to curb the colonies,
but of the transition taking place in English constitutional
development in the direction of parliamentary supremacy.
But it was chiefly the problem of defense which demanded
attention.   The French and English realized that the

[7] A memorialist wrote in 1697, "The English colonies being
planted at severall times and by distinct grants from the Crown
having different interests in Trade, looke upon themselves as so
many distinct Principalities, are jealous of each other, and stand
upon their separate Laws & Customs to the prejudice and weakening of the whole." *Cal. State Paps., Col.*, 1696-1697, 338.

Treaty of Aix-la-Chapelle did not settle the claims of the contending parties in North America; the final decision rested with the judgment of the sword. In view of the impending crisis, the home government laid plans to combine the forces of the colonies for defense and to centralize the management of Indian affairs. Such a policy was of pressing necessity. Colonial disunion led the French to force the issue and the unscrupulous dealings of the colonists with the Indians weakened their friendship for the English cause. Colonial representatives met at Albany in 1754 to make a treaty with the Iroquois and seized the occasion to frame a scheme of colonial federation. In the same year the Board of Trade drafted a plan of military union, but the unanimous rejection of the Albany plan made the acceptance of the board's plan improbable. The refractory and obstinate conduct of the colonies was largely responsible for the failure of the attempts of Washington and Braddock to check the first advances of the French and provoked colonial governors and commanders to urge colonial union and taxation by act of Parliament.[8] In 1756 England declared formal war against France and such schemes were simply laid aside to a more convenient time.

The events of the war revealed completely the unwieldy and disjointed character of the structure of the Empire. Indifference to the security of the frontier, intercolonial jealousy, conflicts between governors and assemblies, and local interference in the raising and direction of the troops contributed to retard military operations, limited their scope, and made necessary large bounties from the home government to encourage the colonies to greater activity. Some colonies acted with great spirit, others in a half-hearted manner, and the rest were sadly deficient in conduct. Indifference and the plea of poverty accounts only in part for the delinquency of Pennsylvania in particular;

[8] Beer, *British Col. Policy, 1754-1765*, 28-30, 43-51.

a fundamental constitutional principle was at stake. The assembly with unfaltering determination refused to allow either the crown or the proprietors to interfere in the taxation of proprietary estates, the issue of paper currency, the expenditure of public funds, and the control of the militia. This firm devotion to abstract principles of self-government led the assembly to place the rights and liberties of the subject above the security of the province and the welfare of the Empire and caused the colony to falter in its duty in the earlier years of the war and rendered it helpless after 1760. Moreover, the merchants of Pennsylvania and other colonies were deeply implicated in a treasonable trade with the French, whereby the enemy was supplied with provisions and the efforts of the English naval and military forces were in part neutralized. This trade was furthered by the unfaithfulness and greed of governors and customs officials and by the partiality of admiralty judges. It was evident that there was little spirit of loyalty to the Empire and a sense of pride in the imperial connection on the part of a considerable number of the colonists.[9]

With the advent of peace in 1763 the English government was confronted with the problem of reorganizing the colonial system. The exaltation of British power over the French created a strong sentiment of imperialism similar to that which followed the Restoration of 1660 and the Revolution of 1689. The large additions of territory to the Empire and the defects in the system of administration revealed by the war necessitated a reconstruction of the colonial policy in both its economic and political features. The laws of trade were modified and extended to bring the new dominions within the scope of the mercantile

[9] Governor Morris of Pennsylvania wrote in 1755 of the colonists, " I cannot accuse them of disaffection to the Royal Family now upon the Throne, but they are certainly disaffected to Government itself, and consequently to his Majesty's Office and Authority." *Pa. Archives*, 1st. ser., II, 439.

system. In order to enforce the laws of trade absenteeism in the customs service was abolished, the authority and power of the customs and admiralty officials was strengthened, and men of war were employed as revenue cutters. The over-issue of legal tender paper currency and its deleterious effect on trade and commerce led to the prohibition of this financial policy. English troops were placed on the western frontier to hold in check hostile Indians and disaffected Canadians and to guard against the probability of renewed French attacks. Plans were laid to make the Indians the wards of the imperial government in order to protect their interests and preserve their friendship. The events of the French war and Pontiac's Conspiracy showed conclusively that the colonies could not be depended upon to guard the frontier. The heavy drain upon the English exchequer to save the colonies from foreign conquest justified in the minds of English statesmen a parliamentary tax upon the colonies to support in part a standing army in America. Such were the objects which the Currency and Sugar Acts of 1764, the Stamp Act of 1765, and other measures, parliamentary and ministerial, were designed to accomplish. These reforms did not spring from motives of oppression, nor did they originate as party measures. They had been urged repeatedly by colonial administrators in the period prior to 1763 and were now forced upon the imperial government by the stern logic of the events of the war.

The reconstruction of the colonial policy fell upon an unpropitious time. Two factors in the main tended to hold together the unstable structure of the Empire; the particularism of the colonies and their dependence upon the imperial government for support. Time and again the agents of the central government had interpreted the resistance of the colonies to the sovereign will as indicative of a determined effort to throw off English rule.[10] This

[10] Beer, *British Col. Policy, 1754-1765*, 167-169. Chalmers, *In-*

charge the colonists consistently repudiated. Keith, Dummer, Pownall, Shirley, and Franklin pointed out that intercolonial prejudices and jealousies were too strong to permit of a union without which they could not hope to sever the imperial relation.[11] The chief factor which kept in check the forces of disintegration was the need on the part of the colonies of the naval and military protection granted by the home government. In fact, some held that Canada in French hands was desirable in order to perpetuate the utilitarian bond of union.[12] The removal of French power from Canada broke that tie and gave scope to the centrifugal forces within the Empire, and the assumption by Parliament of an authority which violated long established customs and threatened to undermine the independence of the colonies furnished them with a principle of union.[13] Substantial unity of action, disobedience to the recent regulations of Parliament, attacks upon royal officials and a general spirit of defiance are not accounted for solely on the ground of intensity of attachment to abstract principles of self-government. The arguments against the new system were as much economic as political. The commercial restrictions upon a foreign trade which formed the basis of colonial prosperity, the prohibition upon the issue of legal tender paper currency which the colonists considered necessary to their welfare, and the collection of the new taxes in specie when the colonies were drained of their gold and silver by a balance of trade in favor of England, together with the existing economic distress, intensified the spirit of opposition to parlia-

troduction to the Revolt of the Colonies, II, quotes frequently from the letters of royal officials to show that the colonies were consciously aiming at independence from the mother country.

[11] Dummer, *Defence of the Charters* (London, 1721), 36; Franklin, *Works* (Smyth ed.), IV, 41, 70-71; Pownall, *Administration of the Colonies* (ed. 1768), 93.

[12] Beer, *British Col. Policy, 1754-1765*, 142-147; Channing, *Hist. of U. S.*, II, 596-597; Franklin, *Works* (Smyth ed.), IV, 70-77.

[13] Beer, *British Col. Policy, 1754-1765*, 171-173.

mentary interference. Moreover, the controversy revealed the partial nature of the colonial policy. The colonists felt that it was unjust to force them to contribute to the support of guarding Canada in view of the heavy debt they had incurred on behalf of the conquest of a territory of which the mother country reaped the sole advantage; and they felt grieved that the interests of the continental colonies should be sacrificed to the advantage of a few British planters in the West Indies.

The clash of interests provoked a final scrutiny into the nature of the constitution of the Empire. Both sides professed to draw their arguments from the principles and precedents of English law, and their claims varied little from those urged formerly in the contest between the provincial governors and assemblies. English and colonial statesmen were of one accord on the principle of '' no taxation without representation,'' one of the basic doctrines of English constitutional liberty, but they disagreed fundamentally on the interpretation of that principle. In America, the generally accepted theory considered the Empire as composed of a number of separate and independent political entities in which their several legislatures were '' entitled to a free and exclusive power of legislation . . . in all cases of taxation and internal polity,'' subject to the accustomed negative of the crown.[14] The colonists conceded to Parliament the right to levy taxes upon their trade for the purpose of regulating the commerce of the Empire, but they claimed that the assumption of a power to tax them for revenue purposes was unconstitutional.[15] They interpreted the provisions of the

14 Ford, *Journals of Continental Congress*, I, 68.
15 Samuel Adams, *Writings* (Cushing ed.), I, 18, 24-26, 157, 171; Hopkins, *Rights of the Cols. Examined*, (R. I. Col. Recs., VI, 423, 426); Otis, *Rights of the British Cols. Asserted*, and Dulany, *Consideration on the Propriety of imposing Taxes in the Cols.*, (Almon, *Tracts*, London, 1766); Dickinson, *Letters from a Farmer*, *Works* (Ford ed.), 316, 320, 328-335; Pa. *Votes of Assembly*, V,

Magna Charta and Bill of Rights which guaranteed the subject against taxation without his consent as a constitutional limitation upon the power of Parliament.[16]   Therefore, the colonists concluded that since the principle of representation was alone preserved in the local assemblies, they only were legally competent to levy taxes.   Franklin saw that in this distinction between taxation and legislation in other respects "no middle ground could be well maintained." He said that "Something might be said for either of the extremes, that Parliament has a power to make *all laws* for us, or that it has a power to make *no laws* for us," and he advanced to the more logical conclusion that the Empire consisted of separate states bound together exclusively through the crown.[17] With this theory John Adams, James Wilson, Hamilton, and Jefferson concurred.[18]   Hamilton and Adams conceded to Parliament a power to regulate the trade of the Empire as a matter of expediency, but not of right.[19]   On the other hand, English statesmen and jurists would recognize no theory which denied the supremacy of Parliament in all cases whatsoever, and held that the colonists were virtually

361, 376. Dickinson held that "parliament unquestionably possesses a legal authority to regulate the trade of Great Britain, and all her colonies," but entered a "total denial of the power of parliament to lay upon these colonies any 'tax' whatever." *Works*, 312, 328.

[16] Franklin contended that although the charter of Pennsylvania contained a reservation of the right of Parliament to tax the colonists, yet it had no right to do so under cover of that clause until it had admitted representatives from the province.   *Works* (Smyth ed.), IV, 445.   Pitt and Camden in Parliament also looked upon this principle as a fundamental law binding upon the power of Parliament.   Hansard, *Parl. Hist.*, XVI, 168, 169, 171, 179, 195.

[17] Franklin, *Works* (Smyth ed.), V, 115; see also V, 280.

[18] John Adams, *Novanglus*, *Works* (Adams ed.), IV, 33, 37, 38, 46, 48, 49, 99; Hamilton, *The Farmer Refuted*, *Works* (Lodge ed.), I, 76, 77, 81; Jefferson, *Summary View of the Rights of British America*, *Writings* (Ford ed.), I, 421-447.

[19] Hamilton, *The Farmer Refuted*, 109, 112, 115, 123, 163; Adams, *Novanglus*, 105-107, 113, 115.

represented in the imperial legislature.[20] In point of law
this theory of parliamentary omnipotence was unassailable
and in point of precedent nothing could be urged against
the late statutes which was not equally true of the acts
of trade. Theoretically, there was no disparity between
the realm and dominions over-sea; in law the colonies were
provinces or municipal corporations on the same footing as
their prototypes in England, subject to the will of the
sovereign legislature, and so they were considered in England.[21] But the theory of parliamentary supremacy was
hedged about with serious limitations as far as colonies
were concerned. It was a principle of government peculiar to England itself and by reason of limitation of
place it contained no solution of the problem of governing
dependencies. The colonists felt, and justly so, that " Parliament cannot wisely and well make laws suited to the
Colonies, without being properly and truly informed of
their circumstances, abilities, temper, &c. This it cannot
be without representation from thence." [22] But the actual
inclusion of the colonies within the English representative
system, the incorporation of the dependencies into the
body politic, was rendered impracticable not only by reason of distance, but by the strong attachment of the colonists to the principles of home rule. In fine, geographical
separation, difference in social structure, in institutions,
and in economic needs precluded the possibility of a consolidated and centralized imperial fabric. The idea of
complete independence and separation was repudiated by

[20] Hansard, *Parl. Hist.*, XVI, 161, 164, 165, 167, 173.

[21] Bernard, governor of Mass., wrote, " In Britain the American
governments are considered as corporations, empowered to make
bye-laws, existing during the pleasure of Parliament; who hath
never done anything to confirm their establishments, and hath at
any time a power to dissolve them." *Select Letters on Trade* (London, 1774), 32.

[22] Franklin, *Works* (Smyth ed.), V, 17-18, 241.

the colonists until the hope of reconciliation was lost.[23] What they wished was the restoration of the relations which existed between the colonies and the mother country prior to the entrance of Parliament into the domain of legislation and taxation hitherto left to the colonial assemblies.[24] In this way the constitution of the Empire had developed by a natural growth and a recognition of this fact was necessary to the permanence of the Empire. But the mutual failure of the colonists and English statesmen to understand and appreciate the needs and desires of each other rendered compromise impossible and in the end it led to the disruption of England's first Empire in the West.

[23] Ford, *Journals of Continental Congress*, I, 15-30; II, 13-23; 155, 160; IV, 142-143.

[24] Hopkins of Rhode Island likened the Empire to the old German Confederation: "In an imperial state, which consists of many separate governments, each of which hath peculiar privileges, and of which kind it is evident the empire of Great Britain is." *R. I. Col. Recs.*, VI, 420. John Adams wrote that the "Patriots of the province desire nothing new; they wish only to keep their old privileges. They were, for one hundred and fifty years, allowed to tax themselves, and govern their internal affairs as they saw best. Parliament governed their trade as they thought fit. This plan they wish may continue forever." *Works* (Adams ed.), IV, 116, 121, 131.

BIBLIOGRAPHICAL NOTES

A.—Manuscript Sources.

A considerable part of the present work has been based upon manuscript sources, chiefly the papers and journals of the Board of Trade and Plantations. A large part of the material was drawn from the transcripts of these volumes made from the original manuscript in the Public Record Office, London, for the Historical Society of Pennsylvania, as follows: *Journals*, 1675-1782, 90 vols., (London, 1895-1898); *Papers, Proprieties*, 1697-1776, 25 vols., (London, 1901-1904); *Papers, Plantations General*, 1689-1780, 28 vols., (London, 1904). The *Journals* contain a record of the meetings held, the members present, and minutes of the debates, procedure and action of the board on colonial business. The *Papers* embrace copies of memorials, petitions, complaints, letters, reports of legal advisers, and orders in council sent to the board. The division of these documents into two separate series of volumes, *Proprieties* and *Plantations General*, is based on the relation of the colonies to the central government, the former comprising the charter colonies under indirect control, and the latter the royal provinces under direct crown control.

The original volumes of the *Entry Books, Proprieties* and *Plantations General* in the Public Record Office, and lacking in the collection of the above named historical society, have been used. This series contains the out-letters of the board, reports and representations to the Privy Council and Parliament, and the commissions and instructions issued to colonial governors.

In addition the following collections in the Public Record Office have been of particular help: (a) *America and West Indies, No. 28*, a bundle which includes letters from Governors Keith and Thomas, James Logan, Thos. Penn and others to the Duke of Newcastle concerning Pennsylvania affairs; *No. 599*, a bundle containing various petitions, letters, memorials, legal opinions, etc. concerning Pennsylvania. (b) *Customs Books*, a series of manuscript volumes containing entries of warrants issued by the Lords of the Treasury for granting commissions and the payment of salaries to the customs officials at home and in the colonies, as also minutes of the reports of the Customs Board to the Lords of the Treasury. (c) *Admiralty Books*, a series containing entries of warrants issued by the Lords of the Admiralty for commissioning officials of the vice-admiralty courts, minutes of the reports of the judge of the High Court of Admiralty to the admiralty board, etc.

Among the *Rawlinson MSS.* and *Clarendon MSS.* in the Bodleian Library, Oxford, were found a few papers relating to Pennsylvania, and a few relating to the vice-admiralty jurisdiction in America.

Some use was made of the transcripts of the British Museum *Additional MSS.* deposited in the Congressional Library, Washington.

A valuable and detailed description of the colonial records in various British archives may be found in two articles by Professor C. M. Andrews of Yale, *American Colonial History*, (American Hist. Asso., *Reports*, 1898, pp. 55-60), *Materials in British Archives for American Colonial History, (Amer. Hist. Rev.*, X, 325-349). A hand-book of the greatest value for investigators is C. M. Andrews and F. G. Davenport, *Guide to the Manuscript Materials for the History of the United States to 1783, in the British Museum, in Minor London Archives, and in the Libraries of Oxford and Cambridge*, (Washington, 1908). The description of documents and pamphlets and their location is of the highest value to the student of our colonial history. A similar guide for the materials in the Public Record Office is now in preparation under the editorship of Professor Andrews and Miss Davenport. Professor Andrews has also compiled a very useful *List of the Journals and Acts of the Thirteen Original Colonies preserved among the Colonial Office Papers in the Public Record Office* (Amer. Hist. Asso., *Report*, 1908, I).

The following collections of the *Penn Papers*, in the Library of the Historical Society of Pennsylvania, were of considerable importance for the light they threw not only upon the relations of the proprietary system to the colonists, but also on the relations of the colony to the home government: *Official Correspondence*, 1683-1817, 12 vols.; *Letter Books*, 1729-1834, 12 vols.; *Forbes-Penn Collection*, 2 vols., (catalogued in *Pennsylvania Magazine of History*, April, 1904) ; and the *Saunders-Coates Collection*, 1720-1766, 1 vol. In the same library the *Customs House Papers*, a collection of the papers of the collector of the port at Philadelphia, have been of some value in throwing light on the administration of the acts of trade after 1750.

B.—General Collections of Printed Sources.

1. English.

Calendar of State Papers, Colonial Series, America and West Indies, 1574-1701, 14 vols. (London, 1860-1911), contain extracts from the colonial office papers. This series

has not progressed beyond the opening of the eighteenth
century, and further, although the calendaring is well done,
it does not take the place of the complete document for
the investigator. The gap for the eighteenth century is
partly filled by the publication of the *Documents Relative to
the Colonial History of New York*, 14 vols., (Albany, 1856-
1883), of which vols. III-VIII contain the London Documents; *Documents Relative to the Colonial History of New
Jersey*, 26 vols., (Newark, Paterson, 1880-1904); and *Colonial Records of North Carolina*, 10 vols. (Raleigh, 1886-
1890). These three collections contain many of the state
papers in full. To a great extent the gap for the eighteenth
century is filled by the recent publication of the *Acts of the
Privy Council, Colonial Series*, 1613-1766, 4 vols. (Hereford,
1908-1911). With the appearance of this admirably edited
series, which prints many of the papers in full, much light
is thrown on the policy, procedure, and organization of the
Privy Council acting on colonial affairs. (These volumes
are well reviewed by Professor C. M. Andrews in *American
Hist. Rev.*, XIV, 590, XVI, 119, 638, XVII, 130.) *Calendar
of Home Office Papers of the Reign of George III*, 4 vols.
(London, 1878-1899), are of value for the revolutionary
period. *Calendar of Treasury Papers*, 1557-1728, 6 vols.
(London, 1868-1889), and *Calendar of Treasury Books and
Papers*, 1729-1745, 5 vols. (London, 1897-1903), contain some
material bearing on the administration of the acts of trade,
fiscal matters, etc.

Journals of the House of Lords and *Journals of the House
of Commons* are of considerable value for the history of imperial legislative action. They contain minutes of the houses
on colonial matters, reports of various boards, and addresses
to the crown. For typical reports of the Board of Trade
to Parliament, such as those on 1702 and 1703, consult the
Bulletin of New York Public Library, X, no. 5, XI, no. 10.
William Cobbett, *Parliamentary History of England* (1806-
1820), is of some value. Of course the *Statutes of the Realm*,
to 1713, 12 vols. (1810-1828), and the *Statutes at Large*,
Danby Pickering, 109 vols. (1762), are indispensable. *House
of Lords MSS. new series*, 1693-1704, 5 vols. (London, 1900-
1911), in continuation of the series started under authority
of the Hist. MSS. Commission, are valuable for a study of
the legislative attacks on the colonial charters.

George Chalmers, *Opinions of Eminent Lawyers on various
points of English Jurisprudence, chiefly concerning Colonies,
Fisheries, and Commerce of Great Britain*, (Burlington, 1858),
is of first rate importance as a convenient hand-book of the
opinions of crown lawyers and English jurists on matters
of law affecting the colonies. *Reports and Arguments of Sir*

John Vaughan, Lord Chief Justice of Common Pleas (London, 1706), contains several illuminating opinions on the legal relations of the colonies to the mother country given in the time of Charles II.

2. Colonial Records.

Adelaide R. Hasse, *Materials for a Bibliography of the Public Archives of the Thirteen Original Colonies* (Amer. Hist. Asso., *Report*, 1906, II), furnishes a list of the official archives and is valuable as a guide to the documentary material of the colonies. For colonial charters and constitutions consult, F. N. Thorpe, *Federal and State Constitutions, Colonial Charters, and other Organic Laws*, 7 vols. (Washington, 1909); and B. P. Poore, *Federal and State Constitutions and Colonial Charters*, 2 vols. (Washington, 1878). Volume II of *Anniversary History of the Constitution of the United States*, H. L. Carson, 2 vols. (Philadelphia, 1889), gives in full the various plans proposed for a union of the colonies.

The most valuable of the colonial records are: *Colonial Records of North Carolina; Documents Relative to the Colonial History of New Jersey; Documents Relative to the Colonial History of New York*, (these collections have been cited above); *Public Records of the Colony of Connecticut*, 15 vols. (Hartford, 1850-1890); *Records of Rhode Island and Providence Plantation*, 10 vols. (Providence, 1856-1862).

For Pennsylvania in particular the following public archives have been indispensable; *Minutes of the Provincial Council of Pennsylvania*, 1683-1776, 10 vols. (Harrisburg, 1851-1852); *Pennsylvania Archives, first series*, 12 vols. (Phila., 1852-1856); *second series*, 19 vols. (Harrisburg, 1874-1893); *Votes and Proceedings of the House of Representatives of Pennsylvania*, 1682-1776, 6 vols. (Phila., 1752-1776).

For a study of the royal disallowance, the *Acts and Resolves of the Province of Massachusetts Bay*, 1692-1760, 16 vols. (Boston, 1869-1909); *Laws of New Hampshire*, 1679-1702, 1 vol. (1904); and the *Statutes at Large of Pennsylvania*, 1700-1793, 14 vols. (Harrisburg, 1896-1909), are of first-rate importance. They contain the procedure of the home government on the laws of the colony and the reasons for disallowance. The appendixes of the *Statutes at Large of Pennsylvania* are of particular value in these respects, for they include in full the minutes and reports of the Board of Trade, the reports of crown lawyers and other officials on the laws of the colony, and the orders in council affirming or annulling laws.

The following collections have been of assistance for the history of the English Church in the colony; G. M. Hills, *History of the Church in Burlington, N. J. . . . from original, contemporaneous sources* (Trenton, 1876); W. S.

Perry, *Historical Collections relating to the American Colonial Church*, 5 vols. (1870-1878), of which vol. II gives the papers relating to Pennsylvania.

C.—Correspondence, Writings, Tracts.

1. The correspondence of English officials in the colonial service with the authorities at home is necessary to a proper understanding of colonial administration. The following collections may be cited as having particular value, *Belcher Papers*, 2 vols. (Mass. Hist. Soc., *Collections*, VI, VII, Boston, 1893-1894) ; *Official Letters of Robert Dinwiddie, 1751-1758*, 2 vols. (Va. Hist. Soc., *Collections*, n.s. III, IV, Richmond, 1883-1884) ; *Papers of Lewis Morris, 1738-1746*, (N. J. Hist. Soc., *Collections*, IV, N. Y. 1852) ; *Official Letters of Alexander Spotswood, 1710-1722*, 2 vols. (Va. Hist. Soc., *Collections*, n.s. I, II, Richmond, 1882-1885) ; *Correspondence of Horatio Sharpe*, 3 vols. *(Maryland Archives*, VI, IX, XIV, Baltimore, 1888, 1890, 1895). The letters of these provincial governors contain highly valuable data for a study of constitutional development in the provinces, and for the relations of the governors to the central government. Much of the correspondence of the governors of New York, New Jersey, and North Carolina may be found in the records of these colonies already enumerated. The letters of Governor Dinwiddie of Virginia, of Governor Sharpe of Maryland, and the *Correspondence of William Pitt when Secretary of State with Colonial Governors and Military and Naval Commanders in America*, 2 vols. ed. by G. S. Kimball (N. Y., 1906), are essential for a knowledge of the attitude of the colonies toward the question of imperial defence during the French and Indian War. *Letters and Papers of Edward Randolph*, 7 vols. (Prince Society, *Publications*, Boston, 1890, 1899, 1909), are invaluable for a study of the administration of the acts of trade prior to 1703.

The Correspondence of the Governors of Rhode Island, 1723-1775, 2 vols. ed. by G. S. Kimball (N. Y., 1902) ; *Penn-Logan Correspondence*, 2 vols. (Hist. Soc. of Penn'a, *Memoirs*, IX, X, Phil., 1870, 1872) ; and the *Talcott Papers*, 2 vols. (Conn. Hist. Soc. *Collections*, Hartford, 1892, 1896), are important for the relations of the corporate colonies of R. I. and Conn., and the proprietary province of Pennsylvania with the home government. A few letters of William Penn of much importance may be found in *Duke of Portland MSS.*, III, IV, (Hist. MSS. Com., *Reports* 14, pt. 2, and 15, pt. 4).

The following essays by English officials who had served in the colonies throw considerable light on the character and defects of the system of colonial administration, and also contain proposals of remedial measures; Francis Bernard, *Select Letters on Trade and Government of America* (London,

1774), Thomas Pownall, *Administration of the Colonies* (ed. London, 1768), Sir William Keith, *Collection of Papers and other Tracts written occasionally on various Subjects* (London, 1740).

2. Of the writings of English statesmen, the *Correspondence of John, Fourth Duke of Bedford*, 3 vols. (London, 1842); *A Narrative of the Changes of Ministry*, by Duke of Newcastle, (Camden Society, *Publications*, London, 1898); Horace Walpole, *Memoirs of the Reign of King George the Second*, 3 vols. ed. by Lord Holland, (2d. ed., London, 1847); *Letters of Horace Walpole*, 9 vols. ed. by Cunningham, (London, 1891); and a few letters of Lords Dartmouth, Hillsborough, and Chesterfield in the *Dartmouth MSS.*, III, (Hist. MSS. Commission, *Report* 15, pt. 1), contain some material dealing with history and personnel of the Board of Trade. Of more importance on this point are H. R. Fox Bourne, *The Life of John Locke*, 2 vols. (London, 1876), which includes extracts of letters relative to the establishment of the board in 1696 and some account of the activity of Locke as a member of the bureau; *Life of William, Earl of Shelburne, with extracts from his Papers and Correspondence*, ed. by Lord Edmond Fitzmaurice, 3 vols. (London 1875), which contains letters valuable for the later history of the board, as also the activity of Shelburne as president of the board and as secretary of state during a critical period. Charles Davenant, *Political and Commercial Works*, ed. by Chas. Whitworth, 5 vols. (London, 1771), are valuable for a discussion of the British Colonial Policy in its economic and administrative features. *Works of Edmund Burke*, Bohn ed., 6 vols. (London, 1872), contain much of great value on the relations of the colonies to the mother country and on the colonial policy in general. *Grenville Papers, Correspondence of Richard Grenville*, etc., ed. by W. J. Smith, 5 vols. (London, 1852), throw light on the reformations of the colonial policy in 1763-1765.

3. Of the colonial statesmen Benjamin Franklin, *Writings*, ed. by A. H. Smyth, 10 vols. (N. Y., 1905), have been especially helpful for a knowledge of the popular attacks on the proprietary system in Pennsylvania, of Franklin as a colonial agent in London, and for controversial material concerning the parliamentary regulations after 1763. John Dickinson, *Writings*, ed. by P. L. Ford, (Hist. Soc. of Penn'a., *Memoirs*, XIV, Phila., 1895), contain pamphlets of importance on the conflict between the popular and proprietary parties in Pennsylvania, as also on the controversy with Great Britain after 1763.

William Smith, *A Brief State of the Province of Pennsylvania, 1755*, (Sabin Reprint, N. Y., 1764), is an attack on the Quaker power in Pennsylvania politics. Jeremiah Dummer, *A Defence of the New England Charters* (London, 1721), contains much of value on the administrative side of the colonial policy.

For the constitutional and economic arguments put forth by colonial leaders consequent upon the passage of the Sugar and Stamp Acts the following have been especially helpful; John Adams, *Novanglus: or a History of the Dispute with America, Works*, IV, ed. by C. F. Adams (Boston, 1851); Samuel Adams, *Writings*, I, ed. by H. A. Cushing (N. Y., 1904); Alexander Hamilton, *The Farmer Refuted, Works*, I, ed. by H. C. Lodge (N. Y., 1885); Stephen Hopkins, *The Rights of the Colonies Examined*, 1764, *(R. I. Col. Recs.*, VI, 416-427); Thomas Jefferson, *Summary View of the Rights of British America*, 1774; *Works*, I, ed. by P. L. Ford (N. Y., 1892); James Otis, *The Rights of the Colonies asserted and proved*, 1764, (Almon, *Tracts on the Colonies*, I, London, 1766); and the pamphlets in the *Writings* of Dickinson and Franklin cited above. An analysis and discussion of this controversial material is found in M. C. Tyler, *Literary History of the American Revolution*, 2 vols. (1897).

D.—Secondary Works.

No claim to completeness is made in the following list of secondary works, and only such books and articles as the present writer has found of particular assistance will be cited.

The neglected phases of British-American history have been well pointed out in C. M. Andrews, *American Colonial History*, (Amer. Hist. Asso., *Report*, 1898); *Some Neglected Aspects of Colonial History* (Paterson, 1896); William Macdonald, *A Neglected Point of View in American Colonial History* (Amer. Hist. Asso., *Report*, 1902, I); H. L. Osgood, *Study of American Colonial History (ibid., Report*, 1898); and also the addresses by G. L. Beer and H. L. Osgood, at the Conference on Research on American Colonial History, *(ibid., Report*, 1908, I, pp. 111-121).

General works on the political conditions in England; W. E. H. Lecky, *History of England in the Eighteenth Century*, 8 vols. (N. Y., 1878-1890); I. S. Leadam, *History of England from the Accession of Anne to the Death of George II, (Political Hist. of Eng.*, X, London, 1909); Grant Robertson, *England under the Hanoverians* (London, 1911); G. M. Trevelyan, *England under the Stuarts* (London, 1904).

General works dealing more particularly with the history of the imperial policy, H. E. Egerton, *A Short History of British Colonial Policy* (2d. ed., London, 1908), gives a general view of the subject on historical lines. George Chalmers, *Introduction to the Revolt of the Colonies*, 2 vols. (Boston, 1845), is a work of importance for the unity it gives to colonial history, although written from a prejudiced point of view. H. L. Osgood, *American Colonies in the 17th Century*, 3 vols. (N. Y., 1904, 1907), is a work of authority. Volumes I and II deal entirely with the development of purely local institutions, and vol. III is confined to a study of the development and application of a system of imperial control. Such an able treatment of our colonial history from these points of view for the 18th century still remains to be written. G. L. Beer, *Origins of the British Colonial System, 1578-1660* (N. Y., 1908), and *British Colonial Policy, 1754-1765* (N. Y., 1907), are eminently judicial in tone and are models of historical workmanship. The former traces the beginnings of the colonial policy, chiefly in its economic features, and the latter deals with the character of the imperial system during the critical period of the French and Indian War and with the reorganization of the system as a result of the events of that conflict. C. M. Andrews, *Colonial Self-Government* and E. B. Greene, *Provincial America, (American Nation Series*, V, VI, N. Y., 1904, 1905), include well-written chapters on the imperial relation, and contain excellent critical essays on authorities for the colonial period. Edward Channing, *History of the United States*, 2 vols. published (N. Y., 1905, 1908), especially vol. II on the period 1660-1760 includes chapters of value on the imperial system.

On the commercial policy of England, the best general account is G. L. Beer, *Commercial Policy of England toward the American Colonies* (N. Y., 1893). Mr. Beer's *Origins of the British Colonial System* and certain chapters in his *British Colonial Policy*, both cited above, are important for the economic features of the colonial policy. G. S. Callender, *Selections from the Economic History of the United States* (Boston, 1909), is a valuable handbook of extracts from sources throwing light on the economic history of the colonies and the commercial system of the mother country. Chapters i and ii of Andrews, *Colonial Self-Government* and chapter vii, vol. III, of Osgood, *American Colonies* (cited above), are excellent discussions of the principles of the commercial policy of England and the administration of the acts of trade in the 17th. century. W. J. Ashley, " England and America, 1660-1760," in his *Essays Historical and Economic* (1900), is an attempt to show that the commercial regulations were in general not oppressive. Theodora Keith, *Scottish Trade with the Plantations before 1707 (Scottish Hist. Rev.*, October, 1908), and *The Economic Causes for the Scottish Union, (English Hist. Rev.*, January, 1909), give the conditions surrounding the passage of the statute of 1696 which strengthened the administration of the acts of trade.

Little of a comprehensive character has been written on

the subject of the central institutions of colonial control.
C. M. Andrews, *British Committees, Commissions, and Councils of Trade and Plantations, 1622-1675, (Johns Hopkins Studies*, XXVI, nos. 1-2, 1908), gives the early history of the development of a colonial office. Mary P. Clarke, *The Board of Trade at Work, (American Hist. Rev.*, XVII, October, 1911, pp. 17-43), is interesting for the light it throws on the organization, staff, and procedure of the board. W. R. Anson, *Law and Custom of the Constitution*, 2 vols. (2d. ed., Oxford, 1892); Alpheus Todd, *Parliamentary Government in England*, 2 vols. (2d. ed., London, 1887), contain helpful material on the Privy Council, the secretaries of state, the Lords of the Treasury, and the Lords of the Admiralty. C. H. McIlwain, *The High Court of Parliament and its Supremacy* (New Haven, 1910), contains a very valuable chapter on the history of the theory of parliamentary supremacy and the attempt to apply it to the governance of an empire. Bernard Holland, *Imperium et Libertas* (London, 1901), includes a good discussion, with extracts from contemporary opinions, of the principle of parliamentary supremacy as applied to the colonies. Chapter i, vol. III, Osgood, *American Colonies*, is an excellent discussion of the nature and organs of imperial control in the 17th century.

C. M. Andrews, *Connecticut Intestacy Law, (Yale Review*, 1894, reprinted in *Anglo-American Legal Essays*, I); O. M. Dickerson, *The British Board of Trade and the American Colonies* (Mississippi Valley Hist. Asso., *Proceedings*, 1907-1908); A. M. Davis, *Frost vs. Leighton, (American Hist. Rev.*, II); and H. D. Hazeltine, *Appeals from the Colonial Courts to the King in Council* (Amer. Hist. Asso., *Report*, 1894), about conclude the list of articles on the very important subjects of the royal disallowance and appeals to the Privy Council. Louise P. Kellogg, *The American Colonial Charter* (Amer. Hist. Asso., *Report*, 1903, I), is a good monograph dealing with the attempts to bring the chartered colonies into closer administrative relations with the crown, and with the efforts to abrogate the charters. E. P. Tanner, *Colonial Agencies, (Political Science Quarterly*, XVI), is a useful essay on the colonial representatives in London.

E. C. Benedict, *The American Admiralty, its jurisdiction and practice* (3d. ed., N. Y., 1894); R. G. Marsden, *Select Pleas in the Court of Admiralty*, 2 vols. (VI, XI, Selden Society, *Publications*, London, 1894, 1897); Josiah Quincy, Jr., *Reports of Cases Argued and Adjudged in the Superior Court . . . of Massachusetts, 1761-1772*, (Boston, 1865); and W. S. Holdsworth, *History of English Law*, 3 vols. (London, 1903, 1909), have been helpful for the study of vice-admiralty jurisdiction in America.

On the questions of imperial defence and Indian policy, J. W. Black, *Maryland's Attitude in the Struggle for Canada (Johns Hopkins Studies,* X, no. 7, 1892) ; C. E. Carter, *Great Britain and the Illinois Country, 1763-1774* (Washington, 1910) ; and certain chapters in Francis Parkman, *Half Century of Conflict, Montcalm and Wolfe, Conspiracy of Pontiac,* are useful. More particularly, Beer, *British Colonial Policy, 1754-1765,* contains excellent chapters on these subjects during the critical period of the French and Indian War. J. W. Fortescue, *A History of the British Army,* 2 vols. (London, 1899), II contains useful chapters on the history of the British forces in the colonies.

Questions of coin and paper currency have been treated in C. J. Bullock, *Essays on the Monetary History of the United States* (N. Y., 1900) ; A. M. Davis, *Currency and Banking in Massachusetts Bay,* 2 vols. (Amer. Economic Asso., *Publications,* 3d. ser., I, II) ; and certain chapters in Smith, *South Carolina,* cited below.

On the English Church in America consult, J. S. M. Anderson, *History of the Church of England in the Colonies,* 3 vols. (rev. ed., 1856) ; S. E. Baldwin, *The Jurisdiction of the Bishop of London,* (Amer. Antiquarian Society, *Proceedings,* n.s., XIII) ; A. L. Cross, *The Anglican Episcopate and the American Colonies (Harvard Historical Studies,* IX, 1902) ; David Humphreys, *An Historical Account of the Society for the Propagation of the Gospel in Foreign Parts* (London, 1730).

The best general account of the provincial governor and the constitutional development in the provinces is to be found in E. B. Greene, *Provincial Governor (Harvard Historical Studies,* VII, 2d. ed., 1907). For particular provinces there are: E. J. Fisher, *New Jersey as a Royal Province, 1738-1776 (Columbia Univ. Studies,* XLI, 1911) ; W. H. Fry, *New Hampshire as a Royal Province, (ibid.,* XXIX, 1908) ; M. D. Mereness, *Maryland as a Proprietary Province* (N. Y., 1901) ; C. L. Raper, *North Carolina* (N. Y., 1904) ; W. R. Smith, *South Carolina as a Royal Province* (N. Y., 1903) ; C. W. Spencer; *Phases of Royal Government in New York, 1691-1719* (Columbus, 1905) ; H. R. Spencer, *Constitutional Conflict in Provincial Massachusetts* (Columbus, 1905) ; E. P. Tanner, *The Province of New Jersey, 1664-1738, (Columbia Univ. Studies,* XXX, 1908). These special monographs are valuable for the light they throw on the interaction of colonial and imperial interests, particularly in the royal provinces. Everett Kimball, *The Public Career of Joseph Dudley, (Harvard Historical Studies,* XV, 1911), deals with the colonial policy of the Stuarts in New England, 1660-1715.

On the history of Pennsylvania, W. R. Shepherd, *Proprie-*

tary Government in Pennsylvania, (Columbia College Studies, VI, 1896), and C. H. Lincoln, *The Revolutionary Movement in Pennsylvania,* (Univ. of Penn'a., *Publications,* 1901), have been of great assistance. Isaac Sharpless, *A Quaker Experiment in Government* (Phila., 1898) gives a fair-minded view of the religious and political principles of the Quakers. Other works on Pennsylvania history found useful: Benjamin Dorr, *An Historical Account of Christ Church* (Phila., 1859); S. M. Janney, *The Life of William Penn* (2d. ed., Phila., 1853); C. J. Stille, *Life and Times of John Dickinson* (Hist. Soc. of Penn'a., *Memoirs,* 1891); J. F. Watson, *Annals of Philadelphia and Pennsylvania in the Olden Times,* rev. by W. P. Hazard, 3 vols. (Phila., 1877).

INDEX